W9-CEC-714

HOW TO PREPARE FOR THE
ADVANCED PLACEMENT EXAMINATION

AP
UNITED STATES
HISTORY

FOURTH EDITION

William O. Kellogg
St. Paul's School
Concord, New Hampshire

BARRON'S

BARRON'S EDUCATIONAL SERIES, INC.

Acknowledgments

Thanks are due to the copyright owner for permission to reprint the
following copyrighted material:

George Weidenfeld & Nicolson Limited for three maps, appearing on
pages 91, 92, and 96. Reprinted with permission of the publisher from *The
American History Atlas* by Martin Gilbert, cartography by Peter Kingsland.

© Copyright 1993 by Barron's Educational Series, Inc.
Prior editions ©1988, 1983, 1977 by Barron's Educational Series, Inc.

All rights reserved.
No part of this book may be reproduced in any form, by photostat, microfilm,
xerography or any other means, or incorporated into any information
retrieval system, electronic or mechanical, without the written permission
of the copyright owner.

All inquiries should be addressed to:
Barron's Educational Series, Inc.
250 Wireless Boulevard
Hauppauge, New York 11788

Library of Congress Catalog Card No. 92-37455
International Standard Book No. 0–8120–1437–5

Library of Congress Cataloging-in-Publication Data

Kellogg, William O.
    AP United States history / William O. Kellogg. – 4th ed.
        p.   cm.
    Rev. ed. of: How to prepare for the advanced placement examination
AP, American history. 3rd ed. c1988.
    Includes biblographical references.
    ISBN 0-8120-1437-5
    1. United States—History—Examinations, questions, etc. I. Kellogg,
William O. How to prepare for the advanced placement examination AP,
American history. II. Title.
E178.25.K4   1993
973'.076—dc20   92-37455
                                                                    CIP

PRINTED IN THE UNITED STATES OF AMERICA

3456 100 9876543

Contents

Preface to the Fourth Edition

Writing, rewriting, and editing this book for the Advanced Placement examination has been most interesting and educational for me. I only hope it proves to be the same for the students and teachers who will use it to further their study and understanding of that always intriguing subject: the history of the American people. While the material included in the book is mine and I am responsible for the emphasis and interpretations, over 3,500 St. Paul's students during the past 38 years have strongly influenced my understanding and method of presenting American history. They, together with the many colleagues, particularly J. Carroll McDonald, with whom I've worked both at St. Paul's and elsewhere, have my heartfelt thanks for providing ideas and the stimulating atmosphere that have made teaching such an exciting endeavor. Also, during the preparation of this book and the subsequent revisions for the later editions I have had great help and support from the St. Paul's School research librarian, Anne Locke. Her support, enthusiasm, and untiring effort are greatly appreciated.

Since the third edition I have had the privilege of writing a text on American history for Barron's. Help from the publisher, editor, and my many colleagues in the Advanced Placement Program made these endeavors a pleasure. Many of the ideas developed in this process have been included in this new edition, especially material dealing with the chronology in Part Five.

I would also like to express my gratitude to my typist of the first and second editions, Judy Morin, who had an uncanny ability to decipher scratchings, turning them into words and to follow arrows making words into sentences. Without her this manuscript would never have emerged, and she is greatly missed. My thanks also go to the editors at Barron's who have helped with the four editions. They have all worked to improve the book.

PART ONE

Using This Book

This book was written to help students prepare for the Advanced Placement examination. It can be used three different ways. First, it can be used as a supplement to a regular course in American History. The student wishing to take the Advanced Placement examination and not enroll in an advanced course can use this book to provide depth of coverage. If the student writes the essays and answers the multiple-choice questions, he or she will be well prepared for the Advanced Placement examination. In addition, supplemental readings are suggested in the bibliography and these can be pursued as the student wishes.

The second way this book may be used is as part of an advanced placement course. The teacher can assign chapters in the book to supplement work in class. The suggested essay topics in each chapter can be assigned at the teacher's discretion.

The third way the book may be used is by a student who has already had a course in American history and wishes to simply review before attempting the Advanced Placement examination. A student using the book in this way will want to practice the multiple-choice questions in each chapter. These would be a good starting place to test how much information the student already has at hand.

To the Student

A careful study of this book will provide you with many of the skills needed on the examination. Writing the practice essays will help prepare you for that important part of the examination. The multiple-choice questions will remind you of just how much you already know. It is important to take the practice Advanced Placement examination in a situation that simulates the real exam as much as possible. Directions are included as to how to do that in Part Four.

While it is important that you move at your own pace in working through the book, it is also important that you look at the material in each chapter. Do not skip chapters, because there is important information included in each one.

You may wish to read through Part Five to remind you of the many aspects of American history that will be covered on the Advanced placement examination.

To the Teacher

This book can be used to supplement work in class. The chronological material in Part Five provides a good overview of important issues in our history. You may wish to assign that as you work with each time period of American history. Part Five and Part Three are divided in the same manner chronologically.

If you are teaching a regular section of American history, the book can provide the supplementary stimulation needed to prepare an excited student to take the Advanced Placement examination. You may in this case wish to suggest additional reading, but if you do not have enough time in class to review it all, this book will help that student prepare for the exam. If you are teaching an advanced placement course, the book can be broken up in segments and assigned as you find appropriate.

Organization of This Book

Part Two provides a general introduction to the study of American history and presents a method of writing essays. It can prove very helpful for a student wishing to prepare for the essays on the Advanced Placement examination or writing any essays. Part Three focuses on periods of time in American history, and in each chapter the important issues of the period are listed. In each chapter a different type of essay question is analyzed and sample answers are included. Among the types of questions considered are: evaluate this statement, assess the validity, describe . . . explain, and other essay formats. Also in Part Three different types of multiple-choice questions are presented and analyzed. Included in each chapter are five sample essay questions and at least 15 multiple-choice questions. These deal with the time period included in the chapter or with preceding time periods. This is not to suggest that only these types of questions will be asked on that particular era of American history. As you work through the book, your knowledge of American history will be broadened. Part Three ends with the presidential campaign of 1992.

Part Four presents a sample Advanced Placement examination. Also included are suggestions as to how to take the examination and how to do the final review before the exam.

As mentioned above, Part Five of this book presents a chronological outline of important events in American history. While this book is not meant as a complete textbook, using this section should stimulate your recall of important issues and developments in our history. It can provide a good last-minute review of American history before taking the exam or it can be used to supplement your chronological study of American history in a textbook.

This volume was designed to be used in a flexible way. It can be read straight through or different sections can be chosen at random to help your review and in-depth study. It has proven very helpful to many students of American history and it has been used in a variety of courses throughout the country.

The Nature of the Advanced Placement Examination

Advanced Placement examinations are offered in a wide range of subject areas. The structure of each of these examinations differs somewhat, and therefore all information offered in this book regarding Advanced Placement examinations refers only to the American history examination.

Grading

Advanced Placement examinations are offered annually in May. Final grades are reported on a five-point scale as follows:

5   extremely well qualified
4   well qualified
3   qualified
2   possibly qualified
1   No recommendation

In granting credit or advanced placement, many colleges honor grades of 3 or higher. The policies of colleges vary: some automatically grant credit or advanced academic standing; others respond individually to each situation.

It is interesting to note that roughly 75 percent of the students taking the American History Advanced Placement examination are high school juniors. The college board presents AP Scholar Awards to students obtaining a 3 or better on three AP course examinations and who have obtained a strong grade average. They also notify colleges connected with the AP program of students who have done well on AP examinations in their sophomore or junior year. This is a benefit for those applying to college and an incentive to take an AP examination before the senior year.

The Types of Questions

The American history AP examination consists of three types of questions: the multiple-choice question, the document-based essay question (often abbreviated as DBQ), and the standard essay question. In evaluating the examination, the two essay questions are weighted equally, and together the answers to these two questions form one-half of the examination grade. It is thus clear that writing skills are extremely important in achieving a good score on the Advanced Placement examination, as essay answers account for 50 percent of the grade.

The Multiple-Choice Questions

The multiple-choice questions test a student's knowledge of specific information, as well as how effectively the student can apply that knowledge to answer other less factual questions. The following questions are typical of those that appear on the examination:

1. "A well-regulated militia being necessary to the security of a free state, the right of the people to keep and bear arms shall not be infringed."
   All of the following are true in relation to the above quotation EXCEPT:
   (A) It is the second amendment to the U.S. Constitution
   (B) It is considered part of the Bill of Rights
   (C) The "right to bear arms" has been a major political issue in post World War II United States supported by the National Rifle Association
   (D) The National Guard of each state is an example of a "well-regulated militia" as mentioned in the statement
   (E) The statement assumes that all people will serve in the military

2. Among the scandals connected with the Grant administration are
   (A) Credit Mobilier and Watergate
   (B) Teapot Dome and the Whiskey Ring
   (C) the Whiskey Ring and Credit Mobilier
   (D) Watergate and Teapot Dome
   (E) the Whiskey Ring and Watergate

3. Which of the following is true about the concept of neutrality?
   (A) Its aim is to avoid involvement in foreign wars.
   (B) It has been successfully applied by the United Nations.
   (C) It has been an important concept since first proclaimed by President Monroe in the Monroe Doctrine.

(D) It prolonged World War II.

(E) It was the basis of U.S. policy in Central America in the 19th century.

There will be further information on multiple-choice questions in Part Three of this book. Questions in this section of the exam will be based on recall of information as well as questions on interpretation of information presented on the exam. These latter questions are often referred to as "stimulus" questions. They may be based on political cartoons, tables and charts, maps, or documents. Questions on the multiple-choice section of the examination will draw on information from social and cultural history, including possibly a question or two on literature and art, as well as the more traditional ones on political and economic history.

Answers to Sample Questions

1. E   2. C   3. A

The Document Based Essay Question (DBQ)

The essay section of the examination consists of two parts: the document-based question (DBQ) and the standard essay question. The DBQ will be based on documents but not necessarily famous documents such as the Constitution. The documents may include writings by well known individuals, Supreme Court decisions, other important national documents, or newspaper articles, and may also include charts, graphs, maps or cartoons. There is no limit as to the type of document that may be used. The document-based question is designed to test your analytical skills as well as your ability to relate the material to the main issues of American history. The DBQ will not necessarily be directly related to a major issue of American history which you have studied in detail. The DBQ will, however, require an understanding of the major issues of the time period of the DBQ. These major issues form what is referred to by the historians who develop the Advanced Placement examination as the "mainstream" of American history. You must be able to introduce ideas and information from this "mainstream" in your DBQ answer. For example, the question might be on the intricacies of U.S. foreign policy between 1795 and the outbreak of the war in 1812. The documents included would reflect the various aspects of this foreign policy and might include selections from treaties, the XYZ correspondence, or the embargo of 1807. You would then be expected to interpret these documents and show how they relate to the mainstream developments of those years. For instance, you should be able to express the views of the Federalists and the Anti-Federalists, of John Adams and Thomas Jefferson, of New Englanders and settlers on the issues raised by the documents. You must include such information in your DBQ answer if you wish to achieve a good grade. Your answer cannot be based simply on the documents. You must also include additional or "outside" information from the "mainstream" of American history.

The DBQ is discussed in greater detail in Part Three, Chapter 5, where a sample question is included. There is also a sample DBQ included in the model exam found in Part Four.

The Standard Essay Question

The second part of the essay section includes five essay questions and instructs the student to choose one. You should choose the question about which you know the most and pick your facts carefully to substantiate your opinion on the particular subject. In each chapter of Part Three of this book a different type of essay question is presented. These are analyzed and sample answers are presented. The examples are chosen from different periods in American history that are presented chronologically. Thus, as you work through this book you will be studying both American history chronologically and and in different types of essay and multiple-choice questions. The fact that a particular type of question is included in a chapter on the Civil War period does *not* mean that all questions on the exam dealing with the Civil War will be of that type. Of course, any type of question can be asked on any period. This combination of chronology and questions has proven to be an effective way to organize the presentation of material for an efficient review of American history while preparing for the Advanced Placement examination. Be sure to read all of Part Three.

A great deal of American history is included in the essay answers, and while some of it is not presented well, there are no factural errors in these answers, and therefore these answers can provide a helpful review of American history.

Study carefully each of the question types. Following are three typical essay questions of the type likely to appear on Advanced Placement examinations:

1. "The English founded colonies to escape oppression in England." Evaluate this statement.
2. How do you account for the entrance of the United States into World War I after a century free of United States entanglements in European wars?
3. "The proposals of the Populists as to how to handle the economic conditions of the early 1890s were not enacted but these proposals provided the framework for the New Deal's response to the economic conditions of the early 1930s." Assess the validity of this generalization by discussing both the Populist proposals and the New Deal's use of them.

Time Allotment on the Exam

The American history exam is three hours in length. You are given 75 minutes to answer the 100 multiple-choice questions. You are then allotted one hour and 45 minutes for the essay section. This is divided so that you have 15 minutes to read the DBQ and the five other essay questions, 40 minutes to write your DBQ answer, and 50 minutes to answer one of the five essay questions, for a total of 105 minutes on the essay section.

Content Covered on the Exam

The AP exam has traditionally been given in May, and plans indicate that this will continue. Since this mid-May date falls at a time when many high school courses have not yet gone beyond 1970 in their chronological study, the AP exam has placed less emphasis on the post-World War II period, especially on the essay questions, than on other periods of our history. Also, since a number of schools today devote little time to colonial history and concentrate on the period after 1763, the AP exam has placed less emphasis on pre-1763 American history than on later history, although students should have an understanding of the interaction between native American culture and that of the European settlers in the colonial period. Over the years the exam has particularly emphasized the following periods: the Revolution and Constitution; the Jacksonian Era; Sectionalism and Nationalism; the coming of the Civil War, the Civil War, and Reconstruction; the Populist and Progressive movements; the Great Depression and New Deal; and international and domestic developments in the post-World

War II era, especially those relating to the Cold War. On the multiple-choice section of the exam approximately one-sixth of the questions come from the period prior to 1789, approximately one-half of the questions deal with the period from 1790 to 1914, and approximately one-third of the questions deal with the period from 1914 to the present. This tests the coverage of American history normally achieved by the mid-May examination date.

The Advanced Placement program has always emphasized and acknowledged the independence of each classroom teacher in designing an advanced-level course. Any CEEB publication on the subject of history curriculum will offer general guidelines. Although the topics listed above will be particularly emphasized, other concepts and periods will be included.

In designing your study, all periods of American history should be considered, but one should certainly give extra time to the seven periods mentioned above. In considering these periods you should keep in mind that political institutions and behavior account for approximately one-third of the questions on both the multiple-choice and essay sections of the examination. Another third of the questions will deal with the general areas of social and economic change. The remaining third of the exam will deal with issues of diplomacy, foreign policy, cultural and intellectual developments. The essay questions may require relating two or more of these types of issues, such as economic implications of foreign policy moves or the political response to economic crises. To address these issues, students might investigate the following topics in depth while preparing for the Advanced Placement examination: American expansion, both on the continent and overseas and its social and economic impact on the nation; the Constitution and its interpretation; the changing role of government throughout our history; population and immigration issues, including treatment of the Native American population; economic changes both in business and labor practices and attitudes; slavery and the role of minorities in American life; the cause and effect— economic, political, and social—of major wars on the United States; the many -isms in our history, such as progressivism and popularism and their relationships; the growth of an American culture in the nineteenth century and its flowering in the twentieth.

One should include in any investigation of American history material peripheral to the political chronology. When considering literature, one should study it as it reflects changing attitudes and values in American history and not as a work of literary art. The same holds true for any consideration of art and philosophy. Gender, ethnic and racial differences, socio-economic conflicts as well as changing historiographic interpretations of major developments in the mainstream of American political history should be considered, although historiography will not be questioned directly on the examination. Of course not all of this material can be included so choices must be made. However, be certain to study several of these topics in depth. There are many literary anthologies, TV documentaries, and collections of documents that can help you gain the understanding you need.

These varying descriptions of exam content may seem confusing. Just realize that no two courses in Advanced Placement American history will be the same, thus you must decide what areas to concentrate on. The core of the exam will be economic and political history supplemented with items from social and cultural history. You need to consider the major events in the "mainstream" of the nation's history. There will be less emphasis on the period prior to 1763 and after 1970 than on the other times, with approximately half the multiple-choice questions covering material between 1790 and 1914.

You are now ready to begin your study or review of American history. In the next section are some general guidelines on studying history and writing essays. In Part Three you will follow chronologically the development of American history from the colonial period to the present. Following this section is a sample Advanced Placement exam. Finally, there is a chronological overview to help you in your study.

CLEP Examination

Several years ago the College Entrance Examination Board introduced the College Level Examination Program (CLEP) to provide a method for students to gain college credit for work and life experience outside the classroom. Some high school students have used the exam to gain college credit. However, the Advanced Placement Program is designed for such students and is the exam you should plan to take. Information on the CLEP Exam can be obtained from the College Board.

Publications of the College Board

It is most important that you, your teacher, or your guidance counselor check with the CEEB for the latest details on AP exams and with the colleges to which you are applying as to how they respond to AP grades. Colleges have very different ways of awarding placement and credit based on the AP exams, and you should have the correct information. The CEEB has a publication, *College Placement and Credit by Examination*, which provides some information. It should be consulted by all students considering taking AP examinations.

There are also yearly changes in the program, test dates, and centers. For the latest information, check with the guidance department of your high school or write directly to:

The Advanced Placement Program
The College Board
45 Columbus Ave.
New York, New York 10023-6992

In addition to specific information on the AP and CLEP programs and on testing dates, the CEEB publishes a variety of pamphlets that can help you. These may be obtained by writing to:

The Advanced Placement Program
P.O. Box 6670
Princeton, New Jersey 08541-6670

Among the more helpful publications are:

A Guide to the Advanced Placement Program Bulletin for Students, AP Program
Some Questions and Answers About the Advanced Placement Program
1993 AP Course Description in History
Grading the Advanced Placement Examination in American History
Teacher's Guide to AP Courses in American History
CLEP General and Subject Examinations

Helpful Hints for Studying American History

In studying any subject there are certain techniques and approaches that make understanding the material easier for the student. Many students approach all subjects with the same methods and become frustrated when they fail to achieve success in one area with techniques that proved successful in other subjects. For example, the study of history requires a great deal of reading, but if you read history the way you read a novel, you will not find success, since you may miss many of the important details you must know.

Each student studying history will develop his or her own very personal approaches to material. Some will underline in the books they own, others will take extensive notes on the reading, while others will outline the chapters. Each of these three approaches will make the material more meaningful to the individual and each is a personalized variation of note-taking as described below. Other techniques each history student will want to develop involve the pre-reading of material; the identifying of authors' prejudices; the making of time-lines; the reading of charts, graphs, and maps; the building of vocabulary; the developing of methods to review for tests; and, most important, the writing of essays in a clear and patterned manner. In this chapter comments will be made on all except two of the above. Essay writing, since it is so important, will be the topic of Part Two Section B, and Parts Three and Four will focus on developing methods to review for tests in terms of question and analysis and essay writing.

Reading History Material

Any student planning to take the Advanced Placement examination should be a good reader, since he or she will have to read extensively in history books and will need to be prepared to read quickly and with understanding. Many students read all written material in the same manner. They start at the beginning and go to the end. In a novel or in other literary works and in pleasure reading, this is a satisfactory approach, but another method is more beneficial when you are attempting to learn the details presented in the written material and when the subject is strange or unfamiliar to you. This method is to pre-read the material.

Pre-Reading

In pre-reading one looks over the chapter quickly, reading titles and sub-headings when they occur and, when they do not, reading the first sentence of paragraphs to get the sense of what will be presented in the reading. Often one will find review questions or a summary at the end of a chapter, and these should be read as part of the pre-reading. Once you have looked over the reading you should have a good idea of what it is about. You should have some questions for which you need answers. These questions may have been at the end of the chapter. They may be ones you have developed from reading the summary and discovering items that were not clear to you. They may simply be ones that have occurred to you as a result of looking over or pre-reading the chapter. These questions should be written down or marked or underlined in the book *if you own it*.

Underlining

This raises another issue about reading. Many students who own books develop techniques of underlining or making marginal notes in the books to identify the information that will answer the questions they have developed. This can be a very helpful technique, but one should limit the amount of underlining that is done. Too much underlining is worse than none, since it defeats the purpose of underlining, which is to clearly mark those items in a book that you think are important to remember. Underlinings, slash marks through important sentences, and circles around key words are all helpful techniques. Each student fortunate enough to own his or her history books will develop a technique that will make reviewing written material easy and will enable the student to answer questions developed in pre-reading. In addition to underlining, students will also want to take notes on the material read as indicated below.

Once you have completed your underlining or note-taking you are ready for the final step of effective reading. Look back at the questions you developed in your pre-reading and be sure you can answer them. This amounts to a review of the chapter. If you are taking a history course, you will want to do this reviewing as close to the class meeting time as possible. If you are studying independently, you will want to look over your notes at regular intervals. If you have good notes on the material you study, you will find it very helpful to read these during the week before you take the Advanced Placement exam. You will find it exceedingly difficult to review all the reading you do in an advanced level course the week before the exam, so your notes will be most important.

Summary

In studying for a history course or exam, you should first pre-read all material. While doing this you should develop questions that will provide the focus for your reading. You should then read the material, underlining or taking notes to prepare answers to the questions. Finally, before class or before going on to the next reading, you should review the material by checking the answers you have prepared for the questions you developed in your pre-reading. You will also want to review your answers to questions before any test and especially before taking the AP exam.

Taking Notes

Note-taking is an important skill for every history student to develop. There are several approaches one may follow. As suggested above, one method of note-taking is to develop questions about your reading and then take notes to develop answers. This method allows the student to restructure the material in a book into patterns that he or she has developed. If you follow this method, you will have put yourself into the role of the historian, collecting and reordering factual information to provide answers to questions of interest to you. If you consider the question as a sort of thesis and the factual information you put in your notes as the data to prove it, this method of note-taking will be excellent practice for writing essays as presented in Part Three.

Outlining

Another valuable method of note-taking is outlining. In this approach the student simply summarizes or condenses the information in the book. The summary does not reorder the information, but retains the important data in a short version that can be referred to for review or before the exam. The student is not involved in being the historian in preparing such notes, but will have at hand in a brief version the information he or she needs to discuss issues or to prove given hypotheses. Both methods have advantages; whichever method of note-taking you follow is a personal choice. Each student should try both and find which is more helpful in his or her study.

Most students will keep their notes in a notebook. A looseleaf book is suggested since you can add or rearrange pages that you may find helpful. However, many students do find a bound spiral notebook satisfactory. A few students will take notes on index cards. This is a valuable technique when writing a research paper, but can become rather burdensome when simply taking notes on a text.

Time-Line

In addition to taking notes on the general content of the material read, there are several types of specialized note-taking techniques that can be invaluable to the student of history. The first involves making a time-line. Dates are important in history since they provide the key to the cause-and-effect relationship that is at the heart of understanding history in the Western world. Unless you know the chronological order in which events happened, you cannot explain the relationships among them. Therefore, as you read it would be wise to keep a list of major events and the date on which each occurred. This can be a simple list in which you merely record the date and the name of the event. For instance, a time-line can be as simple as the following:

> 1763 — Treaty of Paris
>   — Proclamation Line
>
> 1764 — Grenville Program
>   — Sugar Act
>
> 1765 — Stamp Act
>   — Stamp Act Congress
>   — Boycott
>
> 1766 — Stamp Act Repealed
>   — Declaratory Act

You can make your time-line more complex by adding the day and month of each event, which is sometimes very important, by adding the names of people and places, and even going so far as to briefly describe each event, person, or place.

Part Five includes a simple time-line. You may wish to add to this one or make your own as you study. If you make your own, emphasize what is important to you and not what someone else has decided you should learn. This is an important part of any study—to make the information yours.

Lists of Individuals

A second specialized type of note-taking, and one that might be combined with a time-line, is that of keeping a list of important individuals. Your notes might group them by activity, such as political leaders, business leaders, reformers, inventors, and the like, or by time periods. In Part Five such lists are presented but again you should develop your own lists as you study or, at the very least, add names as you study.

The third type of specialized note-taking deals with vocabulary building and deserves a separate section.

Building Vocabulary

Every disicipline has its own vocabulary. We often do not realize this as we study English or history, since most of the vocabulary is familiar to us from our daily usage. However, there are many words that are used in a special ways in history. As you study, you should develop a list of words with which you were not familiar when you began your study. In the list after each word you should write a definition.

Many words used in history change their meaning during the course of time. You must be aware of the *shifting use* of words as well as of their meanings in the last quarter of the twentieth century. For instance a person labeled as a *liberal* in 1830, in 1912, and in 1968 might stand for very different points of view. As you read, be certain you can identify these shifting meanings of such a word.

Also, many terms or phrases used in history refer to much more than is meant by the word alone. For instance, the word *frontier* has different meanings and different connotations depending upon how it is used. If by *frontier* one means the edge of unsettled land, you react in one way. However, if you mean *frontier* as understood by the very important American historian Frederick Jackson Turner, then you need to react in many other ways. *Frontier* is simply one example of many words that have particular meanings for history.

Key Phrases

Historians also have adopted many phrases used by politicians and others through the years to convey certain concepts. For instance, the New Frontier of President Kennedy has a specialized meaning with which you should be familiar. Keep a list of such words and phrases as you study for you will find them to be invaluable in aiding your understanding of American history. Many questions on the examination will assume a knowledge of such phrases and words.

In the Appendix to this book you will find a Glossary that contains many of the specialized words used by historians. This can be of help to you as a model for your own list or in helping you find the meaning of some words. But as in the case of the time-line, do not rely on the Glossary to supply your understanding of historic terms. Develop your own list.

The sample multiple-choice questions in Chapter 8 deal with vocabulary. By the time you get to those questions you should have developed your own vocabulary list and thus should find these questions easy. Of course, all questions dealing with history require some knowledge of the vocabulary of history. Thus, throughout this book as well as throughout your study of history, you need to expand your vocabulary. Continually add new words to your vocabulary notes.

Analyzing Authors' Viewpoints

As every student of history must realize, history is a very personal subject. Every writer has his or her own ideas about the relationship of different happenings, the importance of certain individuals, the motivations behind various actions, and the significance of each event. No two historians will agree on their interpretations, and so the question "What is history?" must be considered by every student.

Personal Viewpoints

History is certainly what has happened in the past, but it is also what different men and women tell us in their writings or films or pictures. The individual's personal interpretation of events we call his or her bias, and every historian, even the writer of the apparently most objective history textbook, has a bias. As a student of history, you should train yourself to identify each author's bias and to take that into account as you read his or her works. For example, if you are reading one of the *Federalist Papers* written by James Madison, it is important to realize Madison's biases in favor of the Constitution, of education, and of wealth and his biases against the poorer and less educated. When you see Madison quoted in a text, you will want to keep these points in mind. Likewise, if you are reading Charles Beard, one of the great American historians of the first half of this century, you will want to be aware of his biases. If you are not aware, you might accept without question Beard's interpretation of the Constitution as a document written by wealthy men for the protection of their own wealth. Knowing that Beard was an economic historian and that he interpreted history, as does a Marxist, in terms of economic pressures and class divisions based on wealth, you might not accept all Beard has to present. Charles Beard made many important points in his famous book, *The Economic Interpretation of the Constitution*, but many of his assumptions have been questioned or tempered by later scholars, such as Richard Brown, who based their interpretations on other assumptions, some of which are also being questioned. The point is that historians interpret events based on their personal viewpoints and the student must learn what these viewpoints or biases are as well as learn the evidence the historian presents. Further reading may make you aware of how much information was left out or overlooked by the author of a particular book.

Each reader of this book will have his or her own views, and you must be aware of these—your own biases and prejudices—as you study. Also, do not overlook the fact that I, too, have biases that are incorporated in this text. Can you identify some of them?

Biases and prejudices are not necessarily bad, although we often use the word *prejudice* negatively. They are simply a part of being human and thus are a part of history. The greater your awareness of the biases of the authors you read, the greater your understanding of events will be.

Identifying Biases

There are many ways to identify biases. Such simple devices as the date of publication and the home of an author will give some insights. Prefaces, biographical sketches, and reviews will also provide information. The most important way to discover bias, however, is through a careful reading of the material. For instance, the words chosen to describe the slave in America may reveal certain attitudes. Is he Sambo, a *shuffling* character who *benefited* from his *master's* religion? Or was he an *exploited* worker—more exploited than those in the factories of England since he could never be *free*? Such words reveal a lot about the author, as will the manner in which various events are described. As a test of author's biases, try reading about the same event in several different books. Most historians in considering Lincoln's signing of the Emancipation Proclamation would include the same so-called hard facts—i.e., date (1863), documents (Emancipation Proclamation), and specific events (the signing ceremony). How each uses these facts to explain Lincoln's reasons for signing reveals the author's bias. Textbooks compared this way can reveal a great deal.*

Summary

As you read, look for the biases and prejudices of the author. Try to identify your own biases and prejudices. When you make judgments about the past, what we will refer to in Part Two Section B as developing your own thesis, keep your biases in mind. As you collect material to support or prove your thesis, be sure to remember the source from which your information came.

Bibliography

When students or teachers first look at the amount of material available in the field of American history, both in hardcover editions and in paperbacks, they are often overwhelmed. The quantity, much of it of high quality by outstanding historians, is so discouraging that the teacher or student often retreats to a safe textbook within the covers of which will be found brief presentations of all the important events of American history, at least as understood by one or several authors. It is hoped that the users of this book will not fall into that trap, but rather will use a variety of sources for the study of American history. A textbook is often a fine starting place, but for the truly interested student-scholar, it should be only that—a starting place. With this point in mind, each of the chronological review chapters in this book contains a bibliography of special works dealing with the period covered in the chapter. In no way could a student in a one-year course be expected to read all these works, but they are included to serve as

---

*What Happened on Lexington Green: An Inquiry into the Nature & Method of History by Brown and Halsey is an excellent introduction to bias and prejudice history. There are other works that approach history in the same way, and it would be worthwhile to read one of them if you have not considered this topic previously.

examples of the type of material one might read to supplement his or her study of the period in question. Many of the works in these bibliographies cover one aspect of the period, such as the post-Civil War condition of the blacks in the South or the Great Crash of 1929, and students should pursue special interests of this type as they study.

Reference Works

The bibliography in this section is different from the chapter bibliographies. Included in it are general works that cover in one volume the history of a particular aspect of American history, such as *American Economic or Diplomatic History* or special reference works such as the *Encyclopedia of the American Constitution*. Students should read parts of at least one work from each chapter to supplement textbook reading or read several of the more general works from the list below. Under no circumstances should a student consider himself or herself prepared for the Advanced Placement exam if he or she has simply read a textbook, even if it is one of the best.

In looking over the bibliographies, teachers and students will recognize some of the better known American historians. Since one aspect of history of which you should be aware is how different historians interpret events and how these interpretations change, you may wish to look at several of these works. It is impossible to prepare a definitive list of the currently recognized great American historians. Every teacher has his or her own favorites, and the list of important interpretations continually changes. For instance, there are differing interpretations now on everything from the role of the "people" in the American Revolution to the origins of the Cold War. While there will be no specific information required concerning historiography on the AP exam, a well-prepared student should be aware of major changes in interpretations of U.S. history.

To help you, the student, make decisions as to what historians are of special significance and what interpretations are held, you may wish to consult some of the learned history journals that carry articles on recent research. Consulting such journals is a good supplement to your regular study. At least one or two of these journals should be available in your school library or in the local public library. They supplement any study of American history. Also, there are works that include selections from different historians on the same topic, such as that edited by E. C. Rozwens, *The Causes of the American Civil War*. It is probably the best known series of this type for advanced work next to the so-called Amherst Pamphlets. In reading one you will see how interpretations change and historians differ.

If you are studying independently in preparation for the Advanced Placement examination, your first step should be to decide if you will pick a text from the bibliography, or use several different reference works for your study, If you are in an Advanced Placement or regular class, the teacher will have already made this choice.

Summary

The works listed in the bibliographies are meant to be suggestions for further study. There are other works that would serve as well, but it would be overwhelming to list them all. These are merely examples of the types of works you might use and those that reflect the author's personal prejudices.

Textbooks

There are innumerable textbooks in American history. Among those that might be used in an advanced-level course are the following:

Bailey, T.A. and Kennedy, David M. *The American Pageant*. Lexington: D.C. Heath and Co., 1991. (An old favorite of many teachers written in an easy and chatty style).

Blum, John, et al. *The National Experience: A History of the United States*. New York: Harcourt Brace Jovanovich, Inc., 1988. (A standard college-level text book written by several of the nation's best known historians.)

Garraty, J.A. and McCaughey, Robert. *The American Nation: A History of the United States*. New York: HarperCollins, 1987.

Kellogg, W.O. *American History: The Easy Way*. Hauppauge, NY: Barron's Educational Series, Inc., 1991. (A recent, brief overview of American history that serves well as a text and can be supplemented by specialized works.)

Norton, M.B. et al. *A People and a Nation: A History of the United States*. Boston: Houghton Mifflin, 1988. (A recent addition to the textbook field written by several authors who emphasize the social history of the nation.)

General Works

Bailey, T.A. *Diplomatic History of the American People*. New York: Appleton-Century Crofts, 1980.

Corwin, Edward S. *The Constitution and What It Means Today, 14th Edition*. Princeton: Princeton University Press, 1979.

Curti, Merle, *The Growth of American Thought*. New York: Transition Books, 1981.

Hofstadter, Richard. *Age of Reform*. New York: Random House, 1966.

——. *American Political Tradition and the Men who Made it*. New York: Alfred A. Knopf, Inc., 1973.

Karsten, Peter, ed. *The Military in America: From the Colonial Era to the Present*. New York: Free Press, 1986.

Kennan, G.F. *American Diplomacy*. Chicago: University of Chicago Press, 1985.

Quarles, Benjamin. *The Negro in the Making of America*. New York: Macmillan, Inc., 1987.

Smith, H.N. *Virgin Land*. Cambridge: Harvard University Press, 1978.

Woodward, C.V. *The Burden of Southern History*. Baton Rouge: Louisiana State University Press, 1968.

Special Reference Works

Adams, J.T., ed. *Atlas of American History*. New York: Charles Scribner's Sons, 1985.

American Council of Learned Societies, Garraty, J.A. ed. *Dictionary of American Biography*. New York: Macmillan, 1981.

Carruth, Gorton and Ehrlich, Eugene. *The Harper Book of American Quotations*. New York: HarperCollins, 1988.

Deconde, S.M., ed. *Encyclopaedia of American Foreign Policy*. New York: Macmillan, 1978.

Dictionary of American Biography. New York: Charles Scribner's Sons, 1931.

Encyclopedia of the American Constitution. New York: Macmillan and Free Press, 1986.

Evans, J.M. ed. *Two Thousand Notable American Women*. Raleigh, NC: American Biographic Institute, 1987.

Freidel, Frank, et al., eds. *Harvard Guide to American History*. Cambridge, MA: Belknap Press, 1974.

Gilbert, Martin. *American History Atlas*. New York: Macmillan, 1968.

Gonick, Larry. *Cartoon History of the United States*. New York: HarperCollins, 1991.

Heffner, Richard, ed. *A Documentary History of the United States*. New York: NAL Dutton, 1985.

Hofstadter, Richard and Beatrice. *Great Issues in American History: From Reconstruction to the Present Day 1864–1981*. New York: Random House, 1982.

International Encyclopedia of the Social Sciences. New York: Macmillan and Free Press, 1969.

Morris, R.B., ed. *Encyclopaedia of American History*. New York: Harper & Row, Publishers, 1982.

——.*Witnesses at the Creation*. New York: NAL Dutton, 1989.

Porter, Glenn, ed. *Encyclopaedia of American Economic History*. New York: Macmillan, 1980.

Sowell, Thomas. *Ethnic America, A History*. New York: Basic Books, 1983.

Journals and Magazines

American Heritage Magazine
American Historical Review
Current History
Foreign Affairs
Journal of American History
Journal of Negro History
William and Mary Quarterly

Seven Steps to Make Essay Writing Easy

Why the Essay Technique Is Important

A good essay style is the key to success on the Advanced Placement American History examination. This may appear to be an extreme statement, but it can be defended. In this three-hour examination, you will have one hour and 45 minutes in which to organize and write two essays: the first, the DBQ is a required question in which you must analyze the given documents and incorporate in your answer both your analysis of them and information from the mainstream of American history, and the second is to be chosen by you from five given alternatives. In grading the exam, the two essays are weighted equally in the formula* used to determine the student's grade. Each essay counts one-fourth of the total grade. So you can see how important it is to do well on the essays if you want to get a good grade on the examination. You may be well trained at analyzing documents, and you may have mastered the factual content of American history, but if you cannot express yourself in writing, the reader of your exam paper will never know how much you understand and how much work you have done.

Because of this, we will spend substantial time considering essay questions and how to answer them. As you will learn when reading Chapters 1–8 in Part Three, there are many ways in which essay questions may be phrased. In each chapter we will consider different types of questions, so that as you work through this book you can read and practice the different types of essay questions used on the Advanced Placement examination.

Considering the Essay Question

The term *essay* is often used to mean a composition or a piece of writing in which a question is answered. Actually the word *essay* is defined as a literary composition, analytical or interpretive, dealing with its subject from a more or less limited or personal standpoint. According to this, it is not simply a rambling piece of writing that answers a question. As essay is literary; it is analytical or interpretive, and it deals with the subject in a somewhat limited way that may include a personal standpoint. All three of these points are important for you to understand about the essay, but the idea that the essay presents a personal viewpoint is most significant. We will refer to this personal viewpoint as the thesis of the essay, and we want you to develop your personal opinion on each essay topic presented in this book. Your thesis will distinguish your essay answer from those of other students; and how well you convince the reader that your view is correct will determine the grade your receive for your essay.

The first type of essay question we will look at is the *Evaluate this statement* type. It is a common and effective type of question. The test designer presents a statement that may or may not be controversial. The student can use the

---

* The formula is a ratio of 2 : 1 : 1 in which two points are given to the multiple-choice questions, one to the document-based essay, and one to the standard essay.

statement as the thesis of an answer, but it need not be so used. The word *Evaluate* is crucial in this type of question. The student must be prepared to judge the validity of the statement, to weigh the pros and cons, and to reject or accept the truth of the statement after analysis. Often the directions for this type of question on the AP examination will be phrased, "Assess the validity of this statement or generalization." Phrased this way, the question asks you to do the same thing as *Evaluate this statement*. Chapter 7 of Part Three will introduce other variations of the *Evaluate this statement* essay question. A thorough treatment of the *Evaluate this statement* essay question can be found in Chapter 1 of Part Three.

This first sample *Evaluate this statement* essay question deals with the geography of the colonial regions. Following the question are two sample introductory paragraphs. We will analyze these introductions and then look at several complete essay answers to the question. After analyzing these answers, we will present some general guides for the writing of essays, which you should follow throughout your study. First, however, let us look at several examples of student's essay answers and see how they offer some general guidelines for all essay answers.

Sample Question	"The geographic conditions of the three major areas of English settlement in America—New England, the mid-Atlantic region, and the South—were the primary factors in determining the differences in the colonial way of life in these three areas." Evaluate this statement.

Sample Introduction 1

Virginia had a fairly mild climate and fertile soil in the tidewater area where many rivers supplied transportation to the plantations. The mid-Atlantic region also had fertile soil, but it lacked the rivers into the interior to aid transportation and the winters were less mild. With cold winters and hot summers, New England was climatically the least attractive of the three colonial regions, and the soil was very rocky. Therefore, New Englanders turned to business and the sea in order to make a living.

Sample Introduction 2

Geography is an important factor in the lives of all people. This was certainly true in the English colonies in America, where the barren New England soil and the harsh climate contrasted sharply with the rich soil and comparatively mild climate of the South. However, to say that geography accounts for the differences in the colonial way of life in the three areas of English settlement— New England, the mid-Atlantic, and the South—is an exaggeration. The types of settlers, the reasons for settlement, and the relations with the mother country had a major impact on the colonial way of life.

Comments on Sample Introduction 1

Sample Introduction 1 is a typical student response to the given question. It clearly illustrates the greatest problem students have in writing essay answers—the problem of analysis of the question. Under the pressure of limited time, students too often begin their writing before they have thought about what the question asks. Many students respond to questions without considering what they are being asked. Such a response can lead to disaster on the Advanced Placement examination. Let us look at this introduction and see what the student has done.

The student has immediately grabbed the idea of three regions and focused on an example of one, Virginia, and in the first sentence has proceeded to present three items of information connected with geography—climate, soil, rivers. The student demonstrates good factual information, referring to "tidewater" Virginia and to the plantation economy. In the second and third sentences, general information is presented about the two other regions. There is a structure to the paragraph, to these three sentences, and to the way they are constucted. You might wonder, therefore, why this paragraph is being criticized as an introduction. The problem, of course, is in defining or understanding the purpose of an introduction to an essay.

The Opening Paragraph

An effective opening paragraph *must* contain two essential points:
1. a statement of the topic under consideration (i.e., the question)
2. a statement of the author's opinion on the topic (i.e., the thesis)

A good opening paragraph will also contain:
1. a rather broad comment on the topic in general
2. no factual information (this should be saved for the body of the essay)

The most effective opening paragraphs have the thesis as the last sentence of the paragraph, and the earlier sentences present the question and the broad comment on the general topic. Now look at the last sentence of Sample Introduction 1 and decide what thesis this student is presenting. Is this sentence the thesis of the essay? Reread the paragraph and write down what you consider is the topic of the essay based on this introductory paragraph. If you cannot determine that the topic is a comparison of the geographic features of New England, the south, and the mid-Atlantic states, you would agree with the author of this book. Yet what does the actual question ask? This illustration should impress upon you the importance of that first step in writing any essay—*analyzing the question.*

Comments on Sample Introduction 2

For contrast, read Sample Introduction 2. What factors distinguish Introduction 2 from Introduction 1? Can you determine what the topic under consideration is for the second introduction? Can you determine what that writer's opinion is on the topic?

Sample Introduction 2 is one type of effective opening paragraph for an essay. The topic of geographic influences in history is introduced in the first two sentences. It is a broad comment on the general topic of the question. The specific topic is presented in the third sentence, and the author's personal opinion, or the thesis of the essay, is presented in the last half of the third sentence and in the fourth sentence. This introduction paragraph answers two questions that must be dealt with in every essay and usually are treated most effectively in the introductory paragraph. These two questions are: "What is the topic?" and "What is the author's opinion on the topic?" Obviously, for the writer to deal with these two questions, he or she must take the first step in essay writing—*analyzing the question.*

Now let us look at the body or remainder of the two sample answers to this same essay question. As you read the body of sample essays 1 and 2, first pay particular attention to the organizational structure used by each writer. Second, consider the way specific information is used in each essay.

Sample Essay 1   The Pilgrims were the first settlers in New England. They farmed, taught by the Indian Squanto, and as a result of their production, they celebrated the first Thanksgiving. The later Puritan settlers based their life around the church and lived very strict and limited lives. Because they believed that God rewarded those who worked hard, the Puritans were very industrious. Boston became a thriving seaport and many merchants were soon involved in the triangular trade with England or Africa, the West Indies, and Boston, trading slaves, sugar, and rum. Lumber for ships of the English navy also made fortunes for many Bostonians.

Tobacco was the crop that produced the wealth of Virginia. Rice and indigo were important in South Carolina as fortunes were made there in the 18th century by plantation owners. The southerners sold their crops to England and in return imported fine English furniture and china. Some of the plantations in Virginia, such as Westover, rivaled the finest English homes and showed that the southern colonies had come a long way from the log houses of Jamestown. The Virginia plantation owners imported blacks from Africa to work the tobacco fields as slaves, while the owners developed the first legislative body in America in the House of Burgesses.

Pennsylvania, in the mid-Atlantic region, had its own system of government. The colony was the private estate of William Penn. He ruled it as such, but because he was a Quaker, he allowed religious toleration in the colony. Pennsylvania prospered, with many small farms producing staple crops. When Ben Franklin came to Philadelphia, he worked as a printer, showing how advanced Philadelphia was as a city. The city was well planned with straight streets and fine buildings.

In this paper I have tried to show how different the colonies were. Virginia was the best place to live because it was easiest to make a living on the plantations. New England and Pennsylvania were not as good, although many people in both colonies made money in trade.

Sample Essay 2   The majority of settlers in New England came there for religious reasons—the Pilgrims to separate from the Church of England and the Puritans to purify the church. Later settlements such as those founded by Roger Williams and Anne Hutchinson were established essentially for religous reasons. This fact colored the colonists' outlook on life and led to such events as the great preaching of Cotton Mather in Massachusetts Bay Colony and the Salem witch trials. The emphasis upon religion and the Bible required that people could read and led to public-supported schools and the founding of Harvard College. The Puritan view of life held that work was essential and success God-given. Therefore, the New Englanders were driven to seek employment and use their resources—lumber— and experience with the sea to become sailors and merchants in the triangular trade. New Englanders sold rum in Africa, brought slaves to the West Indies, and imported sugar or molasses to New England for the production of rum.

English mercantilist policies, incorporated in various Acts of Trade and Navigation, such as the Molasses Act, attempted to control this trade. The attempts led to antagonisms between England and New England. The struggle between the two affected colonial life, and the basis for the antagonism may be traced to religious differences. Of course, geography provided the harbors and the lumber of ships involved in the triangular trade and for the British navy, but it was their religion that was most important in setting the life-style of New Englanders.

Virginia's life-style (and it may be considered representative of the South) was plantation based; therefore, one might consider that soil and climate determined Virginia's life-style. That is partly true, but what was crucial in Virginia was the London Company's motivation in founding the colony—to make a profit. Until tobacco was discovered and a market was found in England, Virginians struggled. Once a money-making product was found—it could as easily have been gold, which would have changed the life-style greatly—Virginia's future was determined. Slaves, large farms or plantations, a close connection with England— sons were sent there for education and plantation homes such as Westover were built on Georgian models—all developed as a result of economic motivation and the finding of a cash product. Geography may have determined the product, but the type of people and their contacts with England helped determine the life-style.

Pennsylvania, in the mid-Atlantic region, was founded at a time of economic prosperity, which allowed the colony to grow rapidly. William Penn, a Quaker, was an idealist who believed in religious toleration. This attracted numerous Germans to the colony. Many became small farmers in the rich valleys—a geographic factor—but it was Philadelphia that typified the colony. Here merchants flourished in the well-planned port city. The quakers believed in equality and provided good hospitals and charity for the poor, setting an example followed later by the United States. Because of his religious convictions, Penn set very liberal laws for the colony, and a group of elected officials helped the proprietor run the colony. Thus it was the attitudes of the settlers and of Penn himself, more than the geographic conditions, which determined the colonial way of life in Pennsylvania.

The colonial way of life differed in the three areas of settlement. The types of people who settled and their reasons for colonizing—religious or economic— played a key role in determining these differences. Of course geography—climate, ports, soil, and available crops—affected what people could do, but it was the people themselves who made the difference. Even F. J. Turner, who later suggested that the frontier determined American history, would say that the people made the frontier. The settlers made the colonial way of life as we make ours.

Comments on Sample Essays

It is clear that each writer followed the easy yet effective method of organizing material by geographic areas. It should also be clear that after that, the writer of Essay 1 simply presented factual information as it occurred to him with little attempt to relate the facts to each other and with no attempt to relate these facts to the topic. The writer of Essay 2, however, has organized material within each paragraph to follow the same pattern; motivation for settlement, effect of motivation on life-style, acknowledged geography. He or she also continually relates the ideas to the thesis and to the overall topic.

To illustrate this point, prepare an outline of the second answer, following traditional outline form. The form is as follows:

I. Major Topic 1
   A. Primary evidence
      1. Secondary evidence
         a. Tertiary evidence
II. Major Topic 2
   A. Primary evidence
      1. Secondary evidence
         a. Tertiary evidence
. . . and so forth.

Bascially, outlines are merely an organizational format. They are not always easy to develop, but for the question considered in this chapter, several organizational formats are possible. You could organize your answer either by life-style in each geographic region or by climate in each geographic region. The organizational format or structure then follows easily. A formal outline of Essay 2 would look like this:

I. New England
   A. Why settlement?—Religion
      1. Cotton Mather
      2. Salem witches
      3. read
         a. public school
         b. Harvard
   B. Life-style: Success for God
      1. work
         a. resources
         b. sea
         c. merchants
      2. triangular trade
   C. Struggle with England: Mercantilism
   D. Geography
      1. harbors
      2. lumber
II. Virginia (the South)
   A. Why settlement?—Profit
      1. London Co.
      2. tobacco
   B. Life-Style
      1. slaves
      2. English education
      3. plantations
   C. Geography
III. Pennsylvania
   A. Why settlement?—Penn's idealism
      1. economic prosperity
      2. religious toleration
   B. Life-style
      1. Philadelphia
         a. port
         b. equality
         c. hospitals
      2. religion
         a. liberal laws
         b. legislature
   C. Geography
IV. Conclusion
   A. Different life-styles
      1. types of people
      2. reasons for settling
   B. Geography
      1. climate
      2. ports
      3. soil
      4. crops
   C. Settlers made life-style; so do we

The writers of answers 1 and 2 are both knowledgeable students. They both include the type of effective factual information required for Advanced Placement work. They are aware of details, and their sentence structure is sound. The writer of Essay 2, however, has demonstrated two additional skills that clearly mark him or her as an above-average student. These skills are that of organization and analysis. The writer of Essay 1 clearly demonstrates a lack of analytical work, and the reader is left wondering if the student understood the question. Because of this the student would receive a mediocre grade on the Advanced Placement examination.

As a student, when you write a practice essay, you would be very wise to make formal outlines of this type after writing the essay. For many years it was the style to ask students to make a full formal outline prior to writing a paper. Students usually used so much time on the formal outline that they had little time to write or polish the essay. The technique presented under Step Two later in this section has proved to be very effective for organizing essay answers. The brief notes should be sufficient to provide an organizing format for writing the essay. To help you write the body of the paper, these brief notes can be numbered in a logical order for you to follow in introducing the ideas in your answer. If these answers are then outlined in detail after the writing, the student can learn how well he or she is following the logical sequence in presenting information. It is strongly urged that students make formal outlines of their answers after writing the essays as a technique in developing a good clear style. When writing an essay on the AP examination you will want to make only a brief outline. Remember that timing is important on the examination and you will not have enough time to develop a full formal outline.

We have now looked at two sample answers for our first essay question, and, in doing so, we have presented several definitions and rules for the writing of essay answers. As you study and review American history, you will want to practice writing essays. The technique presented here, summarized as Seven Steps in Essay Writing, if mastered, will provide an effective method for answering all types of essay questions and for writing all kinds of essays for your classes. As you perfect your technique, you may wish to try variations on this style, but first master this method for writing an essay.

Seven Steps in Essay Writing
Step One—Analyzing the Question

In writing an essay, the first step is always to analyze the question. Without a clear undestanding of what the question is, you cannot possibly write an adequate answer. Let us now look at the question again.

> "The geographic conditions of the three major areas of English settlement in America—New England, the mid-Atlantic region, and the South—were the primary factors in determining the differences in the colonial way of life in these three areas." Evaluate this statement.

The question presents a statement and then asks the student to evaluate the statement. The key word here is, obviously, *evaluate*. What does it mean? According to the dictionary, it means to determine the value of or to appraise carefully. In other words, the question is asking the student to determine the value of the statement. Is it true or false, or is there some truth that must be qualified? In other words, you are to appraise the question as a jeweler appraises a diamond to determine how valuable it is.

The *Evaluate this statement* format is a popular type of essay question on Advanced Placement examinations. As stated above, it allows innumerable ideas or potential theses for essays and it forces the student or writer to judge or appraise the suitability of these theses. In many ways, it is one of the easiest forms of questions for the student. The statement can be accepted or rejected as the thesis of the essay. The writer is not required to express a personal opinion or thesis in his or her own words. As you will see later, the formulation of one's own thesis is often the most difficult aspect of producing good, effective essay answers.

This particular question presents a thesis involving geographic influences on the development of patterns of living. The word *geographic* in this question may be understood to mean environmental geography. The general topic of geography or environmental influences on human activity is an important one historically. Most historians have strong opinions on the topic, and every student of history has confronted the question directly or indirectly at some point. Therefore, it is a good topic for the Advanced Placement examination and a good topic with which to begin a study or review of American history. The quotation suggests that the extreme environmentalist interpretation of history—that the colonial way of life was determined by geographic influences—is the correct view. The quotation assumes three different geographic regions in the English colonies and a different way of life in each. It uses general terms for these three regions— South, mid-Atlantic, New England—so the writer is forced either to supply specific names for colonies in these regions or to deal in generalizations. It is always better to be specific, so you should immediately focus on one or two colonies in each region. You would then use these colonies to illustrate the way of life of the region as well as the geography of the region. The essence of the question, then, is the relationship between the geography and the way of life in each of the three regions as illustrated by the three or more colonies you have chosen.

Most histories of colonial America emphasize Virginia in the South, Pennsylvania in the mid-Atlantic region, and Massachusetts Bay Colony in New England as typical of the three regions. This division is clear, easy, and a valid one to make. Therefore, you would probably pick these three colonies to illustrate your answer. Thus, having decided on specific illustrations for the three regions mentioned in the question, the next step in the analysis would be to focus on the phrase *colonial way of life*. What was the colonial way of life in each of these three colonies? That is, how did the people live and make a living? A few ideas should come quickly to mind. If they do, you may decide this is a question you wish to answer. Then you must decide if geography was the primary factor in determining that way of life.

You have now completed the analyis of the question. You have taken the question apart, considered the definition of words and decided what is being asked. You are ready to proceed.

Step Two—Collecting and Sorting Information

Once you know what the question asks, you should move on to the next step: *collecting and sorting your information.* For this question, under the name of each colony you have decided to use as an illustration, you could write a few simple phrases illustrating the way of life in the colony. Also a few brief phrases, illustrating the geographic conditions, will help in analyzing the second part of the question. The notes might look something like the box shown here (the columns and letters are referred to later in the text; they would not be part of your actual note taking):

Notes for Answering Question

Column M
(Way of Life)

Column O
(Geography)

Virginia
e. plantations
r. Church of England
   London Co. for Eco. Reasons
e. Slaves
p. House of Burgesses

warm mild
river transport
tobacco
good soil

Penn.
e. merchants
r. Quakers / Germans
p. Wm. Penn., proprietor
   melting pot

mix of S. and N.E.
little river transport
grains and vegetables

Mass. Bay
e. merchants / sailors
r. Puritans
p. town meetings

cold
rocky soil
lumber
harbors

There are, of course, other ways of organizing the answer to this question. Looking at the brief notes in Column M, you will see that r under each region refers to religion, p to political developments or organization, and e to economic activities. You might organize your answer with a section on religion in all three regions, followed by sections on political developments and economic activities. This organization would appear more complicated, but it illustrates the variety of ways in which one can organize answers. The idea of organizing an answer around religion, politics, and economics jumps at you from the notes. This is one reason why note-taking is so important in preparing essay answers—it focuses attention on possible ways of organizing material.

Therefore, as you make notes for your essay answer and sort through the facts that you know are relevant, consider also the various ways of presenting this information.

Step Three—Developing Your Thesis

As mentioned previously, every essay *must* have a thesis. Your thesis is your personal opinion on the given topic. In this seven-step method of essay writing, a stated thesis should be included in the introductory paragraph so the reader learns immediately of your reaction to the question.

The writer of Sample Essay 1 decided to agree with the statement that geography was the primary factor in determining the life-style in the colonies but that fact is never clearly stated in the essay. Does this make sense to you? That is the great weakness of Essay 1.

The writer of Sample Essay 2 did not believe that the statement made complete sense. This writer saw an alternative explanation or cause for the differences in the way of life of the three colonial regions. He or she accepted the fact of differences in geography and in the colonial way of life in the three regions. In the last sentence of that introductory paragraph the writer presents his or her personal opinion or thesis on the issue. The writer only partly agrees with the statement. Part of answering any question completely is the presentation of a thesis. What would your thesis be for this question? Would you accept the view expressed in the quotation after analyzing the question, or would you qualify it, as the author of Essay 2 has done, or would your reject it totally? As you analyze the question and as you collect your information, you should develop your own thesis. You are expected to present your opinion in every essay you write and, if you fail to do so, you risk getting a lower score on the Advanced Placement examination.

Step Four—Writing the Introduction

An introductory paragraph should answer two questions: "What is the question?" and "What is the author's opinion on the question?" When these two questions are not answered, the reader is confused. Usually the statement of the topic comes in the first part of the paragraph, and the writer's opinion or thesis is the last sentence of a paragraph. Remember: the thesis of an essay is the statement of the writer's opinion on the topic under consideration.

In Sample Introduction 2, the question is quoted and the author's opinion, without stating it as "my opinion" or "I believe," is clearly stated in the word *exaggerated*. The thesis then follows in the last sentence and is clear to the reader.

This introductory paragraph also illustrates another very important aspect of the essay introduction. The sample begins with a general comment on the topic, slowly narrows the focus of the topic to the specific question, and then narrows it more to the thesis. The introductory paragraph is like a lighthouse or a flashlight beam.

This beam catches the viewer in its broad beam and then brings his or her attention to the source or, in this case, the thesis. Your introduction should always work like a lighthouse beam, starting broad enough in scope to get the reader's interest, and then directing attention to a specific point.

Step Five—Writing the Body of the Essay

Once the crucial introduction is completed, you are ready for the fifth step: *the writing of the body of the essay.* It is in this section that the factual information to prove your thesis should be presented. The facts should be organized in a logical sequence. Each major set of facts should be presented in a separate paragraph. These paragraphs might be considered as the separate batteries that power a flashlight, thus making a beam. Each must work separately, yet they must be connected. There are many ways to achieve such connections—similar ideas, linking words (such as however, therefore, but), or repetition of an aspect of the question. Look again at Essay 2. Paragraphs 1 and 2 are linked by the idea of trade and 2 and 3 by repeating the word life-style.

Often, in defending a position, you will come across several strong arguments that can be used against your view. If your are able to refute any of these arguments, you should do so. Otherwise it can be useful to admit that they exist in the first paragraph of the body of your essay and to then present your strong facts in the succeeding paragraphs, ending with your strongest point. This is a good lawyer's or debater's technique, and in your essay you are like a lawyer arguing a case.

When you jotted down your brief notes as part of Step Two, you were collecting information which can now be used to prove your thesis. Look at your brief notes and arrange them in the most effective sequence for proving your thesis by numbering the items 1, 2, 3, etc. At this point, your numbered items should provide the basis for a separate paragraph or for several sentences within different paragraphs as you expand on the concept represented by each item. For example, in the brief notes presented earlier, the single word *Puritans* could easily be expanded into several sentences within a paragraph. This is the way you will use your brief notes to help write the body of your essay.

In the case of this sample, the notes jotted down on the colony of Virignia might logically be presented in the order numbered 1-6. You might leave out the

House of Burgesses and the Church of England, as they seem to have little relation to geography. You could include river transportation as number 7 as a link to Pennsylvania's lack of rivers.

COLUMN M	COLUMN O
(Way of Life)	*(Geography)*
Virginia	
5. plantations	2. warm mild
Church of England	7. river transport
4. London Co. for Eco. Reasons	3. tobacco
6. Slaves	1. good soil
House of Burgesses	

Remember in writing the body of the essay that you must use paragraphs that stand like the batteries in a flashlight—each linked together at the contact point (your paragraph links), but each a separate unity giving power to the beam of light. The batteries are held together by the casing, which provides the structure for the flashlight, just as your brief outline and numbers provide your essay with a structure.

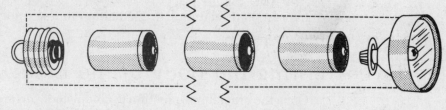

Step Six—Writing the Conclusion

Once you have completed the body of the paper, you are ready for the sixth step: *writing the conclusion*. The conclusion of the essay is as important as the introductory paragraph. The conclusion holds the essay together and might be compared to the cap on the end of a flashlight, which holds the batteries in and forces them into contact to make the beam. Without a good cap, the flashlight does not work; without a good conclusion, the essay also does not work.

The conclusion should bring the reader back to the question and back to the thesis. An excellent preparation for writing the conclusion is to read your introduction and the body of your essay through before writing the conclusion. Then, keeping in mind what you have said and what your thesis is, write a paragraph that reintroduces the thesis and the topic without merely repeating the introduction. If possible, you should end your conclusion with an indication of the applicability of your thesis to other situations, thus leaving the reader with the idea that you have proven something of general significance.

There are two things one should avoid doing in the conclusion. The first thing to avoid is presenting a summary of all you've included. There is nothing worse than the conclusion that begins, "Now I have shown that. . . ." It is insulting to the reader. If you have "shown that," then it should be obvious to the reader and you do not have to tell it again. Secondly, do not introduce new evidence in the conclusion—evidence that will help prove your thesis. Get all the evidence into the body of the paper. The conclusion is simply your flashlight cap, and it is not one of the batteries. For many students these two former methods seem the obvious way to end an essay, but they are simplistic, boring, do not do anything to help your case, and antagonize the reader.

With these two negative warnings in mind, you might wonder how you can possibly write a conclusion. The conclusion to Essay 2 provides a fairly effective example to look at and follow. The conclusion to Essay 1 is a poor one because the writer began by saying what he or she had done, introduces new materials, does not reintroduce the topic or the thesis, and makes no attempt to relate his or her ideas to other situations. Other sample conclusions will be discussed in later chapters.

Step Seven—Reading Over Your Essay

When you have completed writing your essay, there is one step left—reading it over to check the spelling, style, and consistency. It is very helpful if you start reading with your conclusion and then read the introduction, checking to see that they agree. Often students who have not analyzed the question well and who have not devleoped an effective thesis will contradict themselves in these two paragraphs. Make sure you have not done that, then read the body of the paper and the conclusion. Correct any spelling or punctuation errors and check to see if the paragraphs link together smoothly.

As your work through this book, studying and reviewing for the Advanced Placement examination, you will want to use these seven steps. They should become habit for you so that you do not have to think about them. Once you can write effective, well-organized, and factually sound essays using these steps, then you will want to try a few variations on the format. First develop this technique. Follow the seven steps as you prepare essay answers for questions in this book. Make formal outlines of these answers after you have written the essays until you are satisfied that you are organizing good answers.

One Final Reminder . . .

There is one last item to consider about the essay style. Most essayists avoid the use of the personal pronoun *I*. The reader assumes that everything in the essay is what the writer believes, so "I think" or "I believe" is redundant. The usual pronouns used are those of the third-person editorial *we* or the impersonal *one*. Although there are times when an author uses the *I* with great effect, it is rare. Stylistically it is better for the beginner to avoid using *I* in essay writing.

To recapitulate, the seven steps to make essay writing easy are:

1. ANALYZE THE QUESTION
2. COLLECT AND SORT INFORMATION
3. DEVELOP YOUR THESIS
4. WRITE THE INTRODUCTION
5. WRITE THE BODY OF THE ESSAY
6. WRITE THE CONCLUSION
7. READ OVER THE ESSAY

As you use these seven steps, keep in mind the image of the flashlight. It should prove a valuable image for you as you construct your essays.

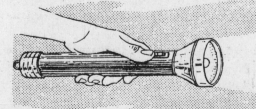

PART THREE 1 Colonial America Before 1763

Important Facets of This Period

It is generally acknowledged by historians that the foundations for the American nation were laid during the colonial period. If this is accepted, then in studying the colonial period an important focus would be to identify these foundations. The more one can identify links among periods and begin to develop meaningful cause-and-effect relationships, the more effective a study of the past will be. The identification of these relationships should provide the basic pattern for the study of the colonial period before 1763 and for all the study done for the Advanced Placement examination in American history.

Today many courses in American history begin with 1763. The feeling is that the period after the Treaty of Paris in 1763, which ended the French and Indian War, brought to a climax the differences between the colonists and the British. These differences had evolved over the preceding 150 years of settlement. In American history courses, as these differences are studied as steps to the American Revolution, a quick look is taken at the origin of the differences in the early colonial period. The Advanced Placement examination acknowledges this trend in American history teaching, and therefore on the examination less emphasis is placed on the history of America before 1763 than on other periods.

In spite of the acknowledgment that many courses do not begin until 1763, however, there will be multiple-choice questions on the colonial period before 1763, and there may be an essay question for which information from this period will be of importance. If, in studying this period, one focuses on the connections between the colonial period and later periods of American history, he or she will be prepared to answer questions and to use the information effectively. Although the sample essay questions presented below are restricted to the colonial period before 1763, the information required for effective answers is related to many later developments in American history.

Among the important developments of the colonial period that have a bearing on later history are:

1. The relations between the Native Americans and the colonists
2. The geographic differences among the regions of settlement
3. The motivation for the settlement of the different European colonies, especially the English colonies
4. The economic development of each colony and the English mercantilist system
5. The development of social and cultural attitudes and differences among the colonies
6. The evolution of a sense of local identity in each colony
7. The attempts at unity among various colonies
8. The establishment of local political institutions in each colony
9. The westward expansion of each colony
10. The military conflicts between the English settlers and both the native Americans and other European settlers

Sample Essay Question—Assess the Validity/Evaluate This Statement

In each chapter we will present and analyze different types of essay questions. We will also present in each chapter a sample answer to at least one essay question. The essay questions presented in this chapter are examples of the *Evaluate this statement* form discussed in Part Two and a very popular variation of that type, the *Assess the validity* form.

In Part Two we presented two sample answers to a question dealing with the colonial period. The following question deals with that era, but it goes beyond the colonial period and calls for information from the period of the American Revolution. As stated above, essay questions on the exam may require knowledge of the colonial period in this way. The question is adapted from the Advanced Placement American History Examination of 1969.

Sample Question

> In the 1600s the major issues of U.S. colonial history revolved around theological issues. In the 1700s, the major issues revolved around political issues.
> Assess the validity of this statement.

Comments on Sample Question

Recalling our Seven Steps in Essay Writing, we must first analyze the statement. For some students the understanding of centuries is difficult, and this would be the first matter to clear up. In the Christian dating method, those dates since the birth of Christ are designated as A.D.. Because we must designate the years 1-99 the first century A.D. (the first 100 years) The second century begins with the year 100 and goes to 199 even though the dates begin with one. All centuries in this era are likewise one number higher than the first or first two digits of the number of the year. Therefore, dates in the 17th century are those years starting with 16, so that 1607, 1620, 1688 are all 17th-century dates and 1701 and 1756 are 18th-century dates. Until that matter is clear, the question cannot be analyzed.

The next concern in analyzing this question is to determine the meaning of the words *theological* and *political*. As you study American history, be certain you understand the specialized vocabulary used. Work at building your vocabulary. To help you, a Glossary of important terms is included in the Appendix of this book.

Theological comes from the Greek words *theos*, meaning God, and *logos*, meaning word or speak. *Theology*, therefore, means speaking about God and *theological* is the adjective form of the word. Theological issues are issues dealing with God or religion. *Political* is an adjective. It means pertaining to the conduct of government. It too has a Greek origin, coming from the word *politikos*, meaning of the citizens. Students often find it helpful to learn the origins of words; it is an excellent way to build vocabulary.

Once you are certain of the meaning of the words and time period, it should be clear the statement suggests that the great concerns of one century revolved about religious issues while the concerns of the next were "largely political." You are asked to assess the validity of the statement. Assess means to determine the value of something as a tax collector assesses the value of property to determine how much tax a person should pay. You must determine what value or truth there is to this statement. Is it true or only partly true or is it false? What do you think? Following the Seven Steps in Essay Writing, you will next want to jot down information about the theological and political issues in two columns labeled 17th century and 18th century. Once you have done that you'll be ready to write your thesis, since you will have determined your opinion on this topic. Then you will go on to write your essay following Steps Four through Six. You may wish to write your own answer before proceeding to read the following sample answer.

Sample Answer   Religion and politics always seem to be important issues in people's lives. Beginning with the first colonists in America during the 17th century, theology was an important issue. Indeed, the greatest reason that many of the colonists had for moving to America was the desire to find freedom of religion in a new land. Many of the fundamental concepts that emerged in the first colonies founded for religous reasons were later, in the 18th century, the ideals for which colonists fought political battles.

At first, the North American continent did not reward individuals who migrated to win a fortune. Several attempts—such as that of Sir Walter Raleigh in the Carolinas—of businesspeople tyring to get rich searching for gold or hoping for big farming profits, failed. Therefore, people generally went to America in search of freedom from the political, economic, social, and especially religious binds of European society.

The Puritans were a prime example of religious development in America. They had become social outcasts in England, where they had little voice in matters, and so they migrated to America. There they set up the Massachusetts Bay Colony, which flourished. With religious motivation to fulfill a "covenant" with God to establish the "New Jerusalem," a successful model colony in America, they laid many of the foundations that would later be of great political importance. They established a two-part representative body or legislature elected by the people and had a single leader, or executive, who for many years was John Winthrop. Winthrop might easily have preserved all legislative power to himself, but he did not, perhaps inspired by a theological view that believers within the community are all equal.

The Massachusetts Bay Colony had many conflicts that revolved about the meaning of the word *believer*. With the Puritans, if you did not agree with them, you were damned and could not live in their "perfect society." People such as Roger Williams became involved in these conflicts and had to found new colonies. The poor witches of Salem show how theological issues dominated the century.

Other colonies also were involved in theological conflicts; the Quaker William Penn founded Pennsylvania for religious freedom, and the Catholic Lord Baltimore supported religious toleration in Maryland when it was not the popular stand. Even Virginia had religious Blue Laws and the colony grew rapidly as Church of Englanders fled England during the rule of the Puritan Cromwell. The century was full of religious conflict, both in England and the colonies.

Under the influence of Puritan ideas as well as the philosophies of many other men, such as John Locke and Montesquieu and leaders of the European Enlightenment, state legislatures were formed in each of the colonies; and charters or constitutions, though requiring approval by the king, were written. Objections began to arise when the lack of power of these representative legislatures was felt.

After 1763, when England had ended its Seven Years' War with France, it turned its attention to America to try to find a way of paying the expense of war. Internal taxes, such as the excise tax on paper (Stamp Act) to which there was strong objection, and external taxes on trade were enacted by Parliament without the consent of the colonial legislatures. Puritan tradition was one force that warned America that "taxation without representation" was wrong. The theological issues of the 17th century — who was a believer and could live in a colony? — gave way to the political issues of the 18th century — who would control the life of the colonies? When the Acts of Trade and Navigation were enforced and other acts were enacted, expecially the Declaratory Act, emphasizing the power of Parliament to tax and legislate without the consent of the colonists, the colonists felt that their political rights had been infringed upon, and they revolted.

The period of Articles of Confederation was a testing period in American history. There was trust in the workability of a true democracy, and though an attempt at this was made, the federal government, unable to tax or enforce any laws, was too weak and could not tie the nation together. The political issue had become one of how to set up a new government.

The Constitution brought all the political ideas of Americans together in compromise. Puritan ideals were certainly present here, but the issues were not theological but political. The political conflicts between industrial and agrarian influences and those of framers and financiers would persist for many years, but a new government was formed that allowed way for political issues to be compromised. This had not been done with 17th-century theological issues.

In the 17th century, theological issues were not compromised, but in the struggle over these issues ideas of identity and self-government were developed that became the great political issues Americans fought for in the 18th century. Religion and politics were important colonial issues.

What is your evaluation of the above essay? What are its strong points and its weak points? You should make a formal outline of the answer in order to identify the structure of the essay. Once you have made your own evaluation of the essay, you should compare your notes with the following teacher comments.

Teacher Comments on Sample Answer

"The student answering this question on theological and political issues has written an adequate but not an outstanding paper. The paper includes enough factual information to provide a very good answer, but the student fails to use this information to respond to the question asked. The student does not understand the difference between reciting information and using information to support a particular thesis.

"The student has written an introductory paragraph and has presented a thesis in the last sentence of the introduction. The thesis is interesting and could be developed, but as worded, the thesis does not relate to the 'great issues' of the 17th and 18th centuries. What is suggested is that the 'great' theological issues of the 17th century became the 'great' political issues of the 18th. Unfortunately, in the body of the paper this relationship is not clearly explored.

"Instead, the student describes important theological incidents in the 17th century, such as the Salem witch trials, and only briefly focuses on issues, such as the role of legislative bodies, which became important later. Still, the 17th-century material is better presented than the 18th-century information.

"In the 18th century, the student too often loses sight of the relationship he or she is trying to establish between the issues in the two centuries. Although the student refers to Puritan ideas in the section, he or she falls into the all-too-open trap of listing information without using it to advance the argument. When discussing the Articles of Confederation and the Constitution, it seems the student is most interested in presenting his or her knowledge of the struggle over the development of the U.S. government, and that he or she has forgotten the theological issues of the 17th century, which, according to the original thesis, had become the major political issues of the 18th.

"The student has an adequate conclusion in which the thesis is restated. He or she avoids repeating arguments and also makes an attempt both in the conclusion and introduction to relate the question to a broader time period. The organization follows a clear pattern established by the quotation — the pattern of the two centuries. Apparently the student did not consider the possibility of organizing the paper around those issues which were theological in the 17th century and political in the 18th century. Such an organization would appear to have a closer connection to the thesis than the organization he or she followed, and it might have helped the paper.

"In the future the student needs to be more careful in analyzing the question and in using information as it relates to the question. The student had fully adequate information, and the body of his or her paper has an obvious if not highly effective organization. The student should receive an above average but not a top grade."

Did your analysis develop the same points as the teacher's? If you did not agree, then reread the sample answer and see where you and the teacher diverged.

The *Assess the validity* question has been very popular on recent Advanced Placement examinations. It allows the student great freedom of choice in designing the answer, as the statement may be accepted or rejected and the specific information to be used is determined by the writer.

There are many variations of this basic type of question. The directions may ask you to *evaluate* or *discuss* a statement or generalization, and again the writer has many choices as to what position to take and what evidence to use. The important point is to stay on the subject and evaluate or judge the statement if the direction says to evaluate. If you are asked to discuss, be certain to write about the statement in the essay discussing it using historical evidence. Sometimes more directions will be given, as in the following examples of this type of question.

Sample Directions

1. Evaluate this statement as it relates to the years 1763-1776 and indicate to what extent you agree or disagree with it.

2. Assess the validity of this generalization for the period 1763-1776.

3. Discuss the validity of this quotation as it applies to the presidencies of George Washington, John Adams, and Thomas Jefferson.

4. Judging from evidence drawn from the years 1763-1776 and 1850-1861, assess the validity of this viewpoint.

You will want to practice your own writing ability and develop your knowledge of the colonial period by writing essay answers to several of the following questions. These questions, as with all of those presented in this book, are not inclusive of all the issues that might arise on the Advanced Placement examination. These questions are representative examination questions, and they will help you organize your knowledge of American history.   These five questions will give you practice with the popular *Assess the validity* and *Evaluate this statement* types of essay questions. Remember this type of question can be used to test material from any period of American history.

Practice Essay Questions

1. "The English founded colonies to escape oppression in England." Evaluate this statement.

2. "The British colonies were so antagonistic to each other that they were unable to unite to face the attack of common enemies." Assess the validity of this statement.

3. "Before 1763 British mercantilist policy, while restricting colonial economic development, allowed colonial political life to develop unhampered by the Mother Country." Evaluate this statement.

4. "The colonial wars fought between the British and the French for domination of the North American continent created a sense of national spirit among the British colonies and created the basis for later unity."· Assess the validity of this statement.

5. "As long as the French controlled parts of North America, they accepted the native American population as equal, whereas the British colonists viewed them as hostile." Evaluate this statement.

Comments on Question 1

Note that question 1 focuses on the reasons for colonization. The quotation suggests that there was one cause for colonization. This would appear an oversimplification. In your answer you would probably explore other reasons for colonization and compare several different British colonies.

Comments on Question 2

The second question raises the entire issue of colonial rivalry and jealousy. There are many examples of antagonism, but there are also important examples of cooperation among the colonies, especially after 1763, and you should note here there is no limit set on the time period covered. As in the sample question in this chapter, you should plan to deal with information up to the independence of the American colonies.

Comments on Question 3

A definite time period is set in the third question, which is also a more complex and perhaps more interesting question. It requires an understanding of historic terms and of a particular historical policy. The question involves a double relationship, and therefore it resembles the sample essay in this chapter. The quotation offers an organizing method for the answer, and this should allow you to avoid being overwhelmed with detailed information.

Comments on Question 4

Question 4 introduces the topic of colonial wars and their impact on the colonists. Military events provide an important element in American history, but one should not merely study battles. Here the question forces you to deal with the impact of war on the life of the colonies. It requires you to know the wars, but you must also include causes and results, peace terms, frontier developments, and, most important, the psychological impact upon the people. Again, since there is no time period, you will need to consider the aftermath of the French and Indian War, which ended in 1763.

Comments on Question 5

The last question raises an interesting and timely topic, that of British racial attitudes as expressed in colonial history. The question assumes a difference in the attitudes of two European colonizing powers, and you need to test this difference. Since the French were essentially forced out of North America in 1763, you might stop your analysis with that date, but you could bring the analysis up to independence. The question requires information from different sources to properly evaluate the quotation, so do not be trapped by the word *hostile* into discussing wars and massacres only. Hostility can manifest itself in a variety of ways. The question, then, becomes a complex one and one that may be more challenging since it does not deal directly with the topics considered in the usual history book.

These brief analyses should start you on your way to writing effective and well-prepared essays on the five sample topics. The questions should help you study and review key information from colonial American history and to be aware of the information you need to know for the Advanced Placement exam.

Multiple-Choice Questions—The Chronology Question

As indicated in the Introduction, the Advanced Placement examination includes one hundred multiple-choice questions. In each chapter of this book, sample questions dealing with information from the different periods will be presented. Different types of multiple-choice questions will be analyzed in each chapter and the correct answer for each question will be discussed. This is done to stimulate your thinking about different periods. Although many topics will be introduced, these questions alone cannot provide a full review of American history.

In scoring the multiple-choice section of the AP examination, one-fourth of a point is taken off for each incorrect answer. Therefore, one should not guess blindly at answers, but rather analyze the choices. If at least one of the five choices can be eliminated then you should mark a selection, since statistically you have at least an even chance, and if you can eliminate two or more choices you have a better than even chance, of gaining a point. As the sample multiple-choice questions in each chapter are analyzed, methods to eliminate incorrect choices will be suggested.

In this chapter we will look at the most obvious type of multiple-choice question — the type that requires a factual recall of chronological information. Many people find historic dates boring and difficult. Some dates are important, however, and in the Western concept of historical cause and effect, a knowledge of the chronological order of events is essential. You should know important dates, but you must also know the order in which events occurred. As suggested in Part One, the making of time charts dealing with related events can be a very valuable device in studying history. In sample 1 below, a time chart focused on the dates of the founding of the British colonies would provide the information requested.

One thing to remember is you may make marks on the test booklet. As you eliminate possible answers on a difficult multiple-choice question you may find putting an x beside the choice or crossing it out to be helpful. You should also skip questions you are uncertain of and return to them. A check (√) by the number will alert you to which questions you skipped. However, after skipping a question be sure and check that you are placing a black pencil mark in the correct oval.

Sample Question 1

> Which of the following British colonies was founded last?
> (A) Plymouth
> (B) Pennsylvania
> (C) Georgia
> (D) Massachusetts Bay Colony
> (E) Virginia

Comments

The correct answer is (C) Georgia. The same question could be phrased, "Which colony was founded first?" In any case, you must know the chronological order and preferably the dates of the founding of the colonies. There is very little you can do with a question of chronology unless you know the chronology. However, if you recognized some of the events but not all, you may be able to arrive at an answer. Sample Question 2 is an example of such a question.

Sample Question 2

> Which of the following English acts or documents was issued first?
> (A) Iron Act
> (B) Proprietary Grant to William Penn
> (C) The Charter of the Dominion of New England
> (D) Molasses Act
> (E) Massachusetts Bay Company Charter

Comments

The correct answer is (E) Massachusetts Bay Company Charter. You are probably familiar with the Molasses Act and the Iron Act. They both deal with the regulation of trade, which was not a major issue until after 1660, by which time the majority of the colonies had been founded. Logically, since several of the choices deal with colonial charters, you would suspect that these two trade acts did not come first. You are then left with three acts, one of which, the Charter of the

Dominion of New England, is probably unfamiliar. It dealt with the union of New England and New York under one royal governor, as an idea for efficiency in colonial rule developed by James II about 1685. The last two, choices B and E, are probably vaguely familiar. The wording of each choice should give you the subject dealt with.

The founding of colonies is a major part of colonial history. If you know when colonies were founded then you would know that Massachusetts came before Penn's Pennsylvania. You should also be able to deduce that one colony in New England would be granted a charter before one would be granted for the entire area. This type of analysis of the choices offered as answers to multiple-choice questions dealing with chronology will often help you to locate the correct answer. Usually, however, it is essential that you know the chronology or dates of the events offered as possible answers.

Study the following multiple-choice questions. How well can you do on them? The various types presented will be analyzed in later chapters. Following the sixteen questions are brief analyses of each correct answer.

Practice Multiple-Choice Questions

1. "It being one chief project of Satan to keep man from the knowledge of the scriptures . . . it is therefore ordered by this court [Assembly] . . . that every township within this jurisdiction after the Lord hath increased them to the number of fifty householders, shall then forthwith appoint one within their towns to teach all such children as shall resort [apply] to him to write and read, whose wages shall be paid either by parents of masters of such children, or by the inhabitants in general . . . provided that those who send their children be not oppressed by paying much more than they can have them taught for in other towns."

   This passage sets forth basic American attitudes concerning the
   - (A) separation of church and state
   - (B) the power of the state over the power of Satan
   - (C) political power of townships
   - (D) importance of education
   - (E) value of fair and equal taxation

2. All of the following important colonial cities are correctly paired with the colony EXCEPT
   - (A) Williamsburg - Virginia
   - (B)   Annapolis - Maryland
   - (C) Salem - Rhode Island
   - (D) Charlestown - South Carolina
   - (E)   New London - Connecticut

3. Which of the following events occurred first?
   - (A) Bacon's Rebellion
   - (B) Glorious Revolution in England
   - (C) War of Spanish Succession
   - (D) Formation of the New England Confederation
   - (E) French and Indian War

4. Which of the following was NOT the leader of the settlement paired with his name?
    (A) John Smith - Jamestown
    (B) General Oglethorpe - Savannah
    (C) William Penn - Philadelphia
    (D) Roger Williams - Hartford
    (E) William Bradford - Plymouth

5. All of the following acts were part of British mercantilist policy EXCEPT
    (A) Act of Toleration   (D) Sugar or Molasses Act
    (B) Hatters Act   (E) Woolens Act
    (C) Iron Act

6. The chief significance of the Great Awakening was that it
    (A) led to the foundation of colleges
    (B) provided Jonathan Edwards with an opportunity to preach
    (C) was the first genuine unified movement of the American colonists
    (D) revived intolerance
    (E) created new interest in the churches

7. The most significant difference between the pilgrims and the Puritans is that the Pilgrims
    (A) arrived in New England first
    (B) obtained a grant of settlement from the London Company
    (C) wished to separate from the Church of England
    (D) had a strong leader
    (E) celebrated the first Thanksgiving

8. In which region is Fort Duquesne located?
    (A) 1   (D) 4
    (B) 2   (E) 5
    (C) 3

9. The first permanent English settlement on the mainland of North America
   was at
   (A) St. Augustine   (D) Jamestown
   (B) Plymouth   (E) Raleigh
   (C) Quebec

10. The Treaty of Tordesillas
    (A) divided the New World between the Spaniards and the Portuguese
    (B) established Spanish as the official language of South America
    (C) resolved the French and English claims to Martinique
    (D) determined the border between Florida and Georgia
    (E) proclaimed the Papacy's desire to prevent warfare between colonies
        and native Americans

11. The Native Americans did all of the following EXCEPT
    (A) aid the Pilgrims in Plymouth
    (B) split in their support of the French and English in the 18th century
        colonial wars
    (C) felt their way of life was threatened by the territorial expansion of the
        colonists
    (D) converted to Christianity in very limited numbers
    (E) organized effectively to block English expansion west of the Appa-
        lachians

12. Which of the following men explored in North America for the French?
    (A) Magellan   (D) Frobisher
    (B) Coronado   (E) Champlain
    (C) Hudson

13. The trial of Peter Zenger in New York has often been considered an
    important step in the development of
    (A) religious toleration   (D) the right to bear arms
    (B) freedom of the press   (E) concepts of privacy
    (C) trial by jury

14. The Albany Plan was
    (A) the first plan for city development
    (B) a scheme to make money
    (C) a plan for colonial union
    (D) a plan for attack in King William's War
    (E) a plan to build a canal connecting Albany with the west

15. Which of the following was NOT an important cause of the French and Indian
    War?
    (A) Formation of the Ohio Company
    (B) Desire of Massachusetts colonists to clear the French out of Canada
    (C) Washington and Braddock's attack on Fort Duquesne
    (D) trade limitations imposed by the Acts of Trade
    (E) French exploration in the Great Lakes region and westward

16. Which of the following had the least significance in providing experience and concepts that were used by the colonists in their arguments and fight for independence?
(A) French and Indian War
(B) New England town meetings
(C) use of the Power of the Purse by the Virginia House of Burgesses
(D) the Albany Plan
(E) development by the colonists of crops for export

Answers and Answer Explanations

1. D	2. C	3. D	4. D
5. A	6. C	7. C	8. C
9. D	10. A	11. E	12. E
13. B	14. C	15. D	16. E

1. (D) Local financing and control of public education has been an important American attitude towards education since Massachusetts Bay Colony passed this, the "Olde Deluder Satan" law.

2. (C) Salem in Massachusetts is famous as the location of the colonial witch trials. The other cities are correctly matched.

3. (D) The formation of the New England Confederation was the first attempt at colonial union. This was formed to combat the Indian threat to frontier settlements. The other events involving violent actions occurred later in colonial history.

4. (D) Roger Williams was the founder of a colony on Narragansett Bay, which joined several other colonies as the federated Colony of Rhode Island and the Providence Plantations. Connecticut was settled under the leadership of Thomas Hooker. The other men were leaders of the named colonies.

5. (A) The Act of Toleration was first passed in Maryland in 1649, granting religious toleration in that colony. It was soon repealed. The other acts were all passed by Parliament with the purpose of controlling trade and manufacture in the colonies.

6. (C) The Great Awakening was the first movement of religious revival experienced in all the colonies. Although each choice offered is true, the chief significance of the Great Awakening would be its unifying nature, and therefore (C) would be the best answer.

7. (C) Again, all the choices are true, but the most significant difference between Puritans and Pilgrims lies in their relationship to the Church of England. The Pilgrims wished to separate from the church and start their own congregational form of worship. The Puritans initially were interested in purifying or reforming the Church of England.

8. (C) Fort Duquesne was founded by the French in western Pennsylvania (area 3). The British changed the name to Fort Pitt when they captured the fort, and it later became the city of Pittsburgh.

9. (D) The first permanent English settlement on the mainland of North America was at Jamestown.

10. (A) The Treaty of Tordesillas in 1494 redefined the demarcation line by which one year earlier the Pope had assigned the Americas to Spain and Africa and India to Portugal. With the new demarcation line Portugal was given a claim to Brazil.

11. (E) The Native Americans did all of the items listed except organize effectively to block English expansion westward. Many tribes supported the French in the French and Indian War. They later tried to block the westward movement of the colonists and of independent whites, but they were not successful.

12. (E) Each of these men were early explorers of the New World, but only Champlain, for whom Lake Champlain in New York State is named, explored under the French flag.

13. (B) The trial of Peter Zenger is often cited as the true beginning of the free press in America. The trial was one of the most important in the colonies although some historians now believe its significance has been exaggerated.

14. (C) The Albany Plan was drafted by Benjamin Franklin in 1754 in an attempt to get the colonies to unite for their common defense. It was not adopted, but many features foreshadowed the Articles of Confederation and the Constitution.

15. (D) There were many causes of the French and Indian War, but the limitation on trade under the British Acts of Trade and Navigation was not one of them. The acts were a major cause of the American Revolution.

16. (E) The first four events listed provided the colonists with the experience and/or concepts to be used in the fight for independence. Fighting methods were developed in the war. Town meetings and the Power of the Purse (appropriation of money) gave good arguments for the rights of English subjects. See Number 14 above for the Albany Plan. While the development of export crops and subsequent trade was essential in creating viable colonies, the process supplied little experience useful in the fight for independence.

Bibliography

As every student of American history is aware, there are innumerable books and pamphlets one may read on the topic. Many adults are history buffs and do all their recreational reading in American history; some even focus on one aspect of American history, such as the Civil War or colonial history. With this mass of material available, it is very difficult for the young student or the experienced teacher to pick and choose the most important or the most interesting material from each period to supplement the standard textbooks mentioned in the bibliography in Part One. To provide some direction at the end of each chapter, a few works will be suggested that may stimulate your study. In this chapter more than the usual number of works are listed to give you a sense of the range of works and topics from which you might select. As stated above, you do not need to read all of these books for the Advanced Placement exam. You should, however, read beyond the standard textbooks in areas that interest you. Texts include suggested bibliographies, and you may find listed there books that relate more to your interests than any of those books listed at the end of chapters. It is important that you supplement your textbook reading, but it is unimportant whether it be with books of the age, such as Franklin's *Autobiography*; with collections of documents, such as Commager's *Documents of American History*; with secondary historical accounts, such as Wright's *The Atlantic Frontier: Colonial American Civilization, 1607–1763*; or with good fictional accounts that supply the feel of a period, such as Miller's play *The Crucible*.

Bailyn, Bernard. *New England Merchants in the 17th Century*. Gloucester, Massachusetts: Peter Smith, 1955.

Brandon, William. *Indians*. New York: American Heritage, 1985.

Dickerson, O.M. *The Navigation Acts and the American Revolution*. New York: Octagon Books, 1974.

Franklin, Benjamin. *Autobiography*. New York: Amsco School Publications, 1970.

Leach, D.E. *Roots of Conflict 1677–1763*. Chapel Hall: University of North Carolina Press, 1989.

Morgan, E.S. *The Puritan Dilemma: The Story of John Winthrop*. Boston: Little, Brown & Co., 1962.

Peckham, H.H. *The Colonial Wars*. Chicago: University of Chicago Press, 1965.

Wertenbaker, T.J. *The First Americans*. Saint Clair Shores, MI: Scholarly

Wright, L.B. *The Atlantic Frontier; Colonial American Civilization: 1607–1763*. New York: Cornell University Press, 1963.

Yale, Elizabeth. *Amos Fortune, Free Man*. New York: Puffin Books, 1989.

Fiction

Cather, Willa. *Shadows on the Rock* (Quebec). New York: Random House, 1971.

Hawthorne, Nathaniel. *House of Seven Gables* (Salem). Oxford University Press, 1991.

Miller, Arthur. *The Crucible* (Salem Witch Trials). New York: Penguin, 1976.

Roberts, Kenneth. *Northwest Passage* (French & Indian War). Ashland, NH: Haas Ent., 1983.

PART THREE **2** The Era of the American Revolution 1763-1789

Important Facets of This Period

The issues and conflicts that led to the independence of the British colonies, the winning of that independence, and the establishment of the new nation — the United States of America — are the major themes of this period. It is a crucial period for understanding American history and one that should be studied in all American history survey courses. One can expect questions dealing with various aspects of this era on any American History examination.

Questions on this period can be designed in several ways. They might deal with one aspect of the period, such as the steps leading to independence, or questions might compare two periods, as is done in the sample question that follows, taken from the 1960 Advanced Placement examination. A third type of question might ask you to consider the relative importance of social, economic, or political factors in determining an event. An alternative, and one that should be kept in mind as you study, is comparison questions in which you are asked to analyze or compare specific aspects of two separate periods of American history. The last sample essay question, number five, is of this type. Since you may find such questions difficult to answer at this point in your study, more examples of this type of essay question will not be introduced until later in this book.

As mentioned in the previous chapter, today many courses in American history begin with the Treaty of Paris in 1763, which ended the French and Indian War (Seven Years' War in Europe). In these courses any reference to colonial history are incidental. The rationale for this is that the two hundred years of independent history are more important than the colonial history and that those issues and ideas of the colonial period that had an impact on our independent history can be studied when the impact is felt. Such ideas include: Puritanism; attitudes towards slaves, Indians and free blacks; religious toleration; economic independence, especially in trade and manufacturing; self-government; the legal status of the individual and the right to vote; access to free land and the settlement of the West. All these issues and ideas had important manifestations and developments immediately after 1763 and should form part of one's study of this period, but their roots can be found in the colonial era. Courses beginning in 1763 usually take a quick look at these roots.

As implied above, the years 1763-1789 logically separate into three separate but related time periods. These are: the steps to independence, 1763-1776; the War of the American Revolution, also called the War for American Independence, 1775-1783; the establishment of an independent government, 1783-1789. This latter period is sometimes referred to as "the critical period," a phrase coined by the American historian John Fiske in the 19th century and used ever since in history texts.

In studying these periods there are many separate points that need to be understood. There are also several important questions that run through all three periods. Among these are:

1. Who will control the frontier lands across the Appalachian Mountains?
2. Who has the power of taxation of citizens?
3. Who will control the legislative power?
4. What are the "inalienable rights" of human beings?
5. Should government be democratic, republican, oligarchical, or monarchical?
6. When are protest, civil disobedience, and revolution legitimate instruments of political action?

Sample Essay Question—Describe . . . Explain

The following question is adapted from the Advanced Placement examination of 1960. It is a fine example of a type of question used on the exam over many years. It is also a very good question for covering the history of 1763-1789, since it ties two of the three time periods together in a comparison. The question is of the *Describe . . . explain type*, which often gives the writer a wide choice for the content or focus of an answer.

Sample Question

> Between 1763-1776, the colonies faced many problems in their relations with the Mother Country. The principal problems reappeared in state/federal relations under the Articles of Confederation (1780-1789). Describe three of the problems and explain how the government under the Articles of Confederation attempted to solve them.

Comments on Sample Question

Following our first step in essay writing, we now need to analyze the question. For your benefit, before you proceed, read the question carefully and decide what is being asked. You may even wish to make a few notes on your ideas so you can compare them with the following analysis and see how well you are doing.

The directions in the *Describe . . . explain* type of essay are clearly stated. The writer is asked to describe one or more particular situations, relationships, or, as in this example, problems and then to explain something about the situation, relationship, or problem described. The question allows the writer to pick the situation. This becomes an important decision, since you must pick a situation about which you not only know the facts, but one for which you can describe the relationship. The choice is yours, but the success of your answer will be determined by how wise a choice you make.

There should be no difficulty in understanding the word *describe*. The difficulty in this type of essay comes in how well you describe the situation. The word *explain* should also present no difficulties. Here again, however, how valid an explanation you present determines your success. Also, sometimes it is not easy to interpret what explanation is desired. Fortunately, Advanced Placement questions are usually very clear because they have been developed and carefully analyzed by a committee over a period of at least a year. In this 1960 question it is clear that a discussion is wanted of how the government under the Articles of Confederation attempted to solve the problems you have described.

The above general comments on the *Describe . . . explain* type of question apply to all of them. Now let's look closely at this particular question. What are you asked to describe? Obviously it is problems, but what "problems?" The question states "Between 1763-1776, the colonies faced many problems in their relations with the Mother Country." This should not be too difficult to understand. The colonies are the British colonies in North America and the Mother Country is England. The history of the period 1763-1776 in America usually focuses on difficulties or problems between these two groups. This part of the question appears, therefore, to be asking for a rewriting of the history of the thirteen years, but be careful! Note the rest of the question, "The principle problems reappeared in state/federal relations under the Articles of Confederation (1780-1789)." The question is tighter than the first part would lead you to suspect. *Problems*—and note, *principal problems*—is the key to the question. You must not simply rewrite the history of 1763-1776; you must identify the problems of that era which recur in the years 1780-1789 *and* recur in state/federal relations as the problems had occurred in colony/Mother Country relations earlier. You can now begin to determine what problems you will deal with in your answer. You must at the time you pick the problems remember to "explain how the government under the Articles of Confederation attempted to solve them." Therefore, you must pick problems: (1) that you can describe; (2) that recurred; (3) such that you can explain how they were dealt with under the Confederation. This should not be difficult, but it illustrates how carefully you should analyze even the simplest-appearing question.

You are now ready for the second step—collecting and sorting your information. You should do that now, following the points mentioned above. That is, pick the three problems faced between 1763–1776 that you wish to write on, note some specific information about them, and finally, jot down information on how the problems were dealt with between 1780–1789. After this, move on to the third step—developing your thesis. In this type of question, some people would say no thesis is required. If that is the case, you would not be writing an essay, but merely a historic composition. This question *does* require you to determine personal viewpoint. You must pick the problems, explain what the Confederation did about them, and, looking at the word *attempted*, decide if the Confederation solved the problems or not. Your thesis or personal opinion might well revolve around the word *attempted*. Unlike the *Evaluate this statement* type of essay question, the *Describe . . . explain* type forces you to write your thesis in your own words. You should do that now. Then follow the remaining four steps in essay writing and write an answer to this question.

After you have written your own essay on this question, read the following student answer. You will then want to outline the student answer and your own to compare the outlines. You will also want to compare the teacher's comments on this student essay with your own comments on it.

Sample Answer

Taxation, currency, and defense are three problems every government and people must deal with. In the period between 1763 and 1776 they were problems to the colonists and the British. Later in 1780-1789, these three problems involved relations between the Confederation and the states. All four groups—colonists, Mother Country, states, Confederation—had ideas on how the problems should be resolved and attempted to do so, but no real solution was found until the Constitution was written in 1789.

The main problem from 1763 to 1776 was that of taxation. The colonists insisted that as members of the British Empire, they were entitled to the same rights that other members, such as Canada, enjoyed. They propounded that taxation without representation was unfair and that taxation for the sole purpose of raising revenue was equally unjust. Actually, what they were demanding was Dominion status, something not granted to Canada until 1839.

In 1764 the Grenville Ministry passed the Sugar Act. Shortly thereafter, the Stamp Act appeared. These taxes the colonists considered far too heavy. They felt that they had been made law without colonial consent. The colonists became very agitated. When, in 1773, a tax was enacted that gave the Dutch East India Company a virtual monopoly on all tea imported to America, the colonists were furious. In December they staged the Boston Tea Party, an act that resulted in the "Coercive" or "Punitive" acts.

Another cause for grievance between the colonies and the Mother Country was the currency situation. In 1764 the Grenville Ministry passed the Currency Act, which was, in effect, a prohibition against the coining of money. The colonists, except in certain specific cases, were forbidden to coin their own currency or to issue paper money through their own banks. This, though not as controversial as the taxation situation, did arouse a considerable amount of protest, especially on the frontier and in North Carolina. The colonists felt that they deserved a certain amount of self-government and that they understood the need for currency better than Parliament. After all, they were a group of different colonies, many of them with different backgrounds and different modes of living, and each with its own debtor-creditor problems as well as a need for cash.

A third point of disagreement between the colonies and the Crown concerned the raising and housing of troops. Parliament, naturally, assumed that since America was a colony just as Canada was a colony, it needed to be protected and could not provide its own army. Consequently, British regulars would have to be sent over and housed in the colonies. This situation first arose in all its seriousness with the Quartering Act, which followed close upon the heels of the Stamp Act in 1765. This act stated that Americans must house British Regulars and they must help pay for the latter's maintenance. This seemed absurd to the colonists, who felt that they themselves could, with less expense and more efficiency, raise the requisite troops for protection as they had been doing since 1607. As stated above, in 1774, in response to the Boston Tea Party, the "Coercive" Acts were passed. One of the provisions of these acts stated that the colonists must within 24 hours comply with any troop quartering regulation that might be enacted. This was especially harsh since the Americans had viewed with disgust the 1770 Boston Massacre, in which five Bostonians were shot by some British Regulars who panicked at a crucial moment.

Taxation under the Articles of Confederation was just as important as it was during the period just discussed. The Congress's main weakness was that it did not have the power to tax the states. As one can see, the problem was entirely different in substance. Instead of the central government forcing the taxes upon the people, it could only tax with the people's (states') acquiescence. However, the situation is in one respect similar. The states and the people protested against any taxation idea that would come up simply by refusing to consider such an idea. For instance, when Congress asked the states to supply the debt-ridden nation with 10 million dollars, they only received 1.5 million. In 1781, 1782, and 1783, when Robert Morris was Secretary of the Treasury, he tried three times to impose taxes but met with failure every time. When he tried to resign from the thankless job, his resignation was not accepted. We see, then, that the Articles of Confederation attempted to remedy the taxing problem of 1763-1776 by simply asking for taxes rather than demanding them. They found, however, that the states were equally as unresponsive as the colonies had been.

The Congress under the Articles of Confederation met currency problems by saying that the states could coin their own money. However, this engendered new complications. People found that there were so many currencies that it was difficult to distinguish the worth of each one. When one state refused to issue huge amounts of currency and farmers demanded that it do so, the result was Shays' Rebellion of 1786. There was so much currency and so many different currencies that inflation soon appeared. Farmers were unable to pay their debts and merchants were unable to purchase the raw materials necessary to increase their business and prosperity.

Finally, the Articles of Confederation attempted to solve the troop question by leaving it up to the states themselves. Congress was not permitted to raise an army; instead, each state would have its own army or militia that could be called upon by Congress when needed. This, however, created new difficulties. It made it impossible for the country to have a central army, centrally trained and operated. And what was to happen if one state army refused to cooperate with another?

Although these three problems of taxation, currency, and army were apparently solved in the new Constitution in 1789, the solutions have been questioned at other times in history. These problems seem to reflect continual concerns of the American people.

Teacher Comments on Sample Answer

"This essay is an excellent answer to the question. It is very effectively and clearly organized with both introductory and concluding paragraphs. The student's personal view on the question is stated in the last sentence of the introduction and again in the conclusion. Although the body of the paper does not deal specifically with the thesis, it is obvious in the presentation of the information and in the discussion of it that the student believes no solutions to the problems were discovered in either period.

"The factual information presented to describe the three problems is excellent. The student illustrates a clear understanding of the steps leading to the revolution and mentions many of them, but not in a mere recitation of events. Instead, the student carefully chooses particular events to illustrate the three problems under discussion. Use of the currency situation in the colonies and under the Confederation is particularly interesting, as it is often not covered or understood by students. Taxation and the army are good choices to illustrate problems.

"Considering the student's thesis, it was wise not to include the problem of western lands or the frontier as an illustration. The problem in this area *was* settled effectively by the Confederation government."

Do you agree with these teacher comments? Overall this essay is excellent. Students should study its organization and the choice of vocabulary and information as both a review of this time period and an example of an answer that would have received a high grade on the Advanced Placement American History exam.

Practice Essay Questions

1. Between 1763 and 1789, the use and control of the frontier regions presented problems to both the British and the Americans. Describe the problems involved in the use and control of the frontier and explain how both the British and the Americans attempted to solve them.

2. After 1763, in the face of recurring crises, the colonists slowly developed a theory of political independence and government. Describe these recurring crises and explain how they led the colonists to develop their theory of political independence and government.

3. The government under the Articles of Confederation has been considered a failure. Describe three actions of the Confederation government and explain how these actions may or may not be considered failures.

4. "The Declaration of Independence issued a call for a democratic government of equal citizens that was rejected by the writers of the Constitution, who created an aristocratic government that benefited only the wealthy few." Assess the validity of this statement.

5. The American people experienced periods of revolutionary change brought about by political action in the years 1783–1789 and 1890–1914. Describe two political changes in each time period and show how these changes were revolutionary.

Before you read the brief comments on the above questions, you may wish to make your own analysis of the questions and write out answers to them.

Comments on Question 1

Question 1 is very similar to the question from the 1960 exam analyzed above. It narrows the choice of problems to those involved with the frontier, but other than that the format is the same.

Comments on Question 2

Question 2 changes the format from one of describing problems to one of describing crises. The time period is narrower than for the other questions, thus requiring a more detailed knowledge of the period 1763–1776 than is needed for the other questions. As you describe crises be clear in your mind how the situation furthered the colonists' development of a theory of political independence and government. Do not just describe all the steps leading to independence, but carefully pick those that can help you illustrate the developing theory of political independence and government.

Comments on Question 3

The third question is a slight variation of the *Describe . . . explain* type. It has a similarity to the *Evaluate this statement* type, since the first sentence is a statement that you are then asked to evaluate as you "explain how these actions may or may not be considered failures." You are expected to describe situations and then evaluate them as you explain. Did you spot this slight variation in the type of question? Were you ready to evaluate the actions as you wrote the answer?

Comments on Question 4

The fourth question is typical of the *Assess the validity* type. The issue raised by the statement is one of major interest to historians and one on which you should have ideas.   The question basically asks, "Did the Constitution reject the principles set forth in the Declaration of Independence?"

Comments on Question 5

The last question uses the *Describe . . . explain* form but deals with two widely different time periods. It also uses the word *show* in place of *explain* but this type of variation should not upset your analysis. You should expect different words to be used from time to time. You may not be prepared to answer this question now because you may lack knowledge of the 1890-1914 period. It was included here to illustrate how differing time periods can be used. The wording of this question may seem to force you to accept the political changes as revolutionary. Actually, in spite of such wording, you always have the option of arguing the other side of a statement and, in this question, you could argue against the political changes being revolutionary. Do not be trapped into taking positions you do not believe in by the wording of a question, but at the same time, do not lose sight of the point of the question as you defend an unusual position. You should feel free to state and defend your personal opinion or thesis on every question.

Multiple-Choice Questions—The Quotation Question

On the Advanced Placement examination there are a number of multiple-choice questions that are not strictly recall questions. These questions are often referred to as "stimulus" questions because they provide you with information that should stimulate your thinking. The information provided can take many forms—quotations, charts, maps, graphs, cartoons—and we will present information and analysis of various ways such stimulus questions may be presented. In this chapter we present the quotation-based question, which is a very important type of multiple-choice question.

A variety of questions can be developed based upon quotations. The most obvious type is the one in which the student must identify the author or the source of the quotation. Such quotations will either be obvious and well known or the content of the quotation will be easily identifiable with the position or viewpoint of the author or with the content of an important document. The documents might include letters, speeches, laws, party platforms, or anything else that could be read to reveal the history of a period. Other multiple choice questions based on quotations or historical documents will require you to understand the content of the passage in view of the history of the time, to identify the philosophical viewpoint expressed, or to analyze the passage to reveal your own analytical and interpretive skills.

The quotation-based multiple-choice question has many forms. Samples will be included in each chapter, but we will analyze several of the possible variations in this chapter. Although we are discussing documents from the era of the American Revolution, you must realize that you may have documents from any period of American history on the examination. We have chosen to present this type of stimulus question here for several reasons. First, there are many documents that are discussed in all American history texts dealing with the era of the American Revolution and you should be familiar with them. Using these documents will illustrate how quotations from any period might be used. The second reason is that quotations are often connected with individuals. In this unit and throughout the remainder of your study, you will read about many important people and as you do, you should relate particular ideas and positions to important individuals. The type of specific information needed to answer many of the quotation-based multiple-choice questions can be acquired as you study your history, if you know what to look for. Names and authors of documents and important laws, the changing concept and interpretation of the laws as they apply to economic and social activity, major speeches and who delivered them, the changing attitudes of people living in various parts of the country—all of this information can be absorbed as you study the past. Another reason is that on the DBQ on the Advanced Placement examination you will have to read, analyze, and interpret information taken from various documents. If you begin now to practice reading documents to find key ideas and relate these to the mainstream of traditional development of our history, you will be preparing all through your study or review for the DBQ. Read the quotations looking for the key ideas and connect these to individuals and the history of the time.

As the following examples of quotation-based multiple-choice questions are studied, it should become clear how various types of information will help you respond to such questions.

Sample Questions 1-2

"So soon as there shall be 5,000 free male inhabitants of full age in the district, upon giving proof thereof to the Governor, they shall receive authority, with time and place, to elect representatives from their counties or townships to represent them in the General Assembly: *Provided*. That, for every 500 free male inhabitants, there shall be one representative, and so on progressively with the number of free male inhabitants shall the right of representation increase, until the number of representatives shall amount to 25; after which, the number and proportion of representatives shall be regulated by the Legislature . . . ."

---

1. The above quotation is most likely from
   (A) the U.S. Constitution
   (B) Galloway's Plan of Union
   (C) Quebec Act
   (D) Northwest Ordinance
   (E) Stamp Act

2. The previous quotation (from the Northwest Ordinance) established the basic American political concept of the
   (A) equality of men
   (B) right of governors to set election dates
   (C) size of legislature
   (D) right of 5,000 free men to have elections
   (E) right of free men to govern themselves through their own legislatures

Question 1 is a most common form of question. It requires you to be familiar with five acts and be able to understand the passage. The passage states how and when a legislative body will first be set up. You might remember the line "5,000 free male inhabitants," as many books point out that this clause has set the pattern for the government of territories and the admission of states into the union throughout our history. Chances are, however, that you will not recognize the quotation but that you will be able to understand its content and purpose.

You must then look at the choices offered in this question to determine which one most likely contained the quotation. As is often the case, several choices will be very familiar. All students should know the U.S. Constitution well enough to realize that it does not establish the pattern for creating legislatures. State legislatures were in existence and the Constitution establishes the two branches of the U.S. Congress only. The U.S. Constitution can obviously be eliminated.

You should be aware of the Stamp Act. It would then be obvious that the Stamp Act did not deal with legislatures. Therefore, it can be quickly eliminated. You are now left with three choices, each of which is a possibility. You should recall the Quebec Act, Galloway's Plan of Union, and the Northwest Ordinance, all of which deal with the establishment of government. The Quebec Act of 1774 extended the Province of Quebec to include all the land north of the Ohio River under the authority of the Provincial government. It also continued the French method of government. There was no place in such an act for the establishment of new legislatures.

The same holds true of Galloway's Plan of Union of 1774. It is probably the least familiar of your choices, but the title alone should identify it as an attempt to unite the already established colonies. The goal of the plan was the union of existing colonies, not the creation of new ones.

By elimination, we come to the Northwest Ordinance, which was designed in 1787 to provide organized government for the land between the Ohio River and the Great Lakes west to the Mississippi gained in the 1783 Treaty of Paris—the area known as the Northwest Territory. Various states claimed the land but ceded their claims to the federal government under the Articles of Confederation at the insistence of Maryland and New Jersey. The territory lacked a governmental system, and this ordinance established it. The concept of new and equal legislatures formed by free men when the population of a territory reaches a certain point is one of the great contributions of the American people to the concept of colonial government. You may have been familiar with the document and the idea and have been able to identify the Northwest Ordinance immediately. However, if you find that with such questions you cannot immediately spot the answer, think through the choices and see if you can come to the correct answer.

Question 2 has been phrased to see if you understand the significance of the content of the question. In this version you need not identify the document as it is given to you in the statement. Even if the name of the document were eliminated (note the parentheses), you could still identify the political concept stated in the passage. The multiple-choice question now becomes one of checking your analytical and reading abilities — those two skills essential for every historian.

You may know that the Northwest Ordinance dealt with the establishment of governments in the territories that were to be free and equal to governments of the original thirteen colonies. In this case you would probably consider choices

A and E and eliminate the others. Since A is very general and equality is not mentioned in the passage, you would quickly decide on choice E, which is a summary of the main idea in the quotation.

Simply reading the passage you would realize that choices B, C, and D are all included in the quotation. However, none of these should qualify as a "basic American political concept." It is true that the Northwest Ordinance allowed the governor to set the election date, but governors do not do that today. Again the passage allows 5,000 free men to have an election, but that has no relation to basic American political concepts. The passage does state a rule concerning legislative size, but that also is not a basic American political concept. This leaves you with choice E, which is very basic to American political life. It is the correct answer since choice A, although a basic American political concept, is not mentioned in the passage.

Sample Question 3

---

3. The previous quotation (from the Northwest Ordinance) establishes
    I.   The right of free males to vote for members of a legislature
    II.   The authority of the legislature to set its own size once there are 25 members
    III. The control of the governor over the legislative body
    IV.   The power of the governor to set the time and place for the first voting of the legislature

    (A) I and II
    (B) I and III
    (C) I, II, and IV
    (D) I, III, and IV
    (E) I, II, III, and IV

Comments on Question 3

The format of this question is somewhat different from that used previously. Instead of having five choices lettered A-E you have four statements lettered I-IV and five combinations of those four Roman numerals lettered A-E. Your task is to determine which statements with Roman numerals are correct. Then find the letter that lists those correct statements. To make your analysis easier, you should mark with a check ($\sqrt{}$) the correct or appropriate items that have Roman numerals. If you read the quotation carefully you will find that statements I, II, and IV are correct. The correct answer is thus C and so the oval lettered C on your answer sheet would be filled in. The quotation established the right of free males to vote for a legislative body when there are 5,000 free males in the district. The governor is the one to set the time and place for the first voting. Finally, once the General Assembly (legislature) reaches 25 members they may decide the future size of the legislative body. The quotation does not set the governor's control over the legislative body.

This format will be used in a variety of questions and *not* only with quotations. You will find examples of this format in the following chapters. It is an interesting format, as you analyze the four choices offered and determine their accuracy. It is often more difficult to eliminate choices, as these questions often rely less on recall and more on analysis. However, if you read the questions carefully, analyze the statements, and think of the history of the stated or implied time period, you will easily master this format.

On the Advanced Placement examination sometimes more than one question will be asked about the same quotation, map, chart, or cartoon. We have presented three questions here based on the same quotation and will often present two questions about one item in these sample stimulus questions. This is done deliberately to illustrate various types of questions that could be asked although it is rarely done on the exam itself. As in the case of the essay section, in the multiple-choice section of the Advanced Placement examination the first crucial step toward achieving success on multiple-choice questions is to analyze the question.

Let us look at several other quotation-based multiple-choice questions. Read them carefully, analyze the question, and decide on your answer. Then read the brief descriptions of the questions that follow.

Sample Questions 4-5

"All communities divide themselves into the few and the many. The first are the rich and well born, the other the mass of the people. The voice of the people has been said to be the voice of God; and however generally this maxim has been quoted and believed, it is not true in fact. The people are turbulent and changing; they seldom judge or determine right. Give therefore to the first class a distinct, permanent share in the government. They will check the unsteadiness of the second, and as they cannot receive any advantage by a change they therefore will ever maintain good government. Can a democratic assembly, who annually revolve in the mass of the people, be supposed steadily to pursue the public good? Nothing but a permanent body can check the imprudence of democracy. Their turbulent and uncontrolling disposition requires checks."

4. The writer believed all of the following EXCEPT
   (A) the people are quick to change ideas
   (B) there should be stability in government
   (C) the rich and well born deserve a permanent share in the government
   (D) government should be headed by a king
   (E) government should be designed with checks and balances

5. The above statement is most likely to be found in
   (A) the *Virginia Resolves*
   (B) *Notes of the Debates in the Federal Convention in Philadelphia*
   (C) *The Letters of a Pennsylvania Farmer*
   (D) an account of the Boston Tea Party
   (E) the Peace of Paris 1783

Comments on Questions 4-5

The quotation is from a speech by Alexander Hamilton at the debates on the Constitution in 1787 and is found in the *Notes on the Debates of the Constitutional Convention.* It briefly summarizes the position held by Hamilton until his death. He believed in government by the few who are rich. Unlike Jefferson, who believed that the people, especially the small farmers, should be the deciding power in government, Hamilton distrusted the people, who had no economic stake in society.

Question 4 requires that you understand the paragraph. There is no mention of rule by a king, although it may be implied. The hasty reader might miss this point.

A statement of this type would not be suitable for a treaty or for a description of an action-packed event, such as the Tea Party. The remaining three choices for question 5 must be recognized if you are to analyze them properly. The *Virginia Resolves* and the *Letters* will then be understood to present a pro-people position. The Debates remains the correct answer and you might have suspected this type of statement would be in a debate where a particular opinion is being expressed.

Sample Questions 6-7

"That government is, or ought to be instituted for the common benefit, protection, and security of the people, nation, or community; of all the various modes and forms of government, that is best which is capable of producing the greatest degree of happiness and safety, and is most effectually secured against the danger of maladministration; and that when any government shall be found inadequate or contrary to these purposes, a majority of the community hath an indubitable, unalienable and indefeasible right to reform, alter or abolish it, in such manner as shall be judged most conducive to the public weal."

6. The philosophy expressed in the above quotation most closely resembles that held by
    (A) Jean-Jacques Rousseau
    (B) Montesquieu
    (C) John Locke
    (D) Voltaire
    (E) Hobbes

7. The philosophy expressed in the above quotation finds its most famous expression in American history in the
    (A) Declaration of Independence
    (B) Constitution
    (C) Articles of Confederation
    (D) Northwest Ordinance
    (E) Virginia Bill of Rights

Comments on Questions 6-7

The quotation forms part of the Virginia Bill of Rights, a document adopted in 1776. It is an excellent statement of John Locke's philosophy as stated in his *Two Treatises on Government*. Locke's philosophy was well known to the colonial leaders and provided the philosophical basis of the Declaration of Independence. In the Declaration Jefferson adopted Locke's ideas about inalienable rights and the "right of revolution." The latter is the main idea in this passage. The other men listed in question 6 were important philosophers of the 17th and 18th centuries and their ideas were important to many of the colonial leaders, but Locke's ideas were crucial in the Declaration.

In question 7 the other choices are all important documents, but all students should recognize the similarity between this passage from the Virginia Bill of

Rights and the Declaration of Independence, which is the most famous American document to express Locke's idea of the right of revolution.

Sample Questions 8-10

Quotation A

"Resolved. That the first adventurers and settlers of this His Majesty's Colony and Dominion of Virginia brought with them, and transmitted to their posterity . . . all liberties, privileges, franchises, and immunities, that have at any time been held, enjoyed, and possessed, by the people of Great Britain . . .

"Resolved therefore, That the General Assembly of this Colony have the only and sole exclusive right and power to lay taxes and impositions upon the inhabitants of this Colony . . .

"Resolved, That His Majesty's liege people, the inhabitants of this Colony, are not bound to yield obedience to any law or ordinance whatever, designed to impose any taxation whatsoever upon them other than the laws or ordinances of the General Assembly aforesaid."

Quotation B

"The inhabitants of this country in all probability in a few years will be more numerous than those of Great Britain and Ireland together; yet it is absurdly expected by the promoters of the present measures, that (the colonists') property shall be disposed of (taxed) by a House of Commons at three thousand miles distant from them; and who cannot be supposed to have the least care or concern for their real interest: who have not only no natural care for their interest, but . . . every burden they lay on the colonists is so much saved or gained to themselves. The colonists have been branded with the odious names of traitors and rebels, only for complaining of their grievances; how long such treatment will, or ought to be borne, is submitted (offered for debate)."

8. The writer of Quotation A bases his argument upon the idea that
    (A) colonists brought with them their rights as English subjects
    (B) colonists do not have to obey English laws
    (C) English people are better than people of other nationalities
    (D) England is a small country and the colonies are large
    (E) the Virginia General Assembly has the exclusive right to tax

9. The writer of Quotation B bases his argument upon the idea that
    (A) the king of England has no power to tax his subjects
    (B) the rights of colonists are the same as those of English subjects
    (C) the colonists should not be called traitors
    (D) England will have fewer people than the colonies
    (E) members of the House of Commons have no real interest
        in the colonists

10. Although the writers of Quotations A and B differ as to the bases of their arguments, according to the quotations, they agree on all the following EXCEPT

   (A) the House of Commons does not have the right to tax the colonies
   (B) the colonists have the right to complain about their grievances
   (C) the number of inhabitants in a territory should affect the legal power of the territory
   (D) the English actions are curtailing American rights
   (E) the right of taxation is at the heart of the disagreement

Comments on Questions 8-10

Quotation A is from the *Virginia Resolves*, introduced into the Virginia House of Burgesses by Patrick Henry, and Quotation B is from a letter by Sam Adams. It is unusual to include two quotations in one multiple-choice question, but this format allows for a comparison of ideas and can test the student's reading and analytical abilities. The reasoning used in the *Resolves* appears much more sound than that used by Adams, but both agree on many points.

The *Virginia Resolves* assumed that the colonists brought with them to America their rights as English subjects, and this is the answer to question 8. The passage states that the Virginia Assembly has the right to tax and that the colonists do not have to obey English laws, but these two points are the *result* of the argument, not its *basis.*

In question 9 the answer would be the House of Commons' lack of interest in the colonies. The passage talks about traitors and about comparative population, but the basis of the rather flimsy argument seems to be the interest of the House of Commons in the colonies.

In spite of the differences in the basis of their arguments, the two documents agree on four points given as possible answers to question 10 — they agree about taxation, the right to complain, and the curtailment of American rights, but the *Virginia Resolves* makes no reference to population.

Sample Questions 11-12

"But with the greatest submittion we beg leave to informe your Honours that unles something takes place more favourable to the people, in a little time att least, one half of our inhabitants in our oppinion will become banckerupt—how can ittt be otherwise—the constables are dayly (selling at auction) our property both real and personal, our land after itt is appraised by the best judges under oath is sold for about one third of the value of itt, our cattle about one half the value, the best inglesh hay thirteen shilings per tone, intervale hay att six shilings per ton, and other things att the same rate. And we beg leave further to informe your honours that sutes att law are very numerous and the atturneys in our oppinion very extravigent and oppressive in their demands . . . What can your honours ask of us unles a paper curancy or some other medium be provided so that we may pay your taxes and debts."

11. The quotation most nearly reflects the views held by a(n)
    (A) English gentleman in 1783
    (B) Virginia planter in 1787
    (C) Boston merchant in 1788
    (D) settler in Kentucky in 1784
    (E) frontier farmer of western Massachusetts in 1786

12. The quotation discusses a recurrent issue in American history, the concern of the
    (A) merchant for a fair income from investment
    (B) farmer for easy credit
    (C) attorney for a living wage
    (D) judge for equal justice
    (E) legislator for fair laws

Comments on Questions 11-12

The spelling and grammar have not been changed in this quotation. The meaning should be perfectly clear, but the language of the quotation may slow down your reading. The spelling and style will often provide a clue as to the date of the writing.

The quotation is from the Petition of the Town of Greenwich, Massachusetts, in January 1786. It is a post-revolutionary war document and focuses on a new aspect of the taxation/money issue. Here the small farmers of the western part of the state are protesting high prices, tight (or limited amounts of) money, and what seemed to be unfair bankruptcy laws and judges.

The answer to question 11 is, therefore, a frontier farmer in 1786. The other choices are not suitable, as these complaints were not issues to an English gentleman, a Virginia planter, or a Boston merchant, and Kentucky was not yet organized enough in 1784 to have farmers' complaints formalized.

The quotation is an early example of a recurrent issue in American history, the farmer's desire for easy credit, and this is the answer to question 12.

The Sample Questions illustrate the variety of questions that can be asked about documents. There will be further examples in each review chapter. As you study American history, look for important quotation and document selections that might be used in multiple-choice questions. Practice analyzing the content or meaning of these various selections so you can answer questions such as 1, 5, 6, 7, 8, and 12. Practice identifying the philosophy or attitudes of American leaders and groups so you can answer questions such as 3, 4, 9, 10, and 11. Questions 2 and 5 illustrate the need for knowing certain documents, and, therefore, as you learn the factual information, include such documents among your facts.

Practice Multiple-Choice Questions

Questions 1-3 refer to the following map

1. The First Continental Congress met in the region numbered
    (A) 1   (D) 4
    (B) 2   (E) 5
    (C) 3

2. The British surrender at Yorktown took place in the region numbered
    (A) 1   (D) 4
    (B) 2   (E) 5
    (C) 3

3. The region numbered three on the map is remembered as including the site of:
    I.   the Battles of Lexington and Concord
    II. the signing of the Mayflower Compact
    III. the meetings of the House of Burgesses
    IV. the Battle of Saratoga
    (A) I   (D) I and IV
    (B) I and II   (E) I, II and IV
    (C) I, II and III

4. All of the following played a role at the Constitutional Convention of 1787 EXCEPT
    (A) George Washington   (D) Benjamin Franklin
    (B) Alexander Hamilton   (E) James Madison
    (C) Thomas Jefferson

5. "To make all laws which shall be necessary and proper for carrying into execution the foregoing powers, and all other powers vested by this Constitution in the Government of the United States . . ." has been referred to as the

   (A) elastic clause
   (B) Bill of Rights
   (C) commerce clause
   (D) Power of the Purse
   (E) checks and balances clause

6. Which of the following British acts was enacted first?
   (A) Tea Act
   (B) Intolerable Acts
   (C) Stamp Act
   (D) Townshend Revenue Act
   (E) Declaratory Act

7. *Common Sense* by Thomas Paine is considered a most effective
   (A) logical argument for independence
   (B) propaganda work for independence
   (C) handbook for guerrilla warfare
   (D) condemnation of Whig philosophy
   (E) attack on the Stamp Act

8. The *Federalist Papers* were written by
   (A) Hamilton, Jefferson, Jay
   (B) Hamilton, Madison, Washington
   (C) Hamilton, Madison, Jay
   (D) Hamilton, Jefferson, Adams
   (E) Madison, Jefferson, Adams

9. Which of the following was NOT a reaction of the American colonists to the Stamp Act?
   (A) The Stamp Act Congress
   (B) Virginia Stamp Act Resolutions
   (C) Instructions of the town of Braintree on the Stamp Act
   (D) Non-importation measures
   (E) Declaratory Act

10. Which of the following was NOT a reason for the calling of the federal Constitutional Convention?
    (A) Northwest Ordinance
    (B) Shays' Rebellion
    (C) Annapolis Convention
    (D) Near-bankruptcy of the Confederation government
    (E) Lack of executive leadership in the confederation

11. Thomas Jefferson's philosophical position during the period prior to 1789 could best be described as
    (A) aristocratic and internationalist
    (B) monarchical and agrarian
    (C) democratic and mercantilist
    (D) democratic and agrarian
    (E) socialistic and internationalist

12. The Bill of Rights was added to the Constitution primarily to
    (A) curtail state power
    (B) protect the states from the power of the federal government
    (C) protect individual liberties from the power of the federal government
    (D) protect individual liberties from the power of state and local government
    (E) protect the states from the power of the church

Questions 13-14 refer to the following quotation

" . . . The power of Parliament is uncontrolable, but by themselves, and we must obey. They only can repeal their own Acts. There would be an end of all government, if one or a number of subjects or subordinate provinces should take upon them so far to judge of the justice of an Act of Parliament, as to refuse obedience to it. If there was nothing else to restrain such a step, prudence ought to do it . . . Reasons may be given, why an Act ought to be repeal'd, and yet obedience must be yielded to it till that repeal takes place."

13. The argument presented in the above quotation is based on the assumption that
    (A) government is a blessing for mankind
    (B) the state of nature is one of conflict and war
    (C) Parliament derives its power from the consent of the governed
    (D) the people are at the complete mercy of the ruling authority
    (E) laws should be obeyed until they are changed or modified by legal means

14. The above statement is most likely to have been made by a(n)
    (A) English gentleman in 1775
    (B) frontier settler in 1763
    (C) Boston merchant in 1773
    (D) moderate colonist in 1765
    (E) Virginia planter in 1776

15.   "You are to be diligent in the execution of the powers and authorities given you by several Acts of Parliament for visiting and searching of ships, and for seizing, securing and bringing on shore any goods prohibited to be imported into, or exported out of said plantations; or for which any duties are payable, or ought to have been paid, by any Act of Parliament."

The above quotation sets forth the British theory that Parliament had the right to
    (A) dominate the seas
    (B) regulate production in the colonies
    (C) seize missing seamen
    (D) control colonial trade
    (E) issue Bills of Attainder

16. The following items all dealt with relations between the thirteen English colonies and the English government EXCEPT
    (A) Acts of Trade and Navigation
    (B) Stamp Act
    (C) Quartering Act
    (D) Quebec Act
    (E) Olive Branch Petition

Answers and Answer Explanations

1. B	2. D	3. B	4. C
5. A	6. C	7. B	8. C
9. E	10. A	11. D	12. C
13. E	14. D	15. D	16. D

1. (B) The first Continental Congress met at Philadelphia in the colony of Pennsylvania in 1774. Region 2 includes Pennsylvania, New York, and New Jersey.

2. (D) Yorktown, Virginia, is in Region 4.

3. (B) The Battles of Lexington and Concord and the signing of the Mayflower Compact by the Pilgrims took place in New England, which is Region 3 on the map. The House of Burgesses was the Virginia assembly and met in Williamsburg, Virginia (Region 4), and the Battle of Saratoga took place in New York (Region 2). This is a good example of the question format that uses four statements, any combination of which may be correct.

4. (C) Thomas Jefferson did not attend the Constitutional Convention. He was in Europe. The other men all played crucial roles at the Convention.

5. (A) The clause from the Constitution is often referred to as the elastic clause. It has been interpreted to give extensive powers to the federal government covering all things "necessary and proper" (i.e., helpful in carrying out all the other powers given to Congress).

6. (C) The Stamp Act (1765) was the first of these five acts enacted.

7. (B) Thomas Paine's pamphlet *Common Sense* is considered an excellent propaganda piece. The arguments he used in presenting his case for independence are not very logical, but they persuaded many colonists to support the rebellion.

8. (C) The *Federalist Papers* were written by Hamilton, Madison, and Jay to support the Constitution. The papers helped win votes for the Constitution in New York and elsewhere. They are considered one of the finest analyses of the new federal system of government and they provide excellent examples of 18th-century essay style.

9. (E) The Declaratory Act of 1766 was passed by Parliament at the same time the Stamp Act was repealed. The act declared that Parliament had the right to tax the colonies even though the StampAct was being repealed as a response to the violent reactions of the colonies.

10. (A)   The Northwest Ordinance was one of the successes of the Confederation government and was not a cause for calling the Constitutional Convention.

11. (D)   Thomas Jefferson was a strong believer in the yeoman farmer—the agrarian—as contrasted with the mercantilist interest in society. He also supported the people, which would suggest his support for democracy—not yet a commonly used term. His support of the people is illustrated in his writing of the *Declaration of Independence*. Selection D best summarizes Jefferson's philosophical position.

12. (C)   The Bill of Rights was added to the Constitution to protect the liberties of the individual from the power of the new federal government. The Constitution written without these protections almost failed ratification. Massachusetts ratified the Constitution with the provision that the Bill of Rights be added, and several other states followed that lead by ratifying the document with this qualification.

13. (E)   James Otis, in this selection from his *Rights of the British Colonies*, 1764, bases his argument on the assumption that laws should be obeyed until they are changed or modified by legal means. He believes Parliament has the wisdom to understand when its laws are oppressive and that Parliament will change these laws.

14. (D)   The argument presented in this document would most likely be held by a moderate colonist as was James Otis before the development of major controversies between colonies and Mother Country. Choice D is the best answer.

15. (D)   This quotation, from a summary of the British Acts of Trade made in 1769, clearly assumes the right of the British Parliament to control colonial trade.

16. (D)   The Quebec Act (1774) established the framework for the government of Canada, which the British acquired by the Peace of Paris in 1763.

Bibliography

The following books will allow you to explore different issues of the Era of the American Revolution 1763–1789.

Andrews, L.M. *Colonial Background of the American Revolution*. New Haven: Yale University Press, 1961.

Bailyn Bernard, ed. *Pamphlets of the American Revolution*. Cambridge: Harvard University Press, 1965.

Becker, Carl. *The Declaration of Independence*. Magnolia, MA: Peter Smith.

Farrand, Max. *The Framing of the Constitution of the United States*. New Haven: Yale University Press, 1962.

Jameson, J.F. *The American Revolution Considered as a Social Movement*. Princeton: Princeton University Press, 1940.

Middlekauff, Robert. *The Glorious Cause: The American Revolution 1763–1789*. New York: Oxford University Press, 1985.

Morgan, E.S. *The Birth of the Republic*. Chicago: University of Chicago Press, 1956.

Storing, Herbert J. *What the Anti-Federalists Were For, The Political Thought of the Opponents of the Constitution*. Chicago: University of Chicago Press, 1981.

Documents

There are many collections of documents relating to American history that can be used to supplement textbook readings and to provide experience in analyzing important writings. In addition to those listed at the end of Part One, the following may be useful:

Morris, R.B., ed. *Basic Documents in American History.* Melbourne, FL: Krieger, 1980.

Biographies

For those students particularly interested in studying history as reflected in the lives of important individuals, there are many excellent works to choose from. Check your library to find biographies of people who interest you.

Fiction

Many works of fiction supply the feel for an era. These two works listed are particularly good in this aspect, although they will not help broaden your factual knowledge.

Cannon, L.G. *Look to the Mountain.* Woodstock, VT: Countryman, 1991.

Edmonds, W.D. *Drums Along the Mohawk.* Cutchogue, NY: Buccaneer Books, 1981.

PART THREE 3 The New Nation 1789-1824

Important Facets of This Period

The adoption of the Constitution by the United States in 1789 ushered in a new phase of our history. The Constitution is a remarkable document and should be studied carefully by all students. It will be clear that the Constitution established the simplest framework for the new government, a framework that had to be fleshed out with laws, policies, and programs and by the development of customs. This filling out of the framework of the Constitution occurred in the generation after 1789 against a background of international tension and war.

The period from 1789 to 1824 often seems confusing as the manipulations on foreign policy are followed. The intrigues of the British, French, Spanish, and Americans brought the nation close to war several times and finally resulted in the War of 1812. The problems of control of the western frontier were as complicated, and throughout this period there were dramatic developments internally, as seen in the Hamilton-Jefferson, Hamilton-Burr, Federalist-Republican conflicts. All of these issues are of importance, but probably the most important development in the era was the establishment of those laws and the setting of those policies that provided real substance to the new nation.

These laws and policies have affected all later U.S. history and should therefore be understood by every student. The developments of the years 1789-1824 should be studied from this perspective. Among the more important developments of the years 1789-1824 are the following:

1. The creation of political parties or factions
2. The establishment of the judicial system and its functioning, especially under Chief Justice John Marshall
3. The imprint George Washington put on the new government
4. The development of conflicting interpretations of the Constitution as exemplified by Alexander Hamilton and Thomas Jefferson
5. The continuing conflict with the British over both the 1783 Treaty of Paris and the idea of freedom of the seas
6. The relations of the United States with the revolutionary government of France
7. The growing sense of nationalism manifested in the country, especially after 1814
8. The physical growth of the United States

If you have a factual knowledge of these major developments and are able to see their interrelations and to develop parallels to other periods of our history, you should have an excellent understanding of this era.

Sample Essay Questions—Who? What? When? Where? Why? How?

A common type of essay question is the type based on one of those crucial six words the historian continually uses—Who? What? When? Where? Why? How?

Every historic event and development can be studied by applying these words. All six words do not always apply to each event, but if you know the *Who?* or *What?*, the *When?* and *Where?* you will be able to identify the event, and when you understand the *How?* and/or *Why?* you will have mastered the causal relationship of events, that is at the heart of Western civilization's understanding of the process of history. These six little words are decisive in one's study of history.

In this chapter we will look at several essays built around these six words. Our analysis of multiple-choice questions will focus on the cause-and-effect relationship suggested by the two words *Why?* and *How?* This chapter, therefore, should leave you prepared to approach historic material as a historian trained in Western civilization, to think in terms of cause-and-effect relationships, and to identify events by using the four W's—*Who? What? When? Where?*

The meaning of these words and what they ask you to do should be familiar to you. For instance, *When?* requires an indication of time—either a date or a period such as "the presidency of John Adams." *Where?* requires an indication of place—either a city, state, region, or country. *Who?* requires an indication of the participants, while *What?* requires specific information not involving people—either laws, actions, or details of actions. The words *Why?* and *How?* are the more important and complicated ones. They require an analysis of the information collected in answering the other four words. The analysis must seek the reasons for the actions and an explanation of the relationships between all the information or data collected.

Sample Question	How was war with England and France avoided in the years 1793–1810?

Before you read the student answer to this question, you should follow the first three steps in writing an essay answer—analyze the question, collect and sort information, develop a thesis. Then you will want to compare your notes with the answer and the teacher comment.

Sample Answer

War is a concern to all people, and avoiding war has been a major desire of the United States throughout our history. We were more successful avoiding war in the early years of the country than we have been since 1914. The newly independent country avoided war with England in 1794, with France in the years 1797–1800, and with both countries in the early 1800s. The way or reason we were able to avoid war then was that the presidents, unlike recent ones, refused to lead the nation into war. They—Washington, Adams, Jefferson—put domestic concerns ahead of schemes to prove our strength or to right "wrongs," and they were willing to *compromise** on issues of "honor."

For instance, Washington was willing to *compromise* our 1778 alliance with France. The French had allied with us in our Revolution, and the alliance stated it was to be "forever." The Jeffersonians were thrilled by the outbreak of the French Revolution and wanted to support them, but Washington felt that the struggle was not ours. When England and France went to war in 1793, Washington proclaimed our neutrality in spite of the alliance, thus compromising

---

*See Teacher Comments on Sample Answer.

our "honor" in the eyes of the world, to borrow a modern term. The Jeffersonians were angry but could do nothing except receive the French envoy, Citizen Genet, with open arms. He misread the American mood, ordered warships built for French use, and praised the Republicans. These actions infuriated the Federalists, and Washington asked the French to recall him, which was done. Washington did not want the nation provoked into war. He knew we were not prepared and faced many *economic* and other *problems* at home, which took priority over "honor."

One *economic problem* involved our expanding merchant fleet. As a result of the English-French war, the British needed more sailors for their ships. They practiced impressment—the seizing of British or suspected British citizens off American ships and seized American ships that were trading with the French. Impressment was wrong in the eyes of Americans, and a cry rose up to have our government force an end to it, to defend our rights on the sea, and to protect our ships. At the same time there were problems with the British. They had ignored the clause in the 1783 peace treaty and had never evacuated the frontier forts, such as Detroit. These issues seemed to justify war in the eyes of many Americans, especially the Jeffersonians, but instead of asking for a declaration, Washington sent John Jay to negotiate a treaty with the British. The terms were not very good; the British agreed to evacuate the forts, which they had already promised to do in their 1783 treaty, and they agreed to pay for ships already seized, but they made no mention of future impressments, and the Americans agreed to pay all pre-1776 debts to the British. Washington was not pleased with the treaty, but he strongly supported it in the Senate, knowing the terms were the best the United States could get and that to reject them meant war. Again he compromised on an issue and may have sacrificed our "honor" in the process, but war was avoided and the nation gained time to *expand* and grow.

Our westward *expansion* was affected by frontier wars against the Indians and Washington negotiated the Treaty of Greenville with them, which granted to the United States certain Indian lands north of the Ohio River. It was another attempt on his part to avoid war, as were the 1795 negotiations with Spain. Pinckney's Treaty provided free shipping on the Mississippi. It gained this "right" for the frontier farmers by a step short of war and without establishing *alliances*, which Washington warned against in his Farewell Address.

John Adams's four-year term was full of international intrigue and turmoil, but he too avoided *alliances* and kept the peace. The French had been furious over Jay's Treaty and began seizing American ships to retaliate. Adams sent men to Paris to negotiate, but when the French asked for bribes, the men came home and a great cry about war, rights, and "honor" broke out. "Millions for defense but not one cent for tribute" became a slogan as the Federalists pushed for war with France. The Navy department was expanded, Congress agreed to expand the Army, and Washington said he would take command, but preferred a younger man to lead the forces. The Federalists in Congress passed the Alien and Sedition Acts to keep out foreign (read French) ideas and to suppress opposition to government policy. War looked inevitable, but then the president reversed the movement by announcing he would send a new ambassador to France. An agreement was negotiated, the Convention of 1800, which again compromised the issues. The Alliance of 1778 was ended, but the Americans had to agree to pay for seized shipping. Adams followed in Washington's footsteps in compromising to avoid war. He infuriated Alexander Hamilton and other

Federalists, and historians believe his courage in going against the popular opinion for war cost him the *election* of 1800.

Jefferson won that *election*. During his first term relations with England and France were calm. However, after 1805 it was clear that neither England nor France could win militarily, so they turned to indirect attacks. The British began impressing American sailors again, the French and English battled via economic boycotts, and both seized American ships. Again the time seemed ripe for war. Jefferson, by his actions against the Barbary pirates, had shown that he was not a total pacifist, as some had suspected, but he, as had Washington and Adams, moved to avoid proving our strength and trying to right wrongs. Instead of a war declaration, he asked for an embargo on all U.S. trade. The French "helped" enforce the embargo by seizing U.S ships, but even that did not provoke Jefferson to war. The embargo was replaced with a Non-Intercourse Act (no trade with England and France) in 1809. The embargo was not popular; it compromised American "honor" and it seemed to say we would not defend what was right. It did have some beneficial results, as American manufacturing increased, but no one saw that at the time. People were angry at the embargo, but again war was avoided by the strength of presidential action in the field of *foreign policy*.

NOTE: We have talked about the importance of a conclusion. Before you read on, write your own conclusion for this essay. Then read the three conclusions presented below. How do they compare? Which one is most like yours? The teacher comments include reactions to all three conclusions. Do you agree with the teacher? You may find it helpful to write your own conclusion to other sample essays in this book. Conclusions are difficult to write, but a good conclusion is an important part of every essay.

Conclusion A

Clearly, there is a consistency in the *foreign policy* actions of Washington, Adams, and Jefferson. The three were not to be provoked into war and were willing to compromise on important issues. By avoiding war they may have sacrificed American "honor," but we owe them a great debt because their astute policies and farsightedness permitted the nation to grow strong. Mid-20th century presidents could learn a great deal on how to handle foreign policy by studying the actions of our first three presidents.

Conclusion B

As you can see, Washington, Adams, and Jefferson all followed the same type of *foreign policy* actions. I have shown how they compromised and went against popular opinion: Washington with the Neutrality Proclamation and in Jay's Treaty; Adams by arranging the Convention of 1800; Jefferson by pursuing the embargo. These men were great presidents, and we could learn a great deal from them. I hope our president will learn.

Conclusion C

Washington's, Adams's and Jefferson's *foreign policy* actions were taken to avoid war, and they were ready to compromise and to go against popular opinion. By their actions they gained time for the nation to grow and develop. In 1812 the war hawks from the frontier areas gained control of Congress and forced a declaration of war against England. Later presidents also led us into war. This ended the "avoid war" policies of our first three presidents. These were wise presidents following a wise foreign policy, and presidents today could learn a great deal from them.

Teacher Comments on Sample Answer

"This is an excellent essay answer. The *How?* question asks the writer to explain the way or manner in which a certain event or events took place, that is, to explore the cause and effect relationships among events. In this answer the writer has presented a clear thesis to explain the way or manner in which war was avoided, i.e., by strong presidential action. Sound evidence is presented from the presidential terms of Washington, Adams, and Jefferson to support the thesis. The evidence is factually correct and in enough detail for the reader to understand what is being proven. His or her chronological organization is clear and an obvious organizational device to use for the answer.

"The writer has paragraphed his other information smoothly. The reader moves easily from one paragraph to the next as the writer has repeated a word from the last sentence of one paragraph in the first sentence of the next. (See italicized words). There are other ways to link paragraphs in the body of the paper (i.e., to make the contact between the batteries in our flashlight image of the essay). This repetition of words is one way, and it is a very effective technique as seen in this essay.

"Of the three conclusions offered, Conclusion A is the most effective. The writer's thesis and the question are restated but in slightly different ways than in the introduction. The information in the body of the essay is pulled together by the word *consistency*, and the writer's interest in honor, which he or she makes a major point of the essay, is commented upon again. No new information is introduced. The writer's thesis is expanded to a broader context because he or she suggests modern presidents can learn from the first three. All of these elements are part of a good conclusion.

"Conclusion B is the poorest. The writer links it to the previous paragraph, but his or her use of the phrases *as you can see* and *I have shown* belittle the reader, who does not need to be told about what has been read. The writer summarizes what is said in the essay, yet fails to restate either his or her thesis or the question. Although he or she applies the question to a larger area than early America, he or she does not clearly state what we might learn from these 'great presidents.'

"Conclusion C also links the conclusion to the previous paragraph and applies the topic to a broader context. He or she indicates his or her thesis and the topic, but introduces new material about the War Hawks and the War of 1812. The question ended with 1810. If this information were to be introduced, and it is not called for by the question, it should have been presented in the body of the essay. This is a common error in conclusions, and yet it is one the student can easily learn to avoid.

"Basing the judgment on the use of Conclusion A, the writer of this answer would receive an excellent grade. It is a fine paper and one students could well use as a model, although it may be a little more detailed and a little longer than essays usually written for the Advanced Placement examination."

Summary—How to Write a Conclusion

An effective conclusion is different from a simple summary in which you repeat what you have already stated in the body of the paper. The best AP papers will have a conclusion that restates the thesis and suggests the larger implications of the thesis.

A good conclusion *must* include:

- a restatement of the thesis
- an indication of what the question was

A good conclusion *should* include in addition to the above:

- a reference as to how the thesis affects other broad issues

A good conclusion should NOT include:
- new evidence or facts not included in the body of the essay
- the pronoun *I*
- a statement saying "It is now proven" or similar wording
- a simple listing of the evidence included in the essay

Practice Essay Questions

The following essay questions have as their roots one of the six little words. Read the questions over and analyze them as in Step One of our essay-writing technique. You should write down some notes on these questions before reading the analyses given below. You will want to prepare answers for several of the questions either by collecting notes, making an outline, or writing out answers. Any of those approaches will help your review by giving you practice with essays and forcing you to recall events of American history. You should do this for each chapter.

1. Why were political parties formed in the new nation and what were the major differences among political parties in the years 1791-1820?

2. What events on the frontier had a major impact on national history in the years 1789-1820?

3. Each of the following individuals expressed strong opinions concerning the policies of the new nation. What opinions were expressed by two of the following? Of the two, whose opinions had the greatest impact on the new nation?
   (A) George Washington
   (B) Alexander Hamilton
   (C) Thomas Jefferson
   (D) John Marshall

4. How did the Republican party's policy of economic boycott in the years 1807-1812 affect the new nation?

5. Why did the United States not go to war against England in 1794 and against France in 1798-99?

Comments on Question 1

On a first reading, these questions may appear to call simply for a recitation of events in a logical cause-and-effect sequence. They may appear to have no place for a personal opinion or thesis and thus would not qualify as essay questions. Of course, as in the case of the *Describe . . . explain* type of essay noted in Chapter 2, this is not true. In each of these questions you need to determine your personal opinion on the question (Step Three in essay writing) before you can organize the factual material into a meaningful and effective answer. *Why? What? How? Who?* questions all require a personal opinion stated as a thesis.

In question 1, your thesis might not be very original, since most textbooks and special works on the origin of political parties pretty much set forth the same information and explanations. Therefore, you may use a familiar or already stated thesis if your personal opinion agrees with it. In writing the paper you will then need to recall the information you have to support that thesis. However, you should not study history by simply learning others' opinions or theses. You will retain information better and enjoy the study more if you become personally involved in each topic. That is why you are asked to develop theses and answers to the essay questions presented in the book. There is room in this question for some originality and a great deal of choice of factual information to support your answer.

Question 1 has two parts, each introduced by one of the six little words—*Why?* and *What?* The issue being considered in each part has to do with political parties. First, the writer must explain the origin of parties and, second, he or she must clarify the differences between parties in the early years of the republic — 1791-1820. As a study of these years reveals, there was no provision for parties, or factions as they were then called, in the Constitution. In fact, one of the major concerns of George Washington was the growth of these factions during his administration. Responses to such questions as, "Why was he concerned?" "Why did he oppose factions?" "Are factions bad?" would provide one aspect of your answer to the first part of the question. These three subquestions allow for a variety of answers and provide a place for you to present a personal opinion or thesis. You also need to have a personal opinion as to the events or issues on which people disagreed and which led to the formation of parties.

The issue usually cited as decisive in separating groups in Washington's first administration was Hamilton's economic program, and specifically his plan for a Bank of the United States. This is by no means the only issue that divided citizens into two opposing camps, but it is a major issue and one usually cited in all books. There are many subquestions you can ask about the bank and about economic policies. What has emerged in our analysis of the first half of question 1, the *Why?* half, is that there are many subquestions to ask yourself. The raising of these subquestions is an excellent illustration of what you do in Step One of essay writing — analyzing the question.

In question 1 these subquestions involve attitudes, values, and events. Each one must be traced to a cause if you are to do what the word *Why?* demands. In the dictionary, *why* is defined as, "For what cause, reason, or purpose; on what account . . ." As already stated, *Why?* demands the establishment of a cause-and-effect relationahip among events, ideas, and attitudes. For instance, how do you explain George Washington's fear of political parties when, to most Americans and for almost 200 years of our history, the political life of our nation has revolved around such parties? Was it because he was a military man and he saw the disruptive quality of warfare? Was it because parties were not anticipated in the Constitution? Was it because he understood British politics and understood how British factions aided the colonists in the revolution? When you determine what you consider the cause of George Washington's attitude, then you are answering the *Why?* question historically. This is the type of information expected in your answer to the first half of question 1. It is the type of approach expected for every *Why?* question. For example, question 5 also requires the same approach.

The second half of question 1 asks a What? question — "What were the major differences among the political parties?" This provides a great deal of room for personal opinion or a thesis, since it asks for major differences, and who is to decide this but you? Since you are given a long period of time (29 years) in which to present major differences, you cannot possibly list all the differences, so you must make choices as to the differences you will discuss, and this again provides an excellent opportunity for the expression of personal opinion. Thus, you can see that this combined *Why? What?* question demands a thesis and is an excellent essay question.

But what does *What?* mean or require in an answer? First of all, grammatically considered, *what* is an indefinite pronoun and corresponds to the substantive pronoun *who,* which is used to refer to people. (Therefore, the information presented here about *what?* also applies to *who?*) Secondly, *What?* is an interrogative and refers to the nature or identity of an object or matter. In a *What?* question, therefore, you must explain or identify the nature or identity of the object or matter. Specifically, in question 1 you must explain or identify the nature of the major differences in political parties.

This may seem very complicated or you may believe all that has been said about question 1 is obvious. It *is* obvious, but an understanding of the question, an understanding of the meaning of the words used, and an understanding of what is needed in an answer are *essential* if you wish to do well in Advanced Placement work.

Question 1 presents a challenge organizationally. The two questions within the question suggest dealing with each separately. This is one possibility. Another would be to indicate two or three differences that manifested themselves during the years 1791-1820. This approach is complex, but would make an interesting and effective answer. Of course, there are many other ways you might organize the material. As a general rule, one interrelated answer to double questions makes the best and most sophisticated answer, but it is the most difficult approach.

Comments on Question 2

Now let us look at essay question 2. Again it is a *What?* question. You need to identify or explain those "events on the frontier" that "had a major impact on national unity." Again, you can indicate your personal opinion or thesis by choosing the events to be discussed. You might even decide that no frontier event had a major impact and thereby produce a rather unexpected answer. The answer should be rather easy to write once you have analyzed the question (knowing how to respond to *What?* questions) and determined your thesis. The inclusion of the phrase *years 1789–1829* presents an easy method—chronological—for organizing your answer, although your brief notes may provide other organizational ideas.

Comments on Question 3

The third question combined several types of essay question. It begins with a statement of fact similar to the "Evaluate this statement" form, but you are not asked to evaluate the statement, which is very simple and almost noncontroversial. The question then presents a *What?* and a *Who?* (*Whose?*) section and includes a choice of individuals. As you realize many types of essay questions can be written to include a choice from which you must pick one or more items to discuss in your answer. We will include more examples of this type of question in succeeding chapters. It is of utmost importance in this type of question that you choose those items about which you know the most *as they relate to the question asked.* All four men mentioned in question 3 had strong opinions, some of which had a great impact throughout our history, such as Marshall's Supreme Court decisions and Washington's attitudes towards "entangling alliances." But what impact did these opinions have "on the new nation"? You must decide *that* before answering the question.

To analyze this particularly complex question you must:
1. pick two individuals to write about
2. present the nature of and identify the opinions of the two men in regard to "policies of the new nation"
3. indicate "whose opinions had the greatest impact on the new nation."

There is plenty of room for the development and presentation of a thesis as you follow these three steps.

Perhaps the most difficult point in answering question 3 will be in organizing your material. Chronology is not important. As you follow Step Two in essay writing and make brief notes, several organizational frameworks may emerge. One would be to present the opinions of one man followed by the second and then present in a paragraph which opinions had the greatest impact. Another way would be to present the opinions of the two men on specific policies, such as the development of parties, the chartering of a Bank of the United States, U.S. relations with England and France, the interpretation of the Constitution (loose or strict construction), the Louisiana Purchase, or other policies that had to be determined by the federal government. As each policy is discussed, you could indicate which man's opinion had the greatest impact, then you could present your estimation of which individual's impact was greatest (that is your thesis) in your conclusion. Although the organization of this essay may be complicated, there are several organizational schemes that could be very effective.

Comments on Question 4

Question 4 is a *How?* question. In the dictionary *how* is defined in several ways, all of which provide help in understanding what is expected in the answer. *How* means, "in what manner or way; to what degree or extent; in what state or condition; for what reason; why . . .; what?" In answering question 4, you must deal with the manner, degree, and state or condition in which "the Republican party's policy of economic boycott" affected the nation. The question also requires specific knowledge of the Republican party's policy, and this entails an understanding of another frequently used historic term — *boycott.* If you do not have this information, do not answer the question. If you have the facts, then you can develop a thesis presenting your views on the manner and degree of impact of the economic boycott on the new nation. The most obvious organizational scheme is to pick different examples of the impact of the boycott, such as its impact on New England merchants, on the Federalist party, and on a frontier settler and to explain in separate paragraphs the manner in which the impact was felt by each.

Comments on Question 5

Question 5 is similar to the sample essay question for this chapter; the questions involve essentially the same information. They both require knowledge of U.S. foreign policy in the years 1791 to 1812. Yet the questions are different in terms of the expected answer. Question 5 asks *Why?* — "The reason or purpose; on what account" — and the sample asks *How?* — "The manner, degree, state" — by which we avoided war in the first 23 years of our nation's history. These two questions were included to show the similarity of *Who? What? Why? and How?* questions, but also to show what a difference there can be. They also illustrate how carefully questions are constructed in order to extract the expected answer and how carefully they must be analyzed. They seem so much alike, but each question seeks a different answer.

Multiple-Choice Questions — How? Why? Cause-and-Effect

The majority of multiple-choice questions are based on those previously discussed six little words — *Who? What? When? Where? Why? How?* The usual student response to these words is factual. How often have you been asked questions such as, "Who won the battle of Tippecanoe?" or "When was the battle of New Orleans fought?" or "Where was the Cumberland Road?" These questions lend themselves naturally to short, factual answers. The *When?* multiple-choice type of questions was analyzed in Chapter 1. *When?* multiple-choice questions are those requiring a knowledge of dates or chronology. *Where?* multiple-choice questions require geographic information. Sometimes these questions involve maps, as in the sample multiple-choice questions in Chapters 1 and 2, and sometimes they simply require factual recall of places. We will consider *Where?* questions and particularly multiple-choice map questions in Chapter 4. *Who?* and *What?* are behind the majority of the remainder of multiple-choice questions. They are usually quite direct and rather easy *if* you know the facts. However, some multiple-choice questions, particularly the more complex ones, require *How?* or *Why?* knowledge. These *How?* or *Why?* multiple-choice questions are really designed to test the student's ability to analyze the cause-and-effect relationships that underlie, as has been stated several times, the whole interpretation of history in Western civilization. In what form will these *How?* and *Why?* questions appear on the multiple-choice section of the AP exam?

The chronological-type question discussed in Chapter 1 can be a way of asking a *Why?* or *How?* question. Very often the student will be asked to learn chronology, such as the British acts which led to the Revolution, because the teacher wants the student to understand how one event has caused another. As you develop chronologies and time charts, use them as keys to cause-and-effect relationships. This will help you a great deal in answering some multiple-choice questions. Do not use them simply as lists of dates to be learned.

Many times a seventh little word, *Which?*, will be used to introduce a *Why?* or *How?* question. *Which?* as a pronoun is often used to refer to objects while *Who?* is used to refer to persons or animate objects. Therefore, what has been said about *Who?* also refers to *Which?* The word *which* can also be used as an adjective; it then seeks the one or ones out of a group that are most relevant to the question asked. Sample Question 1 provides a good example of a *Which?* question.

Also, often a *Why?* or *How?* cause-and-effect relationship is sought without using those words. In such questions you can easily tell a causal relationship is asked for by switching the wording of the question to use *How?* or *Why?* Sample Question 2 illustrates this and will be discussed below.

Sample Question 1

> Which of the following was NOT a cause of John Adams's defeat in the presidential election of 1800?
> - (A)   The Alien and Sedition Acts
> - (B)   The XYZ Affair
> - (C)   Alexander Hamilton's disagreement with John Adams
> - (D)   British impressment of American sailors
> - (E)   The failure of Adams to support war with France

Comments on Question 1

Although the question does not contain one of the six words, it should be obvious that the question is asking a *Why?* question and could be worded, "Why did John Adams lose the presidential election of 1800?" It is an excellent example of a *Which?* question when *Which?* is used as an adjective asking which one. To answer this question the student must not only know the facts, such as the XYZ Affair and the meaning of impressment, which are presented as possible answers to the question; he or she must also understand a cause-and-effect relationship.

In simplest terms, we are acknowledging that Adams was defeated for many reasons, and the student is expected to know the reasons. Since the word *cause* is used in the question, it should be obvious that a cause-and-effect relationship is being sought.*

Not all multiple-choice questions asking a *How?* or *Why?* question are as obvious. For instance, another question might ask the following.

Sample Question 2

> The declaration of war against the British in 1812 illustrates the importance of the
> (A)   establishment of a regular army
> (B)   native Americans in the frontier area
> (C)   Congressional representatives from the newly admitted western states
> (D)   growth of manufacture in New England
> (E)   Department of the Navy

Comments on Question 2

Again the question does not use a little word, but the question is asking, "How did the declaration of war in 1812 get passed?" or "Why did we go to war in 1812?" The question does not mention the words *cause* or *effect*, but essentially a cause-and-effect relationship is being sought. The student must know what issues led to the War of 1812, and from that knowledge he or she must analyze the choices offered. It is a complex process, but it illustrates how many forms of multiple-choice questions seek cause-and-effect relationships and are really asking *How?* or *Why?* questions in shorthand form. The same analytical process and the same type of information is required to deal with the multiple-choice question, which seeks a cause-and-effect relationship, as is needed to write an essay on such questions. To repeat, the six little words are crucial in developing an understanding of history and should be continually used as you study.**

The following forms of multiple-choice questions all seek a cause-and-effect relationship. They are asking *How?* or *Why?* Note, however, that we have not given five choices for each answer. You may make up your own choices as you study this period of history. The choices offered for answers are not the important point now. Instead it is to understand in how many different ways questions can be asked.

1.   The chief reason for the formation of the party known as the Jeffersonian Republicans was . . .
2.   Because of the attitude of the frontier settlers toward whiskey, the first major domestic crisis under the Constitution of 1789 involved . . . .

---

* The correct answer would be D, "British impressment of American sailors." Although the British were still following this practice, it was of minor significance in 1800 compared with our relations with France. Hamilton and the war faction of the Federalist party wanted to fight France, so Hamilton attacked Adams when he refused to support the war. The XYZ Affair in Adam's presidency illustrated the tension in our relations with France, and the Alien and Sedition Acts were part of our preparation for war. The XYZ Affair and the Alien and Sedition Acts antagonized many citizens who therefore voted for Jefferson and the Republicans.

**The correct answer is C. The major force in pushing for war were the so-called War Hawks, the young Congressional representatives from the new western states. Our army and navy were unimportant at the time. The native Americans were a concern, but their activities did not cause this war — in fact, General William H. Harrison had defeated the Indians at the Battle of Tippecanoe in 1811. New Englanders generally opposed the war and voted against it in Congress. If it had not been for the representatives of the new states, we would not have fought the War of 1812.

3. The impressment of American sailors by the British led the United States to . . . .

4. The Hartford Convention of 1815 was a result of . . . .

5. The Jeffersonian Republicans supported the French in the years immediately after the start of the French Revolution because . . . .

6. Which of the following was most directly responsible for Napoleon's offer to sell Louisiana to the United States . . .?

7. The XYZ Affair affected relations between the United States and France by . . .

8. How did members of the Federalist Party respond to Washington's Proclamation of Neutrality in 1793 . . . ?

9. The chief reaction to Jay's Treaty in 1794 was . . .?

10. Why do the terms of the Treaty of Ghent suggest that the War of 1812 was a useless undertaking . . . ?

As you analyze these, you will begin to realize that there are other ways to phrase such questions. Practice making up such questions as you study American history. Involve yourself in the material as a teacher would. Look for relationships, make up questions about the relationships, and see how many different ways you can phrase questions to obtain the information sought when one uses the six little words. These words can be your greatest friends when studying history, so never forget to ask as you study American history — *Who? What? When? Where? Why? How?*

Practice Multiple-Choice Questions

1. The Rush Bagot Agreement called for
   (A) the expulsion of the British from Canada
   (B) a new boundary in Florida
   (C) the expulsion of aliens
   (D) mutual disarmament of the Great Lakes
   (E) commemoration of Perry's victory

2. Which of the following is NOT true concerning the Treaty of Ghent?
   (A) It was signed before Jackson's victory at New Orleans.
   (B) It stated the British would rebuild the burned city of Washington.
   (C) It referred boundary disputes to arbitration committees.
   (D) It called for no exchange of territory.
   (E) It made no reference to impressment.

3. Who of the following was NOT a Federalist?
   (A) Alexander Hamilton   (D) John Marshall
   (B) George Washington   (E) Albert Gallatin
   (C) John Adams

4. Which of the following treaties granted the right of navigation on the Mississippi to the U.S.?
   (A) Pinckney's Treaty   (D) Treaty of Utrecht
   (B) Jay's Treaty   (E) Treaty of Ghent
   (C) Treaty of Greenville

5. The Supreme Court decision in Marbury v. Madison established the
    (A) doctrine of judicial review of Congressional legislation
    (B) principle of state control over local legislation
    (C) doctrine of Supreme Court review of state laws
    (D) principle of sanctity of contract
    (E) sanctity of Congressional control of interstate commerce

6. Where did the Whiskey Rebellion of 1794 take place?
    (A) Ohio   (D) New York
    (B) Massachusetts   (E) Virginia
    (C) Pennsylvania

7. What was the key frontier post held by the British in spite of the Treaty of
    1783?
    (A) Tippecanoe   (D) Genet
    (B) Detroit   (E) Erie
    (C) Greenville

8. The Hartford Convention of 1815
    (A) nominated candidates for president
    (B) called for repeal of the Alien and Sedition Acts
    (C) was a meeting of disaffected Federalists
    (D) rejected the Treaty of Ghent
    (E) supported another invasion of Canada

Questions 9-10 refer to the following map

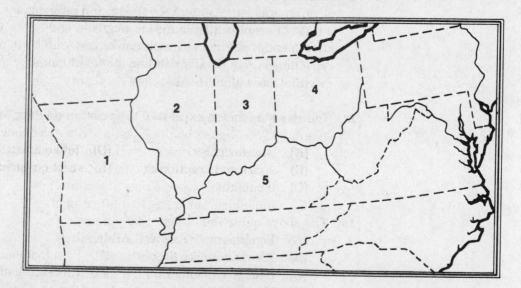

9. Which state's southern boundary of 36°30' was the basis of the Compromise
    of 1820?
    (A) 1   (D) 4
    (B) 2   (E) 5
    (C) 3

10. What state did Henry Clay represent in the U.S. House of Representatives?

    (A) 1   (D) 4

    (B) 2   (E) 5

    (C) 3

11. How would one best explain the location of Washington, D.C.?

    (A) It was at a natural ford in the Potomac River.

    (B) The rapids in the river provided power for water mills.

    (C) It was convenient to George Washington's home at Mount Vernon.

    (D) It was selected as a compromise between the claims of New York, Boston, Princeton, and Philadelphia.

    (E) The land was granted by the state of Maryland to the federal government as the site of the capital city.

12. Why would the average frontier settler in Illinois most likely support the United States' acquisition of New Orleans?

    (A) It would provide a good market for midwestern corn.

    (B) It would prove the nation supported expansion.

    (C) It would provide convenient access to a large slave market.

    (D) It controlled the Mississippi River trade route.

    (E) It was an urban center with a cosmopolitan lifestyle.

Questions 13-14 refer to the following quotation

"Now it appears . . . that this general principle is inherent in the very definition of government, and essential to every step of the progress to be made by that United States, namely: that every power vested in a government is in its nature sovereign, and includes, by force of the term, a right to employ all the means requisite and fairly applicable to the attainment of the ends of such power and which are not precluded by restrictions . . . in the Constitution, or not immoral, or not contrary to the essential ends of political society . . . "

13. The above quotation expressed the position on the Constitution advocated by a

    (A) states-righter   (D) Jeffersonian

    (B) loose constructionist (E) strict constructionist

    (C) Federalist

14. The above quotation is most likely from

    (A) Washington's Farewell Address

    (B) The "Kentucky Resolutions"

    (C) Jefferson's "Letter on the Constitutionality of a National Bank"

    (D) Hamilton's "Letter on the Constitutionality of a National Bank"

    (E) Marshall's decision in *McCulloch v. Maryland*

15. ". . . How unfortunate, and how much is it to be regretted then, that whilst we are encompassed on all sides with avowed enemies and insidious friends, that internal dissensions should be harrowing and tearing our

vitals. The last, to me, is the most serious, the most alarming, and the most afflicting of the two. And without more charity for the opinions and acts of one another in governmental matters, or some more infallible criterion by which the truth of speculative opinions before they have undergone the test of experience are to be forejudged than has yet fallen to the lot of fallibility, I believe it will be difficult, if not impracticable, to manage the reins of government or to keep the parts of it together. . .

The author of the above quotation is concerned with the
   (A)   threat of foreign enemies
   (B)   problem of spies within the government
   (C)   best way to organize dissension
   (D)   problem of states' rights
   (E)   issue of faction or party in government

Answers and Answer Explanations

1. D	2. B	3. E	4. A
5. A	6. C	7. B	8. C
9. A	10. E	11. E	12. D
13. B	14. D	15. E	

1. (D) The Rush Bagot Agreement between the United States and Great Britain in 1817 established the principle of the undefended border between Britain's Canadian colony and the U.S. It called for the disarming of the Great Lakes. It was a result of an arbitration committee established under the terms of the Treaty of Ghent in 1814 and illustrates the growing cooperation between the U.S. and Great Britain.

2. (B) The Treaty of Ghent in 1814 essentially reestablished the situation as it existed before the war. Those issues that had led to war were not mentioned, and the British made no offer to repair damages inflicted during the war, such as their burning of the nation's capital.

3. (E) A. Gallatin was Jefferson's very successful Secretary of the Treasury and a Jeffersonian Republican. The other four men were all Federalists.

4. (A) Pinckney's Treaty with Spain was signed in 1795. It permitted navigation on the Mississippi. At the time Spain owned the Louisiana Territory and controlled the city of New Orleans, so Spain controlled navigation by owning one side of the river and the port at the mouth. France later acquired Louisiana from Spain and we bought the territory from France in 1803. The other treaties dealt with various international issues in the years 1713-1814.

5. (A) John Marshall, a Federalist, believed in strengthening the power of the federal government and of the Supreme Court within the government. The famous case of *Marbury v. Madison* established the right of judicial review of Congressional legislation by the Supreme Court, which is not stated, but is

implied in the Constitution. This use of implied powers allows for a loose construction or interpretation of the Constitution.

6. (C) The Whiskey Rebellion of 1794 was a protest by Pennsylvania farmers over a tax on whiskey by the federal government.

7. (B) Detroit was a key frontier post that the British refused to evacuate after 1783 in spite of the terms of the Treaty of Paris in that year. It was later evacuated according to the terms of Jay's Treaty in 1794.

8. (C) The Federalists of New England were opposed to the War of 1812, and when it looked as though the U.S. would be badly defeated, they called a secret meeting at Hartford to discuss what might be done, including the possibility of secession from the union. The Convention is considered the death knell of the Federalist party. It never again held national political power.

9. (A) The southern boundary of Missouri is the parallel 36°30′, which, with the exception of Missouri, became the boundary between slave and free states in the area of the Louisiana Purchase, according to the terms of the Missouri Compromise of 1820.

10. (E) Henry Clay, a War Hawk elected to Congress first in 1812, represented Kentucky.

11. (E) The state of Maryland granted the site of Washington, D.C., to the federal government as the site of the federal capital. It was a compromise location between the North and the South but not between the cities listed. It did not grow up as so many cities did because of fords or water power. Being close to Washington's home in Mount Vernon had no bearing on the situation, as New York City served as the capital throughout Washington's presidency.

12. (D) A frontier settler in Illinois would most likely support the acquisition of New Orleans because it controlled the Mississippi River trade route to the ocean and thus to the East Coast, Europe, and the Caribbean. Illinois was a non-slave state, so there would be no interest in the slave market. New Orleans would provide only a small market for corn. The other two are true of New Orleans but would have little importance to a frontier settler as far away as Illinois.

13. (B) The quotation expresses the idea of loose construction of the Constitution. It says that if a power is *not* specifically *denied* in the Constitution, is not immoral or opposed to the ends of political unity, and if it is needed to carry out one of the powers expressly mentioned in the Constitution, then the federal government should have that power. Loose construction has been advocated by different parties at different times. Usually the party in power supports the concept. The Federalists did in the 1790s, but opposed loose construction at the time of the Louisiana Purchase and after 1812. The Jeffersonians opposed it during John Adams' administration.

14. (D) The quotation is from Alexander Hamilton's "Letter on the Constitutionality of a National Bank," a strong statement on loose construction, which was written in opposition to Jefferson's statement on the Bank, a statement that opposed a bank since the power to establish one was not specifically mentioned in the Constitution. At that time, 1790, Jefferson was a strict constructionist. Marshall supported the concept of implied powers in Marbury v. Madison.

15. (E) The author of this quotation, George Washington, was greatly concerned about factions (division or disagreements that led to the formation of political parties) in the government. He believed, as indicated here, that unity against the foreign foe was essential and that all groups within the nation should work together for the benefit of the new country.

Bibliography

The following books focus on different important issues of the years 1789-1824. To supplement your textbook, you may wish to read sections in different books about matters of particular interest to you.

Cunliffe, Marcus. *The Nation Takes Shape 1789–1837*. Chicago: University of Chicago Press, 1959.

Goodman, Paul (ed.). *Federalists vs. the Jeffersonian Republicans* (Am. Problem Series). Melbourne, FL: Krieger, 1977.

Landenberg, Thomas. (Am. Hist. Ser.) Boulder, CO: Social Science Editors, HarperCollins, 1989.

Madison, James et al. *The Federalist Papers*. New York: Viking Penguin, 1987.

Perkins, Dexter. *The Monroe Doctrine 1826–1867*. Magnolia, FL: Peter Smith.

Sears, L.M. *Jefferson and the Embargo*. New York: Octagon Books, 1967.

Stinchcombe, W.C. *The XYZ Affair*. Westport, CT: Greenwood Press, 1980.

Thayer, James B. et al. *John Marshall*. Chicago: University of Chicago Press, 1967.

PART THREE 4 Jackson and the West 1824-1850

Important Facets of This Period

The central figure in this period of American history is Andrew Jackson. He has given his name to the age, which is considered by some historians as the adolescence of the nation. It was a period marked by many social and economic changes. The age is recognized as the start of the operation of the political system as we know it today. It was a time of contrasts — of great intolerance and of great concern for the underprivileged. Jackson's presidency was followed by economic depression and a decade of expansion for which the slogan became Manifest Destiny. Manifest Destiny culminated in the acquisition of Oregon and the Mexican War. These events in turn opened up the issue of the spread of slavery, which was temporarily settled at the end of this time period with the Compromise of 1850.

Expansion and Jacksonian Democracy are the two chief issues of these years; Jackson, the dominant figure, is in the eyes of one historian, J.W. Ward, the symbol of an age. Many accept this view and, therefore, in preparation for the Advanced Placement examination every student should have a thorough understanding of Jackson's career and of the meaning of Jacksonian Democracy.

Among the topics one would want to consider in studying these years would be the following:

1. The reasons for the break-up of the Era of Good Feelings, which culminated in the election of 1828
2. Jackson's "War on the Bank of the United States"
3. The tariff issue and Calhoun's ideas on nullification
4. The growth of sectionalism and the distinguishing features of the three sections — Northeast, South, and West
5. Emerging social concerns and attitudes as exemplified by educational, institutional, and literary developments
6. The Panic of 1837 and its impact upon the nation
7. Manifest Destiny and the presidency of James K. Polk
8. The Mexican War and its aftermath
9. The spread of slavery to new territories.

Sample Essay Question—In What Ways . . . ?

The question that begins *In what ways*...is a common type of essay question and one that has many variations, such as *In what manner*...or *In what respects ...* or *To what extent*...Basically, this form is a version of the simple *What?* type, but with the addition of the other words, the writer is given more specific direction as to what must be done. Therefore, in the *In what ways*...type the important word becomes the one after *what*. How do you approach answering an *In what ways?* question? The key word in this type of question is *ways*. The word *ways* implies a progression or movement from one point to another and suggests a chronological organization by which the writer can illustrate how an event or idea led to other events or ideas.

What do you do when you are asked to focus on the *manner* in which something occurred? The word *manner* means a mode of procedure or customary way of acting. The focus of the answer to this type of essay would be less on the sequence of events and more on what lay behind them. Why did they occur, or what made people act the way they did, would be the important part of the answer.

If you are asked *In what respects . . .* you are being asked about relationships again. *Respect* is defined as relation or relationship, regarding an act of noticing with attention. This version of the basic type is very similar to the *In what ways . . .* version and would require a cause-and-effect approach with events carefully related together. You would want to dwell on the reasons, paying strict attention to all the *whys* and *wherefores* you can consider. There are other variations of the *In what ways* type of question and the key is always to look at and analyze the word after *what*.

The *In what ways . . .* question often presents a clear idea for organizing the answer. Because of the introductory word *in*, it should be clear that the question seeks your personal opinion on the progression, the mode of procedure, or the relationship. *In*, in this type of question, means both inclusion with respect to scope or influence and indicating limits with respect to manner or means. You are the one who must determine what will be included and what is to be limited. When you decide on these two points, you will determine your personal viewpoint and thus establish your thesis on the question.

The variation *To what extent . . .* changes the preposition. In this case *to* means indicating effect or resulting condition, indicating . . . accordance . . . or disagreement and indicating the final or full degree. As in the other variations of the *In what ways . . .* question, the key word is the one after *what*. Here it is the word *extent* that means degree, measure, proportion. You are asked to indicate the final or full degree, measure, proportion to which the given information has an effect on or agrees or disagrees with other information given in the question. This variation obviously requires your personal opinion. There are other words that can be used in place of *extent* and, to repeat, this is the word to which you should pay particular attention in analyzing the question.

Sometimes the *to what extent . . .* variation will have added the phrase *Do you agree or disagree?* This phrase can be attached to many essay questions and simply reinforces the invitation to argument. **Remember, in every essay answer you are arguing a case as a lawyer or debater does**. You may take any personal view you wish on any issue, and the quality of your paper will be judged on how well you argue and prove your personal opinion or thesis. The *Do you agree or disagree?* phrase simply makes it clearer that your personal opinion is being sought. The phrase is another way of asking the writer to evaluate the statement, and much of what was said about that type of essay question in Part Two applies to any essay question in which you are asked to agree or disagree.

A typical *In what ways . . .* essay question is the following:

Sample Question

> In what ways did the emerging sectional conflicts within the United States manifest themselves in the election of Andrew Jackson and in the domestic policies of the nation in the years 1828–1837?

Comments on Sample Question

The question asks you to consider the "ways" — that is, the progression or movement from one point to another in which "the emerging sectional conflicts within the United States manifested themselves" in two areas. In order to answer the question you must know that the word *manifest* means to reveal or else you would be in trouble with the question. You must deal with the two areas also — the election of Andrew Jackson in 1828 and his domestic policies. It is important that both areas be treated thoroughly.

You will want to begin your analysis by deciding what the sectional conflicts were and then listing the issues of the election of 1828 and Jackson's domestic policies. If you have knowledge of the latter two and can identify the emerging sectional conflicts, then you are ready to answer the question. After you have worked up notes or written your answer to this question, following the Seven Steps in Essay Writing, you will want to read and judge the following student answer to the question.

Sample Answer

Andrew Jackson was elected president in 1828, having run and been defeated in 1824 by J.Q. Adams, whom he beat in 1828. The campaign was a dirty one, the first really dirty campaign. In fact, Jackson later felt that the accusations against his wife and her divorce from her first husband were the cause of her death, which took place early in his first administration.

J.Q. Adams was a very intelligent man, but he was not a very good president. This helped defeat him, as some members of his own party, including the later president Van Buren, left Adams to support Jackson. Jackson, on the other hand, had proven himself a fine general by winning the Battle of New Orleans. He was called Old Hickory and his supporters claimed he was born in a log cabin. Actually, Jackson was wealthy and had a beautiful plantation home, the Hermitage, but the log cabin idea caught on and many men running for office during our history have capitalized on their log cabin backgrounds.

When Jackson became president, he used the Spoils System to put his friends in office. He did not start the system, as it used to be believed, but he used it extensively. Jackson believed any American could operate the government, and since the government was the people's, he appointed ordinary citizens to fill important posts. Jackson also believed, since he was the only official in the federal government elected by all the people, that he represented the people. This encouraged him to act as a strong president. An example of this position is when Chief Justice Marshall declared in a case that Georgia had no claim to Indian Territory in the state. Rather than enforce the ruling, which he disapproved of, Jackson said, "Marshall made the decision; let him enforce it." Along with the Spoils System, Jackson used a Kitchen Cabinet. These were men who were his friends and gave him advice on various domestic and foreign issues. They did not hold government positions, yet they were more important than the regular cabinet.

During Jackson's administration, the sale of western lands was important. There was a lot of speculation in the land sales and this led to inflation, which Jackson didn't like. He therefore issued the "specie circular," which forced people to pay for lands with gold or silver. This was a cause of the Panic of 1837.

The name Jackson is connected with the word *democracy*. Many historians believe the nation really became democratic during the 1830s. To support this idea they report the spread of universal male suffrage. Also, behind this coming of age of democracy are many other important developments, such as the spread of free public schools, the growing rate of immigration, the growth of industry, and the rise of labor unions, which supported the common man. Industry grew the most in the North, and the South remained agricultural. The West wanted roads and transportation, so the idea came to have a high tariff on imports to help the North's industry and to use the money to build roads. The South didn't like the high tariff. Jackson's reelection in 1832 was involved with this tariff mess. Another issue of Jackson's time was the bank issue, which involved a long fight with Nicholas Biddle and a refusal to recharter the second bank. Then there were problems with Indians, England, and picking Jackson's successor. These all affected different people and sections.

As in the case of the other sample essays, reflect on this one before you read the teacher comments. The making of a formal outline of this answer will help you understand better what the writer has done. What are its good features? What are its bad features? Do you think the writer followed the Seven Steps in Essay Writing? What grade would you give to it? What advice do you have for this student? Have you ever written an essay similar to this one? What did the teacher tell you?

Teacher Comments on Sample Answer

"The writer of this essay has plenty of important factual information at his or her command, but he or she has simply spewed it out with no reference to the question at all. It is a tragic case of rushing into answering a question. The writer has recited a few words, in this case *election* and *Andrew Jackson*, and written what he or she knew about those words with no reference to how the words are used in the question. The student's references to Van Buren's desertion of Adams, to the "specie circular," to the purchase of western lands, to the North, South, West split over internal improvements, and to the tariff reveal that he or she has valuable information to develop a viewpoint on "emerging sectional conflicts." Unfortunately, in no place does the student present a personal viewpoint or thesis on the topic under consideration, nor ever mention what the topic of the question actually is. A thesis is badly needed, preferably in an opening or introductory paragraph, and in some way the reader should have been made aware of the question.

"The writer presents detailed information on the Spoils System, the Kitchen Cabinet, and Jacksonian Democracy. All of these items could have been used to illustrate sectional differences, although the Kitchen Cabinet may be a little far-fetched as an illustration. Still, the idea of the use of friends and the common people to run the government could be used to illustrate the change in government brought about when the West took the presidency from the educated, aristocratic East.

"The writer of the essay uses several paragraphs, but the last one includes several ideas — democracy, industry, tariff, and bank — which should be presented in separate paragraphs. There is no clear linkage of the paragraphs and although there is some vague organization — a mixture of topic and chronology, i.e., election, when first president, western land, democracy — the answer is confusing. Finally, the essay just stops; there is no conclusion. Therefore, in spite of the fine information this writer has, the failure to answer the question and the poor essay style earned a low grade. It is an all too common failure among students. It is particularly unfortunate in this case since the student obviously is bright and knowledgeable. If the student had thought before he or she had written, had organized the paper, and had used a better essay style, he or she should have been able to earn a very good or outstanding grade."

Practice Essay Questions

The above student essay clearly demonstrates the importance of the Seven Steps in Essay Writing. Before you read and prepare the answer to the following essay questions, you may want to check back to Part Two and review these Seven Steps in Essay Writing. Also, as you prepare to deal with these five essays, do not forget our image of the flashlight. Your essay needs a beam to catch the reader, connected batteries to make the beam shine, and a cap to hold the batteries in contact and to make the whole flashlight work.

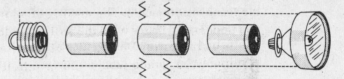

1. In what ways did the concept of Manifest Destiny affect the foreign and domestic policies of the United States in the years 1840-1850?

2. To what extent did Jacksonian Democracy reflect social and economic developments in the nation and in what ways did Jacksonian Democracy further such social and economic developments?

3. In what respects did each of the following represent in their expressed opinions and actions the viewpoint of the section of the nation from which he came?
   (A) Calhoun—The South
   (B) Clay—The West
   (C) Webster—New England

4. "Both the Jacksonian Democrats during 1824-1840 and the Populists during 1890-1896 attacked and sought to rule out special privilege in American life. The Jacksonian Democrats attained power and succeeded; the Populists failed." Assess the validity of this view.

5. In what manner did the Jacksonian Revolution mark the establishment of democracy in America whereas the Jeffersonian Revolution merely marked the arrival of a new party in political power?

Comments on Question 1

Question 1 is typical of the *In what ways...* type of question. It is seeking a cause-and-effect relationship as in a *What?* question, and it asks you to present the manner in which this relationship came about. This particular question is dependent upon your understanding the concept of Manifest Destiny. This is one of those phrases that summarizes a whole series of attitudes and beliefs held by the Americans at a particular point in history. It is one of those phrases every student should know.* Once you have the meaning of the phrase clear in your mind, then you should list some of the foreign and domestic issues of the years

---

* Manifest Destiny summarizes the idea that it was the destiny of the United States to control the continent. The idea guided most American attitudes on foreign policy in the late 1830s and '40s. Americans then believed their destiny should be manifest or obvious and clear to everyone, especially all foreigners.

1840 to 1850. Once you have done that you will want to ask youself the question, "How did Manifest Destiny relate to the issues listed?" Your answer to that question will be your thesis; your list of issues should provide organizational clues, and so you should be ready to write.

Comments on Question 2

The second question is one variation on the *In what ways . . .* type discussed above. The *To what extent . . .* form is a *What?* question seeking cause-and-effect relations, but it clearly asks for your personal opinion about the question and in that sense it is asking you to agree or disagree with the material. This particular question is seeking your judgment on the relationship between Jacksonian Democracy and social and economic developments and is a good example of a question dealing with social history. It asks you to focus on social and economic developments and determine whether they are causes of or simply reflections of political changes and developments. This is an interesting question and one of the first sample questions in this book to require a thorough knowledge of social developments. It is a difficult question, which may be hard to organize, but if you struggle with it, the personal satisfaction gained from writing a good answer will be great.

Comments on Question 3

The third question, an *In what respects . . .* form, is another variation on the *In What ways . . .* type. It is another one of those questions in which a personal opinion may appear not to be needed, but as always, you must make and express a judgment. In this case you must know the opinions of three important leaders of the period before 1850, you must know the viewpoints of the three major sections of the nation in those years, and you must know how the three men expressed their opinions and what their actions were. If you are in command of details involving all of these points, then you can develop your thesis and prepare to answer the question. In this question the obvious organizational format would be to discuss each man in turn and write introductory and concluding paragraphs that tie the three men together with the general topic.

Comments on Question 4

The question from the 1976 Advanced Placement exam is a typical *Assess the validity (Evaluate this statement)* type of question. The quotation asks you to deal with two specific movements in American history in two different periods, which is sometimes done on Advanced Placement examinations. They are major movements that all students should be familiar with, but the focus of the question is on eliminating "special privilege" in American life—an aspect of these movements that may not be as familiar. The question illustrates how an AP examination question may focus on an unusual aspect of the period. If you are not in control of such information, it would be wise not to attempt the question. In this case, once you have analyzed what you know about eliminating special privilege in these two eras, you must decide if you agree that the Jacksonians were successful and the Populists were not. Obviously, your decision on this issue will provide you with the thesis statement. The question requires information from different time periods, but it is not a difficult question.

Comments on Question 5

The last question presents the *In what manner* variation of the *In what ways. . .?* form. The question asks for a comparison of time periods, and in this case you are comparing two periods with which you should be familiar by now if you are studying American history chronologically as you read this book. The issue raised — when did the United States become a democracy? — is one investigated in most U.S. history courses. The Jackson and Jefferson revolutions are often compared. The question takes an extreme position, and you should be able to react strongly with a personal opinion. The facts should then follow, and they should supply you with an organizational framework. Finding such a framework may be the most difficult task with this question.

Multiple-Choice Questions—Maps

As indicated when discussing the sample essay in Part Two, many historians believe that geography or environmental factors are at the heart of history. They believe these factors determine and control the choices people can make about their lives. This is perhaps an extreme interpretation, but it does illustrate how central geography is for understanding history. For you, as a student of American history, geography *must* be learned and understood. A knowledge of the location of states and of geographic features, such as rivers and mountains, and of their importance in the development of the nation and of the movement of people must be understood. Your knowledge of this information may be needed in essay answers (see question 3 above), or it may be tested in multiple-choice questions. Map questions are a good example of a stimulus question. They also provide an excellent way to gain fundamental information about American history and to help the student review basic information. Map questions have already been included in the sample multiple-choice questions in Chapters 1, 2, and 3, and will be included in the remaining chapters. The following examples of multiple-choice questions involving maps will illustrate the wide range of questions that can be asked based directly on maps and on the analysis of maps. Many other questions might be asked in addition to these. These questions should make you realize the importance of geography, of studying the maps in the textbooks, and of locating places where events took place as you read about those events.

Sample Questions 1-3

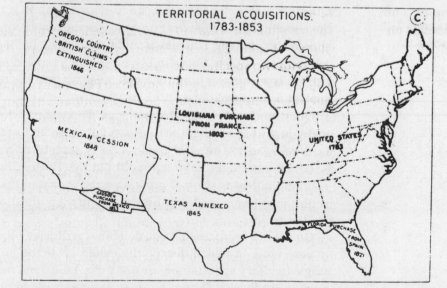

SOURCE: Charles O. Paullin, *Atlas of the Historical Geography of the U.S.* Courtesy of Carnegie Institution, Washington.

1. The map indicates our largest single territorial acquisition
    after independence was the

    (A) Oregon country
    (B) Mexican Cession
    (C) Gadsden Purchase
    (D) Louisiana Purchase
    (E) Florida Purchase

2. The Gadsden Purchase was particularly important because it

    (A) gave us a more defensible border with Mexico
    (B) included a new source of gold
    (C) included the best southern route for a railroad to the
         west coast
    (D) provided land for an Indian reservation
    (E) smoothed our relations with Mexico after the strain
         of the Mexican War

3. The map indicates the period of greatest territorial growth of the
    United States was in the decade

    (A) 1790-1800
    (B) 1800-1810
    (C) 1820-1830
    (D) 1840-1850
    (E) 1850-1860

Comments on
Questions 1-3

Question 1 assumes that you can read a very familiar map. There should be no
question that the Louisiana Purchase was the largest single territorial acquisition
shown on the map. You may want to say Alaska, but it is *not* on the map and *not*
offered as a choice. Sometimes your recall knowledge will *not* be offered as a
choice for an answer, and then you must analyze the data given to pick the best
answer from the choices.

Question 2 tests learned knowledge. There is no way from looking at the map
that you will know that the Gadsden Purchase included the best southern route
for a railroad to the west coast. That is something you should have learned,
although you might have figured it out by eliminating the other choices or by
realizing railroads were of growing significance in the 1850s and the purchase
is on the extreme southern border. Some map questions will simply test your
factual recall.

Question 3 requires that you combine territories acquired in the same decade
to determine in which decade the nation grew the most. Although the largest
single territory acquired before 1853 was Louisiana in 1803, we acquired more
territory in three different sections in the decade of the 1840s. The question is
an easy test of map reading skill.

**Sample Questions
4-6**

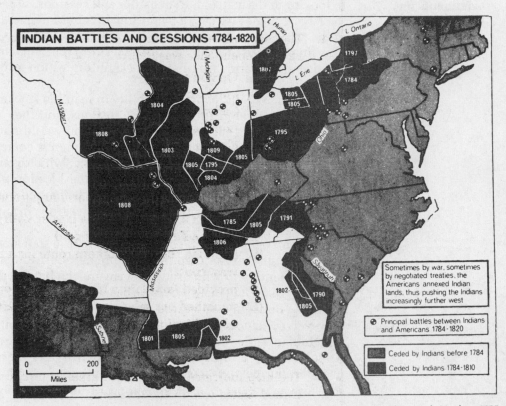

SOURCE: From *The American History Atlas*, Martin Gilbert, George Weidenfeld & Nicolson, Ltd. London, 1985.

4. According to the above map, the largest SINGLE area ceded by the Indians after 1784 was
    (A) the original colonies
    (B) south of the Arkansas River
    (C) west of the Mississippi River
    (D) bordered by the Great Lakes
    (E) along the Ohio River

5. There were fewer Indian battles in the years 1784-1820
    (A) in the areas not ceded to white settlers by the Indians
    (B) in the original thirteen colonies
    (C) west of the Mississippi River
    (D) in the area ceded by the Indians after 1784
    (E) in the areas ceded to white settlers by the Indians

6. From studying this map, one could conclude that
    (A) those Americans living along the mid-Atlantic seacoast were safest from Indian battles
    (B) Indians and white settlers believed in treaties
    (C) white settlers were greedy for land
    (D) the Indians made money from the sale of lands
    (E) the Supreme Court under Marshall protected the Cherokee lands in Georgia

Comments on Questions 4-6

In looking at the map of Indian battles and cessions, 1784-1820, one can see that the largest single area ceded by the Indians after independence was the area west of the Mississippi River and north of the Arkansas River. It was ceded in 1808. You simply need to be able to read the key to the map and to be able to compare the size of the various grants. It is a simple question testing your ability to read a map.

Question 5 again requires an ability to read the key and the map. The given choices divide the map into specific regions, and then you need to count the symbol indicating battles in each region. You would *not* have this information before the exam, as this multiple-choice question is *not* testing recall of information, but rather a specific skill, map reading, which you should have learned. Question 5 does assume that you know the location of the original thirteen colonies, but the other four choices can all be figured out from the map. There were fewer battles west of the Mississippi River than in any of the four other areas described.

Question 6 offers several choices that are true statements but for which there is no evidence on the map. The Supreme Court under Marshall did protect Cherokee lands and white settlers were greedy, but the map doesn't prove it — it may suggest it, but there may have been other motivations for the Indian cession of lands. Belief in treaties and money is not mentioned on the map. You can, however, conclude that Americans along the mid-Atlantic seacoast were safest from Indian battles between 1784 and 1820. There are no symbols along the mid-Atlantic coast (Carolina to New Jersey). There is only one battle symbol anywhere near the northeast seacoast and only an additional three symbols along the southern coast. Statement A does appear true based on evidence from the map.

Sample Question 7

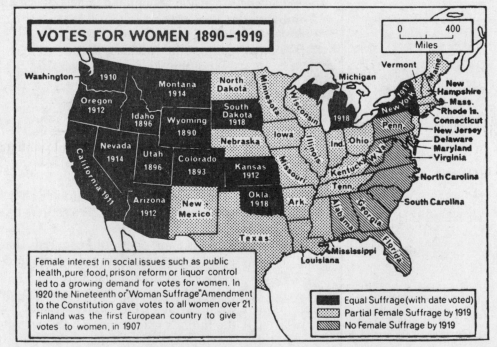

SOURCE: From *The American History Atlas*, Martin Gilbert, George Weidenfeld & Nicolson, Ltd. London, 1985.

7.   Which of the following generalizations could NOT be supported
by information presented in the map?
(A) The western half of the nation was more responsive to
the issue of women's suffrage than the eastern half.
(B) Wyoming was the first state to establish votes for women.
(C) It would be impossible in 1919 to get a Constitutional
amendment passed giving the vote to women.
(D) States along the eastern seaboard would be most likely
to reject a Constitutional amendment giving the vote
to women.
(E) New York was the most liberal state of the original
thirteen on the issue of votes for women.

Comments on Question 7

Question 7 again asks you to confirm generalizations or speculations based on evidence from a map. It is a good test of map reading ability. The map on votes for women would support all the generalizations given, except that it would be impossible to get a Constitutional amendment passed in 1919 giving the women the right to vote. You might assume this, but there is no way of knowing how the states with partial female suffrage would vote. You would *suspect* the states with equal suffrage would support the amendment and those states with no female suffrage would vote against the amendment, but there is no way to be sure from the map how they would vote or how that crucial group of 24 states with partial suffrage would vote. One must be careful not to assume too much from the map. The other four assumptions would appear quite safe. Certainly Wyoming was the first to establish women's suffrage (1890), and of the original thirteen, only New York allowed women to vote equally with men. The western states all had granted female suffrage. If liberal means to grant suffrage, then the west and New York are liberal. It might be argued that there is no certainty the eastern seaboard would vote against a Constitutional amendment. However, since they don't allow women to vote, it would seem likely they would vote against an amendment, which is all the question suggests. The generalization does not suggest certainty on this matter, as does option C with the word *impossible*.

Sample Questions 8-9

THE UNITED STATES TO 1837

8. According to the map, AFTER the original thirteen states, the first three states admitted to the union were admitted in the following order
    (A) Ohio, Indiana, Illinois
    (B) Kentucky, Tennessee, Ohio
    (C) Kentucky, Ohio, Louisiana
    (D) Vermont, Kentucky, Ohio
    (E) Vermont, Kentucky, Tennessee

9. What was the first state admitted to the Union from the Louisiana Purchase territory?
    (A) Mississippi
    (B) Louisiana
    (C) Missouri
    (D) Ohio
    (E) Kentucky

Comments on Questions 8-9

Questions 8 and 9 are even less complicated tests of map reading ability. Simply by reading the dates of admissions you can establish that the first states admitted to the union in order after the original thirteen were Vermont, Kentucky, Tennessee; of course, you must know which states were the original thirteen. A fast reading of the map might lead you to miss Vermont and then you would have picked the wrong answer—Kentucky, Tennessee, Ohio. Question 9 requires you to know the area of the Louisiana Purchase, and then you can easily see that Louisiana is the first state admitted to the union from that territory.

Sample Questions 10-11

10. The Northwest Ordinance applied to the region on the map numbered
   (A) 1
   (B) 2
   (C) 3
   (D) 4
   (E) 5

11. On the map the region numbered 4 is considered the
   (A) birthplace of all great presidents
   (B) place of the first permanent white settlement in North America
   (C) area of strongest support for the Mexican War
   (D) center of American Transcendentalism
   (E) region of outstanding development of new forms of
       land transportation

**Comments on
Questions 10-11**

The map for questions 10 and 11 is a type commonly used in multiple-choice questions. The type requires that you know the geography of the United States so that you can identify regions, states, major cities, and territories. In question 10 you must know that the Northwest Ordinance applied to the Northwest Territory and be able to recognize this region on the map. It is 2—the area east of the Mississippi River, north of the Ohio River, south of the Great Lakes, and west of Pennsylvania. The question tests recall and factual geographic knowledge. Question 11 does the same but it is a little more sophisticated, requiring you to identify a region with an activity. It also tests literary knowledge—an example that map questions can be used to bring about a recall of all types of information. In this question, area 4 is New England, the center of Transcendentalism—the American version of a European philosophical movement. Its leaders were Emerson and Thoreau, but many other intellectual leaders of New England, such as Hawthorne and Parkman, were connected with Transcendentalism. Some people may believe that all great presidents are New Englanders, but that is ridiculous. The first permanent white settlement was in Florida. New Englanders opposed the Mexican War, and new land transportation was developed in the west while New Englanders concentrated on clipper ships and the sea. Question 11 is a good use of the simple map question where you need to know the geography of the country and to recall factual information about it.

Sample Questions
12-13

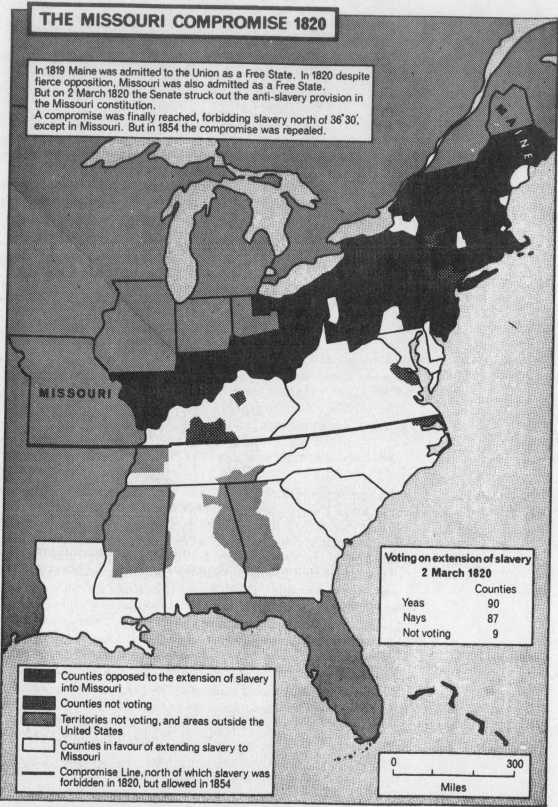

THE MISSOURI COMPROMISE 1820

In 1819 Maine was admitted to the Union as a Free State. In 1820 despite fierce opposition, Missouri was also admitted as a Free State.
But on 2 March 1820 the Senate struck out the anti-slavery provision in the Missouri constitution.
A compromise was finally reached, forbidding slavery north of 36°30', except in Missouri. But in 1854 the compromise was repealed.

MAINE

MISSOURI

Voting on extension of slavery
2 March 1820

	Counties
Yeas	90
Nays	87
Not voting	9

Counties opposed to the extension of slavery into Missouri

Counties not voting

Territories not voting, and areas outside the United States

Counties in favour of extending slavery to Missouri

Compromise Line, north of which slavery was forbidden in 1820, but allowed in 1854

0   300

Miles

SOURCE: From *The American History Atlas*, Martin Gilbert, George Weidenfeld & Nicolson, Ltd. London, 1985.

12. According to the previous map, which one of the following statements is true?
    (A) There were no southern states in favor of the extension of slavery into Missouri.
    (B) Of those eligible, only delegates from southern counties failed to vote.
    (C) No New Englanders favored extending slavery into Missouri.
    (D) Florida was a non-slaveholding territory.
    (E) There was a decided division between the North and the South on the issue of the extension of slavery to Missouri.

13. The map illustrates that
    (A) Henry Clay proposed the Missouri Compromise
    (B) the South always voted as a block
    (C) the North could not unite on issues
    (D) the Missouri Compromise line was approximately the same latitude line as the southern border of Virginia and Kentucky
    (E) there were many territories about to be states

Comments on Questions 12-13

Questions 12 and 13 are good tests of map reading skill. For number 12 the map clearly shows that there were some New Englanders in favor of the Missouri Compromise and that some delegates from all regions failed to vote. Of course the map shows nothing about slavery in Florida. Choice A of question 12 is very tricky. You might read it quickly and say it was true, but, of course, it is just the reverse of the truth. Be careful in your reading. The map shows there was a decided division between the North and the South on the issue of the extension of slavery into Missouri, which is the correct answer for question 12. You might have known this, but again your knowledge is confirmed by the map. The map also shows that the compromise line follows the southern border of Missouri and, if extended east, would run parallel to and just south of the southern border of Kentucky and Virginia, which is the correct answer for question 13. Block voting and unity cannot be shown by a map and the map illustrates nothing about territories becoming states nor who introduced the Missouri Compromise.

Practice Multiple-Choice Questions

1. All of the following were provisions of the Compromise of 1850 EXCEPT:
   (A) admittance of California into the union as a free state
   (B) a strict fugitive slave law
   (C) establishment of Utah and New Mexico as territories with squatter sovereignty
   (D) the redrawing of the Texas boundary
   (E) the prohibition of the slave trade in Washington, D.C.

2. The Independent Treasury plan called for
   - (A)   a bank of the United States
   - (B)   the funding of the U.S. debt by the Treasury
   - (C)   the use of silver coinage for debt payment
   - (D)   the use of state banks by the Treasury
   - (E)   the deposit of U.S. tax revenues in the Treasury rather than in banks

3. Which of the following events occurred first?
   - (A)   Tariff of Abominations
   - (B)   The Force Bill
   - (C)   South Carolina's nullification of U.S. tariff laws
   - (D)   Clay's Compromise Tariff of 1833
   - (E)   Calhoun's resignation as vice-president

4. The Gag Resolution passed by the House of Representatives in 1836 was passed to prevent
   - (A)   publication of Garrison's *Liberator.*
   - (B)   Nat Turner's rebellion
   - (C)   southerners' fears of debate of antislavery appeals
   - (D)   the growth of sweatshop factories in the North
   - (E)   organization of the Free Soil party

5. Which of the following was a reaction to the desire of some members of Congress to lower the price of western land?
   - (A)   Mormon move to Utah
   - (B)   Hayne-Webster Debate
   - (C)   Seneca Falls Convention
   - (D)   American Colonization Society
   - (E)   Manifest Destiny

6. Jackson had the "specie circular" issued in 1836 because he
   - (A)   disliked the Bank of the United States
   - (B)   thought it would win his party the presidency
   - (C)   feared the high rate of debt and the speculation brought about by the sale of western land.
   - (D)   hoped it would force England to open West Indian ports
   - (E)   felt there was enough gold and silver in the country

7. All of the following men are connected with the development and admission of California to the union EXCEPT
   - (A)   Thomas Larkin   (D)   Washington Irving
   - (B)   John Sutter   (E)   John Slidell
   - (C)   John C. Fremont

8. Which of the following would NOT be considered part of Jacksonian Democracy?
   - (A)   Actions of Dorothea Dix to help the insane
   - (B)   The establishment of labor unions and their recognition by the courts
   - (C)   The spread of free public schools
   - (D)   The growth of railroads
   - (E)   The extension of universal male suffrage

9. Of those 19th-century inventions listed below, each is correctly paired with its inventor EXCEPT
    (A) Reaper — McCormack
    (B) Vulcanization of rubber — Goodyear
    (C) Sewing machine — Howe
    (D) Steamboat — Fulton
    (E) Telegraph — Bell

Questions 10-11 refer to the following quotation

"The modifications of the existing charter proposed by this act are not such, in my view, as make it consistent with the rights of the States or the liberties of the people. The qualification of the right of the bank to hold real estate, the limitation of its power to establish branches, and the power reserved to Congress to forbid the circulation of small notes are restrictions comparatively of little value or importance. All the objectionable principles of the existing corporation, and most of its odious features, are retained without alleviation . . . .

"If we must have a bank with private stockholders, every consideration of sound policy and every impulse of American feeling admonishes that it should be *purely American*. Its stockholders should be composed exclusively of our own citizens, who at least ought to be friendly to our Government and willing to support it in times of difficulty and danger . . . . To a bank exclusively of American stockholders, possessing the powers and privileges granted by this act, subscriptions for $200,000,000 could be readily obtained . . . .

"It is maintained by the advocates of the bank that its constitutionality in all its features ought to be considered as settled by precedent and by the decision of the Supreme Court. To this conclusion I can not assent."

10. The author of the above quotation appears to believe all of the following EXCEPT:
    (A) the bank is not constitutional
    (B) it is dangerous to have foreign stockholders
    (C) a limitation on the bank's holding real estate and establishing branches is not sufficient control
    (D) $200,000,000 cannot be raised by Americans
    (E) the bank is not consistent with personal liberty

11. The opinion expressed in this quotation proved to be that held by the American people as indicated by
    (A) the victory of Andrew Jackson in the 1832 election
    (B) Nicholas Biddle's support of New England manufacture
    (C) the Webster Ashburton Treaty
    (D) Calhoun's doctrine of nullification
    (E) the essays of Ralph Waldo Emerson

12. The important foreign policy known as the Monroe Doctrine

    I.   was first proposed by the British government to the United States

    II.   was presented by President Monroe in a State of the Union message

    III.   was designed to protect United States business interests in the Americas

    IV.   suggested the United States would not become involved in European affairs

    (A)   I and II
    (B)   I, II, and III
    (C)   I, II, and IV
    (D)   II, III, and IV
    (E)   I, II, III, and IV

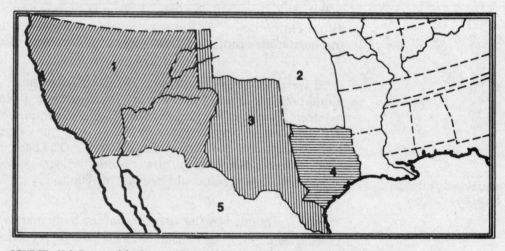

SOURCE: U.S. Bureau of the Census, *Historical Statistics of the U. S., Colonial Times to 1957.*

13. On the map above the area numbered 4 was the

    (A)   area where the U.S. Army was defeated by the Mexican Army in the Mexican War
    (B)   Republic of Texas
    (C)   southern area of the Louisiana Purchase
    (D)   birthplace of Andrew Jackson
    (E)   great cattle grazing region of Texas

Questions 14-15 refer to the following chart

IMMIGRATION TO THE UNITED STATES

Year	Total	Gr. Britain	Ireland	Scandinavia	Germany	Poland
1820	8,385	2,410	3,614	23	968	5
1830	23,322	1,153	2,721	19	1,906	2
1840	84,066	2,613	39,340	207	29,704	5
1850	369,980	51,085	164,004	1,589	78,896	5

14. According to the chart on immigration, all of the following are true EXCEPT:
    (A)   more immigrants came from eastern Europe than from the British Isles
    (B)   the total number of immigrants more than doubled each decade
    (C)   Polish immigration remained rather constant
    (D)   there was a very significant increase in immigration in 1850
    (E)   the smallest number of immigrants from Great Britain arrived in the 1830s

15. The figures in the previous chart on immigration in the period 1820-1850 reveal that
    (A)   the total immigration remained constant
    (B)   Polish immigration increased in 1830
    (C)   in each year shown, the Irish formed the largest single group of immigrants
    (D)   British immigration declined over these years
    (E)   Scandinavian immigrants formed a high percentage of the total immigration

16. Which of the following events occurred last?
    (A)   Purchase of the Louisiana Territory
    (B)   Lewis and Clark Expedition
    (C)   Settlement of Independence, Missouri
    (D)   Extensive use of the Oregon Trail
    (E)   British sending of Vancouver to explore Puget Sound area

Answers and Answer Explanations

1. D	2. E	3. A	4. C
5. B	6. C	7. D	8. D
9. E	10. D	11. A	12. C
13. B	14. A	15. C	16. D

1. (D) The Compromise of 1850 was Henry Clay's (the Great Compromiser) last contribution to national unity. It temporarily resolved the free state/slave state controversy, giving both the North and South certain points they desired. Although slavery had reappeared as a divisive issue as a result of the Texas controversy and the Mexican War, the compromise did not deal with any issue involving Texas.

2. (E) The Independent Treasury Plan was Van Buren's answer to the concept of a Bank of the U.S or the use of state banks by the federal government. It called for depositing federal revenue directly in the U.S. Treasury, thus ignoring banks.

3. (A) The so-called Tariff of Abominations of 1828 set off the entire tariff, state power/federal power, nullification controversy of Jackson's administration. The other four choices all represent key aspects of this controversy.

4. (C) The "Gag Resolution" was passed by the House to eliminate Congressional debate of antislavery proposals, which they feared would lead to federal acts against the interests of the South. Garrison's *Liberator* and Nat Turner's revolt helped provoke this fear, but the "Gag Resolution" was not passed to prevent them.

5. (B) The Hayne-Webster Debate had as its start a proposal to reduce the price of western land. It was one of the most important congressional debates of the 19th century. Its focus became the role of the federal government as opposed to that of state government.

6. (C) Although Jackson disliked the Bank of the U.S., he also disliked paper currency, speculation, and the increase in the level of private debt. The "specie circular" required payment for western lands in gold or silver and was meant to cut down speculation and inflation.

7. (D) Washington Irving is an early American author and member of the Knickerbocker School. The other four men all played key roles in the acquisition of California.

8. (D) The growth of railroads had a great impact on the nation. The railroads cannot be considered a part of social democracy. The other four advanced the democratization of society and represent the great variety of reform movements begun in the 1820s and '30s, which are considered a part of Jacksonian Democracy.

9. (E) Inventions were important in stimulating the economic and industrial growth of the nation, especially of the Northeast. Except for the telegraph, which was invented by Morse and not Bell, these inventions were made before 1850 by the men indicated. Bell invented the telephone later in the century.

10. (D) An analysis of this quotation from Jackson's veto message of the bill renewing the charter of the Second Bank of the United States reveals that he believed $200,000,000 *could* be raised in the United States without foreign support. He also believed the other four points presented as possible choices.

11. (A) The American people apparently supported Jackson's position on the bank since they overwhelmingly voted for him in 1832, and the bank was a major issue of the campaign.

12. (C) The Monroe Doctrine was presented in a State of the Union message by President Monroe, developing a concept suggested by the British government. President Monroe indicated that the United States would stay out of the affairs of Europe just as he expected the European nations to stay out of the affairs of the Americas. United States business interests developed in the Americas but it was not part of the design of the Monroe Doctrine.

13. (B) Region 4 was the pre-Mexican War independent Republic of Texas.

14. (A) An understanding of immigration from different sections of Europe is an important aspect of the analysis of immigration to America and of this question. The question requires an understanding of European geography as does any analysis of European immigration. If you do not have this information, you would have difficulty with this question. It is therefore important to study maps of Europe and other parts of the world as you study American history relating to those regions. Before the 1890s the majority of immigrants came from western and northern Europe, England, Ireland, Scandinavia, and Germany, as this table clearly shows. Therefore, A is incorrect. Poland is the only eastern European country listed, and the number of immigrants is insignificant.

15. (C) The chart reveals that in each year reported, the Irish were the largest single group of immigrants. Scandinavian and Polish immigration was less than that from the British Isles, which makes Choice A incorrect. Later in the century, immigration from eastern Europe did increase. Total immigration greatly increased. British immigration, except for one small drop reported in 1830, did also. Irish immigration remained large through these years. This is a good example of a stimulus question that requires good reading of charts.

16. (D) The Oregon Trail became important after the other events. Vancouver explored the Puget Sound area first. After Jefferson's purchase of the Louisiana Territory, he sent Lewis and Clark to explore it. Trails west were opened later. Independence, Missouri, was the starting point for the Oregon Trail and was settled before the Trail was used extensively.

Bibliography

Brooks, Van Wyck. *The Flowering of New England.* New York: E.P. Dutton, 1936.

Fish, C.E. *The Rise of the Common Man: 1830–1850.* Westport, CT: Greenwood, 1983.

Fogel, R.W. and Engerman, S.L. *Time on the Cross: The Economics of American Negro Slavery.* Lanham, MD: U Pr. of America, 1985.

Franklin, J.H. *From Slavery to Freedom.* New York: Alfred A. Knopf, Inc., 1987.

Gutman, Herbert G. *The Black Family in Slavery and Freedom, 1750–1925.* New York: Random House, 1977.

Hammond, Bray. *Banks and Politics in America, from Revolution to Civil War.* Princeton: Princeton University Press, 1991.

Merk, Frederick. *Manifest Destiny and Mission in American History.* New York: McGraw, 1966.

Remini, R.V. *The Revolutionary Age of Andrew Jackson.* New York: Harper and Row, 1976.

Stampp, K.M. *The Peculiar Institution.* New York: Random House, Inc., 1964.

Ward, J.W. *Andrew Jackson—Symbol for An Age.* New York: Oxford University Press, 1962.

PART THREE 5 The Coming of the Civil War, Civil War, and Reconstruction 1850-1877

Important Facets of This Period

The Civil War has often been considered the great transitional point in American history. In this view the pre-war period was one of territorial growth and the establishment of the framework of the nation. The Civil War intensified all the previous developments and precipitated rapid growth of the nation, which made it an industrial giant and a world power by 1900. Whether this view is valid is not certain, but it certainly is a thesis worth testing in your study of the history of this period. The thesis permits a focus on the Civil War era—the events leading to it, the war itself, and Reconstruction, periods from which factual information will certainly be needed on any American history exam.

As is the case with the era of the American Revolution, the years 1850-1877 logically fall into three time units. The first, 1850-1860, covers those years when the union appeared to be moving inexorably toward war. The second unit encompasses the war years 1860-1865, and the third unit includes the post-war or Reconstruction era, 1865-1877. Questions on these years may cover the entire time span, may require intensive knowledge of one period, or may ask for comparison among the three periods. In your study you may wish to break the time into the three units mentioned above, but be certain you understand the relationship between events in one period and the next.

Although historians place events in time units or periods as they attempt to make sense of the past, you must remember that the events occurred with no division between them. History occurs as a flowing stream. The image of pouring concrete to form a wall comes to my mind when I think of history. The historian sees the solid wall and draws lines on the wall to make the concrete wall appear to be a brick one. In history books we write as though the wall were made of separate bricks, but in reality the wall is one solid mass of material. The bricks help us to analyze, compartmentalize, and master details, but they are not the real history. If you keep this image in mind as you study the periods to which historians have assigned the events of history, you will never lose sight of the Western concept of the chronological interrelatedness of all historical developments.

Among the developments you will want to study in detail from the years 1850-1877 are the following:

1. Events leading to war 1850-1860—political, economic, social, intellectual
2. Secession and the outbreak of war
3. Military and naval war strategy
4. The strengths and weaknesses of the Confederacy and the Union
5. International relations in the war and post-Civil War period

6. Reconstruction plans and policies
7. The presidency of Ulysses S. Grant
8. The social and intellectual changes that took place in both the South and North during the war and Reconstruction
9. The growth and development of the West
10. The election and compromise of 1876

Sample Essay Question—The DBQ

The DBQ or document-based question became a regular and required part of the essay section of the Advanced Placement examination in 1973. The DBQ is a separate and very important part of the examination. In fact, the DBQ essay answer receives a weight of 1 in the 2:1:1 formula used in determining the Advanced Placement scores—the formula where the 2 represents your score on the multiple-choice questions, the first 1 your score on the DBQ, and the second 1 your score on the standard essay question.

The DBQ is also very important because it is a special type of essay question. In the essay-type questions we have discussed so far you must recall all the data or factual material to use in your answer. Until 1981, all the information needed to answer the DBQ was presented in the documents. Starting in 1982, only part of the information you need to answer the DBQ is presented in the documents. **For the DBQ in its present format, you are expected to analyze and interpret the documents and** *at the same time* **relate the documents and your analysis to the mainstream, that is, the main chronological development, of American history, introducing outside information from this chronology that is not found in the documents.** The question asked concerning these documents may be of any essay type. The fact that the form or wording of the DBQ question may be the same as any essay type illustrates how important and widely applicable are the methods of question analysis presented in previous chapters and in the next three chapters. In answering the DBQ, you must begin by analyzing the question, the familiar first step in essay writing. After that step, the second step becomes slightly different. You will still need to make an outline or brief notes, but for the DBQ these notes must be *both* on your reading and analysis of the documents *and* on your recall of information that is relevant to the documents presented and to the question asked.

The reading and understanding of documents lies at the heart of the DBQ, but the real test of the student's ability is in how well the student relates these documents to his or her understanding of the mainstream of American history. The DBQ was added to the Advanced Placement examination as a means of testing the student's training as a historian, to test the analytical and interpretive skills he or she has developed rather than merely to test his or her memory or recall skills. Many multiple-choice questions have been designed to test analytical skills, but they can test skills in a very limited way. The DBQ provides a much greater, in-depth test, since you are allowed fifteen minutes to read, analyze the documents, and make notes, and forty minutes in which to write your answer. For multiple-choice questions you have less than one minute to read, analyze, and decide on your answer. The DBQ may also use maps, graphs, cartoons, and the printed word from many sources, all in one question.

The election of Lincoln and its relation to the abolition of slavery is the topic of the following sample question. All courses in American history will include information on the abolitionist movement, the election of Abraham Lincoln, and the secession of the Confederate States and Lincoln's attitude toward slavery. This is mainstream information. The sample question requires that you have this information, but the documents also present other information that you might not have had at your command. This sample DBQ requires that you relate your factual knowledge of the period from 1837 to 1863 to the various documents presented. In this question there are ten documents. Under the present DBQ format the number of documents will vary as will the type of documents—maps, graphs, cartoons, photographs and written material—from the Articles of Confederation to declarations of war.

The goal of the DBQ is to present a question that will force every student to combine his or her historical research and analytical techniques with his or her recall of historical data in order to answer the question. There is no way a student can memorize or become familiar with all the documents that might appear on the DBQ. The only way to study for it is to practice being a historian as one studies, analyzing documents of all types, questioning statements made by the authors read, seeking cause-and-effect relationships to illustrate one's personal opinion on issues, and continually relating the documents read to the issues in American history. The student who approaches all of his or her material in the way described will do well on the DBQ.

In summary, the DBQ tests your ability to work with historical documents and your knowledge of the mainstream of American history. You are asked to do two related things in a unified essay: to formulate an answer derived from the evidence contained in the documents, as it relates to and bears on events in American history that you must recall from your study; and where relevant to your answer, to assess the value of the documents as historical sources. Reference to historical facts and developments not mentioned in the documents should be included in your answer and, where information is taken from the documents, reference to the documents should be made. It is better not to quote the documents verbatim but rather to paraphrase them or refer to information in them.

Below is a sample DBQ question that follows the style of presentation used on the AP examination. Read the directions, the question, and the documents carefully.

Document-Based Question

Section II
Part A
Suggested Writing

Time—40 minutes*

Directions: The following question requires you to construct a coherent essay that integrates your interpretation of documents A-J and your knowledge of the period referred to in the question. In your essay, you should strive to support your assertions both by citing key pieces of evidence from the documents and by drawing on your general knowledge of the period.

---

* In the general directions for Section II you will be given 15 minutes to read and analyze the documents and prepare your answer. Then you will have 40 minutes to write your DBQ answer.

1.   To what extent was the election of Abraham Lincoln a mandate for the abolition of slavery in the United States?

Document A

The following protest was presented to the House, which was read and ordered to be spread on the journals, to-wit:

"Resolutions upon the subject of domestic slavery having passed both branches of the General Assembly at its present session, the undersigned hereby protest against the passage of the same.

"They believe that the institution of slavery is founded on both injustice and bad policy; but that the promulgation of abolition doctrines tends rather to increase than abate its evils.

"They believe that the Congress of the United States has no power, under the Constitution, to interfere with the institution of slavery in the different States.

"They believe that the Congress of the United States has the power, under the Constitution, to abolish slavery in the District of Columbia; but that the power ought not to be exercised unless at the request of the people of said District.

"The difference between these opinions and those contained in the said resolutions, is their reasoning for entering this protest."

> Dan Stone and Abraham Lincoln
> Representatives from the county of
> Sangamon.
> Entry in the Journal of the House of Representatives of Illinois on March 3, 1837

Document B

My dear Sir, ... You are not a friend of slavery in the abstract. In that speech you spoke of "the peaceful extinction of slavery" and used other expressions indicating your belief that the thing was, at some time, to have an end. Since then we have had thirty-six years of experience; and this experience has demonstrated, I think, that there is no peaceful extinction of slavery in prospect for us. The signal failure of Henry Clay and other good and great men, in 1849, to effect anything in favour of gradual emancipation in Kentucky, together with a thousand other signs, extinguishes that hope utterly. On the question of liberty, as a principle, we are not what we have been. When we were the political slaves of King George, and wanted to be free, we called the maxim that "all men are created equal" a self-evident truth; but now when we have grown fat, and have lost all dread of being slaves ourselves, we have become so greedy to be *masters* that we call the same maxim "a self-evident lie." The Fourth of July has not quite dwindled away; it is still a great day for burning fire-crackers!!

Our political problem now is, "Can we as a nation continue together *permanently—forever*—half slave, and half free?" The problem is too mighty for me. May God in his mercy superintend the solution.

Your much obliged friend, and humble servant,

> Letter from Abraham Lincoln to George Robertson in Lexington, Kentucky—August 15, 1855

Document C

In relation to that, I have my mind very distinctly made up. I should be exceedingly glad to see Slavery abolished in the District of Columbia. I believe that Congress possesses the constitutional power to abolish it. Yet as a member of Congress, I should not, with my present views, be in favor of endeavoring to abolish Slavery in the District of Columbia, unless it would be upon these conditions: First that the abolition should be gradual; second, that it should be on a vote of the majority of qualified voters in the District; and third, that compensation should be made to unwilling owners. With these three conditions, I confess I would be exceedingly glad to see Congress abolish Slavery in the District of Columbia, and in the language of Henry Clay, "sweep from our Capitol that foul blot upon our 'nation.'"

> Abraham Lincoln in the Lincoln-Douglas Debate at Freeport, Illinois, September of 1858

Document D

According to Senator Douglas, the Territorial Legislatures, though prohibited by the Constitution from abolishing slavery within their respective jurisdictions, may lawfully abstain from enforcing the rights of slaveholders and so extinguish the institution by voluntary neglect ... In the name of common sense and common fairness, if slavery is to be prohibited or abolished in the Territories by any legislative tribunal, let it be done by one in which the whole nation is represented, and not by one composed of the representatives of the first stragglers from some over-burdened city or restless border State who happen to squat on the public domain. If slavery is to be prohibited in the Territories by legislation at all, let it be done by the people of the United States. If we must have sovereignty in the case, apart from the Constitution, give us the sovereignty of the American people, not squatter sovereignty. Senator Douglas, as we have seen, gives us the latter—Mr. Lincoln the former. Between the two, no intelligent, discerning patriot can hesitate a moment. Mr. Lincoln's position, aside from its virtually speculative cast, is infinitely less unfriendly to the constitutional rights and just interests of the South. When, furthermore, we reflect that the Supreme Court has pronounced this identical position unconstitutional, and would nullify any Congressional legislation in pursuance of it, the practical consequence of Mr. Lincoln's error vanishes into a political dream. But if it were as vital as it is lifeless, it would be immeasurably less pernicious than the reckless and shameless heresy of Douglas.

> Comments on the Lincoln-Douglas Freeport Debate from the *Louisville* [Kentucky] *Journal*, as quoted in the *Chicago Tribune*—September 4, 1858

Document E

THE QUESTION OF DISUNION

At the hour we write these lines, the American people, in all parts of the United States, are exercising their constitutional privilege of electing a president and vice-president of the United States for the next four years....

But, much as we may deplore the election of Lincoln, because of its calamitous consequences, we choose to put on record now, before the result of the election is declared, that under no circumstances, can disunion be the remedy or redress for the unfortunate choice. Mr. Lincoln may obtain a majority of the election college, and yet receive less than one-third of the popular vote, yet he will nevertheless be constitutionally elected.

... It has been proposed by those who seek a disruption of the Union, that in case Mr. Lincoln shall be elected president the southern states shall withdraw from the Union; ... We wish to place on record now, that ... such secession, being an act not within the constitutional power of any state, will become rebellion and treason on the part of every individual who by an overt act seeks to overthrow the constitutional authority of the federal government in any one of the states. ...

There is another class who propose to "submit" to the *election* of Lincoln, but who propose to secede when he shall attempt to do, or shall do, any unconstitutional act. We do not see that this proposed secession has any higher or more commendatory sanction in law or morals than that which is contingent upon Lincoln's election. ...

If Mr. Lincoln shall in any manner exceed his authority, or violate the constitution, that constitution itself provides the remedy for the wrong. In Article 2, Sec. 4, the constitution provides: "The president, vice-president, and all civil officers of the United States, shall be removed from office, on impeachment for, and conviction of treason, bribery, or other high crimes and misdemeanors". ... We believe that in a clear case of the unconstitutional exercise of power by the president, the Senate would, upon a constitutional form of trial convict Abraham Lincoln and dismiss him from office. ...

Should Mr. Lincoln be elected, great as the calamity will prove to be, still we think it is the duty of every democrat to give to his administration (not his party) every aid and support that the government can constitutionally demand of citizens.

Editorial from the Springfield, Illinois,
Register—November 7, 1860

Document F
ELECTION OF 1860

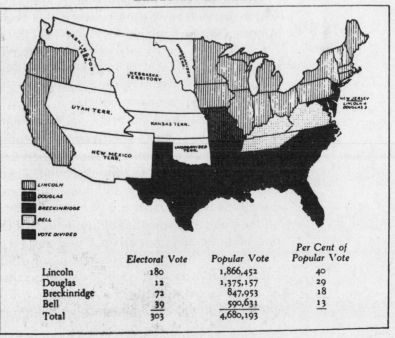

	Electoral Vote	Popular Vote	Per Cent of Popular Vote
Lincoln	180	1,866,452	40
Douglas	12	1,375,157	29
Breckinridge	72	847,953	18
Bell	39	590,631	13
Total	303	4,680,193	

Document G

"It is much to be regretted that in the present crisis of our national affairs, the disposition of events will be, to a great extent, in the hands of mere politicians; and that the sentiments of the masses will be scarcely known. The present unfortunate state of public feelings has, to a great extent, been created by ultra men on both sides, while we believe that the great body of the people, North and South, love the Union, and would deplore its dissolution as the greatest of earthly calamities, and a death blow to the cause of freedom throughout the world ... In so large a party as the Republican, it cannot but be supposed that a great variety of sentiment exists. There are, no doubt, many who voted for Lincoln, who are entirely indifferent to the subject of Slavery, who have never given it any consideration, and have no particular views in regard to it, while, on the other hand, many genuine abolitionists may have voted the ticket, though not the more rabid ones, for these refused to vote at all, and denounced Lincoln more bitterly than did any other of his opponents.

The great mass of the Republican party hold the conservative views so often expressed by Lincoln himself."

Editorial from the Reading, Pennsylvania, *Berks and Schuylkill Journal*—December 15, 1860

Document H

... A geographical line has been drawn across the Union, and all the States north of that line have united in the election of a man to the high office of President of the United States whose opinions and purposes are hostile to Slavery. He is to be intrusted with the administration of the common Government, because he has declared that "Government cannot endure permanently half slave, half free," and that the public mind must rest in the belief that Slavery is in the course of ultimate extinction.

We, therefore, the people of South Carolina ... have solemnly declared that the Union heretofore existing between this State and the other States of North America is dissolved. ...

South Carolina Declaration of Causes of Secession—December 24, 1860

Document I

Apprehension seems to exist among the people of the Southern States that by the accession of a Republican administration their property and their peace and personal security are to be endangered. There has never been any reasonable cause for such apprehension. Indeed, the most ample evidence to the contrary has all the while existed and been open to their inspection. It is found in nearly all the published speeches of him who now addresses you. I do but quote from one of those speeches when I declare that "I have no purpose, directly or indirectly, to interfere with the institution of slavery in the States where it exists. I believe I have no lawful right to do so, and I have no inclination to do so." Those who nominated and elected me did so with full knowledge that I had made this and many similar declarations, and had never recanted them. And, more than this, they placed in the [party] platform [adopted at Chicago] for my acceptance, and as a law to themselves and to me, the clear and emphatic resolution which I now read:

> *Resolved*, That the maintenance inviolate of the rights of the States, and especially the right of each State to order and control its own domestic institutions according to its own judgment exclusively, is essential to that balance of power on which the perfection and endurance of our political fabric depend, and we denounce the lawless invasion by armed force of the soil of any State or Territory, no matter under what pretext, as among the gravest of crimes.

I now reiterate these sentiments; and, in doing so, I only press upon the public attention the most conclusive evidence of which the case is susceptible, that the property, peace, and security of no section are to be in any wise endangered by the now incoming administration. ...

Abraham Lincoln's First Inaugural Address—
March 4, 1861

Document J

1. *Be it Resolved by the Senate and General Assembly of the State of New Jersey*, That this State, in promptly answering the calls made by the President of the United States, at and since the inauguration of the war, for troops and means to assist in maintaining the power and dignity of the Federal Government, believed and confided in the professions and declarations of the President of the United States, in his inaugural address. ...
...(now we) make unto the Federal Government this our solemn

PROTEST

Against the power assumed in the proclamation (Emancipation Proclamation) of the President made January first, 1863, by which all the slaves in certain States and part of States are for ever set free; and against the expenditures of the public moneys for the emancipation of slaves or their support at any time, under any pretence whatever; ...

New Jersey Peace Resolutions — March 18, 1863

Comments on the DBQ

This DBQ divides into three parts. First are the general directions, second is the question itself, and third are the 10 documents, including a map that you are to use analytically in answering the question. Let us consider each of these in turn.

First, the directions specify the time allotted, which is 40 minutes for writing. The directions on the examination will indicate that you are to take 15 minutes to read the documents and to make notes. At the examination you will not be allowed to start writing your answer during these 15 minutes. The examination papers you will be given include space for you to take notes, another indication of the fact that the Advanced Placement examination writers strongly support Step Two in Essay Writing. Incidentally, the directions also tell you where you are to write your answer—keep alert to such details in the directions for any exam. **Read all directions carefully; do not rush over them to get to the question.** This is a fundamental rule of all test taking. After taking notes and organizing your information, you have 40 minutes in which to write the answer.

The directions also briefly indicate the purpose of the DBQ—to test your ability to work with historical documents—and then amplify this to indicate the two things (note how this sentence is structured to clarify that there are two things you must do) expected in the unified essay—(1) "evidence contained in the documents, as it relates to and bears on events in the mainstream of American history" and (2) "to assess the documents as historical sources." As has been stated, it is most important to introduce information from sources outside the documents in your DBQ answer. Clearly, the intention of the DBQ is to test your ability to analyze the documents presented, to relate the material to American history, and to write a unified essay expressing your personal opinion on the question raised.

The DBQ does *not* ask you to simply describe what each document includes; it requires a *unified* essay. In Part Two we presented ideas on writing the unified essay, and you have been practicing with questions from the different chapters, so writing the essay should present no difficulty once you have analyzed the question and the documents.

The second part of the DBQ as presented is the question itself. The question is a *To what extent*...type and, as indicated in Chapter 4, the key word here is *extent*. You are to determine, on the basis of the evidence presented and of your recall of American history, whether Lincoln's election as President of the United States was a mandate for the abolition of slavery in the United States. The word *mandate* may provide some difficulty for you. A mandate is an order. It may not be voiced directly, but rather it is implied by the circumstances. With this interpretation of the word, you can see that the question is asking you to determine if the people of the United States were ordering the abolition of slavery when they voted for Abraham Lincoln. As you will recall from your study and as the documents imply, there were many different views as to what Lincoln stood for and what the election of 1860 meant. You must determine what your opinion is, and from this decide on a thesis for the essay. You will have the limited evidence from the documents and the information you can recall to help you to determine your thesis. As you read the documents and take notes on them, *i.e.*, Steps One and Two in Essay Writing, a thesis should emerge that will determine your approach to the question.

The third part of the DBQ is the documents. As you look at them, remember that you are to write a unified essay and not a mere summary of what is in each document. What are some of the ways you might analyze the documents? What would you look for in making your brief notes? Following are comments on some of the documents. What else would you add?

The first document is an entry dated March 3, 1837 in the Journal of the Illinois House of Representatives in which Lincoln and his fellow representative from his home county protest the legislature's support for the idea of the U.S. government abolishing slavery. Lincoln clearly states that he believes the federal government has no power to abolish slavery in the nation. Is this view a surprise to you? Did Lincoln believe this in 1860? How does this affect your response to the question?

Document B (you may identify documents this way in your answer, but a better way is to identify documents by the author or source) gives a view on slavery expressed privately by Abraham Lincoln in a personal letter. It clearly indicates that he is torn by the question and yet is not prepared to come up with a clear solution. This document is dated 1855. The quotation (Document C) from

Lincoln's address at Freeport, Illinois, in 1858 as part of the Lincoln-Douglas Debate in their race for the U.S. Senate gives another view from Lincoln. Has he changed his mind since 1837? How do you think he will act as president? These are the type of questions you should address as you read the documents and relate them to the question and the mainstream of American history.

The comments (Document D) from a southern newspaper on the Lincoln-Douglas Debate were quoted in a northern newspaper, the *Chicago Tribune* from Chicago, Illinois, and this suggests that both the North and the South might be in agreement on this particular interpretation of the famous Freeport Debate. You will probably have studied the Freeport Debate, one of the Lincoln-Douglas Debates, in your history class. This editorial comment should spark your recall of this major event in the 1850s. It is believed that Lincoln's position lost him the Senate race but endeared him to the Republicans and thus won for him the presidential nomination.

The editorial presented in Document E is from another Illinois newspaper—one that opposed the election of Lincoln. This editorial clearly supports the Constitution and opposes secession as a way to deal with Lincoln's election. Does this support or reject the idea of Lincoln's election as a mandate for the abolition of slavery? This editorial can be a most important document in developing your case.

The map (Document F) can easily be understood. You may have this information in your head, but if not, this could be of benefit to you in developing your argument. Often on DBQs a document other than written words will be included to test your ability to read charts, cartoons, and/or photographs.

The editorial (Document G) suggests that there was not unified support for Abraham Lincoln even in the Republican Party and that view is not supported by the abolitionists.

Part of the actual secession document from South Carolina is presented in Document H. It is a document that you may never have read before, but the issue presented should be familiar to you. How does the document suggest the people of South Carolina viewed the election of Lincoln?

In his first Inaugural Address in 1861 (Document I), Lincoln revealed how he viewed his election. Included in the document is an important quote from the Republican party platform. Does it suggest that Lincoln or the Republicans viewed the election as a mandate for the abolition of slavery? This is the issue that you must resolve in your reading and analysis of the documents.

The final document (Document J), from a series of resolutions passed by the legislature of New Jersey long after the war had begun, clearly suggests New Jersey was not in full support of the war effort. How does this document fit into the overall question? The date is important. As you should know from your study of American history, the Emancipation Proclamation that is alluded to in the Peace Resolutions of New Jersey went into effect on January 1, 1863. Was New Jersey in favor of the abolition of slavery?

These brief comments on the documents may raise many issues. What are your answers to the questions suggested? What other questions do these documents raise in your mind? During the 15 minutes allotted for reading and analyzing the documents and taking notes, you will want to go over documents in this manner. From your notes you should then develop your thesis. You should not feel the need to refer to all the documents in your answer. You should pick *only* those that help you to present your case and to provide your thesis. However, if you have time, you may wish to refute a document that does not support your thesis. If you can do this with evidence from outside sources, it would be to your credit. Unfortunately, in answering the DBQ some students write only a bit telling what each document says, as shown here. You can clearly see this does not answer the question and is an ineffective answer.

At this time you should write your own answer for this DBQ. Use the documents by grouping common ideas found in them. Do not quote what is said verbatim. Do identify the source of the document in the manner used in the brief descriptions previously shown. After writing your own answer read the sample introductions provided here and make your judgment of them. Recall what was said about a good introduction in Part II above. If you have forgotten, go back and read that section again. A good introduction is crucial for a good essay.

Sample Introduction A

Lincoln's election as President of the United States was a mandate to abolish slavery in the United States. It took Lincoln a long time to get around to this act, but in the Emancipation Proclamation, he finally freed the slaves. Although the New Jersey Peace Proposals were opposed to this move, they were certainly not in agreement with the majority of the American people.

Sample Introduction B

Abraham Lincoln was known as the Great Emancipator, and he deserves the title since he freed the slaves.

Sample Introduction C

The political process in America is a very subtle and often confusing one. In every election there are many issues, and to determine clearly what the results of an election mean is a difficult task for any scholar or political historian. Although slavery appears to be the major issue in the election of Abraham Lincoln, there were other factors involved, including the economic balance of the nation, transportation to the West, and the tariff issue. Considering these factors and Lincoln's personal comments on the issue of slavery, it is clear that the election of Lincoln was not a mandate for the abolition of slavery in the United States.

Sample Introduction D

Slavery was a divisive issue at the Constitutional Convention and had been throughout the years of our history to 1860. Compromise after compromise was tried, but as Lincoln asked, "Can a nation continue together permanently— forever—half slave and half free?" The answer was certainly no, and the election of Lincoln in 1860 was a mandate for the abolition of slavery in the United States.

Sample Introduction E

These documents have a lot of conflicting viewpoints. It is very hard to see that anybody agreed on anything. Although Lincoln was consistently opposed to slavery in the District of Columbia, he was not prepared to abolish it. The election in 1860 was viewed in different ways by South Carolina and by the Reading, Pennsylvania, newspaper. Since Lincoln had said that the nation could not be half slave and half free, he must have thought he should abolish slavery. When he did this in the Emancipation Proclamation, which was in agreement with what he had said at Freeport, the country could truly say it was free and all men were created equal.

Teacher Comments on Sample Introductions

As should be very clear, the writers have interpreted the question in a variety of ways. Each position could be defended based on the evidence of the documents and outside information.

Sample B   Considering the literary merits of these five introductions, Sample B is the poorest. The writer fails to set a broad context and fails to introduce the question. This viewpoint on Lincoln does not really relate to the question except indirectly. Sample B confirms the point that a one-sentence introduction is usually not sufficient to set the broad context of the question and your thesis.

Sample E   Sample E is also poorly written. The author has included a good deal of information, much of it from the documents, but there is no clear organization. Instead, a shotgun-spatter-approach has been used, and the topic of the question is not included. A thesis is implied in the fifth sentence, but it is not clearly stated, nor is it related to the election of 1860.

Sample A   In Sample A a thesis is clearly stated in the first sentence, and the question is introduced. Unfortunately, since there is no broad context set, the reader is somewhat taken aback by the opening. The author then elaborates on the thesis in the second sentence. Unfortunately, the last sentence introduces information that somewhat contradicts the thesis—information that could be better used in the body of the paper. It almost appears as if the author of Sample A, just like the author of Sample E, did not take time to organize the material before starting to write. In Sample A one can understand the way the writer's thoughts are moving, but the three sentences do not make as effective an introduction as we find in Samples C and D.

Samples C and D   These two introductions are both good. Each begins with a broad topic related to the question, moves from this topic to the specific topic of the question (Lincoln, his election, slavery), and ends with a clearly stated thesis. The two writers disagree completely as to their interpretation of the meaning of the election of Lincoln. It would be interesting to read their essays and to trace their arguments, as either thesis could be defended. Both Samples C and D conform most closely to what has been set in this book as the pattern for good introductory paragraphs.

Do you agree with the above analysis? Do you see why Samples C and D are considered the best of the five? Do you now have this pattern of an introductory paragraph established in your mind?

Sample Introduction and Conclusion

Introduction

Slavery was an issue in American history starting in 1619. The leaders of the country in the first half of the 19th century shared many different opinions on the topic. Beginning in the 1830s, the abolitionist sentiment was fanned by many events. These events culminated in the election of Abraham Lincoln. Let us consider these events and see to what extent his election mandated the abolition of slavery.

Conclusion

Slavery was abolished as a result of the Civil War. The election of Lincoln determined that this would be so, since it was understood by the Republican party and its leader, Abraham Lincoln, that slavery must not spread to the territories and that ultimately it should be abolished. The election of 1860 ended years of attempted compromise and eliminated slavery as an issue for the American nation.

Were you able to write comparable paragraphs? You see how well they relate together. The introduction sets a broad issue (*i.e.,* slavery) and presents the question (*i.e.,* to what extent was the election of Lincoln a mandate for the abolition of slavery?). The conclusion returns to the question and presents the writer's thesis in the second sentence. It then goes on to bring the question back to the broad issue of slavery as an issue in American history and thereby neatly frames the entire essay. You may wish to experiment with this technique of presenting your thesis in the conclusion, but remember, if your thesis is not presented in the introduction, the reader will have to decide, based on the evidence you include, what your thesis is. What the reader decides may not be what you present as your thesis at the end of the essay. When this happens, you, the writer, are in trouble. Presenting your thesis in the conclusion can be an effective style, but it requires more work than the technique we have presented so far. You may wish to experiment with this new technique, but don't forget that it is more difficult.

Summary of How to Write a DBQ Answer

Several general points were made above about the answer to the DBQ that are worth repeating. They should serve as guides to the writing of the body of the DBQ essay. First, remember that you are writing a unified essay answer involving the documents *and* events in the mainstream of American history. Second, some documents will be more valuable or reliable than others—say so and dismiss the less valuable. Third, identify the documents by author or letter. Fourth, summarize the key idea(s) found in the document, but **do not quote the full document.** Fifth, pick and choose the documents you use and rearrange the order. Be imaginative! Sixth, refer to other events of the age, and clearly indicate how these documents relate to these events and help you gain a better understanding of events in the mainstream of American history. If you keep these six points in mind and remember the Seven Steps in Essay Writing, you should have little difficulty in writing a good answer for any DBQ.

Practice Essay Questions

1. Describe two problems that were important causes of the Civil War and explain how the Civil War and Reconstruction provided solutions to the problems.

2. To what extent do you agree or disagree with the idea that the North had won the Civil War before it began?

3. How do you account for the fact that South Carolina was the leader in the nullification movement over the Tariff of 1828 and in the secessionist movement of 1860?

4. In what ways are the issues that led to the Civil War similar to those that led to the American War for Independence?

5. "The black American in the South during the Reconstruction period was treated better socially and politically than at any other time until the civil rights legislation of the 1960s." Assess the validity of this generalization.

Comments on Question 1

Question 1 is a typical *Describe ... explain* essay question. There should be no difficulty in analyzing what the question requires after your practice in Chapter 2. Whether you have the factual information to deal with this question is another matter, since it is rare that the period 1850-1876 is studied in terms of how the Reconstruction era solved the problems that caused the war. If you are able to organize information in this way, you could write an exciting essay. Among the usual causes of the war cited are slavery and economic differences between the North and the South. How were these affected by Reconstruction and the war? Can you think of other ways of stating these causes or of other causes that were "solved" during the war and Reconstruction? The fact that Congress passed the first railroad construction bill for a transcontinental railroad after the South seceded is one example of economic action impossible before secession. It and other similar examples could be used to illustrate many problems that could not be resolved as long as the union remained united. The question is easy in format, could be easy to organize, but might prove difficult factually.

Comments on Question 2

The second question illustrates the *To what extent ...* type of question used in the DBQ example in this chapter. It adds those familiar words *agree or disagree*, which invite a strong statement of personal opinion. The idea presented is an intriguing one—the idea that the South had lost the war before it began. Considering the length of the war and the difficulty Lincoln had in finding a general to win the war, you might wonder how this could be true, but some historians have suggested that the railroad network of the North plus its industry made it undefeatable. What do you think? This question requires good factual knowledge and good insights into how facts from different sources can be put together to defend a position. The question is completely open as to organizational format and the organization would depend entirely on what you put down in your brief notes. This question illustrates the importance of organizing your essay from the brief notes you make.

Comments on Question 3

Question 3 is a *How?* question and a variation that asks for an explanation or cause-and-effect approach. It needs a personal opinion or thesis that bridges a long time span in which many changes in attitudes, people, and problems occurred, yet during which the position of South Carolina did not change. It is an example of a long-term problem—one that covers a number of years or periods of history—that might occur as one of the five questions on the Advanced

Placement examination. The question requires that you have a general knowledge of southern history from the 1820s to the 1860s and of South Carolina in particular. This general history would be found in any text, but the details of South Carolina's history are something you may have to learn on your own. The question may thus be one some students could not answer and illustrates how many different approaches can be taken to American history. However, if you have the information, a variety of interesting theses and organizational formats could be developed.

Comments on Question 4

The fourth question is a very broad question directly in the mainstream of American history. You are asked to relate two of the most important periods of American history. The question asks you to find the similarities, but, of course, you could disagree with the premise of the question and state that there is no similarity. You will no doubt describe economic issues, majority-minority political issues, and social issues involving differences in life-styles. These three suggestions of issues should be enough to give you some ideas of how these two periods could be compared in terms of similarities. The essay might be best organized around similarities—relating first the Revolutionary War situation and then the Civil War situation before moving on to the next similarity to be treated.

Comments on Question 5

The last question is the broadest question we have had so far in the book. It takes one situation—the treatment of the black American—and places it in the context of *all* American history. Did you notice that the question was not worded to include only the Reconstruction and post-Reconstruction period? You must know something about the way the black person was treated in the South socially and politically during Reconstruction *and* during all the rest of our history. You also must know some of the details of the civil rights legislation of the 1960s. This is asking a great deal. How will you ever organize all this in fifty minutes? Obviously, the question requires you to pick and choose areas to focus on with some detail while quickly passing over others. For instance, you might discuss the entire pre-Revolutionary period, discuss in some detail the disparity among the Declaration of Independence, the Constitution, and slavery, move on to the 1830s and abolitionism, then concentrate on Reconstruction, the growth of Jim Crow, and its culmination in the *Plessy v. Ferguson* case, touch briefly on governmental actions in World Wars I and II and end with the 1960s. This approach or one similar to it in which a few periods are concentrated upon would illustrate your awareness of the total history of the black in America, and that is really what this *Assess the validity* type essay is requesting that you do. Your opinion needs to be clearly stated and the above comments suggest that a chronological organization would be effective. You might decide, however, that an organization focusing on the best and worst treatment of the blacks would be more effective than a chronological approach. Such an approach might permit you to use fewer periods of history to prove your thesis, thus allowing for more detail in the periods you discuss.

Multiple-Choice Questions— Charts and Graphs

A popular type of multiple-choice question used to test analytical skills is one based on charts and graphs. It is an excellent type of stimulus question. Many textbooks today present large amounts of information in this manner. Summaries of election results, votes on various issues in Congress, the pattern of immigration, manufacturing growth or other economic data, even the numbers of enlistees compared to draftees in World War I can be presented in this way. There are a variety of types of charts and graphs—ranging from simple statistical tables presenting raw numbers to complex bar and line graphs where several items are presented for comparison. Today in texts, as well as in magazines and newspapers, we are presented with a great variety of statistical data that we need to understand. As you study, be certain you look at the charts and graphs in your books and learn how to interpret them and get information from them. Do not skip over such items because they form an important method of presenting historic information, and your ability to understand and interpret information in this way will be tested on the Advanced Placement exam. Also, learning to read and interpret charts and graphs and applying this information to the mainstream history you are studying will help you prepare for analyzing documents presented on the DBQ.

Study the following examples of multiple-choice questions based on charts and graphs. There will be other examples in the sample multiple-choice questions at the end of succeeding chapters. The charts and graphs present information from later than 1870 but you should be able to understand the context even if you have not yet studied the time period.

Sample Questions 1-3

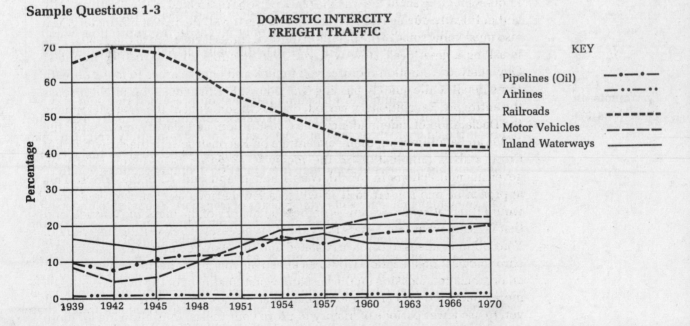

SOURCE: U.S. Bureau of the Census, *Historical Statistics of the U. S., Colonial Times to 1970*

1. According to the graph, which one of the following statements is NOT correct?
    (A) Airline freight traffic is an insignificant part of the total traffic.
    (B) In 1966 inland waterways carried the second smallest amount of domestic freight.
    (C) The percentage of freight carried by the railroads has continually declined.
    (D) Oil pipelines carried more freight than motor vehicles until after 1948.
    (E) Until 1951 motor vehicles carried less freight than did inland waterways.

2. The increase in the percentage of freight carried by railroads in 1942 was most likely a result of
    (A) activities connected with World War II
    (B) the building of new railroads
    (C) a failure to manufacture trucks
    (D) airline crashes
    (E) the discovery of oil in Alaska

3. According to the graph, if you eliminate the airlines from consideration, then
    (A) inland waterways have continually been the second most important domestic freight carrier
    (B) pipelines have always been more important than motor vehicles
    (C) railroads have always carried more than 50 percent of the domestic freight
    (D) inland waterways and pipelines each carried between 15 and 18 percent of domestic freight from 1954 to 1963
    (E) motor vehicles are the only means of transportation which increased its percentage of freight carried between 1948 and 1963

Comments on Questions 1-3

Questions 1, 2, and 3 are based on information presented in a line graph—one of the most common graphs used to present information visually. The graph presents data concerning the transportation of domestic intercity freight, a topic that may not be included in textbooks but is a subject that gives insights into the changing patterns of American life. Question 1 simply requires you to read the graph to get your information. You need to know how to read the key, which tells you which line represents which means of transport. You need to understand that the percentage is presented on the horizontal lines and the years on the vertical lines. Now looking at the graph and locating the symbol for the airlines, you see it hardly appears on the graph, being well below the 1 percent mark. Locating the inland waterway symbol and the 1966 column, you'll see that next to the airlines they carried the smallest percentage of freight. Again looking at the inland waterways line you'll see that motor vehicles carried less freight than did inland waterways, which might surprise you, but is true according to the graph. This is the type of information you can learn from graphs and then apply to mainstream history. It is what you need to look for when reading charts and graphs and the DBQ documents. It may also surprise you that pipelines carried more freight until 1948 than did motor vehicles. Finally, looking at the railroad symbol you'll see that the railroads increased the percentage of freight they carried between 1939 and 1942 and, therefore, C is false. This question requires simple graph reading skills—skills you can practice as you study the graphs found in most textbooks; but, in case your text does not have graphs, you can find graphs in newspapers and news magazines. Graph reading is a simple skill yet an important one.

Comments on Question 2

Most questions based on charts and graphs are testing skills similar to those tested in the DBQ—skills of analysis and interpretation—and most of them are *not* testing recall, although you may need to know the mainstream conditions surrounding the question. For example, in Question 2, Choice A, you need to know the dates of World War II in order to analyze the answer. The question assumes you can read the graph and can identify the increase in freight carried by railroads. It then requires you to think of reasons for this increase, and five possible reasons are suggested. The choices are not very profound, and you could probably eliminate four of them easily, but if you know that we were fighting World War II in 1942 and you realize how disruptive war is for society and how many changes take place then, you would decide on Choice A from a positive approach. Question 2 illustrates how a multiple-choice question based on a graph can test not only a skill but also factual knowledge.

Comments on Question 3

Question 3 simply requires that you read the line graph. This time only one statement is correct and it is D—"inland waterways and pipelines carried between 15 and 18 percent of domestic freight from 1954 to 1963." The other statements are false. For instance, railroads dropped below the 50 percent level after 1954. If you have trouble seeing that, use the edge of a piece of paper placed parallel to the horizontal or bottom line to help you read across on the percentages.

Sample Questions 4-6

LIFE EXPECTANCY AT BIRTH

Year	Total			White			Non-white		
	Both Sexes	Male	Female	Both Sexes	Male	Female	Both Sexes	Male	Female
1976	72.9	69.1	76.8	73.6	69.9	77.5	68.4	63.7	72.4
1966	70.1	66.7	73.8	71.0	67.6	74.7	64.0	60.7	67.4
1956	69.6	66.7	73.0	70.2	67.3	73.7	63.2	61.1	65.9
1946	66.7	64.6	69.4	67.5	65.1	70.3	59.1	57.5	61.0
1936	58.5	56.6	60.6	59.8	58.0	61.9	49.0	47.0	51.4
1926	56.7	55.5	58.0	58.2	57.0	59.6	44.6	43.7	45.6
1916	51.7	49.6	54.3	52.5	50.2	55.2	41.3	39.6	43.1
1906	48.7	46.9	50.8	49.3	47.3	51.4	32.9	31.8	33.9

SOURCE: U.S. Bureau of the Census, *Historical Statistics of the U.S., Colonial Times to 1970*
U.S. Bureau of the Census, *Statistical Abstract of the United States 1981*

4. According to the statistics presented in the table, the individual with the shortest life expectancy at birth was a
    (A)   white male in 1966
    (B)   non-white female in 1936
    (C)   white female in 1926
    (D)   non-white male in 1906
    (E)   white male in 1906

5. The statistics indicate all of the following to be true EXCEPT:
    (A)   The greatest increase in life expectancy for all people occurred between 1936 and 1946.
    (B)   Male life expectancy for white and non-white males has always been shorter than for females in the same year.
    (C)   The white population has always had a longer life expectancy than non-white in the same year.
    (D)   White female life expectancy in 1976 was over twice that of non-white females in 1906.
    (E)   For all whites the smallest increase in life expectancy occurred between 1966 and 1976.

6. The statistics in the chart could most effectively be used to support the idea that
    (A)   more females are born than males
    (B)   life is harder for males
    (C)   it is better to be born non-white than white
    (D)   life expectancy reflects the social and economic condition of non-whites as compared to whites
    (E)   whites are always older than non-whites

Comments on Questions 4-6

Questions 4, 5, and 6 are based on a statistical table, another very common method of presenting a large amount of information. The table deals with life expectancy at birth for the total population, the white population, and the non-white population. These three divisions or headings appear at the top of the table identifying three wide columns, each of which in turn is divided into three parts representing life expectancy for both sexes, for males and females. The careful reading of column headings will save you from many silly errors. The years to be compared are presented in the left-hand column. This is a rather simple lineal table. There is no accumulative data to be presented in peripheral boxes as you sometimes find in statistical tables.

Comments on Question 4

Question 4 offers five choices for the individual with the shortest life expectancy at birth. Looking at the appropriate column for each choice, you see that the life expectancy of a white male in 1966 was 67.6 years, of a non-white female in 1936 was 51.4 years, of a white female in 1926 was 59.6 years, of a non-white male in 1906 was 31.8 years, and of a white male in 1906 was 47.3 years. If you have located these same numbers, then you can read the table. The answer is clearly the non-white male in 1906.

**Comments on
Question 5**

Question 5 involves a comparison of data in the table and you are asked to locate the one untrue statement. It is that for non-whites, the greatest increase in life expectancy occurred between 1906 and 1916, which is choice E. While the increase between 1966 and 1976 for all whites (use column for both sexes) was small—2.6 years—the increase between 1956 and 1966 was smaller—.8 years. In analyzing the question you must read the suggested answers, look up that information in the table, and determine its truth. Look at the total column for both sexes and you will see that life expectancy increased 8.2 years for all people between 1936 and 1946. Comparing all the male statistics with female statistics will show that male life expectancy has always been shorter than female. Again comparing white and non-white statistics, you will find choice C is true. If you look in the box for non-white females in 1906 you will see their life expectancy was 33.9 years; for white females in 1976 it was 77.5 years—well over twice 33.9 years. Thus you see that choices A through D are all true. Another type of question based on these statistics might ask you to explain or account for the timing of this large jump.

**Comments on
Question 6**

Question 6 moves beyond the statistics in the table and asks you to figure out how they might be used. Five possible theses or ideas are presented, and you are asked to decide which would be most effectively supported by these statistics. The best choice would appear to be D—life expectancy reflects the social and economic condition of non-whites as compared to whites. The statistics do not prove more females are born—only that they live longer. In fact, more males are born. Life may be harder for males, but the statistics do not prove it. Unless you find life unattractive and wish to die young, it is certainly not better to be born non-white and, of course, whites are not always older than non-whites—what a ridiculous statement, but one you might accept if you read too quickly! You should know from your study of the mainstream of American history that the living conditions, socially and economically, of non-whites have always been below that of whites in our nation and that living conditions affect life expectancy. The two ideas—living conditions and life expectancy—are related, and these statistics could be used effectively to support this idea. This question thus tests your ability to understand the statistics, to apply them to historic situations, and to make judgments as to the best use of given data. It is a good type of multiple-choice question.

Sample Questions 7-8

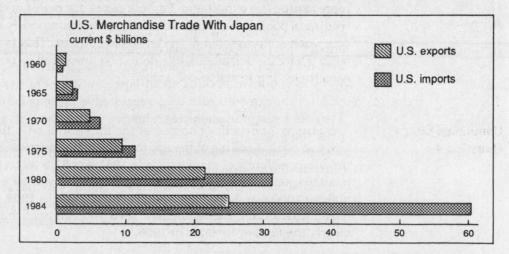

U.S. Merchandise Trade With Japan
current $ billions

U.S. exports
U.S. imports

1960
1965
1970
1975
1980
1984

0   10   20   30   40   50   60

7. In reading the bar graph all of the following are accurate statements EXCEPT:
   (A)   The numbers on the horizontal line at the bottom represents billions of dollars.
   (B)   The graph presents information on U.S.-Japan trade relations.
   (C)   At no time have U.S. exports to Japan exceeded U.S. imports from Japan.
   (D)   The number of years between bars are not always the same.
   (E)   The greatest increase in U.S. imports came between 1980 and 1984.

8. According to information presented in the graph you can conclude that
   (A)   the U.S. trade deficit was a problem from 1960-1984
   (B)   the Vietnam War forced the U.S. to buy from Japan
   (C)   the wages paid to Japanese workers are lower than those paid to Americans
   (D)   the Reagan tax cut program hurt our trade balance with Japan
   (E)   the exports of the U.S. grew more rapidly from 1975 to 1980 than in any other period

Comments on Question 7

Question 7 simply asks you to read the graph. It is a test of your ability to read and understand the information in the key. The numbers at the bottom represent billions of dollars, as it says under the title "current $ billion," and the title tells you that the graph is about *U.S. Merchandise Trade with Japan*. The number of years between bars are five except at the bottom, where only four years are passed; it should be clear that the greatest increase in U.S exports, represented by the hatch marks, came in those years. This leaves choice (C) as the wrong statement—U.S. exports to Japan exceeded imports in 1960. This is a good test of your ability to read all parts of a graph.

Comments on Question 8

Question 8 asks you to interpret the graph and relate information in it to some ideas found in recent mainstream history. The only point you can clearly conclude from the graph and not from outside sources is Choice (E), "the exports of the U.S. grew more rapidly from 1975 to 1984 than in any other period." The U.S. trade deficit was not a problem in 1960, as we exported more than we imported, so Choice (A) is inaccurate. Choices (B), (C), and (D) cannot be proven from the graph. We did not have to buy from Japan as a result of the Vietnam War and you can learn nothing about Japanese wages or Reagan's tax cut from the graph, although both have been suggested as reasons for the imbalance of trade. They are ideas from mainstream history that are important but cannot be proven from the graph.

These sample multiple-choice questions based on charts and graphs should illustrate the range of questions that might be asked. The analysis should provide you assistance in reading the charts and graphs you find as you study. Do not skip over such information, but look at it with care to gain more about the factual content of American history and to gain an understanding of how to read and use charts and graphs.

Practice Multiple-Choice Questions

1. Which is the correct chronological order to illustrate a cause-and-effect relationship among the following events leading to the Civil War?
    (A)   South Carolina secedes, Election of Lincoln, Lincoln-Douglas Debates, Dred Scott Decision, Kansas-Nebraska Act
    (B)   Kansas-Nebraska Act, Dred Scott Decision, South Carolina secedes, Lincoln-Douglas Debates, Election of Lincoln
    (C)   Dred Scott Decision, Kansas-Nebraska Act, Lincoln-Douglas Debates, Election of Lincoln, South Carolina secedes
    (D)   Kansas-Nebraska Act, Dred Scott Decision, Lincoln-Douglas Debates, Election of Lincoln, South Carolina secedes
    (E)   Dred Scott Decision, Lincoln-Douglas Debates, Election of Lincoln, South Carolina secedes, Kansas-Nebraska Act

2. After the South seceded, the Congress was able to pass special legislation to benefit the North and the West, such as the
    (A)   Kansas-Nebraska Act   (D)   Sherman Anti-Trust Act
    (B)   Pacific Railroad Bill   (E)   Chinese Exclusion Act
    (C)   Underwood Tariff

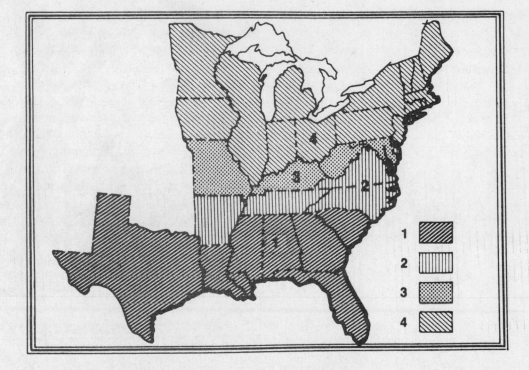

3. On the map, the Confederate States of America are those included in the area numbered
    (A)   1 and 4
    (B)   1 and 3
    (C)   1, 2, 3
    (D)   2 and 3
    (E)   None of the above

4. The so-called border states at the time of the outbreak of the Civil War were those states
   (A) bordering the Atlantic
   (B) which might but did not join the Confederacy
   (C) bordering the Mississippi River south of Missouri
   (D) bordering Canada that Confederate sympathizers could raid from Canada
   (E) which bordered Mexico

5. The following were important Civil War battles
   I. Saratoga
   II. Gettysburg
   III. Bull Run
   IV. Atlanta

   (A) I and II
   (B) I, II, and III
   (C) I, II, and IV
   (D) I, III, and IV
   (E) II, III, and IV

JOHN BULL.

JOHN. "All right, MR. CONFEDERATE—the Money's all right. Call at our Little Shop again, Sir. Fit you out a *Pirate*, or make you *Manacles for Slaves* at shortest notice."

SOURCE: *Harper's Weekly*, December 13, 1862

6. The point the cartoon from *Harper's Weekly* is making centers on the
   (A) way the British industrialists supplied arms and ships for the Confederacy
   (B) way the Confederates could not make manacles for slaves and guns at the same time
   (C) first time the Confederacy was personified in a cartoon as a man
   (D) view of the Union concerning overfed British people
   (E) great wealth and manufacturing skill of the British

7. The leader of the Radical Reconstructionists of the U.S. House of Representatives was

   (A) Andrew Johnson
   (B) Charles Sumner
   (C) Thaddeus Stevens
   (D) Edwin M. Stanton
   (E) Ulysses S. Grant

8. Among the scandals connected with the Grant administration are

   (A) Credit Mobilier and Watergate
   (B) Teapot Dome and the Whiskey Ring
   (C) the Whiskey Ring and Credit Mobilier
   (D) Watergate and Teapot Dome
   (E) Whiskey Ring and Watergate

9. Cattle raising in the semi-arid lands of the West greatly increased as a result of the

   (A) Homestead Act
   (B) invention of barbed wire
   (C) building of the Transcontinental railroad
   (D) cattle drives
   (E) invention of the reaper

10. The National Labor Union, after winning the eight-hour day for government workers, disintegrated because of

    (A) the depression of the early 1870s
    (B) a Supreme Court ruling outlawing unions
    (C) the opposition of President Grant
    (D) the rise of the Knights of Labor
    (E) the failure to admit blacks

11. All of the following comments would apply to *Uncle Tom's Cabin* EXCEPT:

    (A) It was written by a talented woman.
    (B) It originated a common phrase used in black-white relations—*Uncle Tom*.
    (C) It is a story of living conditions under slavery.
    (D) It was an important element in creating antislavery feeling in the North.
    (E) It was not widely read until ten years after publication.

12. The purpose of the Freedman's Bureau was to

    (A) gain the vote for the freed slave
    (B) provide 40 acres and a mule for each slave
    (C) get radical Republicans in positions of power in the South
    (D) feed, adjust, and educate the former slaves, thus aiding their adjustment to freedom
    (E) work against the Black Codes

13.   With malice toward none, with charity for all, with firmness in the right
        as God gives us to see the right, let us strive on to finish the work we are
        in, to bind up the nation's wounds, to care for him who shall have borne
        the battle and for his widow and orphan, to do all which may achieve
        and cherish a just and lasting peace among ourselves and all nations.

The above quotation from a speech expresses the view of the post-Civil
War period held and initiated by

(A) Thaddeus Stevens   (D) Stonewall Jackson
(B) Abraham Lincoln   (E) Horace Greeley
(C) Jefferson Davis

14.   "All persons born or naturalized in the United States, and subject
        to the jurisdiction thereof, are citizens of the United States and of
        the states wherein they reside. No state shall make or enforce any
        law which shall abridge the privileges or immunities of citizens of
        the United States; nor shall any state deprive any person of life,
        liberty, or property, without due process of law; nor deny to any
        person within its jurisdiction the equal protection of the laws."

The above quotation is a key clause in the
(A) Black Code of South Carolina
(B) Gettysburg Address
(C) Thirteenth Amendment to the Constitution
(D) Fourteenth Amendment to the Constitution
(E) Fifteenth Amendment to the Constitution

15.   VALUE OF SELECTED EXPORTS FROM THE UNITED STATES

Year	Total Value* Millions of Dollars	Cotton Millions of Dollars	Leaf Tobacco Millions of Dollars	Wheat Millions of Dollars
1850	101	72	10	1
1853	124	109	11	4
1855	151	88	15	1
1858	157	131	17	9
1860	270	192	16	4
1863	74	7	20	47
1865	154	7	23	30
1868	206	153	23	30
1870	359	227	21	47

*Selected Exports
SOURCE: U.S. Bureau of the Census, *Historical Statistics of the U.S., Colonial Times to 1957.*

According to information presented in the previous table, all of the following would appear true concerning United States exports EXCEPT:

(A)   Export of leaf tobacco was not affected by the Civil War the way the
      export of cotton was.

(B) The export of wheat grew rapidly during and after the Civil War.

(C) The total value of U.S. exports rapidly recovered from the setback and disruption of the Civil War.

(D) Except for the period of the Civil War, cotton accounted for 50 percent of total U.S. exports.

(E) The total value of selected exports from the U.S. increased at a steady rate from 1850 to 1870.

Answers and Answer Explanations

1. D	**2.** B	**3.** E	**4.** B	**5.** E
6. A	**7.** C	**8.** C	**9.** B	**10.** A
11. E	**12.** D	**13.** B	**14.** D	**15.** E

1. (D) Question 1 presents five steps leading to the Civil War in varying chronological listings. The correct answer is D, which is a direct reversal of A. A starts with the most recent event and moves backward and, therefore, cannot reflect cause and effect. D starts in 1854 with the Kansas-Nebraska Act, which had an impact on the Dred Scott Decision in 1857, which affected the Lincoln-Douglas Debates in 1858, which prepared the way for the election of Lincoln in 1860, which was a major cause of the secession of South Carolina in 1860.

2. (B) The Pacific Railroad Bill, providing federal financial aid and land grants for a railroad from St. Louis west, was passed after the South seceded. Until then no bill could be passed because of controversy concerning whether a northern or southern route should be followed. The other four choices are important Congressional acts from other times.

3. (E) The Confederate States are 1 and 2 on the map, a choice not given specifically, so the correct answer is none of the above.

4. (B) The border states at the time of the Civil War were those states which might have seceded but did not. They are identified as 3 on the map in question 3.

5. (E) Saratoga was an important Revolutionary War battle. The other three choices were Civil War battles. Therefore E, which includes II, III, and IV for Gettysburg, Bull Run, and Atlanta respectively, is the correct answer to this question.

6. (A) Question 6 presents the first multiple-choice question based upon a cartoon. It is from *Harper's Weekly* of December 13, 1862. John Bull represents Great Britain and he is shown in front of his little shop, John Bull Variety. His customer is Mr. Confederate, who represents the confederate states. John Bull has received money in the money bag marked CAS—Confederation of American States. Mr. Confederate is loaded up with guns, pistols, swords, and, most importantly, a boat representative of the *Alabama*, which was a privateer built in Great Britain and operated by the Confederacy. It did a great deal of damage to Northern shipping. The point of the cartoon is to illustrate how the British industrialists supplied arms and ships for the Confederacy. The case of the Alabama almost led to war between Great Britain and the Northern states. The claims against the *Alabama* were finally negotiated in 1871-2. The cartoon requires that you can both interpret its parts and place them in the mainstream of American history.

7. (C)   Thaddeus Stevens was the leader of the Radical Reconstructionists in the House. He played a key role in the impeachment of Andrew Jackson and in the development of Congressional reconstruction plans.

8. (C)   A number of scandals are connected with the Grant administration. The Credit Mobilier involving railroad construction and the Whiskey Ring involving the theft of some of the whiskey tax revenue from the Treasury were major scandals in Grant's administration. Teapot Dome is a scandal connected with President Harding's administration, and Watergate is the all-inclusive name given to the scandals of President Nixon's administration.

9. (B)   As a result of the invention of barbed wire, cattle raisers could fence large enough areas of the semi-arid lands of the West to make raising cattle easier. Ranges could be established with set boundaries. The reaper had no relation to cattle raising. Cattle drives to the railheads (shipping points) and the railroads were involved in cattle raising, but were not a cause of the great increase. The Homestead Act allowed for homesteads in the West, but the acreage allotment was too small for cattle raising in the semi-arid areas.

10. (A)   Question 10 asks about the decline of the first major post-Civil War labor union, the National Labor Union, begun in 1866. It was successful during the post-war boom years but collapsed when depression hit the country in the early 1870s. It set a recurring cycle for unions — success in prosperity but trouble during recession.

11. (E)   *Uncle Tom's Cabin*, written by Harriet Beecher Stowe, was published in 1854 and immediately became popular. Its tale of slavery was a major factor in stirring up northern anger at the South's peculiar institution.

12. (D)   The Freedman's Bureau was formed to help the newly freed slaves adjust to their new condition. It was especially important in supplying food and education until it fell under the control of the Radical Reconstructionists, who used it for political purposes.

13. (B)   The quotation in question 13 is from Lincoln's Second Inaugural Address and is often considered a summary of his view for Reconstruction. Certainly the plans for Reconstruction initiated by Lincoln reflect this view. None of the other men, except possibly the *New York Tribune* editor Horace Greeley, expressed such conciliatory sentiments, and Greeley was in no position to initiate action.

14. (E)   Question 14 asks you to identify a section of the Fourteenth Amendment. It is a clause you should know. The Thirteenth Amendment abolished slavery and the Fifteenth granted the vote without regard to color or previous condition of servitude. "Black Codes" restricted rather than granted liberty, and the famous Gettysburg Address was delivered at the dedication of a cemetery and would not include such language or ideas. The Republicans felt they needed to incorporate their ideas in the Constitution and made ratification of this amendment a condition for re-entry of the seceded states into the union.

15. (E)   Question 15 asks you to read a simple statistical table dealing with U.S. exports in the years 1850-1870. In studying the table you will see that all the statements except the last, "The total value of selected exports from the U.S. increased at a steady rate from 1850 to 1870," are true. U.S. exports dropped during the Civil War. You must know that the Civil War years were 1861-1865 in order to interpret the other four choices.

Bibliography

Blassingame, John. *The Slave Community: Plantation Life in the Ante-Bellum South.* New York: Oxford University Press, 1979.

Brown, Richard. *Slavery in American Society.* Lexington, Massachusetts: D.C. Heath and Company, 1976.

Craven, A.O. *The Coming of the Civil War.* Chicago: Chicago University Press, 1990.

Donald, David. *Lincoln Reconsidered.* New York: Random. 1989.

Eaton, Clement. *A History of the Southern Confederacy.* New York: Free Press, 1964.

Elkins, Stanley. *Slavery, A Problem in American Institutional and Intellectual Life.* Chicago: University of Chicago Press, 1976.

Fogel, R.W. and Engerman, S.L. *Time on the Cross: The Economics of American Negro Slavery.* Lanham, MD: U.P. of America, 1985.

Franklin, J.H. *Reconstruction: After the Civil War.* Chicago: University of Chicago Press, 1961.

Parrish, Wm. ed. *Civil War: A Second American Revolution?* Melbourne, FL: Krieger, 1978.

Randall, J.G. and Donald, David. *The Civil War and Reconstruction.* Lexington, Massachusetts: D.C. Heath and Company, 1969.

Rozwens, E.C., ed. *The Causes of the American Civil War.* Lexington, Massachusetts: D.C. Heath and Company, 1972.

Stampp, K.M. *Era of Reconstruction 1865–1877.* New York: Random House Inc., 1967.

Ward, Geoffrey C. *The Civil War: An Illustrated History.* New York: Knopf, 1990.

Woodward, C. Vann. *The Strange Career of Jim Crow.* New York: Oxford University Press, 1974.

Fiction

Benet, S.V. *John Brown's Body.* New York: I.R. Dee, 1990.

Garland, Hamlin. *A Son of the Middle Border.* Irvine, CA: Reprint Series, 1988.

Rolvaag, O.E. *Giants in the Earth.* New York: HarperCollins, 1991.

PART THREE **6** The Growth of Industrial America, Populists, and Progressives 1877-1916

Important Facets of This Period

The two related yet separate reform movements—the Populist and Progressive movements—that bridged the turn of the century are of major significance in gaining an understanding of American history. They should be studied in any survey course either in their own right as significant developments in our history or as part of a general study of reform movements in America, which would include, in addition to these two movements, the Jacksonian period and the New Deal. Changes continually occur in human affairs, but at certain periods these changes seem to occur more rapidly and are, in some cases, the result of deliberate decision. The periods in American history when changes came rapidly have been of particular interest to historians. Why this is so is one of the issues you might explore as you study the Populist and Progressive movements.

The years 1877 to 1916 include many important developments that are peripheral to the reform movements. Some were causes, some results, and some had no real connection to the movements. Such issues include literary and artistic developments, growth of manufacturing methods, our changing relations with England and other European nations, the establishment of the American empire in the Pacific, immigration concerns, and changing life-styles as a result of economic and social developments. These years saw the nation grow to be the world power it has been in the 20th century.

Among those items you will wish to consider in studying these years are the following:

1. The meaning of Populism
2. The changing status of blacks, both in the South and throughout the country.
3. The impact of the growth of manufacturing and the railroads on the farmer
4. The economic or business cycles
5. The meaning of the Progressive movement, especially through a comparison of Theodore Roosevelt and Woodrow Wilson
6. The causes and results of the Spanish-American War
7. The effect of the closing of the frontier on American life
8. American expansion in the Pacific and U.S. relations with the European powers
9. Developments in American literary and artistic expression
10. The growth of cities and of immigration and Americans response to each

Sample Essay Question—Compare

We have mentioned that one type of essay question found on Advance Placement examinations asks that two time periods be considered. A common way of doing this is with a *Compare* type essay. The word *compare* means to represent as similar, to examine the character or qualities of two or more items for purpose of discovering their resemblances or differences. Usually you will be asked to compare two items—people or events—but at times more items may be included. In the definition, it is suggested *compare* implies similarity, but note that the word *differences* is used as well as *resemblances*. In a question asking you to compare, you may go either way in your answer and stress either differences or similarities, but you should consider both.

In a *Compare* question, as in the example below, another word will often be used as part of the question, which helps to specify what you are to do in the answer. In this example, the word is *explain*—a word we have already discussed in Chapter 2 with the *Describe ... explain* type of question. It should be clear by this point that many essay type questions are combinations of several other type questions, and that within every type there are many variations possible. Several variations on the basic *Compare* type are illustrated in the five sample questions below.

Sample Question

> "Under Jacksonian Democracy it seemed in the public interest to separate banking and government; under Wilson's Progressivism it seemed in the public interest to join them." Compare the economic philosophies behind each view and explain the conditions that brought about the change from one to the other.

Comments on Sample Question

The question is quite straightforward. The wording of the last half of the question clearly indicates that you are expected to find differences in the economic philosophies as you analyze the material, but if you find similarities, be sure to include them. The quotation uses the word *seemed*, which leaves the interpretation open since "seemed in the national interest" does not mean it *was* in the national interest. The Congress and the president acted a certain way in each period, but you may decide they acted against the public interest. Such an approach could make an interesting answer. How would you approach this question?

Before writing your own answer and reading the student answer, there are several other items to note. First, the question requires knowledge of economic philosophy, not just of what was done. Philosophy is concerned with the principles behind the actions. Do you know what these were under Jacksonian Democracy and Wilsonian Progressivism? Second, the question is an example of how you can be expected to have information from several periods. You have studied both Wilson and Jackson. Both were great presidents; both were involved with reform movements; both were involved with economic issues. How much do you know of them? Write an answer to the question, doing additional research before you begin if you are not able to deal with the question without it. When you have written your essay, read the following student essay. Again, if you make a formal outline of the answer before you read the teacher comments on the essay, you will be able to see how the student organized the answer and it will help you review the history of the Jackson and Wilson eras.

Sample Answer

Economic philosophy is a complicated matter, and through American history many different economic philosophies have been expressed. Economic issues involving government in banking were important in the administrations of both Andrew Jackson and Woodrow Wilson. A comparison of the policies of these two presidents will clearly demonstrate that in Jackson's time the economic philosophy and the president's idea for the public interest were to have no federal banking. By contrast, in Wilson's time the philosophy and president's attitude called for federal banking. Since we cannot rerun history, we'll never know which policy was truly in the public interest.

In theory, Jackson believed that the states should retain as much power as possible, but he was ready to exercise presidential power. "Andy" Jackson was the first president elected who had been nominated by a popular nominating convention; he was the first president representing the common man.

The Second Bank of the United States had been established in 1816 as a private corporation chartered by the government. As years went by the bank became more and more powerful. Nicholas Biddle, as its head, brought it to its peak in the late 1820s. The bank was up for renewal in 1832. Many people opposed the bank on the grounds that it favored business too heavily. Those in favor of the bank argued that it established a sound currency and aided the government's financial affairs by making borrowing easy and by providing a place for the storage and transfer of tax funds. Biddle began a systematic campaign to ensure the passage of the new bank bill. He threatened to recall loans if the bank was not approved, placed advertisements in newspapers and gave gifts to influential people. Jackson would not tolerate such interference in the politics of the country by one vested interest. He refused to support the new bank in Congress and refused to sign the bill. Instead, after its defeat, he established a system of "pet banks." These pet banks were state-chartered banks that would carry on those functions formerly performed by the Bank of the United States. The pet banks were chosen by Jackson. Hence, both because Jackson disliked federal power when he thought states could do the job and because of Biddle's manipulations, Jackson vetoed the bank bill.

In comparison, when Wilson took office in 1912 conditions had changed radically. The government was too big and diversified to have its monetary matters handled by a few chosen banks. More important, the country had a proven need for a central agency that could control the money situation in some way. Depression in 1837, 1857, and 1893 and other signs of economic instability showed this. By 1912 business was expanding at such a rate that credit regulation was urgent. The business abuses of the previous generation involving stock transactions, misrepresentation of facts on securities, and credit manipulations had all intensified this need for some government regulation. The dealings of Harriman and Morgan are another example of private manipulation against public welfare.

Wilson had realized early the need for a government agency to regulate credit. Wilson's Progressivism included the belief that central government was not necessarily limited by the states' abilities to perform a task similar to that of the federal government. He believed the federal government should intervene to establish an orderly money market and business system for the general public interest.

Hence, Wilson pushed the Federal Reserve Act through Congress as soon as he could after taking office in 1913. The act provided for a Federal Reserve Board of six members appointed by the president. Federal Reserve banks were established and the country was divided into districts. Hence a central organization in Washington could make general polices to be carried out by locally oriented banks throughout the country. The Federal Reserve System could regulate credit by adjusting the prime, discount, and rediscount rates. The flow of money was regulated by the interest rate. The interest rate charged for loans could be changed quite quickly. In theory, inflation and deflation could then be controlled by the central government in the public interest.

Thus Wilson differed from Jackson in that he approved of government intervention whereas Jackson might not have. Regardless of those differences in philosophy, I think that the need was so great, and conditions so changed, that the government would have intervened in some way even if Jackson had been president in 1912.

It is clear that all we are able to do is to illustrate the differences between the two periods—but it is impossible to judge which economic policy was best. This is true of all economic philosophies. We can acknowledge that differences exist, but we cannot tell what is correct, although much of American history has focused on arguments about economic philosophy.

Teacher Comments on Sample Answer

"The student presents very detailed and satisfactory information; however, the thesis avoids the issue by claiming we will never know the answer. The suggested approach—a comparison of the two presidencies—is the logical one to use. Unfortunately, the writer does not present a comparison, and the information presented in the body of the paper does not focus on the thesis. The writer simply presented all the information about Jackson and then all the information about Wilson. The body of the paper gives no clue that the writer's key idea is the policies' relation to the public interest.

"The organization of the essay around Jackson's presidency and Wilson's presidency is fine, but the writer fails to make an effective comparison between the two. He or she is aware of the general economic situation in each period and has an understanding of the Federal Reserve System and the pet banks. The writer is not clear as to the economic philosphies of the two periods nor of what was the public interest at each time, yet his or her comments on Biddle, Harriman, and Morgan illustrate his or her understanding that some individuals were manipulating the country for their own personal interest, which implies it was against public interest.

The writer in the thesis raises an interesting issue concerning the difference between the social sciences and the laboratory sciences when he or she suggests that you cannot 'rerun' history. It is a point he or she might have developed further in the body of the essay, creating an unusual answer.

"In conclusion, this essay is satisfactory in terms of information. There is an obvious organization, but it does not focus on a comparison, which is merely implied, and, although it has a thesis, the body of the essay does not support it adequately. It is an example of an essay with many possibilities that are not fulfilled."

Do you agree with these comments? The introductory paragraph of the sample student essay is a good one. Use it and your formal outline of the answer to rewrite this essay and the conclusion.

Practice Essay Questions

The following essay questions will test your knowledge of this period, and in addition, questions 4 and 5 force you to relate this period of time to others you have studied, as did the sample question above. Types of essay questions we have discussed in previous chapters are used in these five sample questions to provide practice with different type questions.

1. "In understanding the nature of a reform movement it is as important to know what it seeks to preserve as to know what it seeks to change." Compare the Populist and Progressive Reform movements of the late 19th and early 20th centuries in light of this statement.

2. "The nation (United States) whose Constitution is so perfect that no man suggests change and whose fundamental laws as they stand are satisfactory to all . . . The nation in which the right of the minority, the right of property and . . . of free labor are most secure."

   In what ways is this statement an accurate summary of the situation in the United States at the end of the 19th century? To what extent do you agree or disagree with the statement?

3. "The closing of the frontier in 1890 had a profound effect on the social and economic development of the United States in the succeeding twenty years." Evaluate this statement.

4. In the period 1793-1812 the United States was a small nation pushed around by the big powers; in the period 1895-1911 the United States was a big power who pushed around small nations.

   Compare the foreign policy of the United States in these two time periods to test the validity of this generalization.

5. Describe three social and/or political problems that were present in the South in the Reconstruction period and explain what solutions to three problems were offered by the Populists and/or Progressives.

Comments on Question 1	Question 1 is a straightforward *Compare* question. The quotation is an interesting one that could be applied to any reform movement. In this case you are asked to compare two movements that sometimes appear rather similar, but which are quite different. These differences should be clarified in an essay based on this quotation. Your thesis would have to state what you believe each movement sought to preserve, assuming, of course, you don't take the extreme position that the movements tried to preserve nothing. An organization based on similarities and differences in the two movements would seem more satisfactory than a chronological organization. If you have studied these two important reform movements, the question should be rather easy, since there are no unusual words or twists to the question.
Comments on Question 2	Question 2, on the other hand, is long and complicated. It is a typical combination essay type question involving an *In what ways ...*, *To what extent ...*, and an *Agree or disagree* section. Once you figure out what each part is asking you to do, then you need to analyze the quote. The author of the quote is very optimistic about the United States. He believes everything is fine for everybody. He mentions particularly the security of the rights of the minority, of property, and of free labor. These three form an interesting combination. Who are the minority in the speaker's eyes? What is property? What is free labor? These three terms are crucial in understanding the meaning of the quotation and in determining whether you agree or disagree with what the author describes as the situation of the United States at the turn of the century. What is your opinion? Once you decide on your thesis, then factual information can be organized in different ways to answer the question. The question suggests an interesting approach to the period of time at the end of the century.*
Comments on Question 3	Question 3 is a straightforward *Evaluate this statement* type. The quotation uses a familiar idea from the Bureau of the Census report for 1890. The *closed frontier* is the phrase which Frederick Jackson Turner used to develop his important thesis on the significance of the frontier in America. If the thesis is not familiar, you can still develop an interesting essay on the issue of the impact of the frontier on social and economic developments. This essay would best be organized around the various social and economic effects and *not* by chronology.
Comments on Question 4	The fourth essay question again combines several types of essay questions. There is a statement about U.S. foreign policy, but then instead of being asked to evaluate the statement you are asked to compare the two time periods mentioned in the statement with the goal of testing the validity of the generalization. What the writer of this question is seeking in the way of an answer is very close to an

---

*The author of the quote is not given in the question. When you have organized your thoughts, you may be interested to know that the author was Andrew Carnegie, writing in 1873.

evaluation of the statement, but has given directions as to how this is to be achieved—by a comparison. Your thesis will reflect how true you believe the statement to be. Examples of the United States being pushed around in the years 1793-1812 contrasted with the examples of the United States pushing small nations or not pushing them, depending on your personal thesis, in the years 1895-1911, would provide an effective organization. In analyzing the statement you will no doubt recall many examples of U.S. foreign policy activity from which you may choose. In the years 1793-1812 the United States had innumerable dealings with France and England, to say nothing of Spain and the Barbary Pirates, while in the later period we were involved in the annexation of Hawaii, the Spanish-American War, incidents in Panama and Venezuela, and several incidents involving European powers, such as the Algeciras Conference, the Russo-Japanese War, and the Second Hague Disarmament Conference. Again, you will have many examples of foreign policy activity to choose from, so the major difficulty in this question will be in picking information to support your thesis and being certain to refute any major piece of evidence that does not agree with your thesis. For instance, if you do not believe the United States pushed small nations around in the 1895-1911 period, you must not ignore Theodore Roosevelt's use of the "big stick," but either explain that this was an exception to your thesis or that T.R. had certain larger goals in mind. As mentioned in Part Two, when defending a thesis, you are being a lawyer or debater and they often concede points before going on to make their main argument. This technique is important if you wish to win readers to your side.

Comments on Question 5

Sample essay question 5 is a *Describe ... explain* type. It relates the Reconstruction era to that of the Populists and Progressives, and it introduces not merely political problems, but social ones also. There should be no difficulty in analyzing what the question is asking, nor in developing a thesis and an organizing principle. You may find difficulty in focusing on "three social and/or political problems." The social problem of the freed slave is the most obvious one, but there were other social problems involving the economic success of different classes, as well as political problems involving voting and state rule. The question is a difficult one, but a good one in that it makes you consider two time periods and their relation in a new and different way. This question is well worth spending time researching. Also in this question the term *and/or* is used for the first time. It is a connecting term and means both *and* and *or*. In other words you have the choice of picking *three* social problems, *three* political problems, or *any* combination such as one social and two political.

Multiple-Choice Questions—Cartoons and Photographs

In Chapter 5 we discussed multiple-choice questions based on charts and graphs and indicated that the primary purpose of such questions was to test your analytical skills. Another popular type of multiple-choice question designed to test analytical skill more than recall of information is the multiple-choice question based upon a cartoon or a photograph. The cartoon is often a politically oriented one. Although they are not as common, questions are sometimes based on paintings or sketches. As is true in the case of multiple-choice questions based on charts and graphs, when dealing with questions based on cartoons and pictures, you will often be expected to know about the history of the period in which the cartoon or picture was produced. Thus, although the main purpose of such multiple-choice questions is to test analytical skills needed by the student of history, there is also often an element of factual recall involved. Thus, as in the case of the DBQ, in these questions you will often be expected to relate the cartoon or photograph to the mainstream of American history.

The following multiple-choice questions are examples of what you might find on an examination. The cartoons are all from *Harper's Weekly*. There are many other sources for cartoons and sketches, but those that appeared in *Harper's Weekly* are typical of 19th-century cartoons. Many textbooks today use such cartoons to illustrate points, and it would be wise to take time to look carefully at the cartoons and other illustrations as you study. The old expression, "A picture can convey a thousand words," is often true, so look at the illustrations in your books and see what you can learn. These cartoons and pictures and the comments and questions based on them will supply some practice in developing your skill in *reading* illustrations. If your text or the books you are using to study American history lack cartoons and pictures, you can practice by analyzing the cartoons and photographs in the daily papers, in news magazines, or in special books of cartoons such as *The Art and Politics of Thomas Nast*, edited by Morton Keller, or *A Century of Political Cartoons*, edited by Allan Weins and Frank Weitenkampf, or special illustrated histories, such as *The Illustrated History of World War I* by A.J.P. Taylor.

DON'T SWAP HORSES.

JOHN BULL. "Why don't you ride the other Horse a bit? He's the best Animal."
BROTHER JONATHAN. "Well, that may be; but the fact is, OLD ABE is just where I can put my finger on him; and as for the other—though they say he's some when out in the scrub yonder—I never know where to find him."

SOURCE: *Harper's Weekly*

Sample Questions 1 and 2

1. In which of the following years was this cartoon published?
   (A) 1844
   (D) 1940
   (B) 1860
   (E) 1968
   (C) 1864

2. In the cartoon the words in the bushes refer to
   (A) John Bull's economic policies
   (B) the horse trader's promises
   (C) the charter of the city of Chicago
   (D) the main planks in the Democratic party's Chicago Platform
   (E) the goals of the Republican party of "Old Abe"

Comments on Question 1

The first cartoon is from *Harper's Weekly* of November 1864. The artist is not identified. The subject is Abraham Lincoln's campaign for re-election to the presidency. To answer the question you must be able to recall several items that are suggested by points in the cartoon. The biggest point for identification is the reference to "Old Abe." The face on the horse then should be identifiable as Lincoln's. If you recall the years of Lincoln's elections and presidency— 1860-1865—then you have narrowed the choices down to 1860 and 1864. You then need to decide what the title of the cartoon means. *Don't swap horses* is a western expression meaning "don't change." When was Lincoln or the country, represented here by Brother Jonathan, involved in changing? There were times Lincoln changed generals, but this was not a decision made by the country (Brother Jonathan) or of interest to other nations (John Bull representing England). Another change, and one involving the years given as possible answers, was that offered to the country in the election of 1864. Old Abe was president— i.e., the horse being ridden—and the other possible horse was off in the bushes, an "unknown" quantity as Brother Jonathan says. This is further confirmed, if you recognize the face in the bushes as McClellan, Lincoln's Democratic opponent, or if you know the Democrats held their convention at Chicago and their platform called for peace and compromise. Perhaps you were able to identify the years without such a detailed analysis, but this analysis illustrates how you can read cartoons using your knowledge of history to understand what is being presented. Incidentally, the *Don't swap horses* slogan was also used by the Democrats in 1940 to support the third-term election of Franklin D. Roosevelt, with the idea being that we should not change presidents at such a period of international crisis. The year 1844 has no connection to the cartoon; 1968 was the year of turmoil at the Democratic Party Convention in Chicago, where peace and compromise in Vietnam were major issues, but this is irrelevant to the cartoon.

Comments on Question 2

In answering the second question about the 1864 cartoon, you would have to know what the Democrats stood for in 1864. It is a question based more on recall than on analysis, but you might be able to arrive at the correct answer by eliminating the other choices. John Bull's economic policies have nothing to do with the topic of the cartoon, and the cartoon is *not* about horse trading, so you should be able to eliminate those two choices. Although Lincoln was from Illinois and Chicago is in that state, choice (C) about the charter of the city has no obvious connection to the conversation between Brother Jonathan and John Bull, so it should be eliminated. Finally, you are left with two choices involving political parties. If you have identified "Old Abe" as Lincoln, then you would probably be able to eliminate the words in the bushes as being the goals of the Republican party, as you would realize the Republicans were ready to fight the Civil War and not compromise for peace. Thus, with a limited amount of knowledge of the period and by careful elimination, you could probably arrive at the correct answer. Remember that on the Advanced Placement examination it is suggested that you guess at answers provided you can eliminate one or two of the five selections. In preparation for the exam, practice this type of analysis and elimination as you look at cartoons.

THE BATTLE OF THE BULLS AND BEARS.
"Humpty Dumpty on a wall,
Humpty Dumpty got a fall!"

SOURCE: *Harper's Weekly*, September 10, 1872

Sample Questions 3 and 4

3. The cartoonist is chiefly concerned with making a point about
    (A)   wild animal attacks on domestic cattle
    (B)   earthquakes knocking down walls
    (C)   the high cost of pork and flour
    (D)   the high price of stocks on Wall Street
    (E)   a fall in the price of gold on the Wall Street stock exchange

4. All of the following used by the cartoonist are common symbols EXCEPT
    (A)   bulls and bears to represent attitudes toward stock purchases
    (B)   Humpty Dumpty to represent gold
    (C)   a wall to represent Wall Street
    (D)   a bale to represent cotton
    (E)   a barrel to represent pork

Comments on Question 3

The cartoon for questions 3 and 4 is from *Harper's Weekly* of September 10, 1872. The cartoonist is no doubt concerned with the high cost of pork and flour and the high prices of stocks and their fluctuations, but the real point of the cartoon has to do with a fall in the price of gold. Of course, earthquakes and animal attacks have nothing to do with the chief concern of the artist.

Comments on Question 4

The artist has used common symbols to represent various items in his cartoon, and the animals and the wall are examples. Question 4 requires that you be familiar with such symbols from your study. The use of a wall for Wall Street and of a bale for cotton are obvious. Most people today have heard of a *bull* or *bear* market in regard to stock purchases, as these are very common symbols. The *pork barrel* is also a very commonly used expression in American history. Salted pork was stored in a barrel, and whan a person on the frontier had plenty of pork stored, he was considered fortunate and wealthy. Therefore, the political term evolved of dipping into the pork barrel, which meant helping yourself to the wealth or valuable items available for political patronage. This term does not apply to this cartoon, but it illustrates how common terms or symbols develop and become part of common usage. Finally, we come to Humpty Dumpty, as a representation of gold, and this is *not* a common symbol. It is unique to the artist and helps to make his point about the fragility of gold prices and what will happen as they fall, as the artist assumes everyone knows what happened to Humpty Dumpty when he fell off the wall.

Sample Questions 5 and 6

SOURCE: Library of Congress

5. The photograph most likely portrays
   (A) workers on an automobile assembly line
   (B) child laborers in a factory
   (C) Civil War recruits waiting for uniforms
   (D) two boys preparing hot dogs at a baseball game
   (E) Vietnamese boat people

6. The conditions presented in the previous photograph were largely eliminated by
   (A) new industrial methods
   (B) the Child Labor amendment to the Constitution
   (C) Supreme Court decisions before World War I
   (D) legislation under the New Deal
   (E) the Great Depression

Comments on Question 5

The photograph used for questions 5 and 6 is of two young boys working in a glass factory in 1908. It is an example of child labor and reflects factory conditions at a time when the ideas of the Social Darwinists and trust builders dominated American business. Photographs have been used less often for multiple-choice questions than cartoons, but questions can be designed around photographs which do not merely require recognition and recall of facts. By studying this photograph it would be clear that it is not an assembly line or a hot dog stand. The caps may make you think of Civil War recruits, but the chimney tongs and working table make it appear more a factory than a recruiting station. The boys are obviously not Vietnamese. The photograph is a good thought-provoker and is typical of what might be found on an exam.

Comments on Question 6

Question 6 illustrates how a photograph may lead to a multiple-choice question requiring both analysis and factual recall. For question 6 you must recognize the conditions as being those of child labor in a factory, and then you must know how the conditions of child labor were changed in this country. New industrial methods changed working conditions, but many industrialists continued to employ children. The Child Labor Amendment to the Constitution was never ratified by the states, and though it may have had some impact on child labor, it did not eliminate it. Before World War I the Supreme Court was conservative and would not interfere in private business matters, and depressions generally create worse situations for workers; they do not eliminate bad conditions. It was not until the New Deal labor legislation that child labor was eliminated and factory working conditions improved.

Sample Questions 7-8

AMERICAN LABOR pays WAR TAXES on all these articles for the sole benefit of TRUST, MONOPOLY & CO.

IMPORTED, DUTY FREE,
by
TRUST, MONOPOLY & CO.
TO COMPETE WITH
AMERICAN LABOR.

A QUESTION OF LABOR.

"*This question is from first to last, from the beginning to the end, from skin to core and from core back to skin again, a question of labor.*"—JAMES G. BLAINE AT MADISON SQUARE, AUGUST 10, 1888.

SOURCE: *Harper's Weekly,* August, 1888

7. In this cartoon the cartoonist, W.A. Rogers, is protesting all of the following EXCEPT:
   (A) Free immigration
   (B) High taxes on manufactured items
   (C) The power of trusts and monopolies
   (D) James G. Blaine's comment that the immigration issue is "first to last ... a question of labor."
   (E) The poor-quality work of American labor

> **8.** The T.M. & Co. tag on the immigrant's arm stands for Trust, Monopoly and Company, which is
>   (A)   John D. Rockefeller's company
>   (B)   a fictitious organization representing the power of trusts
>   (C)   a company created by the U.S. Congress
>   (D)   a worldwide conglomerate
>   (E)   a government corporation formed to aid immigrants to the United States

Comments on Question 7

W.A. Rogers' cartoon titled "A Question of Labor" provides the basis for questions 7 and 8. It is from the August 1888 issue of *Harper's Weekly*. Question 7 asks what Mr. Rogers is protesting about in the cartoon, and the question is phrased in that very common way that seeks the one point that is incorrect. This phrasing, "All but which of the following," has been used in many multiple-choice questions in this book. It provides a positive approach to the information because four out of the five choices are correct, rather than the reverse where four choices are wrong. In this cartoon you can tell Mr. Rogers is unhappy about free immigration since the sign indicates that the immigrant is imported "duty free ... to compete with American labor." *Compete* is the key word here. He also opposes high taxes he believes only help the trusts. Implied in both these points is Rogers's dislike of the power of the trusts and monopolies, as such phrases as *compete* and *sole benefit* indicate. He is also protesting James G. Blaine's comment, although that is not as easy to see. The title of the cartoon, "A Question of Labor," picked up Blaine's comment, and the impact of the entire cartoon is to indicate that the question is *not* merely a question of labor, it is also a question of labor competition, monopoly control, and high taxes. Rogers is thus protesting the points indicated in the first four choices and he is not protesting "the poor-quality work of American labor," which then is the correct answer for this all-but-one type of multiple-choice question. The answer was arrived at simply by analyzing the cartoon, and there was no need to understand the historical circumstances in which it was placed. These circumstances were a presidential campaign in which Benjamin Harrison, the Republican, was running against Grover Cleveland, the Democrat, whom he defeated. Blaine had been defeated by Cleveland in 1884. Blaine was considered the leading Republican; he was appointed Secretary of State by Harrison; he was a supporter of trusts and big business and was a U.S. Senator from Maine.

Comments on Question 8

In question 8 the T.M. & Co. tag stands for Trust, Monopoly and Company, which is mentioned in the sign under the immigrant's feet. It is a fictitious organization created by Rogers to represent the power of the trusts. The other choices given are all possibilities, and you might pick one of them unless you know a little of the history of the period. The cartoon gives you the date so you do not have to figure that out. Rockefeller's company was Standard Oil; the U.S. Congress was not creating companies at this time—it was done by private enterprise; worldwide conglomerates are a later historic development (in the pre-1900 period national trusts were being created); the United States did very little to aid immigrants in this or any period.

These illustrations of multiple-choice questions based on cartoons and a photograph should help you in your study and analysis of such items in your texts. As you can see, many types of questions can be based on cartoons and pictures, some of which will require simple analysis of the illustrations, some of which require pure recall, and some of which require both. There will be examples of such multiple-choice questions in the following chapters.

Practice Multiple-Choice Questions

1.

SOURCE: *Harper's Weekly*, July, 1872

The cartoonist is making a point concerning the Alabama claims which

(A)   resulted from the attack of the *Alabama* on northern shipping

(B)   were claims of Alabama against British shipping in the West Indies

(C)   were British complaints against the quality of Alabama's cotton

(D)   involved Alabama businessmen and the British government

(E)   resulted from Union attack on the South during the Civil War

2.

VOTE OF THE STATE OF CONNECTICUT 1872-1886

Date	Office	Parties				
		Dem.	Rep.	Gr.	Pro.	Plurality
1872	President	45,880	50,638	....	....	*4758 R.
1874	Governor	46,755	39,973	....	4942	6782 D.
1876	President	61,071	59,034	774	378	2900 D.
1878	Governor	46,385	48,867	8314	1079	2482 R.
1880	President	64,415	67,169	863	448	2656 R.
1882	Governor	59,014	54,853	697	1034	4161 R.
1884	President	67,167	65,893	1684	2489	1284 D.
1884	Governor	67,910	66,275	1379	1636	1636 D.
1886	Governor	58,817	56,920	4687	2792	1897 D.

*Majority.
SOURCE: *Harper's Weekly*, 1888

For the years presented in the table, all of the following are true about political parties OTHER than the Republican (Rep.) and Democrats (Dem.) EXCEPT:
- (A) Votes for only two third parties are recorded
- (B) The Prohibition Party (Pro.) obtained its largest number of votes when it was the only third party
- (C) The two small parties listed polled the largest combined number of votes in the gubernatorial election of 1878
- (D) The votes of the two small parties added to the Democratic votes for president in 1880 would have given the state's electoral college votes to the Democrats
- (E) No votes for third parties were recorded in the presidential election of 1872

3. "The millionaires are a product of natural selection acting on the whole body of men to pick out those qualified few who can meet the requirements of certain work to be done. ..."

The author of the above quotation is most likely
- (A) Woodrow Wilson
- (B) William Graham Sumner
- (C) William Jennings Bryan
- (D) Eugene V. Debs
- (E) Theodore Roosevelt

4. The ideas of natural selection and survival of the fittest, when applied to business and economic activity, are referred to as
    (A) communism
    (B) trust-busting
    (C) anarchism
    (D) Dollar Diplomacy
    (E) Social Darwinism

5. Jim Crowism refers to legislation designed to
    (A) benefit railroad workers
    (B) sell western lands cheaply
    (C) deny equality to the blacks
    (D) keep immigrants from taking jobs away from Americans
    (E) provide economic opportunity for Spanish-American War veterans

6. Which of the following was NOT acquired by the United States as a result of involvement in the Spanish-American War?
    (A) Samoa
    (B) Hawaiian Islands
    (C) Puerto Rico
    (D) Guam
    (E) Philippine Islands

7. The United States' policy toward the Native American changed dramatically with the passage in 1887 of the Dawes Act, which
    (A) treated the tribes as independent nations
    (B) established new and larger reservations for all tribes
    (C) granted full citizenship to all tribal members
    (D) wiped out tribal ownership of property and granted 160 acres to heads of families
    (E) forbade selling alcohol or guns on reservations

8. Theodore Roosevelt named a group of individuals Muckrakers after a character in Bunyan's *Pilgrim's Progress*, but the members of the group gained their real reputation as
    (A) the writers of local-color novels
    (B) reformers who published articles to draw attention to the evils affecting America
    (C) the ten richest men in America
    (D) leaders of conservation movements in the West which brought national attention to conservation
    (E) members of Roosevelt's first cabinet

9. In 1895 President Cleveland turned to J.P. Morgan and a Wall Street syndicate to borrow gold for the U.S. Treasury because

- (A) the U.S. gold reserves were so low the government could not otherwise redeem its outstanding paper money
- (B) Cleveland had Morgan's support in the election and wished to help him
- (C) he could not get Congress to repeal the Sherman Silver Purchase Act
- (D) the government needed the money to pay salaries
- (E) it was the only way Wall Street could recover from the Panic of 1893

10. The major point of difference between the two black leaders Booker T. Washington and W.E.B. Du Bois was over their view of

- (A) the need for education
- (B) the importance of better race relations
- (C) the need for immediate equality for blacks and whites
- (D) the significance of independence for Africa
- (E) using white institutions to help the blacks

11. Starting with the decade of 1890 until Congress passed legislation to control immigration in the 1920s, the largest number of immigrants came from

- (A) Ireland
- (B) Italy, Austria-Hungary, Russia
- (C) England, Germany, France
- (D) Norway, Sweden, Denmark
- (E) Poland

12. The Populist Party platform in 1892 called for

- I. a graduated income tax
- II. government ownership of railroads and the return to the government of land grants held by railroads but not used in their construction
- III. a gold-based currency
- IV. support for initiative and referendum legislation

- (A) I and III
- (B) I, III, and IV
- (C) I, II, and IV
- (D) I and IV
- (E) I, II, III, and IV

13. Each of the following men is correctly paired with an item linked with his name EXCEPT

- (A) Joseph Pulitzer—*New York World*
- (B) Louis H. Sullivan—Skyscrapers
- (C) Thomas Edison—Phonograph
- (D) Bret Harte—*Adventures of Huckleberry Finn*
- (E) Buffalo Bill Cody—Wild West Show

14. Among the major political issues on which Congress passed legislation during the years 1877-1892 were all of the following EXCEPT
   (A) Civil Service Reform
   (B) Civil Rights
   (C) Control of the Trusts
   (D) The Coinage of Silver
   (E) Tariffs

THE FINISHING TOUCH
Drawn by E. W. Kemble

SOURCE: *Harper's Weekly*, November, 1912

15. E.W. Kemble in the above cartoon is particularly commenting upon and making the point that
   (A) Woodrow Wilson was a skilled bullfighter
   (B) campaigns are like bullfights
   (C) there were few issues in the campaign
   (D) lectures delivered by Woodrow Wilson always had a point
   (E) the "Professor" Woodrow Wilson defeated Theodore Roosevelt's Bull Moose party

Answers and Answer Explanations

1. A	2. D	3. B	4. E	5. C
6. A	7. D	8. B	9. A	10. C
11. B	12. C	13. D	14. B	15. E

1. (A) Question 1 refers to a cartoon about the Alabama claims. It appeared in *Harper's Weekly* on June 6, 1872. One piece of paper in the foreground, titled the "Alabama Claims," suggests the topic of the cartoon and requires that you know what the claims were. The *Alabama* was a warship built in Great Britain for the Confederacy during the Civil War. It raided northern shipping. The immediate situation almost led to the North declaring war on Great Britain. The northern financial losses resulting from ships sunk by the *Alabama* were blamed on the British who had built the ship. The situation after the war was referred to international arbitration during Grant's presidency when he "put his foot down." This is a good example of a multiple-choice cartoon-based question requiring recall rather than analytical skill.

2. (D) Question 2 requires that you read the columns other than those marked *Rep.* and *Dem.* on the Table. You will see when you do that all the choices are correct except that the votes in these columns added to the Democratic votes for president in 1880 would not have given the state's electoral college votes to the Democrats. To eliminate this choice you must understand the operation of the electoral college at that time. In 1880 the party with the largest number of votes won *all* the electoral college votes from that state.

3. (B) The quotation in question 3 is from William Graham Sumner, a Yale sociologist who became the chief spokesperson for the philosophy of Social Darwinism. The other men were not active supporters of Social Darwinism.

4. (E) Social Darwinism is briefly described by the two terms used in question four. Social Darwinists believe that Darwin's laws of evolution—natural selection and the survival of the fittest—also apply to social and economic activity. They hold that government should not interfere in such activity but should allow business and social activities to progress naturally.

5. (C) Question 5 also requires you to define a common historic term used widely during these years and since then. *Jim Crow* was a name given to the freed slave, just as John Doe has been used for whites. *Jim Crowism* refers to the legislation designed to deny equality to blacks. Such legislation was widespread and included a great variety of laws. The laws requiring separate but equal school and railroad facilities and laws denying the vote to a person unless his grandfather had voted are examples of *Jim Crowism*. The U.S. Congress did not pass Jim Crow laws, but many states did. The Congress has passed laws involving the four other choices.

6. (A) The answer to question 6 is Samoa. It was not acquired as a result of U.S. involvement in the Spanish-American War; negotiations with Germany led to our acquisition of Samoa. We acquired Puerto Rico, Guam, and the Philippines in the peace treaty and we annexed Hawaii to provide a fueling station for our ships supplying our troops and fleet in the Philippines. The annexation had been rejected earlier, but when we became involved in the war, the situation changed and we annexed the islands.

7. (D) The Dawes Act of 1887 reversed previous policy toward the Native American. Previously, tribes had been treated as independent nations and were placed on reservations. The Dawes Act eliminated tribal ownership of property and provided land for each head of family. It was designed to turn the natives into farmers and *eventually* into citizens. The act did nothing about guns or alcohol, but it did attempt to protect the Indians' claim to their 160 acres and to prepare them for citizenship. It was an attempt to deal fairly with Native Americans, but unfortunately, it was designed to turn them into whites and showed no understanding of their culture.

8. (B) Theodore Roosevelt called those "reformers who used their pens to draw attention to the evils afflicting America" 'Muckrakers' after a character in John Bunyan's *Pilgrim's Progress*. The character spent so much time raking manure that he lost sight of heaven and better things. Roosevelt thought these reformers were too harsh and narrow-minded, although he supported in Congress and in the nation many of the causes these reformers supported. The other choices for question 8 have no significance for the question.

9. (A) Question 9 touches on the monetary problems of the government. A major political issue in 19th-century history involved a freer and more flexible currency. One solution to the problem called for coinage of silver in a ratio with gold and the issuance of paper money redeemable in either gold or silver. When the Panic of 1893 hit, the gold reserves dropped to what Cleveland considered was a dangerous level. The only way he could see to keep the U.S. credit good was to go to J.P. Morgan and his associates on Wall Street to get a loan of gold to redeem outstanding paper money. It created an enraged outcry from the Democrats and Populists, but it maintained America's credit.

10. (C) Booker T. Washington and W.E.B. Du Bois were two outstanding black leaders at the turn of the century. They agreed on many issues, but they disagreed strongly on the need for immediate equality. Washington, the president of Tuskegee Institute, was more popular with whites and was entertained at the White House. He held that first blacks should prove their economic importance and then equality would follow. Du Bois, a graduate of Harvard and an outstanding scholar, wanted immediate equality, and to gain this equality, he helped found the N.A.A.C.P. Both men saw a need for education, but of different types; both men would use white institutions to help blacks and saw the importance of good race relations; African independence was not an issue in Washington's lifetime, so the other choices can be eliminated.

11. (B)   Question 11 focuses on the issue of the "old" and "new" immigration. The "old" immigrants formed the majority of immigrants to the United States until 1890. They came from western and northern Europe—Ireland, England, and Germany. The "new" immigrants became the majority of immigrants in 1890 and came from eastern and southern Europe—Italy, Austria-Hungary, and Russia.

12. (C)   The Populist party platform in 1892 seemed to many a very radical document, but most of its provisions were adopted by 1935. Since the Populists desired a more flexible currency, they did *not* want a gold standard. Instead, they wanted silver and gold as the basis of the currency. They supported a graduated income tax, which would tax the millionaires more heavily than the poor; the return to the government of unused land grants and government ownership of railroads; the initiative and referendum, which they felt would put more political power in the hands of the people. The platform of 1892 provides an excellent statement of the goals of the Populists.

13. (D)   In question 13, five individuals who were important in other than political or economic areas are paired with items for which they are famous. Joseph Pulitzer helped to revolutionize the newspaper business as editor of the *New York World*; Louis H. Sullivan was a famous architect who designed the first skyscrapers; Thomas Edison invented the phonograph; Buffalo Bill Cody was a star of typically American Wild West shows. Bret Harte, although a famous author writing about the West, did not write *The Adventures of Huckleberry Finn*, which was written by Mark Twain.

14. (B)   Question 14 lists four areas in regard to which Congress passed legislation in the years 1877-1892. All the issues except civil rights were major political issues of these years. Congress passed civil rights legislation immediately after the Civil War, but not again until after World War II.

15. (E)   The cartoon in question 15 was drawn by E.W. Kimble in November 1912, as a comment on Theodore Roosevelt and his Bull Moose party's defeat in the presidential election by Woodrow Wilson, then the governor of New Jersey and a former college professor and president. Wilson is portrayed in the cap and gown of the college professor while Theodore Roosevelt is portrayed as a Bull Moose stuck in the sand and stopped by the bullfighter Wilson. The cartoon makes use of such symbols as the Bull Moose representing Roosevelt's Progressive party and the college cap and gown. If you recognize these symbols from your study, interpreting the cartoon would be easier, but if you did not, you still might be able to eliminate several choices.

Bibliography

The following books will expand your knowledge of this period. The books dwell on a variety of issues from immigration to elections.

Cooper, J.M., Jr. *The Warrior and the Priest: Woodrow Wilson and Theodore Roosevelt.* Cambridge: Belknap Press of Harvard University, 1983.

Foner, Philip S. *Women and the American Labor Movement from Colonial Times to the Eve of World War I.* New York: Free Press, 1979.

Handlin, Oscar. *The Uprooted.* Boston: Little, Brown & Co., 1973.

Hofstadter, Richard. *The Age of Reform.* New York: Alfred A. Knopf, Inc., 1955.

————. *Social Darwinism in American Thought.* Boston: Beacon Press, 1955.

Link, Arthur, S. & McCormick, R.L. *Progressivism.* Arlington Heights, IL: Harlan Davidson, 1983.

Meier, August. *Negro Thought in America: 1880–1915.* Ann Arbor: The University of Michigan Press, 1963.

Woodward, C. Vann. *Origins of the New South, 1877–1913.* Baton Rouge: Louisiana State University Press, 1972.

Biography

The following biographies and autobiographies will provide insights into the personalities of the leaders of this period, but will also supply interesting and important background information as to what the age was like.

Adams, Jane. *Twenty Five Years at Hull House.* Champaign, IL: Univ. of Illinois Press, 1990.

Blum, J.M. *The Progressive Presidents.* New York: W.W. Norton & Co., 1982.

————. *The Republican Roosevelt.* Cambridge: Harvard Univ. Press, 1977.

————. *Woodrow Wilson and the Politics of Morality.* New York: Scott, Foresman, 1962.

Holbrook, S.H. *The Age of the Moguls.* Salem, NH: Ayer Pub. Co., 1981.

Link, Arthur S. *Woodrow Wilson and the Progressive Era.* New York: HarperCollins, 1963.

Steffens, Lincoln. *Autobiography.* New York: Harcourt Brace Jovanovich, 1968.

Washington, Booker T. *Up From Slavery.* New York: Viking Penguin, 1986.

Fiction

Two novels written at the turn of the century very effectively reveal conditions of the period.

Churchill, Winston. *Coniston.* Philadelphia: Folcroft Library Editions, 1906.

Sinclair, Upton. *The Jungle.* New York: Viking Penguin, 1985.

PART THREE 7 World War I, the Inter-War Period, and World War II 1916-1945

Important Facets of This Period

The years 1916-1945 include several major events of American history with which every student should be familiar. These are World War I, the stock market crash of 1929 and the Great Depression that followed, the New Deal, and World War II. Every American history exam would include multiple-choice questions involving these events and often the Advanced Placement examination will have essay questions about them. The Great Depression and the New Deal responses to it are two of the major historic developments of this century. These events had tremendous social impact on America as well as political, economic, and international impact. They should be considered from each of these viewpoints. Other events occurred in these years that are also very important, but which have not had the impact the above-listed events had.

The *Roaring Twenties* is a phrase describing the 1920s used to cover a variety of events from the political policy of Normalcy, advocated by President Harding, to the Florida land boom. The phrase *New Deal* incorporates many events in the 1930s, largely economic, social, and political. Phrases such as these are important and help to summarize periods but there are other developments of the '20s and '30s that you should be aware of. The division of the country between isolationists and internationalists and the growth of the urban population are two such developments that should be understood, but which are not strictly part of the Roaring Twenties or the New Deal.

The two world wars and the international relations connected with them involve many issues that are likely to appear on the AP examination. The specific events of each war—general strategy and major battles—are important, but of even greater significance are the events surrounding the wars—the causes, the economic and social consequences, and the efforts at peace keeping. Information on some of these aspects of the two wars appears in Chapters 6 and 8. This illustrates how difficult it is to compartmentalize history into units and chapters.

As we move closer to the present, there seem to be more and more details that are included in the history texts. If you look in the average text you will usually discover that the chapters devoted to recent history (i.e., the 20th century) are more detailed and cover shorter periods of time than the earlier chapters. The closer we are to events, the more information we have. For instance, eyewitness accounts are still available, and it is more difficult to see the important and crucial patterns that later historians develop. Therefore, do not be overwhelmed by the factual details of the history of these years, but use your skills to organize the details into your interpretation of the events. In other words, practice being a historian as you work through the history of recent years, establishing your theses and organizing material to support them as you have been doing in writing essays throughout your study. Studying these recent years should be an enjoyable culmination to your study of American history and to your development of skills of historical research. Be your own historian as you pursue information on the following issues:

1. The reasons for the United States' entrance into World War I, the war strategy, and the Treaty of Versailles
2. The Red Scare of the early 1920s
3. The scandals of the Harding administration
4. The effect of the automobile on the economy of the United States and the social habits of its citizens
5. The causes of the Great Crash of 1929 and the Great Depression
6. The New Deal legislation and its impact
7. The New Deal as an economic, social, and political revolution
8. The social changes in Ameria between World Wars I and II
9. The isolationist policies of the United States after World War I and our relations with Europe and the League of Nations
10. The most significant contributions to American social, intellectual, and cultural history in the years between World War I and World War II
11. The coming of World War II in Europe and Asia
12. The strategy of fighting World War II, including wartime conferences, domestic organization, and the founding of the United Nations

Sample Essay Question—Defending a Position

Occasionally you will be asked to *Defend a position* or to *Define* and/or *Identify* a particular viewpoint. Sometimes the question is to *Discuss* the viewpoint. This type of question is not often used on the Advanced Placement examination as it seems to provide less opportunity for the writer to select a position. The meaning of the word *defend* suggests that you are to argue in favor of the position stated and usually you will want to do that when answering this type of question. However, remember than an essay by definition calls for a thesis and you can present a thesis that the position you are asked to defend is indefensible. Normally, in such essay questions the position presented is the one accepted by most historians. However, with the many revisionist schools of American historians who present new and different interpretations of old positions, you may find that you have studied views other than the one presented in the question. Do not be afraid to argue for the revisionist view.

Define and *identify* type questions have the same difficulties. However, you do have more leeway to express your views in a *define* question. For example, the question, "Defend the actions of the British government from 1763-1774 towards the colonies" appears to provide you with little choice but to argue in favor of them, whereas the question, "Define the actions of the British government from 1763-1774 towards the colonies" or "Identify the actions of the British government from 1763-1774 towards the colonies" appears to allow you to make some choice. In all these cases you may formulate a thesis and argue for it in spite of this apparent difference.

A final type of question in this category is the *Discuss* question. "Discuss the relations of the United States government between 1919 and 1941 with Germany and Japan." This seems to ask for a recall of these relations and yet it should be clear by now that you can make a statement of judgment on the relations and then argue it by presenting the evidence. If you include the selective facts concerning United States relations to prove a point, you are discussing these relations.

In all these cases it is important to remember the definition of the word. That is, you must understand how *define* differs from *defend*, how *defend* differs from *discuss*, etc. In each case you can present a thesis and you must have facts to support your position. You must keep in mind what the question is asking in the word used. Both facts and thesis are important in this type question as in all essay questions.

In this chapter, two student answers are given to the question. Read Sample A *before* you read the question. After reading Sample A, write down what you think the question is that the student was answering. This is a very good test of how well the student has understood the question and how well he or she has responded to it in the essay. When you have written down your ideas as to what the question was, read the sample question.

Sample Answer A

Franklin D. Roosevelt was both autocratic and democratic. Roosevelt had to stop a severe depression and had no precedents with which to work. Many of the measures he took provided both relief and long-range reform, which have proven important for the democratization of American life. His first action was to pass the Emergency Banking Act and thus stop the serious runs on the banks. He allowed them to reopen only after passing tests of stability and gave them loans if needed to prevent the run from occurring again. He provided for an insurance of up to $5,000 on future bank deposits.

To help business recover and to provide jobs Congress passed the N.I.R.A., which gave management wide powers of operation, including the suspension of anti-trust cases, as well as assuring labor's rights to collective bargaining. For the farmers, Roosevelt developed two agricultural acts which paid farmers to reduce and store crops.

To help Americans get jobs several acts were passed. The CCC employed 500,000 working on conservation projects. The FWA provided work for thousands making parks and sidewalks. The WPA was established to coordinate the various programs. He also set up the TVA to provide cheap electric power. When the Supreme Court nullified some of what he thought was his greatest legislation, he tried to get Congress to pass a law allowing him to pack the Supreme Court.

Roosevelt also cleverly supported the British while keeping the nation out of war until the Japanese bombed Pearl Harbor. He then provided strong leadership to the nation and the alliance. Although he died before the final victory, his wartime conferences with Churchill and Stalin paved the way for the unconditional surrender of the Nazis and Japanese and for the United Nations.

Obviously, Roosevelt was a great autocratic and democratic president.

Before you read on, write down what you think the question was for this essay.

Sample Answer B

The power of government has two appearances, one during peace and another during war. Because the president is the head of state and the top official within our system, his power also takes on different appearances. In time of national crisis the president seems to be all-powerful. Franklin D. Roosevelt faced two national crises successfully and in the way he handled them has earned the title of our greatest president.

Of course, other presidents have faced crises and handled them well to preserve our freedom and our nation. For instance, George Washington, while establishing the office of president, had to avoid war with England, and Woodrow Wilson kept us out of World War I for three years before finally entering and winning a victory for democracy. Other presidents faced domestic crises, *e.g.,* Andrew Jackson and the nullification issue or Abraham Lincoln and the Civil War, but only Roosevelt successfully confronted major domestic and international crises and thus deserves his title of greatest president.

Roosevelt ruled the country with an iron hand because he realized his New Deal program had to be instigated if America was to recover economically from the Great Depression. His programs, such as the CCC and the WPA, gave Americans an opportunity to work while improvements in the country were also being completed. Roosevelt set up a program to rebuild the banks, including emergency banking legislation and the FDIC to insure private deposits in banks. He also started reforms of agriculture with the AAA and of business with the NRA. The Supreme Court declared much of the legislation unconstitutional and Roosevelt threatened to pack the Court. The Court soon accepted his measures to combat domestic crises. The United States was in need of a strong man who could understand the circumstances and take definite steps towards improving the nation's conditions. FDR was such a man.

Hitler had come to power at the same time as FDR and by the time the New Deal legislation was enacted, Hitler had transformed Germany into a world power. FDR saw the threat but the American people were devoted to neutrality. FDR aided the British secretly after the war began in 1939 and some say that he set the stage for the Japanese attack on Pearl Harbor. In any case, once America was attacked, he led the allies to victory. His foresight laid the foundations for the United Nations, which was begun in San Francisco in 1945 just after his death.

There have been many types of men who have sat in the White House—intellects, lawyers, professional soldiers—some of whom have been strong and some weak. But during certain times, years of war or depression, the man who heads the government must be strong. Franklin D. Roosevelt was such a man. He faced both a major war and a major depression and found solutions to both. He definitely deserves the title of our greatest president.

The above essays were written as answers to the following question:

Sample Question

> "Defend the position that Franklin D. Roosevelt was the greatest president in the history of the United States."

Comments on Sample Question

How close to this question did you come in formulating a question for Sample Answer A? Where did you differ? Did the answer in Sample A seem to relate to this question? If you have not thought of this topic before, you should write your own answer to the question. A formal outline of each student answer will help you compare the two in detail. You will want to read the teacher comments to see how they relate to your own analysis of the two student answers. Before that, however, there is one important point to make concerning this question.

You will note that the information used for Answer B does not come merely from the years 1916 to 1945. This question seems to ask for information on Franklin D. Roosevelt only, but as in the case of Sample Answer B, you may want to refer to other presidents to prove your case in favor of Franklin Roosevelt. You may wish to reject the statement, in which case it would be essential to introduce information concerning other presidents to prove that Franklin D. Roosevelt was not the greatest. You must think about the broadest implications of a question before starting an answer.

Teacher Comments on Sample Answers

Answer A: "The writer has no introduction and it is not clear just what he or she is discussing until the final paragraph of the essay, when he or she presents a statement indicating that Franklin D. Roosevelt was our greatest president. In the body of the essay there is a lengthy discussion of the actions of FDR and the information is accurate. On the basis of the answer, it is hard to know what the question was, yet the answer has sound information which does relate to the question. The writer is factually knowledgeable about Franklin Roosevelt but he or she overlooks the fact that in defending FDR some comment about other presidents who might be considered great would be helpful. From a strictly factual viewpoint, this is a more than adequate answer, but it is a listing of information rather than an interpretation of a question. From that point of view it is a poor answer. It is hard not to reward the student who knows facts but this essay lacks the thesis and statement of the question and should receive a grade in the 4-6 range."

Answer B: "The writer of this essay is more of a generalist than the writer of answer A. He or she has an interesting introduction with a broad opening and a clearly stated thesis. The writer then goes on to consider other presidents who might be considered the greatest but rejects their claims while focusing in on Franklin D. Roosevelt. He or she presents accurate views with some specific information on the New Deal and quickly summarizes the war. The writer thus covers the two crises, one domestic and one foreign, which he or she mentions in the opening. He or she might produce more detailed information but it is clear that the writer has understood the question and knows the presidency of Franklin D. Roosevelt. The conclusion returns to the general philosophical statement at the opening and restates the thesis. The essay clearly was written by a knowledgeable young writer and deserves a score in the top range on the AP rating scale."

Do you agree with these comments? Do you see how the writer in Answer A missed the question yet had very good information? Essay A is an excellent example of what not to do and of the importance of analyzing the question as suggested in the First Step of Essay Writing. Both writers organized the material well but there is more to writing an essay than that, as you are aware of by now. Writer B clearly demonstrates that he or she analyzed the question and is using information to prove his or her thesis. Writer A is simply spilling out information which he or she has learned about Franklin Roosevelt and has made no effort to analyze the question. Such presentations of information without thought are often referred to by Advanced Placement readers as laundry lists. They are reflections of good memorization but not of great thinking.

Practice Essay Questions

The following essay questions require information from the years 1916-1945 and one other period in American history. They should provide a good review of materials studied earlier as well as of the years covered in this chapter.

1. Defend the position that European culture fascinated Americans in the period 1789-1801 and in the period between World Wars I and II.
2. "War has united Americans more closely than any other activity." Discuss this statement and test its validity by references to American history during the years 1812-1824 and 1912-1924.
3. "The social changes of the Jacksonian Period were greater and more profound than the social changes of the post-World War I period." Assess the validity of this statement.
4. "Republicans have been the party of Big Business and depression; the Democrats have been the party of the Little Man and of war." State whether you agree or disagree with this statement and defend your position with reference to World Wars I and II, the Panic of 1893 and the Great Depression.
5. Defend the proposition that "the proposals of the Populists as to how to handle the economic conditions of the early 1890s were not enacted but these proposals provided the framework for the New Deal's response to the economic conditions of the early 1930s."

Comments on Question 1

Question 1 is a typical *Defend a position* type essay question. You are asked to *defend* a particular statement, which may be difficult to do. You are given specific directions as to the two periods you are to discuss. There should be no difficulty understanding what is expected. There may be, however, difficulty in finding factual information to defend this position. When you find yourself in that situation you have two options, first, not to write on the question and, second, to take the opposite view than that expected and argue that the position is not defensible. This is always an option that you have in writing an essay even though the author has clearly stated what you are supposed to do. In an essay you are always, as you learned at the beginning of this book, expected to express your own opinion.

The word "culture" is one of those commonly used words which is rarely defined. It is important to have a concept as to what culture is before answering this question. Culture is defined in *Webster's Eleventh New Collegiate Dictionary* as "the act of developing intellectual faculties, especially by education; a particular state of advancement in civilization and the characteristic feature of such a stage or state." Usually we think of culture as those aspects of society that are not related to economic or political life. In history we often use the expression economic, political and social in describing events or developments. Many people consider social in this phrase as equivalent to culture, but it is not, since culture is the inclusive term under which economic, political, social, and intellectual all fit as this diagram illustrates

culture

economic   political   social   intellectual

Therefore you can include political and economic ideas in your answer, although the usual approach to this question would be to discuss those ideas we usually consider as social and intellectual—matters concerning manners, attitudes, life-styles, literary and artistic development, religious attitudes and the like. Certainly these latter matters should be discussed in your answer to this question but you would not want to narrow your answer to these matters only.

Finally, the question is saying that European ideas were attractive to Americans in the early years of the nation and in the 1920s and 1930s. What is your viewpoint on that question? That is, what is your thesis?

Comments on Question 2

Question 2 is a typical *Discuss* question. There should be no confusion as to what is wanted in an answer. Again the time periods may be difficult, but as mentioned above, the questions in this chapter cover different time periods and are thus excellent review questions for American history since 1789. You have studied all these periods since you began work on this book. How well you can respond to these questions without doing research will provide a good indication of how well prepared you are for the Advanced Placement exam. The generalization in question 2 is an interesting one requiring a new look at or special theses on periods of American history. You should be able to analyze what is needed and prepare a thesis and outline without much difficulty.

Comments on Question 3

Question 3 is a typical *Assess the validity* question. The question focuses on social change and, therefore, unlike the question on culture, you should *not* include economic and political changes except as they might cause social changes. The two periods—the Jacksonian and the inter-war period, especially the 1920s—were times of great change in the American way of life. Which period do you feel had the more profound and greater changes? In a way this becomes a comparison question without using that word. Certainly a comparison of the changes provides the obvious organization for this question. The chief difficulty in question 3 is to determine how one measures "more profound." You would want to make a statement on this in your introduction and perhaps it would provide the wording for your thesis.

Comments on Question 4

Question 4 is another *Generalization* question where the directions are given in detail. You are to state whether you agree or disagree, which, of course, is what a thesis is, and then it tells you to defend your position, which, of course, is what you have been doing in every essay you have written. The directions should be easy and obvious. The time periods are those you have studied most recently, so they should not be too difficult to handle. The items you are to discuss, "World Wars I and II, the Panic of 1893, and the Great Depression," are all ones you should know about in detail. Therefore, you should have the facts for the answer. The major problem in question 4 is the baldness and simplicity of the generalization. It is the type of statement we often hear, but it is so blatantly broad and unthinking that it is hard to deal with. There is truth in it, which you must discover and present. Your introduction will probably include general comments on the generalization; that is, such matters as its simplicity and the meaning of Little Man and Big Business. Your thesis will then present your interpretation of the generalization. How to organize this question is a challenge. When you make your brief notes on the information, a pattern should emerge which will supply the organizational pattern. The question itself supplies no simple, obvious pattern. This is a difficult question in many ways, but the information should be readily at hand.

Comments on Question 5

Question 5 is another variation of the *Defend* question. The directions are given as to what you are to discuss in your answer. The generalization is quite straightforward, and the question should not be difficult to understand. The major problem in this question centers on how specific your knowledge is of the Populist proposals. The chances are you will have detailed knowledge of the New Deal response to the economic conditions of the 1930s. How well can you relate these to the Populist proposals? This again is an excellent review question. Most essay questions on the Advanced Placement exam will not require this much specific information. The detailed information that is required will be taken from the mainstream of American history and should be familiar to you if you have studied the periods of U.S. history emphasized in this book. Several essay questions may require information from social or literary history or the history of minorities but they will relate to mainstream U.S. history.

There should be no difficulty developing a thesis for question 5. An obvious organization is suggested in the directions—discuss "both the Populist proposals and the New Deal's use of them." Following this direction, you would in each paragraph in the body of the paper make a statement of a Populist proposal followed by a discussion of how the New Deal used or failed to use the proposal. This format would give an excellent structure to the essay.

Multiple-Choice Questions—The Value of Sources

In this chapter are six sample questions, the purpose of which is to test your knowledge of different historical sources, of historical bias and interpretation, and of historical research technique. You should be prepared for these questions as a result of your general study and particularly as a result of any research papers you have done. What sources to turn to first, how you recognize bias, where data are stored are all important matters for the historian. Many of the answers are supplied merely by common sense, but many will have been learned or absorbed from your study. Also, as a result of your study you should be aware of the best sources to use in writing history. Read and answer the questions before reading the comments.

**Sample Questions
1-2**

1. In doing research for a history project, to which one of the resources listed below would you turn first if you were seeking information on the text of Franklin D. Roosevelt's First Inaugural Address?
   (A) *Encyclopaedia Britannica*
   (B) Collection of documents of U.S. history
   (C) A biography of Franklin Roosevelt
   (D) *Books in Print*
   (E) *Dictionary of American Biography*

2. In doing research for a history project, which one of the resources listed below would give you the quickest access to information on the current population of New York City?
   (A) *Encyclopaedia Britannica*
   (B) *Guinness Book of World Records*
   (C) A historical atlas
   (D) A world almanac
   (E) *Facts on File*

**Comments on
Question 1**

Questions 1 and 2 test your knowledge of sources used in historical research. The sources listed in question 1 should be familiar to every history student. An encyclopedia includes informative articles on many items and is often a good source as an introduction to a topic. In doing effective research, it would *never* be your only source. There are many collections of documents related to U.S. history. They usually include famous speeches, important congressional legislation, treaties, Supreme Court decisions, and letters. The contents vary according to the point of view of the editor. A biography of Franklin Roosevelt might include excerpts from his speeches but it is unlikely a complete address would be included; again, what is included would depend upon the writer. *Books in Print* is an important source of information on books currently available. They are listed by author and subject. You could find if any works by FDR are in print but his speech would not be in *Books in Print*. The *Dictionary of American Biography* is an invaluable source of information on famous Americans. It includes brief but thorough accounts of the lives of famous Americans. With this description of the sources that were probably familiar to you, the answer to the question should be rather obvious. The text of Franklin D. Roosevelt's First Inaugural Address would most likely be included in a book of documents, which would be the place to look first.

**Comments on
Question 2**

In the choices for question 2 the *Guinness Book of World Records* is an interesting listing of records but most of them have little historical significance. An historical atlas contains maps and charts relating to geography. *Facts on File* is a compilation of many facts using a chronological presentation. It is helpful in checking on recent events but the best place to find the population of New York City would be in a world almanac.

These two questions test your knowledge of sources and your research ability by finding where you would go first for information. It is one method of testing your knowledge of the value of sources.

Sample Question 3

3. If you were involved in a research project on the Teapot Dome oil scandal during President Harding's administration, to which one of the following would you go for the most complete unbiased report on the scandal?
   - (A) A personal friend of the president
   - (B) A newspaper article written when the scandal first was publicized
   - (C) The records of the oil companies involved
   - (D) The complete transcript of the court trial of the men involved
   - (E) A biography of President Harding

Comments on Question 3

Question 3 is a test of your perception or understanding of the reliability of sources. It does not require that you know the details of the Teapot Dome scandal, but that you can determine how biased sources would be. Obviously, a friend of the president would have a particular case to state, as would the writer of a biography. The report of these individuals might be biased either for or against the case. The records of the oil companies would present only one side of the case. The newspaper account, although claiming to be unbiased, is often biased, and one written when the case was just starting would obviously not have a complete record. The complete transcript of the trial would include information on both sides of the scandal and should include all the information available at the time. It would be a good place to begin your research.

Sample Question 4

4. Which of the following would most likely supply you with information on the wealth of the individuals listed on a voting register for a colonial New England town?
   - (A) The Bible in the local church
   - (B) The tombstones in the churchyard
   - (C) The military roster for the town
   - (D) The original charter for the town
   - (E) The local town rolls

Comments on Question 4

Question 4 tests your understanding of where information can be found. Bias is not involved as there is only one place listed where a person's wealth would be recorded. The question is more a test of your knowledge of types of sources than in research. Local town rolls in colonial New England listed the wealth of the citizens for purposes of taxation. The church Bible and tombstones would be a good source of names of citizens and birth and death dates, but they would not reveal wealth. The military roster would supply the names of males and perhaps ages. The original charter of the town would be of no help in learning about the wealth or anything else about the citizens.

Sample Question 5

5. In the 1970s revisionist historians of the Cold War reinterpreted events to suggest that all of the following are true EXCEPT:
    (A)   Truman overreacted to the post-war developments in Greece
    (B)   The Yalta Agreement was a fair document based on historic circumstances
    (C)   The Communists carefully followed a master plan to bring on the Cold War
    (D)   Blame for the Cold War should be split between the Soviet Union and the Western allies
    (E)   Churchill's goal was more the preservation of British power than world peace

Comments on Question 5

Question 5 tests your understanding of historiography. It is the only question in the book so far which does so. You must know what the Cold War is and you must know what that group of historians who are revising the interpretation of the Cold War is saying. The question tests factual knowledge of a very particular and very important kind. It tests your knowledge of historical interpretation, which in turn reveals the types of sources you have used in your study. As your study of American history has progressed, you should have learned of various interpretations of the facts by the leading historians of the different periods and not just the facts. There are standard and accepted interpretations of the major events of American history, and some of these interpretations have been challenged from time to time. Thus, there are recent revisionist schools on causes of the American Revolution and the Civil War, on the character and politics of Abraham Lincoln, on the Turner thesis concerning the significance of the frontier in American history, on Beard's economic interpretation of the Constitution, on the origins of the Cold War, and on many other events. The books in the bibliographies at the end of each chapter will help you in finding different interpretations. Also, the very important "Amherst Series" on *Problems in American Civilization*, published by D.C. Heath & Co. and mentioned in the bibliography in the Introduction, gives different interpretations of major events by outstanding historians. You should understand by now how historians differ in their interpretations of the past. The Cold War historians are reinterpreting the Cold War and suggest that except for C, the choices given are correct.

Sample Question 6

6. If you read the statement, "Violence was a way of life in pre-Civil War southern society," you would be more inclined to accept it as valid if you learned
   (A) the author was a leading southern historian of the pre-Civil War era
   (B) there were more lynchings in the South than in the North
   (C) that on a per capita basis there have been more volunteers for the army from the South than from the North.
   (D) the writer was a trained psychologist and a leading historian of the South
   (E) the statement was quoted in two textbooks and used in a speech by a historian

Comments on Question 6

The last question in this group of examples, question 6, asks you to make a judgment on the reliability of a statement when you know its source. If you read the statement on violence, you might question it and hopefully reject it if it were solely based on the number of lynchings in the South or southern volunteers in the U.S. Army. Also, simply because textbooks quote ideas does not make them true. *Who* said them is crucial! In this case, if "the writer was both a trained psychologist and a leading historian of the South," you *should* be more inclined to accept the statement than if it were simply made by a "leading southern historian." This is an excellent example of the multiple-choice question designed to test the value of sources. As you review the last years of American history, test your ability to judge sources. The closer we are to events, the more possibility there seems to be for rashness of judgment and bias. Read the material you study carefully to check on such rashness and to help prepare yourself for multiple-choice questions of the type presented here.

Practice Multiple-Choice Questions

1. "The world is so deeply divided into opposing classes that social wrongs can only be corrected by revolution" summarizes a position held by many supporters of
   (A) Socialism
   (B) Nazism
   (C) Isolationism
   (D) McCarthyism
   (E) Communism

2. "There is no reason why the United States should be committed to other political units or involved in entangling alliances" expresses the view held by American
   (A) Socialists
   (B) Immigrants
   (C) Isolationists
   (D) Internationalists
   (E) Clergy

3. The first woman to serve in the United States cabinet was
    (A) Frances Perkins
    (B) Oveta Culp Hobby
    (C) Eleanor Roosevelt
    (D) Marian Anderson
    (E) Sandra Day O'Connor

4. The best way to locate the latest research or discussion of a particular topic of current national concern is to consult the
    (A) Index of *Books in Print*
    (B) Editor of your local newspaper
    (C) *Periodical Guide to Literature*
    (D) *New York Times Index*
    (E) Local television station

5.

COMPARISON OF MANPOWER LOSSES IN WORLD WAR I

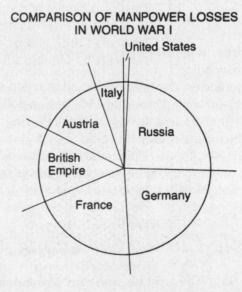

According to the chart above, manpower losses in World War I were
    (A) larger for the United States than for Austria
    (B) greater for Russia than for the British Empire, Austria, and Italy combined
    (C) approximately the same for France, the British Empire, and Italy
    (D) heaviest for the combined Central Powers of Germany and Austria
    (E) approximately equal for Russia and Germany

6. Which of the following legislative acts designed to regulate or control actions of Big Business was part of the New Deal legislative program?
    (A) Clayton Anti-Trust Act
    (B) Sherman Anti-Trust Act
    (C) Federal Securities Act
    (D) Federal Trade Commission Act
    (E) Pure Food and Drug Act

7. Which of the following programs did NOT provide jobs, work opportunities, or direct aid to unemployed or disabled individuals?
   (A) Civilian Conservation Corps
   (B) Federal Emergency Relief Administration
   (C) Works Progress Administration
   (D) National Recovery Administration
   (E) Social Security Program

8. All of the following authors are correctly paired with one of their works EXCEPT:
   (A) Ernest Hemingway—*A Farewell to Arms*
   (B) John Steinbeck—*Grapes of Wrath*
   (C) Eugene O'Neill—*Strange Interlude*
   (D) Sinclair Lewis—*Main Street*
   (E) William Faulkner—*The Great Gatsby*

9. Which of the following developments did NOT occur in the 1920s?
   (A) The first "talking" motion picture
   (B) The development of commercial radio
   (C) The Monkey Trial of John Scopes in Dayton, Tennessee
   (D) The end of Prohibition
   (E) The rebirth of the Ku Klux Klan

10. If you were seeking information on Franklin D. Roosevelt's personal opinions concerning U.S. foreign policy towards Great Britain from 1933-1939, in which one of the following would you be more likely to find the information?
    (A) The Franklin D. Roosevelt Library in Hyde Park, New York
    (B) The National Archives in Washington, D.C.
    (C) The State Department Library
    (D) The Library of Congress
    (E) The British Museum

11.   "For many years numerous Americans have been living in Nicaragua, developing its industries and carrying on business. At the present time there are large investments in lumbering, mining, coffee growing, banana culture, shipping, and also in general mercantile and other collateral business.

    "In addition to these industries now in existence, the Government of Nicaragua, by a treaty entered into on the 5th day of August 1914, granted in perpetuity to the United States the exclusive proprietary rights necessary and convenient for the construction, operation, and maintenance of an oceanic canal. ..."

The above quotation is an example of the United States policy toward Latin America known as
    (A) the Good Neighbor Policy
    (B) the Monroe Doctrine
    (C) Dollar Diplomacy
    (D) Pan-Americanism
    (E) Alliance for Progress

12. Which of the following were events that led directly to the United States involvement in World War I?
    I.   Zimmermann Note
    II.   Russian Revolution of March 1917
    III.   Sinking of the *Lusitania*
    IV.   Unrestricted submarine warfare

    (A)   I, II, and III
    (B)   I, II, and IV
    (C)   I, III, and IV
    (D)   II, III, and IV
    (E)   I, II, III, and IV

13. The United States in the 1920s refused to cancel the war debts of its European allies because the United States
    (A)   wanted to force Germany to pay the wartime reparations
    (B)   needed the money to help pay for economic development at home
    (C)   believed the money paid was needed for loans to Germany
    (D)   considered that all honestly incurred debts should be paid
    (E)   thought debt payment would reduce the arms race in Europe

14. The United States issued a Declaration of Neutrality in 1937 as a result of the
    I.   outbreak of the Spanish Civil War
    II.   growing strength of Hitler in Germany
    III.   Nye Committee's Report on War Profiteering in World War I
    IV.   invasion of Ethiopia by Mussolini's Italy

    (A)   I and II
    (B)   I, III, and IV
    (C)   I and IV
    (D)   II, III, and IV
    (E)   I, II, III, and IV

15. All of the following battles involved American troops EXCEPT:
    (A)   Stalingrad   (D)   Bataan
    (B)   Iwo Jima   (E)   Battle of the Bulge
    (C)   Inchon

16. According to his presentation in the above cartoon, you could assume the artist, Barclay, would support
    (A) the Republicans' not providing direct aid to the unemployed
    (B) the need for slum clearance in Washington
    (C) the Republican interpretation that the depression would be quickly over
    (D) specific action to aid the unemployed
    (E) the Democratic party's program of reform of business

17. An agreement by one group of legislators to support or oppose a particular bill in return for support or opposition for another bill is known as
    (A) balance of power
    (B) logrolling
    (C) bilateral legislation
    (D) a social contract
    (E) a filibuster

18. Which of the following was not a leader of a nation allied with the United States in World War II?
    (A) Winston Churchill
    (B) Charles de Gaulle
    (C) Joseph Stalin
    (D) Benito Mussolini
    (E) Chiang Kai-shek

19.

That's Why It's Not Time for a Change

SOURCE: *Richmond Times Dispatch, November 12, 1944*

In the cartoon, the cartoonist, Fred O. Seibel, is suggesting that
(A)   the colonel has an old-fashioned record player
(B)   Dewey is a poor record salesman
(C)   Virginia will not vote for the Republican candidate for the White House
(D)   Virginia has its own record and is not interested in changing it
(E)   the White House is a loudspeaker for ideas of Virginians

Answers and Answer Explanations

1. E	**2.** C	**3.** A	**4.** C
5. E	**6.** C	**7.** D	**8.** E
9. D	**10.** A	**11.** C	**12.** C
13. D	**14.** E	**15.** A	**16.** D
17. B	**18.** D	**19.** C	

1. (E) The statement in question 1 summarizes a view held by communists in the tradition of Marx and Lenin. There has been some shift away from this "classical view" in recent years in China and the Soviet Union before its disintegration in 1991.

2. (C) Question 2 summarizes the view of American isolationists. It is the opposite of what internationalists believe. Socialists also support cooperation between nations. It is impossible to group immigrants and clergy together to hold any one view.

3.   (A)   Frances Perkins was the first woman appointed to a cabinet post by an American president. She served as Franklin D. Roosevelt's Secretary of Labor. Sandra Day O'Connor was the first woman to serve on the U.S. Supreme Court and was appointed by President Reagan. Eleanor Roosevelt, wife of the president, was active politically and served in the United States delegation to the United Nations after her husband's death. Marian Anderson is a noted black singer who was denied the right to sing in the hall of the Daughters of the American Revolution during Roosevelt's presidency, angering President and Mrs. Roosevelt. Oveta Culp Hobby headed the woman's branch of the Navy during World War II.

4.   (C)   The best source of information on a current national topic is the *Periodical Guide to Literature.* This contains information on all of the latest articles written on a particular matter. It would be more up to date than books, which take longer to appear in print. Therefore, you would consult the *Periodical Guide* before consulting the Index of *Books in Print.* The editor of your local newspaper or your local television station just might have information on your topic but it would be difficult to be certain that they know all of the latest research unless they are experts in the field. The *New York Times Index* would only list articles carried in that newspaper and would not suggest other sources for such information.

5.   (E)   The question is based on a graph of a type not seen so far. It is a pie graph in which a circle is divided into pie slices, each of which represents a percentage of the whole pie. In this chart each slice represents the number of men from the nation named killed in World War I. It provides a quick comparison of the numbers killed. It should be immediately clear from comparing the sizes of the slices that the losses of Russia were greater than those of any other nation, with the United States' losses the smallest. You are not given the actual number killed, only a comparative percentage of the total killed. To compare the percentages in each slice use a ruler, piece of paper, or pencil to measure the distance between the places where the sides of each slice meet the rim of the pie. This segment provides the basis of measurement of the size of each slice. When you do this measurement and then compare the size of the pieces, you will see that the correct answer is E—losses were "approximately equal for Russia and Germany." In fact, the official count of war dead for Russia was 1.7 million and for Germany it was 1.6 million, whereas the United States lost 49,000.

6.   (C)   The Federal Securities Act was part of the New Deal program. The others all came earlier. The Clayton Act and the Federal Trade Commission Act were part of Wilson's New Freedom. The Pure Food and Drug Act was passed in 1906, inspired by the Muckrakers, and the Sherman Anti-Trust Act was passed in 1890.

7.   (D)   One aspect of the New Deal was to provide immediate relief for the unemployed, and each of these acts, except the National Recovery Administration which dealt with business recovery and conditions of labor, provided either direct relief in the form of unemployment benefits or jobs for the unemployed.

8.   (E)   The authors listed in question 8 are all famous writers of the period 1920-1940. Each title mentioned was written in those years, but *The Great Gatsby* was written by F. Scott Fitzgerald, not by William Faulkner. These works all provide important insights into the attitudes of people during these years and

should be read by students of American history. Eugene O'Neill is a playwright; the others mentioned are all novelists.

9. (D)   Prohibition was ended in 1933. Prohibition was in effect during the 1920s. The other developments listed all occurred in the 1920s and reflect different aspects of that very interesting period, the Roaring Twenties.

10. (A)   The five choices in this question are all important depositories of letters and papers dealing with history. The British Museum would be the one least likely to contain F.D. Roosevelt's personal opinions on foreign policy, but it might have some of the Churchill-Roosevelt correspondence. In seeking knowledge of U.S. history you must not confine yourself to American sources only. The Library of Congress, National Archives, and State Department would all have some of the official documents of the Roosevelt years, but the personal correspondence and other personal statements of F.D. Roosevelt would most likely be found in the Roosevelt Library at Hyde Park, which houses his personal papers. Although you might not have been familiar with these five items, you should be able to figure out the best source for information on personal opinions from this list—personal opinions are least likely to be found in official places.

11. (C)   The question is from a message of President Coolidge to Congress, January 10, 1927, in which he sets forth the justification for sending U.S. Marines to Nicaragua at that time. It was a move typical of Dollar Diplomacy and of the attitude of the United States toward Latin America during much of our history.

12. (C)   The Russian Revolution of March 1917 (number II) is not usually considered as an event that led to the United States' involvement in World War I although the establishment of a democratic government in St. Petersburg made Russia a more appealing ally than Tsarist Russia was. Therefore C, which includes I, III, and IV, is correct as those three events are all considered as events that led to our entry into World War I. The Zimmermann Note was a secret message sent by the German Foreign Minister to the German Ambassador in Mexico on March 1, 1917, suggesting an alliance between Mexico and Germany in case the United States entered World War I on the side of the Allies. The message was decoded by the British and turned American sentiment against Germany. When a German submarine sank the British passenger liner The *Lusitania*, 128 Americans lost their lives. After an exchange of messages, German submarine warfare was decreased but its resumption in February 1917 led directly to the Declaration of War on April 7, 1917.

13. (D)   The United States under the Republican leadership of Harding, Coolidge, and Hoover insisted that honestly incurred debts should be paid. With the stock market crash in 1929, Hoover allowed a one-year moratorium on debt payment, but by then it was too late to renegotiate the debts and they were never paid except by Finland.

14. (E)   Question 14 seeks reasons for the U.S. Declaration of Neutrality in 1937 and all four choices offered in I-IV were used as reasons to justify the declaration.

15. (A)   The Battle of Stalingrad was a turning point in World War II. The Russians at Stalingrad stopped the German advance into the Soviet Union without U.S. troops, but with the aid of U.S. supplies. The other four battles involved U.S. troops and are among the most important battles we fought. Iwo Jima was a major step on MacArthur's path back to the Philippines and Japan. The Inchon landings behind the advance of the North Koreans reversed the military balance in the first months of the Korean War. Bataan, a peninsula in the Bay of Manila, fell to the Japanese after a significant holding action which allowed the United States to recover from Pearl Harbor and prepare to wage war in the Pacific during World War II. The Battle of the Bulge was the final attempt by the Germans to prevent the Allied invasion of Germany.

16. (D) The artist, Barclay, is making a comment on the apparent blindness of the Republicans to the fact that there are 15 million unemployed and that living conditions, as depicted in Hooverville, are terrible. He portrays the Republican elephant as blind and insensitive to these conditions. If this is Barclay's idea, then it would seem logical that he would support specific action to aid the unemployed. The other choices do not appear to reflect the viewpoint expressed in the cartoon.

17. (B) When legislators exchange support for each other's special bills, it is called logrolling. The terms are defined in the Glossary.

18. (D) Benito Mussolini was the Fascist dictator of Italy during World War II. The others ruled Allied nations: Churchill — Great Britain; de Gaulle — Free France; Stalin — U.S.S.R.; Chiang Kai-shek — China.

19. (C) The cartoon, drawn by Fred Seibel in October 1944, refers to the Dewey-Roosevelt presidential campaign of that year, when F.D. Roosevelt defeated Dewey winning an unprecedented fourth term. Seibel suggests that the state of Virginia will not vote for Dewey, the Republican (G.O.P.).

Bibliography

Allen, F.L. *Only Yesterday*. New York: Harper-Collins, 1957.

———. *Since Yesterday*. New York: Harper & Row, 1972.

Eisenhower, D.D. *Crusade in Europe*. Garden City: Doubleday & Co., 1990.

Freidel, Frank. *FDR: Rendezvous with Destiny*. Boston: Little Brown, 1991.

Galbraith, J.K. *The Great Crash of 1929*. Boston: Houghton Mifflin Company, 1972.

Goldman, E.F., *Rendezvous with Destiny*. New York: Random House, 1978.

Leuchtenburg, W.E. *Franklin D. Roosevelt and the New Deal 1932–1940*. New York: HarperCollins, 1963.

Lynd, R.S. and H.M. *Middletown*. New York: Harcourt Brace Jovanovich, Inc., 1959.

Perkins, Dexter. *The New Age of Franklin Roosevelt: 1932–1945*. Chicago: University of Chicago Press, 1957.

Schlesinger, A.M. *Crisis of the Old Order*. Boston: Houghton Mifflin, 1988.

———. *The Coming of the New Deal*. Boston: Houghton Mifflin, 1959.

Time Life ed. *World War II: Time Life History of the Second World War*. New York: Prentice Hall, 1989.

Widenor, William C. *Henry Cabot Lodge and the Search for an American Foreign Policy*. Berkeley: University of California Press, 1980.

Fiction

Fitzgerald, F.S. *The Great Gatsby*. New York: Macmillan, 1988.

Lewis, Sinclair. *Babbitt*. New York: Harcourt Brace Jovanovich, Inc., 1989.

Steinbeck, John. *The Grapes of Wrath*. New York: Viking Penguin, 1977.

8 The Post-War Period, the Cold War, and After 1945-1992

Important Facets of This Period

The period after World War II presents many problems for the student of history and for the creators of the Advanced Placement examination. As indicated in the Introduction, since the exam is given in May, those schools that present a chronological history and that continue in session until mid-June will most likely not have studied much of this time period before the May examination. Responding to the problem created by this situation, the Advanced Placement test creators have indicated that, although one-sixth of the multiple-choice questions will be on the time after 1914, very few questions will be on the period after 1970. Likewise, the test creators have indicated that no essay question will focus exclusively on the time after 1970, although in some cases an essay will ask for knowledge of that era as it relates to earlier U.S. history. The 1970 date was set some years ago. It means that such major events as the end of the Vietnam War, Watergate, and the Reagan Presidency will not be the *exclusive* subject of an essay. However, as the years pass this date may be changed. Presently there are multiple-choice questions on post-1970 history. The sample essay questions in this chapter indicate how history after 1970 may be included in essay questions.

Another problem these years present to the student of history is that mentioned in the previous chapter concerning the interpretation of recent events. Until a generation or two has passed it is difficult to be certain what events are important and particularly how these events have truly affected the course of history. For instance, everyone believes the Vietnam War has had a profound impact on American life, but what the impact will prove to be by 2020, when today's high school students are in their 40s is hard to determine. In the meantime, we have a great deal of data about the war to absorb. You need to know the details of war activities, of domestic protest, of presidential politics, of social changes, and all the rest, yet by 2020 the social changes, for example, may have been totally reversed, and we will consider them of little historic significance. Thus, as events recede into the past, we simplify and interpret them to make them more manageable and, we think, more understandable.

Since we are forced to consider all the developments of recent years with equal care, we have much more factual information to absorb. This presents another problem for the history student. One can easily become overwhelmed with the details of the recent past and lose sight of any interpretation or themes. This is particularly true of the years since World War II, during which time the methods of recording information have multiplied so rapidly. Recording devices, copying machines, and television provide us with quantities of factual data we have not had available before. Watergate is an excellent example of how this phenomenon can affect politics and history; Nixon's own tape recordings proved the downfall of his presidency. Sorting out the data to write the simplified history of our time will be a fascinating undertaking, but until it is done, the student has a quantity of information to learn and interpret. The challenge to the student can be exciting and worthwhile, but the amount of raw data does make preparing for the Advanced Placement exam difficult; and that is another reason why the test authors have de-emphasized the period after 1970.

Another matter that makes recent U.S. history more difficult is that from 1941 on U.S. history has really become world history. No longer can we study developments such as those on the frontier and feel we are learning American history. Since 1941 the student must not only know domestic developments, but must also be aware of what has happened to the Soviet Union, what the map of Vietnam looks like, who is ruling France, why the Arab-Israeli conflict seems unresolvable, how the independence of African nations has affected blacks in the United States, and a thousand other points involving nations throughout the world. Until 1941 many Americans and many American decisions ignored these areas. It was probably wrong to do so, but it certainly made American history up to 1941 much easier to study and to understand.

Although the problems stated above make U.S. history more complex, they also offer to the student a chance to be an active historian analyzing primary sources and seeking new information and interpretations. This is excellent practice for the AP examination, especially for the DBQ. As World War II recedes in time, more definitive interpretations of its aftermath are becoming available. The AP examination recognizes this fact and expects the student to be familiar with these interpretations. Many of the trends and concerns of recent years began in the immediate post-World War II era or in the time between the two world wars. Since you are expected to know these time periods on the examination, one helpful way to study the post-World War II period is to analyze it comparing events and trends with those following World War I. Then you should focus your study on the direction the trends took in the more recent past. The trends listed below are some of those that have been identified as significant ones in the post-World War II era.

Some of your study may have to be done in contemporary sources—magazines and newspapers—as some texts will not go up to the present. In fact, if you get in the habit of reading the newspapers and news magazines, this reading will give you a lot of information on recent history; will help your understanding of charts, graphs, and maps; and will often make you aware of events in the distant past, since such events are often referred to in articles. Such reading of newspapers and news magazines is strongly recommended.

Major Trends in U.S. History Since the End of World War II

1. Move toward internationalism—United Nations and treaty commitments
2. The emergence of the United States as world police officer and leader of the free world
3. The development of the Cold War and a sense of the danger of communism
4. The desire for *détente* and cooperation with the U.S.S.R. and other communist nations
5. A concern for undeveloped nations throughout the world
6. A move away from world involvement to a neo-isolationism
7. Greater government control of the business cycle
8. New economic conditions that upset the traditional patterns and understanding of the business cycle, including trade deficits, inflation, and government debt
9. Strong civil rights movements benefiting all minorities

10. A distrust of peoples who can be labeled as different
11. A tremendous growth in service industries, advertising, and general affluence
12. Problems created because a segment of the society continues to be poor and is denied the benefits of affluence
13. Extensive use of natural resources and a growing awareness of the *spaceship Earth*
14. A general distrust of and disillusionment with the political process
15. A growing desire to make government the servant of the people
16. An increasing frankness in human relations and a greater emphasis on free sexual expression
17. A movement to control what is taught in schools and to permit local censorship
18. Exciting experiments in all the arts with debate as to the role of government support for the arts
19. A sense that government is too big combined with a move towards the deregulation of business by government and the desire to cut services and costs
20. An awareness of the interdependence of nations and the threat to life posed by the nuclear arms race, leading to attempts at arms control
21. A perceived breakdown in values with greater emphasis on the individual's wants and on pluralism in society
22. An emphasis on traditional "family" values and conformity to them

As you are aware, there are almost twice as many topics as we have suggested for any other chapter. Also, you can see that many are contradictory, and some might be combined under one heading. These twenty-two trends suggest the complexity and diversity of U.S. history in recent decades. You, the student of history, should be the one to reorder the statements, to narrow them in scope if you wish, and to exercise your historical judgment as to which ones you will study. Based on your study of U.S. history since the start of World War II, what trends do you find? Which ones appear most important to you?

Sample Essay Question—Review

In Chapters 1 through 7 we have presented and analyzed different types of essay questions. We have illustrated the fact that different types of questions are often combined. This means there are innumerable combinations of questions and directions, but in what we have discussed so far, you have been presented with the most important types of essay questions found on the Advanced Placement exam. We have analyzed the different types of questions, and—as you are well aware—this is the first and crucial step in essay writing. In these chapters we have presented sample student essays of varying degrees of excellence for you to analyze. Rather than discuss and analyze another type of essay question in this last chapter, we will present two different questions and one student answer to each. As in all cases so far, we suggest that you write an answer to the question before you read the sample answer and the teacher comments.

Sample Question A

"The Supreme Court's interpretation of the Constitution in the years before the election of Franklin Roosevelt in 1932 made it difficult for the federal government to legislate social policy and changes at the national level, yet from that time until the election of Ronald Reagan in 1980 the situation was reversed." *Assess the validity* of this quotation.

Sample Answer A

The Supreme Court is a very powerful part of the federal government, although it receives much less publicity and notice than the other two branches. In many ways it is the most powerful of the three branches, since the president and congress must abide by its decisions. These decisions are based on the Court's philosophy and interpretation of the Constitution and can change from time to time.

Until the late 1930s the philosophy of the Supreme Court judges and their interpretation of the Constitution made it almost impossible for the president and Congress to obtain "social legislation." By social legislation is meant national laws regulating social and economic relations between individual people, possibly an employer and employee, business person and consumer or starving individuals and those to whom they were forced to turn for handouts.

In 1890 Congress passed the Sherman Act, which forbade any business combination in restraint of (interstate) trade. This act was intended to break up monopolies harmful to the U.S. public and thus was social legislation. However, the Court rendered the act useless by deciding that only those companies that actually and directly controlled interstate commerce were able to restrain interstate commerce and that commerce and manufacturing were separate. In *United States v. E.C. Knight*, the Sugar Trust, a manufacturing company which controlled the sugar industry and whose goods were traded in interstate commerce, was said *not* to affect interstate commerce since control of manufacture did not mean control of trade. Similar interpretations invalidated the Clayton Anti-Trust Act passed by Congress in 1914. Thus, Supreme Court decisions in the early part of the century blocked federal legislation to control big business for the benefit of the people.

In 1916, Congress passed the first child labor act forbidding a company to ship goods in interstate commerce if the company employed children. In *Hammer v. Dragenhart*, a year later, the Court struck down the law as an unjustifiable use of the commerce power to control local labor conditions. A year later, Congress passed a law taxing companies employing child labor. In *Baily v. Drexel Furniture Company*, the Court again struck down the social legislation. Most states eventually forbade child labor, but the Supreme Court had effectively blocked national social legislation in this area.

Even in 1934, at almost the peak of our country's depression, the Court struck down Roosevelt's NIRA in *Schechter Poultry v. United States*. The NIRA had among other things set a minimum wage and a code of fair labor and price policies. This was needed and was beneficial social legislation for the United States, but the Court again seemed to interpret only the literal meaning of the Constitution. Schechter didn't affect interstate commerce directly and therefore the law, which was derived from Congress's commerce power, was unconstitutional.

There were two reasons why the Court had not let Congress pass social legislation. One was because in almost all the laws for social reform, some part or wording of the Constitution was being stretched or broadened. For example, Congress claimed that because the Constitution said "Congress shall have the power to regulate interstate commerce," they had the right to regulate any company involved in interstate commerce even if they sent only 1% of its goods across a state line. They felt that if they once gave such a loose interpretation to the Constitution, Congress would soon be able to justify any law it wished to pass which would be wrong.

The other reason was that the Court was dominated by rather conservative justices who were influenced by the philosophy of Social Darwinism and a laissez-faire approach to economics. These attitudes prevented the Court from regarding social legislation as beneficial to the country.

In the early 1930s the Court continued to uphold its rather literal interpretation of the Constitution. Thus almost no social legislation was approved but most of the decisions were by a 5–4 vote. After the Court invalidated several other items of New Deal legislation, such as the AAA in 1937, Roosevelt attempted to pack the Court, which, although not passed by Congress, scared the Court. Also, one of the elder judges retired and was replaced by a supporter of F.D.R., thus we began to see 5–4 and 6–3 decisions in favor of Roosevelt's social legislation.

The most obvious change in the Court's decisions was in the Bituminous Coal Board case which, indirectly reversing *Carter v. Carter*, said that Congress could regulate the working hours of miners, their pay, and the price of coal. In this case the Court said Congress derived from the commerce power the right to regulate any industry in the best interest of commerce. Moreover, in using any of its powers, Congress could combine other powers with it. In 1941, in *Darby v. United States*, the Court validated a law forbidding child labor, thus reversing its previous position. *Commerce* was defined as totally under congressional control, thus breaking down barriers between state and federal areas of control.

The climax in the Court's change of opinion as to how to interpert the Constituttion probably is marked by *Brown v. Board of Education*, which struck down segregated schools. Although the decision did not involve social legislation, it involved the relations between individuals as established by state and local laws. The case clearly reveals the Court's new position on constitutional interpretation and its support of the individual. The Court interpreted the Constitution loosely and largely based its decision on psychological evidence. This trend continued, and under the leadership of Chief Justice Warren, who retired in 1969, several important decisions, such as that in the Gideon case, gave strong protection to the rights of the individual in opposition to the rights of the state. Later in *Roe v. Wade*, a woman's right to an abortion was upheld. Although, again this was not strictly support of social legislation, it continued the trend established in the 1930s of using the power of government, in this case the courts, to support the individual threatened by large concentrations of power, be they in the hands of private economic corporations or public police departments. After his election, Ronald Reagan called for more conservative decisions, and with his court appointments the court began to reverse itself. The abortion cases of the 1980s and early 1990s clearly illustrate the conservative trend.

The Supreme Court, because of the philosophical position of its members, effectively prevented national social legislation in the early years of the century. After an apparent total reversal of opinion, the Warren Court appeared to be ready not only to approve social legislation passed by Congress, but even to take the lead in bringing on social change. Reagan's appointments reversed this trend, which illustrates that the Court is an important and powerful branch of the federal government.

Teacher Comments on Sample Answer A

"This is an excellent answer to the question on social legislation and the Supreme Court. It is well organized, presents a thesis that is well developed, and contains fine factual details from one of the more specialized area of American history— legal history. The student's definition of social legislation is adhered to in the essay and his or her thesis on the philosophy of the judges and their interpretation of the Constitution is well supported. Only at the end does he or she depart from examples drawn from cases involving strictly social legislation, and the student is aware of this departure and carefully states what might be expected from the Court in the future. The conclusion is well presented as is the introduction, both of which follow well-established techniques for essay writing. This essay would have received a top grade as an answer to this question."

Did you agree with the teacher comments? This answer is one of the best sample essay answers in the book, and was placed here to provide a high standard for comparison now that you have almost completed your study and you have had extended experience writing essays. How did your essay compare with this one? It illustrates how one can effectively use specific information on the exam. You may wish to concentrate on certain areas of study, such as the Supreme Court, when you review for the exam.

This is a typical *Assess the validity* type of question which has been very popular on the AP examination in recent years. What the question was asking for should not have been difficult for you to analyze. Whether you were as well prepared to discuss Court cases and decisions as the writer of the sample essay will depend on how much time you devoted to legal history. You could write an effective answer putting greater emphasis on social legislation and explaining why you believe the trend changed. The directions to the question expect you to deal with issues up to the Reagan years. You should be familiar with some of the recent material if you have read the newspapers and newsmagazines over the past several years. Thus, it illustrates how information from the period after 1970 may be included on the exam. It does not ask you to deal with changes in the Court's decisions that began with the appointment of several conservative judges by President Reagan.

Now let us look at another question and a sample student answer. This question is a good example of the type of essay question you might get on recent history. The question is confined to the post-World War II era and is a clear indication of what a student is expected to know about the period after 1945.

Sample Question B

> In what ways did the administrations of Presidents Eisenhower, Kennedy, Johnson, and Nixon continue the containment policy of President Truman?

Sample Answer B

Americans seem to have a basic fear of those who are different. This has manifested itself often in our history in such occurrences as the Know Nothing Party, the KKK, the Palmer Raids, and the containment policy. The first three were domestic developments directed out of fear against people and ideas that were different. The foreign policy known as *containment*, developed in the Truman years following the ideas expressed in the famous "X" article in *Foreign Affairs*, was a reflection of the fears of the American people and government that the communist Soviet Union (and later China) was a threat to America. The containment policy set by the Truman administration remained the basic foreign policy of the Eisenhower, Kennedy, Johnson, and Nixon administrations.

The containment policy held that the West should meet every aggressive communist move with equal pressure. It became clear that Europe would have to be rebuilt if it were to help in applying this pressure. The Marshall Plan was developed in 1947 to do this. The first clear statement of containment was the Truman Doctrine which, following a Soviet threat to Greece and Turkey, stated the United States would aid any nation threatened by communist power internally or externally. When the Soviet Union blocked the land transportation routes to Berlin in 1948, the Truman administration pushed for the establishment of the North Atlantic Treaty Organization, a mutual defense pact subscribed to by most of the nations ringing the Atlantic area and extending through the Mediterranean to Turkey.

A major test of the containment policy was the Korean War. Truman responded to the invasion of South Korea by sending U.S. troops into battle. Later the United Nations approved of this act and war was fought under the auspices of the U.N. But it was really a U.S. act of containment of communism.

One primary proponent of the policy of containment in later years was John Foster Dulles, Eisenhower's secretary of state. It was Dulles who formed the Southeast Asia Treaty Organization and the Central Treaty Organization, both modeled after NATO and devoted to the purpose of surrounding the Soviet Union and China with U.S. allies.

The foreign aid program was developed to make foreign nations more like us. Aid was given to make undeveloped countries capable of resisting the advances of communism. Foreign aid was first used by President Truman and later by the other four presidents.

It was under Eisenhower that the Domino Theory was first expressed which held that if one country in southeast Asia fell to communism, the other countries would fall like dominoes. The French in Indochina were aided under this reasoning just as the Greek government had been under Truman when we were keeping Greece on our side. This was the beginning of the long U.S. involvement in Indochina to prevent a communist government in Vietnam, Laos, and Cambodia. Other examples of containment at work under the Eisenhower administration were the rearmament of Germany and its admittance into NATO, the maintenance of Chiang Kai-chek on Formosa, the sending of Marines to Lebanon in 1957, and the development of extensive spying techniques exemplified by the U-2. Although there were moves for rapprochement with the Soviet Union toward the end of Eisenhower's administration, the basic foreign policy of the Eisenhower administration was containment by Brinkmanship, Dulles' idea of threatening nuclear retaliation for any aggressive communist moves. We were guided by fear of those who were different from us.

Kennedy enlarged the foreign aid program. The Peace Corps and an increased emphasis upon the Good Neighbor Policy in South America were part of the aid policy. It was rooted in America's fear that Castro's Cuban communism would spread to South America if not blocked by U.S. money. The Cuban missile crisis brought the world to the brink of war, but Kennedy proved that the United States would not permit the Soviet Union to establish a military base in this hemisphere. It was a classic example of the containment policy at work and was designed to keep those who are different out of the country.

Under these four presidents containment became our worldwide policy. Under it lay a fear that other nations, if not like us, would be like the communists. It ranged from Eisenhower's decisions over financing Egypt's Aswan dam project and our involvement in supplying arms to Israel to Kennedy's aiding newly independent African nations to keep them from forming communist governments. In Indochina, the Vietnam War became, with Kennedy's approval of an increase in the amount of military aid to South Vietnam, exclusively an American endeavor to halt the spread of communism.

Kennedy's foreign policy program, cut short by his death, was inherited by Johnson, his successor. The Johnson years were primarily the time of an enlargement of the Vietnam conflict into a full-scale bloody war albeit localized. The Vietnam War was the focus of most of the attention of Johnson's administration and is an excellent example of how he followed the containment policy. Other examples of his pursuing this policy can be seen in the Middle East and in Central America where troops were sent into the Dominican Republic.

Nixon's efforts to end the Vietnam War, to establish good relations with China, and detente with the Soviet Union may appear to go against containment. In reality they were merely other ways of achieving the same goal. Nixon hoped China and the Soviets would contain each other if we were friendlier with each of them.

In conclusion, then, the Eisenhower through Nixon administrations saw the enlargement of the containment policy to include not only western Europe and the Far East, but Southeast Asia, the Middle East, Africa, and South America as well. The programs which have been and are a part of that policy have ranged widely, but the motive behind them has been to block the spread of that fearful quantity known as communism. Each administration has enlarged upon the policies of the previous administration which has served to increase and establish America's position as "police officer of the world." America's motivation in this move to a police officer's role has been fear—fear of international communism.

Teacher Comments on Sample Answer B

"The student essay is a very fine answer to the question. He or she defines the containment policy of the Truman administration and goes on to present excellent examples of the policy in operation under the Eisenhower, Kennedy, Johnson, and Nixon administrations. The student states his or her thesis in the introduction and develops the essay to support it all the way through. The conclusion brings the reader back to the thesis and completes a very effective organization for the paper. Although there are some foreign policy developments in these years that negate the thesis, he or she has chosen to ignore them and to pick very effectively a variety of factual details that do support the thesis. The essay is perhaps longer than the average one, but it is the quality, not the length, which makes this an outstanding answer."

Would you have made the same comments as the teacher did on this answer? As with the first essay, it is a good answer and was placed here to provide a high standard for you as you finish the book. It demonstrates what a student can do with a question based on post-World War II material. Both answers are longer than the average Advanced Placement examination answer. The answer could be condensed by including fewer examples from each administration but if you have the time, include all the evidence you can but do not simply give a laundry list of facts—interpret the question and pick the facts which relate to it.

As you realize, Question B is a version of the *What?* type of essay question. You should have had no difficulty in analyzing and answering the question. By now, with our consideration of basic types of essay questions and with the many essays you have written, you should be well prepared for the essay and DBQ parts of the Advanced Placement exam. You can test your readiness by taking the sample exam in the Appendix. While you are practicing with that exam and when you take the Advanced Placement exam in American History, never fail to use the Seven Basic Steps in Essay Writing:

First — Analyze the question
Second — Make brief notes or outline
Third — Develop your thesis
Fourth — Write the introduction
Fifth — Write the body of the essay
Sixth — Write the conclusion
Seventh — Reread the essay–Introduction, Body, Conclusion

And do not forget the flashlight image.

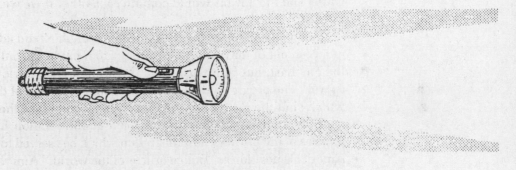

Practice Essay Questions

The following practice essay questions require knowledge of the period since 1945 and one other period from American history. The questions represent different types of essay questions presented in the text. These five questions thus provide an excellent review for the Advanced Placement examination.

1. "... almost all the defects inherent in democratic institutions are brought to light in the conduct of foreign affairs." Evaluate this statement from *Democracy in America* by Alexis de Tocqueville (1835), and compare the conduct of U.S. foreign affairs from 1961 to 1973 with its conduct from 1931 to 1941.

2. How do you account for the fact that in the Populist era both state legislation and federal Supreme Court decisions went against the civil rights of minorities, whereas in the period 1954–1974, both national legislation and federal Supreme Court decisions have supported the civil rights of all Americans?

3. Describe three economic reform measures passed as part of the New Deal Program of the 1930s and explain their importance to the economic growth of the post-World War II period.

4. Compare the efforts for international cooperation and peace in the twenty years after World War I with those efforts for international cooperation and peace pursued in the twenty years after World War II. Why do you believe the latter were more successful in preventing a world war?

5. "Americans have learned that divisive military activity weakens the social life of a democratic society and precipitates moral and ethical decline." *Assess the validity* of this quotation by referring to both the Civil War and the Vietnam War and to both post-war periods.

Comments on Question 1

The first sample essay question is a standard combination type in which an *Evaluate this statement* type is combined with a *Compare* type. The *Compare* part provides specific directions as to what periods of time you are to consider and suggests a chronological organization. You may well decide, however, that a different approach in which similar situations in each of the two time periods are compared and/or contrasted would be a more effective way to organize the material.

The two time periods are interesting and provided real tests of American democracy. The 1930s saw the rise of Hitler and the Japanese aggression in Asia while the 1960s included the Vietnam War and the intensification of the Cold War. Nixon resigned in 1973. The statement itself makes use of an observation by that most astute and perceptive Frenchman, Alexis de Tocqueville, who wrote an outstanding commentary of American life in 1835. His *Democracy in America*, although rather slow reading for present-day students, should be read by all who consider themselves scholars of America's past. This quote is typical of his sharp analysis and clear perception of life in the United States in the Jackson era, much of which is still applicable to the nation today. Do you agree with this statement of de Tocqueville's? What will your thesis be? You should be able to decide on one rather easily by following the usual essay writing technique, since the statement does not include very complicated vocabulary.

Comments on Question 2

The second question is the familiar *How do you account . . .* type. This question asks about the change in attitude toward civil rights and minorities as seen in legislation and Supreme Court decisions between the Populist Era (1890-1898) and the period 1954-1974. Two words—*state, national*—in the question may provide a key to interpretation. For the Populist Era, *state* legislation is mentioned; for the more recent period, *national* legislation is referred to. Why? When you decide on your answer to that you will probably have both your thesis and very likely your organizational pattern. The question focuses on a very important aspect of recent history. You will want to include both the civil rights legislation of the Johnson era and also Supreme Court decisions in the 1954 *Brown v. Board of Education* case (desegregation of schools), the Miranda case (rights of the suspect) and the 1974 *Wade v. Rowe* (women's rights to privacy and abortion).

Comments on Question 3

Question 3 is a *Describe . . . explain* question that asks you to analyze the economic reforms of the New Deal in light of the importance of recent economic history. It will probably force you to take a new and different look at both the New Deal and recent economic history before you will be ready to answer the question. There has not been a great deal of emphasis placed on cause-and-effect relationships between the New Deal reforms and post-war prosperity. It appears to be a rather difficult, narrow, and specialized question, but the general topic— economic history—has been very important in the past sixty years. How much have you learned? Are you ready yet to answer this question? The wording of the question is not complicated, so your analysis should not be difficult, but you may have real difficulty making brief notes without further research. Do not worry if you are not ready to answer this question. On the exam you can assume there will be at least one question on a topic with which you are not familiar, so do not get upset when you find a question you cannot answer. The most logical organization for this question is that discussed for other *Describe . . . explain* type questions in Chapter 2.

Comments on Question 4

The fourth question focuses on the important issue of peacekeeping and uses a *Compare* type of question to get you to make decisions about international cooperation after the two world wars of this century. The question concludes with a second part, a *Why?* part, which forces you to make a judgment as to why we have been able to avoid World War III. The information needed to answer the question should be part of your knowledge of the history of this century. What your thesis will be, however, and how you organize the materials is open to many possibilities. The question falls easily into a description of post-World War I and then post-World War II methods followed by your reasons for the latter avoiding World War III. On the other hand, you might begin with how war has been avoided and use illustrations from the post-war periods to explain the failure in one era and success in the other in avoiding war. This latter organization would provide an exciting essay, but it would require careful thought before writing to determine those successful peacekeeping moves. This is a good question for 20th-century history.

Comments on Question 5

The last sample question is based on a quotation dealing with the moral and political life of our nation. The familiar directions *Assess the validity* have been expanded to include directions to refer to two periods of time. The two wars were very divisive—a civil war is divisive by definition—and many interesting parallels and contrasts come to mind as you consider the two post-war periods—for instance, the scandals of the Grant and Nixon administrations. The question should not be hard to analyze, although the word *divisive* may not be familiar. It is an adjective meaning divided. No dates are given so you must recall the time period of each war—this is why a time line is important. The question focuses on social life rather than the more familiar economic or political activity. You can expect at least one question on the Advanced Placement examination to deal with history other than from a political or economic viewpoint. If you have included any social history in your study you should be able to deal with this question. The question certainly invites a range of theses and a variety of organizations. It is a wide open question dealing with the important issue of war and social life and morality—crucial and recurring issues in history and thus a very good one with which to end this study of essay questions based on American history.

These five questions, as well as those in Chapter 7, provide an excellent review of American history. If you are able to answer them in effective, well-organized essays without additional research, you should be suitably prepared for the Advanced Placement exam.

Multiple-Choice Questions—Vocabulary

Throughout this book we have taken care to define special words used in the questions. Every student of history must know the vocabulary used by the historian. In Part One we suggested keeping a vocabulary list. Throughout the book, questions, both essay and multiple-choice, have indirectly been introduced that tested your specialized history vocabulary.

Every subject has its own vocabulary. You become particularly aware of this when you study a foreign language or begin studying a new field—biology, for instance, has a very specialized vocabulary. Often the student studying history or English does not realize that there is a specialized vocabulary for these subjects because the student has usually used or heard the words all his or her life. We have saved this topic for last because most of the vocabulary you will need will have been absorbed without effort, and there is no need to make an issue of an obvious matter. We have often defined terms, such as *embargo*, and to aid you in your vocabulary development, there is a Glossary included at the end of the book. It is not a list to memorize, but illustrates the types of words you should know and provides a starting place for expanding your vocabulary. If you followed the suggestions for vocabulary building in Part One, you should have your own extensive list by now that should enable you to answer the sample questions below.

The following multiple-choice questions illustrate several ways in which your knowledge of historical terms may be tested directly on the Advanced Placement exam. It should be obvious, however, that your vocabulary will be tested throughout the exam on every question.

Sample Question 1

1. One who moves from place to place seeking agricultural employment is referred to as a (an)
   - (A) displaced person
   - (B) serf
   - (C) migrant worker
   - (D) unemployed agriculturist
   - (E) veteran

Comments on Question 1

Question 1 is a straightforward one in which a definition of a word is presented followed by five choices of words for which you are to pick the correct word for the definition. You are probably familiar with this type of question from English examinations. In this question the correct answer is "migrant worker." If you did not know the term, you might have known other words related to *migrant*, such as *migratory*, *migration*, or *immigration*. In all three words, movement is involved; the phrase *moves from place to place* in the definition might lead you to the word *migrant*. Combining with this the fact that *employment* means work, you would have a good chance of picking "migrant worker" as the correct answer. You might also know the meaning of the other words, thus eliminating them. You can check the meaning of these other words in the Glossary.

Sample Question 2

2. A scalawag was a southern white who after the Civil War believed
   - (A) in segregation
   - (B) in cooperation with blacks and northerners
   - (C) all southern whites should be paid for their freed slaves
   - (D) secession was still legal
   - (E) all blacks should be sent back to Africa

Comments on Question 2

The second question reverses the order of the first and provides a term in the question and five choices for a correct definition. The term *scalawag* was applied to southern whites who cooperated with the freed blacks and northerners in the period after the Civil War. The term is often used in discussing the Reconstruction period. There are groups who believed in the other four choices. *Segregationists* and *Secessionists* are specific terms to refer to the other two groups. The chances are that to answer this question you would have to know the term *scalawag*. It is specialized, but you might have been able to deduce the definition by eliminating several of the choices.

Sample Question 3

> 3.   Which of the following terms is used to refer to the foreign policy of the
>   United States in the years 1844-1850?
>   (A)   Manifest Destiny   (D)   Isolationism
>   (B)   Détente   (E)   Brinkmanship
>   (C)   Alliance for Progress

Comments on Question 3

The third question combines a knowledge of historic periods with a definition of terms. In order to answer the question you must know what the foreign policy of the United States was during the years 1844-1850 and then you must be able to relate it to a specific word. All the choices relate to American foreign policy at different periods. You should recognize them and thus you would have no trouble identifying "Manifest Destiny" as the correct answer. This is a very common expression used in texts to describe U.S. foreign policy of the mid-1840s. The other words can be found in the Glossary. Before studying American history you were probably not familiar with these terms and you would have had difficulty with the question, but the chances are you know all or enough of them now so that you could eliminate most of the choices.

Sample Question 4

> 4.   If you lived in a city slum in the 1890s, the building in which you lived
>   would most likely be a
>   (A)   megalopolis   (D)   trust
>   (B)   condominium   (E)   tenement
>   (C)   skyscraper

Comments on Question 4

Again, question 4 combines a knowledge of specific historic periods with an understanding of words. As in the first and third questions, the definition is given in the question and the choices are of words to fit the definition. In this question the words *city*, *slum*, *1890s*, and *building* should combine to give you the answer—"tenement." *Condominium* is a more recent word for middle- and upper-class apartment houses. A skyscraper, a particular type of tall building usually used for offices, was developed in the 1890s, but not in slums. Trusts were formed in the 1890s, but they were large businesses, and *megalopolis* is a 20th-century term used to describe a huge, sprawling urban center and not a building. If you could not identify "tenement" as the correct answer immediately, you could probably arrive at the answer by eliminating the other terms, which should be part of your specialized history vocabulary.

Sample Question 5

> 5. In the United States today a person who said, "Each state is sovereign" probably means each state has the right to
>   (A) coin money
>   (B) make treaties with other states
>   (C) reject decisions of the Supreme Court
>   (D) raise an army
>   (E) declare war

Comments on Question 5

The last question is a little more complicated in form, but essentially it does what question 2 did. A word is presented in the question and the choices test your understanding of the word. *Sovereign* means ruler or the right to rule yourself. A sovereign nation, such as the United States, can coin money, make treaties, raise an army, and declare war, but in the United States, since the Civil War, it has been established that no state can do those things and very few people advocate that states do them, but many people do believe a state is sovereign in the United States to the extent that it can reject decisions of the Supreme Court. This question tests a very specialized understanding of a very important word.

These five examples illustrate ways in which vocabulary can be specifically tested on the Advanced Placement examination. It is important to remember, however, that all questions on the exam will require a history vocabulary, so be sure to study the Glossary and develop your own vocabulary list.

Practice Multiple-Choice Questions

The following questions illustrate the type of questions one might be asked concerning events since World War II. Remember, however, that only one-third of the multiple-choice questions on the examination will be on the post-1914 period and that not many will be on the post-1970 era. Thus the time period discussed in this chapter, 1945 to the present, will receive less emphasis on the Advanced Placement examination than other time periods. Most of the multiple-choice questions on the period after 1945 will cover the years 1945-1970. These sample questions, however, include many questions of the post-1970 period in order to stimulate your thinking on this period and to illustrate what type of questions *might* be asked on very recent history.

These are the last practice multiple-choice questions in the book. As you begin this final set of practice questions, remember that it is important to read the entire question and all the answers carefully. Do not guess at answers unless you can eliminate several of the possible choices.

1. All of the following individuals are correctly paired with the organization with which they are usually connected EXCEPT:
   (A) Martin Luther King, Jr. — Southern Christian Leadership Conference
   (B) Ralph Nader — Black Panthers
   (C) Malcolm X — Black Muslims
   (D) César Chavez — United Farm Workers of America
   (E) Betty Friedan — National Organization for Women (NOW)

2. All of the following occurred after the fall of the Berlin Wall in 1989 EXCEPT:
   (A) The beginning of Peristroika and Glasnost
   (B) The breakup of the Soviet Union into separate nations
   (C) The outbreak of warfare in Yugoslavia
   (D) The emergence of President Yeltsin as the leader of Russia
   (E) The support of the Russian economy by the International Monetary Fund

3. The Cold War included many events and among them are the
   I.   Cuban missile crisis
   II. U-2 incident
   III. Marshall Plan
   IV. Operation Second Start
   (A) I and II
   (B) I, II, and III
   (C) I, III, and IV
   (D) I and IV
   (E) I, II, and IV

4. One of the chief reasons Americans were willing to accept membership in the peacetime NATO Alliance was because of the
   (A) Truman Doctrine
   (B) Hungarian Revolution
   (C) Berlin Blockade
   (D) Berlin Wall
   (E) Bay of Pigs

5. Since World War II U.S. troops have been sent to the Near East to protect United States interests in Lebanon and the Persian Gulf by United States presidents
   (A) Eisenhower, Nixon, and Bush
   (B) Eisenhower, Kennedy, Nixon, and Bush
   (C) Eisenhower, Ford, Reagan, and Bush
   (D) Eisenhower, Reagan, Carter, and Bush
   (E) Kennedy, Carter, and Bush

6. In retaliation for a supposed attack on U.S. destroyers, the U.S. Congress authorized President Johnson to take any action he deemed necessary to deal with the crisis when they voted
   (A) for My Lai
   (B) the War on Poverty
   (C) support of Escobedo and Miranda
   (D) ICBMs
   (E) the Tonkin Gulf Resolution

7. All of the following terms became part of the American political vocabulary in the 1960s EXCEPT:
   (A) *pig*
   (B) *hippie*
   (C) *dove*
   (D) *flapper*
   (E) *black power*

8. On the map at the right, Vietnam is numbered
- (A) 1 and 2
- (B) 2, 3, and 4
- (C) 2 and 4
- (D) 1, 2, 4, and 5
- (E) 4 and 5

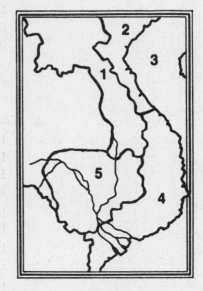

9. All of the following measures were enacted by Congress as part of President Lyndon Johnson's Great Society program EXCEPT:
- (A) establishment of the Department of Housing and Welfare
- (B) abolition of immigration quotas based on national origin
- (C) voting Rights Act of 1965
- (D) the Taft-Hartley Act
- (E) Medicare

10. A major foreign policy achievement of Jimmy Carter's administration was
- (A) the withdrawal of U.S. troops from Vietnam
- (B) the breakup of OPEC
- (C) the overthrow of the Shah of Iran
- (D) the Camp David Accords for Near East peace
- (E) the purchase of the Panama Canal

11. The Supreme Court under Chief Justice Earl Warren was noted for its decisions regarding segregation and the
- (A) rights of the police to punish criminals
- (B) protection of individual rights in criminal cases
- (C) defense of the death penalty
- (D) support of presidential authority
- (E) limit of federal authority in the War on Poverty

12. The 1973 Supreme Court decision in the case of *Roe v. Wade*
- (A) marked the end of the Court's liberal view in support of the rights of suspected criminals
- (B) was strongly opposed by the National Rifle Association
- (C) was very controversial and precipitated strong political reactions both pro and con
- (D) was endorsed by Presidents Reagan and Bush
- (E) was the Court's most sweeping decision in favor of civil rights

13. Which of the following developments relating to nuclear power for military purposes occurred last?
    (A) The signing of the INF Treaty
    (B) The Brinkmanship policy of John Foster Dulles
    (C) The START talks
    (D) The SALT talks
    (E) The Nuclear Test Ban treaty

14. All of the following were characteristic of the 1960s EXCEPT:
    (A) increasing computerization of industry
    (B) Pop Art
    (C) the Beatles and rock-n-roll
    (D) adult movies stressing sex and nudity
    (E) an increase in the quality and number of dramatic programs produced by American T.V.

15.

PERSONS IN POVERTY

Family Situation	Number of persons in millions in given family situations who are poor over total number of persons in that situation.		
	White	Non-White	Total: All Races
Individuals Living Alone	4.0	.08	4.8
	10.8	1.6	12.4
Members of Family Units	16.3	8.5	24.8
	159.6	21.4	181.0
TOTAL Both Situations	20.3	9.3	29.7
	170.4	23.0	193.4

According to the table above for 1966, all of the following statements are true EXCEPT:
    (A) There were more whites living in poverty than non-whites.
    (B) If you are non-white and live alone you have a 50-50 chance of being in poverty.
    (C) Your best chance of avoiding poverty is to be born in a white family.
    (D) More unrelated individuals live in poverty than do members of families.
    (E) Although the total number in poverty for whites is greater, there is a higher percentage of poverty among non-whites.

16. In his first year in office, President Reagan tackled the issue of inflation by
    (A) establishing a Department of Energy
    (B) encouraging Congress to pass a new tax law reducing income taxes
    (C) stopping U.S. military and economic aid to Taiwan
    (D) repealing the minimum wage law
    (E) increasing military support for terrorist activities

Answers and Answer Explanations

1. B	**2.** A	**3.** B	**4.** C
5. D	**6.** E	**7.** D	**8.** C
9. D	**10.** D	**11.** B	**12.** C
13. A	**14.** E	**15.** D	**16.** B

1. (B)   Ralph Nader founded Public Citizen, Inc., an organization that focused on consumer protection. He was not connected with the Black Panthers, who were organized as an activist Black Power group by H. Rap Brown. The other individuals are correctly linked with their organizations, all of which were very important in the Civil Rights Movement of the 1960s and 1970s.

2. (A)   President Gorbachev of the Soviet Union introduced his reform policies of Peristroika and Glasnost soon after his rise to power in 1985. Many believe these policies led to the fall of the Berlin Wall and the end of the Cold War. After the wall fell, a failed coup in the Soviet Union led to the emergence of Yeltsin as the leader of Russia, and the Soviet Union broke up into separate nations. These countries then applied to the International Monetary Fund for support for their economies. Meanwhile, with the end of communism in eastern Europe, Yugoslavia broke into separate nations and warfare between them erupted.

3. (B)   The Cuban missile crisis in President Kennedy's administration, the U-2 spy plane incident during President Eisenhower's administration, and the Marshall Plan begun under President Truman are all events in the Cold War. Operation Second Start was part of President Johnson's War on Poverty.

4. (C)   The Berlin Blockade by the Russians in 1948 was met by a successful airlift of supplies to the beleaguered city. The Soviet action seemed to confirm the danger to the West and to world peace of the communist nations. The result was that the United States was drawn to join a newly formed alliance of Britain, France, and the Benelux nations. This alliance became NATO, our first peace-time alliance since George Washington warned the nation against entangling alliances in his Farewell Address. NATO marks a major shift in U.S. foreign policy. The other items were all Cold War events which helped to confirm the need for the NATO alliance.

5. (D)   U.S. troops have been sent to Lebanon or the Persian Gulf since World War II by Presidents Eisenhower, Carter, Reagan, and Bush. Eisenhower declared the Eisenhower Doctrine to protect our interests in the Near East and sent troops to Lebanon. Carter sent troops in an attempt to rescue the American hostages in Teheran, Iran. Reagan again sent troops to Lebanon. Bush organized Operation Desert Storm through the United Nations and sent troops to force Iraq out of Kuwait. Kennedy sent troops to Vietnam but not to the Near East. Ford and Nixon sent no troops to the Near East.

6. (E)   The Tonkin Gulf Resolution, passed by the U.S. Congress in August 1964 after it was reported that two U.S. destroyers were attacked in the Tonkin Gulf, gave the president authority to take any action he deemed necessary for dealing with the crisis. The Resolution was used to justify the entire U.S. involvement in Vietnam without a declaration of war. The other items relate to different developments since 1960.

7. (D) *Flapper* was a term used in the 1920s to describe the ideal young woman of the period. The other terms are all from the 1960s and have political connotations. *Pig* was used to refer to police; *hippie* was used to describe those young people in the 1960s who first adopted long hair and unisex clothing and who rejected many of the materialistic values of U.S. society; a *dove*, as opposed to a *hawk*, was against U.S. involvement in Vietnam; *black power* was the slogan of some civil rights activists.

8. (C) On the map of the Indochina Peninsula, 2 is North Vietnam and 4 is South Vietnam so the correct answer is C — Vietnam consists of both North and South Vietnam. It does not include Cambodia, which is number 5, and Laos, which is number 1. Three is the South China Sea.

9. (D) President Johnson's Great Society involved many different programs ranging from Medicare to the establishment of the Department of Housing and Welfare. Although the president wanted some revisions in the Taft-Hartley Labor Act, Congress never voted them and the Act, passed over Truman's opposition in 1947, remained in force.

10. (D) The Camp David Accords, which led to the Peace Treaty between Egypt and Israel, were negotiated by President Carter, using his personal persuasion. President Nixon withdrew U.S. troops from Vietnam. OPEC is still in existence as this book goes to press and shows no signs of breaking up. The overthrow of the Shah of Iran is not considered an achievement of the U.S., and we rent but do not own the Panama Canal.

11. (B) The so-called Warren Court is noted for its concern for the rights of all individuals. Many right-wing groups strongly opposed some of the decisions and called for the impeachment of the chief justice, but the Court continued to support the rights of individuals in criminal cases (for example, *Escobedo, Gideon, and Miranda* cases) and desegregation cases (for example, *Brown v. Board of Education*).

12. (C) The Supreme Court decision in *Roe v. Wade* supported a woman's right to abortion during the first trimester of pregnancy. It was a very controversial decision and brought reaction in the political arena where pro-life and pro-choice groups became active. The decision was based on the "right to privacy" and not civil rights. It had nothing to do with the rights of suspected criminals. The National Rifle Association, although an active pressure group, had nothing to say about this decision. Presidents Reagan and Bush opposed the decision and worked to have it overturned.

13. (A) The INF Treaty outlawing intermediate-range nuclear weapons in Europe was signed by Gorbachev and Reagan in December 1987 in Washington and was approved by the Senate and the government of the U.S.S.R. in May 1988. It is the most recent of the developments listed. The START talks between the Soviet Union and the United States on the issue of nuclear disarmament were begun by President Reagan early in the 1980s after the SALT II Agreement negotiated by President Carter and the Soviet Union was not accepted by the United States Senate. The Nuclear Test Ban Treaty was signed in 1963 and Brinkmanship was U.S. policy in the 1950s under Eisenhower.

14. (E) Increased use of computers, Pop Art, rock-n-roll, and adult movies were all characteristic of U.S. culture in the 1960s. Higher quality dramatic T.V. programs were not.

15. (D) The table used for this question presents a different type of chart or graph than has been used so far. It presents information by two categories — first white and non-white; second, living alone and in family units. In the columns it presents information about the totals in these categories for all races and both living situations and finally presents in the lower right-hand corner a grand total indicating all those in poverty. If you read the titles of each column carefully and understand that the fraction represents the total number of persons in each category as the denominator (bottom number) and the number of persons in poverty in each category as the numerator (top number), then you would realize that all the choices except D, "more unrelated individuals live in poverty than do members of families," are correct.

16. (B) During his first year in office President Reagan very successfully pressured Congress into passing a massive income tax cut — a key point of Reaganomics. It was part of his administration's attack on the high inflation rate. Reagan was desirous of eliminating the Department of Energy and not of creating one, of reducing the minimum wage for teenagers but not for everyone, of supporting aid to Taiwan, and of blocking the activities of terrorists and not of supporting them.

Bibliography

Barrett, L.I. *Gambling With History: Ronald Reagan in the White House*. New York: Viking Penguin, 1984.

Bernstein, Carl and Woodward, Bob. *All the President's Men*. New York: Simon and Schuster, Inc., 1974.

Dinnerstein, Leonard and Reimers, David M. *Ethnic Americans, A History of Immigration*. New York: HarperCollins, 1987.

Donovan, R.J. *Tumultuous Years: The Presidency of Harry S. Truman 1949–1953*. New York: W.W. Norton & Co., 1982.

Ganley, A.C., et al. *After Hiroshima: America Since 1945*. White Plains, NY: Longmans, 1985.

Hagstrom, Jerry, ed. *Beyond Reagan: The New Landscape of American Politics*. New York: Viking Penguin, 1989.

Halberstam, David. *The Best and the Brightest*. New York: Fawcett World Library, 1973.

Halle, Louis J. *Cold War as History*. New York: HarperCollins, 1991.

Karnow, Stanley. *Vietnam: A History*. New York: Viking Penguin, 1984.

Kennedy, R.F. *Thirteen Days*. New York: W.W. Norton & Co., 1969.

King, M.L., Jr. *Why We Can't Wait*. New York: NAL Dutton, 1991.

Parker, Thomas. *America's Foreign Policy 1945–1976: Its Creators and Critics*. New York: Books Demand UNI, 1991.

Salisbury, Harrison E. *Vietnam Reconsidered: Lessons from a War*. New York: HarperCollins, 1985.

Sitkoff, H. *The Struggle for Black Equality: 1954–1980*. New York: Hill and Wang, 1981.

White, T.H. *The Making of the President 1960*. New York: Macmillan, 1989.

Williams, Juan. *Eyes on the Prize*. New York: Viking Press, 1986.

Memoirs

Acheson, Dean. *Present at the Creation*. New York: W.W. Norton & Co., 1987.

Carter, Jimmy. *Keeping Faith: Memoirs of a President*. Toronto: Bantam Books, 1982.

Harris, William H. *The Harder We Run: Black Workers Since the Civil War*. New York: Oxford University Press, 1982.

Kissinger, Henry. *The White House Years*. Boston: Little Brown & Co., 1979.

MacArthur, D. *Reminiscences*. New York: McGaw-Hill, 1964.

Malcolm X. *Autobiography*. New York: Grove Press, 1965.

Taking the Advanced Placement Examination: A Summary of Things to Remember and to Do

Points to Remember About the Exam: A Summary

**Multiple-Choice Section
The Questions**

The exam consists of 100 multiple-choice questions. You have 75 minutes in which to answer them. You should keep moving through the questions at a steady pace. If you come to a question that is difficult or confusing, make a checkmark (√) by the question in your question booklet and go on to the next question. When you have finished the 100 questions, you can come back to those you have skipped. The checkmark by the question will help you quickly identify those you skipped.

Material Covered

The questions will test factual knowledge and, in the "stimulus" questions, analytical skills. Approximately one-third of the questions will cover political history, one-third will cover social and economic history, and the remaining one-third will cover other issues such as diplomatic, intellectual, and cultural history. One-sixth of the questions will come from the period prior to 1789, one-half will come from 1789-1914, and one-third will come from 1914 to the present.

Grading

The difficulty of these questions is such that if you answer about 60 percent correctly, you'll receive a grade of three which ranks you as "qualified" on the AP examination.

Thoughtless guessing of answers should be avoided, as one-fourth of a point is deducted for each incorrect answer. However, if in analyzing the question you can eliminate one or two of the five possible choices, selecting what appears the best answer from the three or four choices remaining is recommended.

The Answer Page

Answers to the questions are indicated on your answer page by filling in a small space with a number 2 lead pencil. You should bring at least two sharpened number 2 pencils to the exam. When you skip a question, be sure to leave that space blank on the answer sheet until you come back later. If you realize you have made an error in filling in the spaces, do not panic. Make a note where you realized your mistake, start marking the answers correctly at that point and finish the multiple-choice section. Speak to the test administrator when the multiple-choice question part of the exam is over and tell your teacher when you next attend class. If the Advanced Placement Program Director at the College Board, 45 Columbus Ave., New York, NY 10023-6992, is notified immediately, preferably by phone (212-713-8000), your answer sheets will be hand corrected, not machine corrected.

Essay or Free Response Section

Time

There are two essays to be written in Section 2 of the examination. There is a fifteen-minute required period in which you should read the questions, analyze the documents, and briefly outline your answer(s). You then have 40 minutes to write your answer to Part A — the DBQ — and 50 minutes to write your answer to Part B—one of the five essay questions. You should bring two pens to the exam, since you should write the essays in ink.

DBQ: Section 2, Part A

Remember, the purpose of the DBQ is to test your analytical skills *and* your understanding of "mainstream" American history. You must analyze the question, then read the documents and determine how they relate to the question and to the traditional, chronological history of the period from which they come. In your answer you need to weave together information from both these sources. You should not simply recite what is in the documents.

In writing your DBQ answer you should refer to the documents by the author or sources but try not to quote long passages. Paraphrase the main ideas and discuss *how* they relate to the question and to the political, economic, diplomatic, or social history of the period. A listing of the documents and recitation of what each one says is referred to by the correctors as a "laundry list" and is not well thought of by these readers.

Essay or Free Response Question—Section 2, Part B

Read and analyze the five questions carefully before making your choice. Make a brief outline if you did not have time to do so during the 15-minute reading period. Follow the suggestions presented in this book. Remember the Seven Steps in Essay Writing and the image of the flashlight as you write your essay.

Reviewing the Week Before the Examination

The most important thing to remember as you begin to review for the AP examination is that you have been preparing since you first picked up this book or began your study of American history. Have confidence in yourself and rely on the work you have done all year. A planned review can be helpful but cannot replace the confidence gained by systematic work over a year. Last-minute cramming of factual information can be counterproductive and confusing.

A One-Week Review Plan

Develop a plan that fits your own time schedule. A little review each day or evening is best—an hour should be plenty of time if used well. If you have not yet taken the practice Advanced Placement exam that follows, you should begin your review by doing that. First read this section and then set aside three hours in which to take the model exam.

In planning a five-day review, an easy approach is to review two chapters in Part III each day and use the fifth day for an overview. Each day of the four, begin by going over the sample multiple-choice questions in the two chapters and see how well you do. Then read the appropriate sections in Part V or study your own time-line and notes. Do *not* try to reread the whole text but use *your* notes. Finally, you will want to read over the sample essay questions in the two chapters under review that day and think about answers to them. What your goal is for this review is to get your mind turning again—thinking over material you studied several months ago.

One excellent way to review the essay possibilities is to work with a friend. If this can be arranged, after you have both read over your own notes and answered the multiple-choice questions, discuss possible approaches to the five essays. Share your knowledge.

Remember your AP examination results will be reported by the College Board as a ranking on a scale of 5 to 1. You are not competing with your friends for *the* one top grade in the class. Instead you are going to be ranked in five categories with over 100,000 students who will take the Advanced Placement exam. A score of five means you are "extremely well qualified" and there will be many who achieve this score. Therefore, work together to support each other's efforts to reach a rank of five. Thirty minutes a day spent reviewing your notes and multiple-choice questions and thirty minutes spent discussing the essay questions with a friend will prove an excellent five-day review pattern. On the fifth day you can review whatever information seems appropriate at that time—your own notes, your lecture notes, old tests.

Taking the Exam

The Night Before the Exam

The night before the exam is a time to relax and get a good night's sleep. Some students have found seeing a good movie or watching a favorite TV show a better preparation than last-minute studying. Other students look over special notes or review the chapters that gave them the most difficulty in the final week's review. Another excellent option for this last night review is to read again the model Advanced Placement exam included in Part Four. What is most important, however, on this night is to get a good rest and have confidence that you have prepared well throughout the year. There is nothing worse than to spend all night before the exam cramming facts into your head — facts that only end up being jumbled by morning.

Day of the Exam

Just as a good night's sleep is most beneficial, a good breakfast is important. If you are a coffee-only, non-breakfast person, on this morning take time to eat something. Three hours of exam taking is very draining and you need the energy a good breakfast will supply.

Being Ready Early

Plan to be at school or the exam location in plenty of time. Hunting for a parking spot can be distracting and you want to be focused on American history on this day. Follow whatever directions you have been given by your teacher or guidance counselor about when to report and what to bring to the exam in the way of I.D. material or other information. Remember you will need several number 2 pencils and two pens.

Starting the Exam

Once you arrive at the exam room find a seat where you will feel comfortable. Sitting towards the front often makes it easier to hear all the directions and there will be many instructions given by the person administering the exam. You will have identification material to fill out before beginning the exam. There will normally be a short break between Sections 1 and 2 of the examination. Instructions will be given for both sections. Pay attention but do not hesitate to ask if there is something you do not understand.

Exercises

For many students the three hours of the Advanced Placement exam will be the longest exam time they have experienced. Both the body and mind can feel tired. You want to keep your blood circulating and plenty of oxygen coming into your lungs while you are working on the examination. There are several simple exercises you can do that help to achieve these goals during long examinations. While writing you can clench your fists several times and release them quickly, and squeeze your toes hard and release them several times. These two exercises will get the blood flowing to your extremities. Another excellent exercise is to make what is known in yoga as the Lion's Face. Stick your tongue out as far as you can and open your mouth and eyes as wide as you can. This will get circulation going in your face. These three exercises can be done while you are writing. A fourth exercise is a gentle finger massage of the temples and over the eyes and cheeks; this will help relieve tension and focus your thoughts. It requires putting the pencil or pen down and gently rubbing your fingers over your temples and then the palm of your hands gently over your eye sockets. Some find gently rubbing the cheekbones and forehead also helpful. A minute or less doing this simple tension-releasing exercise will be time well spent. These simple exercises should be done when you seem to be getting tired. They are not distracting to others and can be helpful to you.

If you are allowed to stand at the break between sections of the examination, bend over to touch your toes several times and stretch. Such simple exercises between sections of the examination, plus some good deep breathing spaced through the exam, can make taking the exam much easier.

Sugar Boost

Some people bring a candy bar to eat at the break for quick energy. As we now know, a sugar high is short-lasting but can be very helpful in the middle of the examination. However, be certain eating is permitted by the test administrator before opening your candy bar.

These hints may seem strange and you may feel awkward making a Lion's Face in the middle of the Advanced Placement examination, but such actions can keep you fresher and your mind working—which is important during the long three hours of the examination. You should practice these exercises as you take the model exam that follows.

After the Exam Ends

Follow the directions given at the end of the examination by your test administrator. Ask any questions you have before leaving.

The essays on the Advanced Placement examination are read in mid-June by a large group of experienced college and high school teachers. You will not hear your results until some time in the summer so you should relax and get on with the rest of your school work. Do not worry about how you did on the Advanced Placement Examination. If you have worked steadily all year and reviewed with this book, you have done all you can to achieve well on the examination.

You should now prepare to take the model examination presented in Part Four, Section B.

ANSWER SHEET FOR THE MODEL
ADVANCED PLACEMENT EXAM IN PART FOUR

Name_____

Date_____

Grade_____

FOR SECTION I — MULTIPLE CHOICE

Sample: 1. The American Declaration of Independence was signed in   1. Ⓐ Ⓑ Ⓒ ● Ⓔ

    (A) 1789   (D) 1776

    (B) 1763   (E) 1667

    (C) 1976

Box D is filled in since the correct answer for the sample question 1 is D.

---

1. Ⓐ Ⓑ Ⓒ Ⓓ Ⓔ   26. Ⓐ Ⓑ Ⓒ Ⓓ Ⓔ   51. Ⓐ Ⓑ Ⓒ Ⓓ Ⓔ   76. Ⓐ Ⓑ Ⓒ Ⓓ Ⓔ
2. Ⓐ Ⓑ Ⓒ Ⓓ Ⓔ   27. Ⓐ Ⓑ Ⓒ Ⓓ Ⓔ   52. Ⓐ Ⓑ Ⓒ Ⓓ Ⓔ   77. Ⓐ Ⓑ Ⓒ Ⓓ Ⓔ
3. Ⓐ Ⓑ Ⓒ Ⓓ Ⓔ   28. Ⓐ Ⓑ Ⓒ Ⓓ Ⓔ   53. Ⓐ Ⓑ Ⓒ Ⓓ Ⓔ   78. Ⓐ Ⓑ Ⓒ Ⓓ Ⓔ
4. Ⓐ Ⓑ Ⓒ Ⓓ Ⓔ   29. Ⓐ Ⓑ Ⓒ Ⓓ Ⓔ   54. Ⓐ Ⓑ Ⓒ Ⓓ Ⓔ   79. Ⓐ Ⓑ Ⓒ Ⓓ Ⓔ
5. Ⓐ Ⓑ Ⓒ Ⓓ Ⓔ   30. Ⓐ Ⓑ Ⓒ Ⓓ Ⓔ   55. Ⓐ Ⓑ Ⓒ Ⓓ Ⓔ   80. Ⓐ Ⓑ Ⓒ Ⓓ Ⓔ
6. Ⓐ Ⓑ Ⓒ Ⓓ Ⓔ   31. Ⓐ Ⓑ Ⓒ Ⓓ Ⓔ   56. Ⓐ Ⓑ Ⓒ Ⓓ Ⓔ   81. Ⓐ Ⓑ Ⓒ Ⓓ Ⓔ
7. Ⓐ Ⓑ Ⓒ Ⓓ Ⓔ   32. Ⓐ Ⓑ Ⓒ Ⓓ Ⓔ   57. Ⓐ Ⓑ Ⓒ Ⓓ Ⓔ   82. Ⓐ Ⓑ Ⓒ Ⓓ Ⓔ
8. Ⓐ Ⓑ Ⓒ Ⓓ Ⓔ   33. Ⓐ Ⓑ Ⓒ Ⓓ Ⓔ   58. Ⓐ Ⓑ Ⓒ Ⓓ Ⓔ   83. Ⓐ Ⓑ Ⓒ Ⓓ Ⓔ
9. Ⓐ Ⓑ Ⓒ Ⓓ Ⓔ   34. Ⓐ Ⓑ Ⓒ Ⓓ Ⓔ   59. Ⓐ Ⓑ Ⓒ Ⓓ Ⓔ   84. Ⓐ Ⓑ Ⓒ Ⓓ Ⓔ
10. Ⓐ Ⓑ Ⓒ Ⓓ Ⓔ   35. Ⓐ Ⓑ Ⓒ Ⓓ Ⓔ   60. Ⓐ Ⓑ Ⓒ Ⓓ Ⓔ   85. Ⓐ Ⓑ Ⓒ Ⓓ Ⓔ
11. Ⓐ Ⓑ Ⓒ Ⓓ Ⓔ   36. Ⓐ Ⓑ Ⓒ Ⓓ Ⓔ   61. Ⓐ Ⓑ Ⓒ Ⓓ Ⓔ   86. Ⓐ Ⓑ Ⓒ Ⓓ Ⓔ
12. Ⓐ Ⓑ Ⓒ Ⓓ Ⓔ   37. Ⓐ Ⓑ Ⓒ Ⓓ Ⓔ   62. Ⓐ Ⓑ Ⓒ Ⓓ Ⓔ   87. Ⓐ Ⓑ Ⓒ Ⓓ Ⓔ
13. Ⓐ Ⓑ Ⓒ Ⓓ Ⓔ   38. Ⓐ Ⓑ Ⓒ Ⓓ Ⓔ   63. Ⓐ Ⓑ Ⓒ Ⓓ Ⓔ   88. Ⓐ Ⓑ Ⓒ Ⓓ Ⓔ
14. Ⓐ Ⓑ Ⓒ Ⓓ Ⓔ   39. Ⓐ Ⓑ Ⓒ Ⓓ Ⓔ   64. Ⓐ Ⓑ Ⓒ Ⓓ Ⓔ   89. Ⓐ Ⓑ Ⓒ Ⓓ Ⓔ
15. Ⓐ Ⓑ Ⓒ Ⓓ Ⓔ   40. Ⓐ Ⓑ Ⓒ Ⓓ Ⓔ   65. Ⓐ Ⓑ Ⓒ Ⓓ Ⓔ   90. Ⓐ Ⓑ Ⓒ Ⓓ Ⓔ
16. Ⓐ Ⓑ Ⓒ Ⓓ Ⓔ   41. Ⓐ Ⓑ Ⓒ Ⓓ Ⓔ   66. Ⓐ Ⓑ Ⓒ Ⓓ Ⓔ   91. Ⓐ Ⓑ Ⓒ Ⓓ Ⓔ
17. Ⓐ Ⓑ Ⓒ Ⓓ Ⓔ   42. Ⓐ Ⓑ Ⓒ Ⓓ Ⓔ   67. Ⓐ Ⓑ Ⓒ Ⓓ Ⓔ   92. Ⓐ Ⓑ Ⓒ Ⓓ Ⓔ
18. Ⓐ Ⓑ Ⓒ Ⓓ Ⓔ   43. Ⓐ Ⓑ Ⓒ Ⓓ Ⓔ   68. Ⓐ Ⓑ Ⓒ Ⓓ Ⓔ   93. Ⓐ Ⓑ Ⓒ Ⓓ Ⓔ
19. Ⓐ Ⓑ Ⓒ Ⓓ Ⓔ   44. Ⓐ Ⓑ Ⓒ Ⓓ Ⓔ   69. Ⓐ Ⓑ Ⓒ Ⓓ Ⓔ   94. Ⓐ Ⓑ Ⓒ Ⓓ Ⓔ
20. Ⓐ Ⓑ Ⓒ Ⓓ Ⓔ   45. Ⓐ Ⓑ Ⓒ Ⓓ Ⓔ   70. Ⓐ Ⓑ Ⓒ Ⓓ Ⓔ   95. Ⓐ Ⓑ Ⓒ Ⓓ Ⓔ
21. Ⓐ Ⓑ Ⓒ Ⓓ Ⓔ   46. Ⓐ Ⓑ Ⓒ Ⓓ Ⓔ   71. Ⓐ Ⓑ Ⓒ Ⓓ Ⓔ   96. Ⓐ Ⓑ Ⓒ Ⓓ Ⓔ
22. Ⓐ Ⓑ Ⓒ Ⓓ Ⓔ   47. Ⓐ Ⓑ Ⓒ Ⓓ Ⓔ   72. Ⓐ Ⓑ Ⓒ Ⓓ Ⓔ   97. Ⓐ Ⓑ Ⓒ Ⓓ Ⓔ
23. Ⓐ Ⓑ Ⓒ Ⓓ Ⓔ   48. Ⓐ Ⓑ Ⓒ Ⓓ Ⓔ   73. Ⓐ Ⓑ Ⓒ Ⓓ Ⓔ   98. Ⓐ Ⓑ Ⓒ Ⓓ Ⓔ
24. Ⓐ Ⓑ Ⓒ Ⓓ Ⓔ   49. Ⓐ Ⓑ Ⓒ Ⓓ Ⓔ   74. Ⓐ Ⓑ Ⓒ Ⓓ Ⓔ   99. Ⓐ Ⓑ Ⓒ Ⓓ Ⓔ
25. Ⓐ Ⓑ Ⓒ Ⓓ Ⓔ   50. Ⓐ Ⓑ Ⓒ Ⓓ Ⓔ   75. Ⓐ Ⓑ Ⓒ Ⓓ Ⓔ   100. Ⓐ Ⓑ Ⓒ Ⓓ Ⓔ

Model Advanced Placement American History Examination

The following is a typical Advanced Placement examination in American history. After you have completed your review of the subject and have studied and analyzed the various types of questions that may appear on the actual exam, take this model examination and get a preview of how you will fare on the real examination in May. Be sure to use the answer sheet on the previous page because it does take a little longer to mark answers on a separate sheet.

Section 1

You will be allowed three hours for the entire examination. Section 1, the Multiple-Choice Section, includes 100 questions to be answered in one hour and 15 minutes. This gives you three-fourths of a minute for each question. Since one-fourth of the number of questions you have incorrect will be subtracted from the total number of your correct answers, guessing haphazardly will detract from your score. However, if you can narrow your choices down to two or three because of your general knowledge of the subject, then it may help your score if you pick an answer. You should work quickly. If the question is difficult for you, do not waste time on it but move on to the next question. You may return to the questions you skipped if there is time left after you have gone over all 100 questions. Since preparation varies from school to school, very few students can answer all the questions so do not be discouraged.

Section 2

Section 2, the Essay Section, includes the DBQ and one other essay question to be selected from five questions. These are to be answered in one hour and 45 minutes. The first fifteen minutes consists of a reading period in which you will read the questions and make your choice as to which questions you wish to answer, and then prepare notes for both of your answers. You then have one hour and 30 minutes to write your answers. It is suggested that this time be divided, with 40 minutes for the DBQ and 50 minutes for the essay of your choice. At the examination you will be supplied a small booklet of 8 1/2" x 11" lined pages on which to write your answers. For this sample examination you will want to use your own paper. You should plan to write your essay answers in black or blue ink. This is much easier for the reader to understand. Pencil is difficult for the reader.

Now tear out the Multiple-Choice Answer sheet or xerox a copy of it. Get some lined paper, pencils and pens, and a timer, and sit down ready to spend three hours on this practice exam. If you need to, you may take breaks between the Sections and/or between the two essays. It would be best to find a quiet place with a desk and to work undistracted.

The Model Exam

Section I
Multiple-Choice
Questions

Time—1 hour and 15 minutes

Number of Questions—100 MULTIPLE-CHOICE

Directions: Each of the questions or incomplete statements below is followed by five suggested answers or completions. Select the one that is best in each case and then blacken the corresponding oval on the answer sheet.

1. "The [American] people,... to a greater extent than any other, realize that surplus wealth is but a trust to be administered during life for the good of the community. Nowhere are there so many philanthropic agencies at work." The above statement would describe the attitudes held by all of the following EXCEPT
    (A) A Social Darwinist
    (B) Andrew Carnegie
    (C) An American business person
    (D) John D. Rockefeller
    (E) Eugene V. Debs

(Question 2)

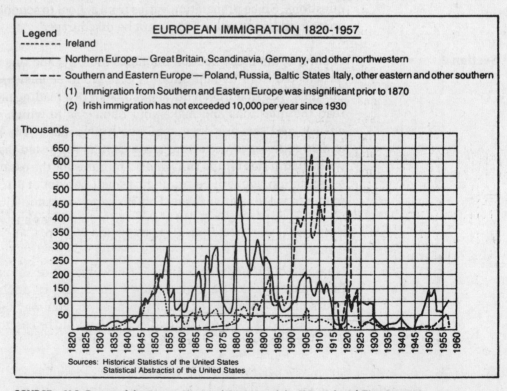

EUROPEAN IMMIGRATION 1820-1957

Legend
-------- Ireland

———— Northern Europe — Great Britain, Scandinavia, Germany, and other northwestern

— — — Southern and Eastern Europe — Poland, Russia, Baltic States Italy, other eastern and other southern

(1) Immigration from Southern and Eastern Europe was insignificant prior to 1870
(2) Irish immigration has not exceeded 10,000 per year since 1930

Thousands

Sources: Historical Statistics of the United States
Statistical Abstractist of the United States

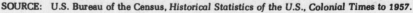

SOURCE: U.S. Bureau of the Census, *Historical Statistics of the U.S., Colonial Times to 1957.*

2. According to the chart showing European immigration,
   - (A) the period of greatest yearly immigration from northern Europe was 1905-1910
   - (B) more Irish came to America in 1850-1855 than in 1885-1890
   - (C) immigration from southern and eastern Europe was insignificant prior to 1930
   - (D) northern Europe includes Great Britain, Scandinavia, and the Baltic States
   - (E) the period of greatest immigration from southern Europe was after 1945

3. Which one of the following events occurred most recently?
   - (A) The ratification of the Articles of Confederation
   - (B) The presentation of the Connecticut Compromise
   - (C) The introduction of the Virginia Plan
   - (D) The drafting of the Declaration of Independence
   - (E) The offering of the New Jersey Plan

4. Which one of the following groups includes individuals all of whom supported the ratification of the U.S. Constitution by the states?
   - (A) Thomas Jefferson, Patrick Henry, Melancthon Smith
   - (B) John Jay, Alexander Hamilton, Patrick Henry
   - (C) James Madison, John Jay, Alexander Hamilton
   - (D) Thomas Jefferson, James Madison, Andrew Jackson
   - (E) James Madison, Samuel E. Morison, Alexander Hamilton

5. Which of the following was NOT offered by Americans as a solution to the problems of the Great Depression?
   - (A) WPA
   - (B) "Share the Wealth"
   - (C) EPIC
   - (D) NATO
   - (E) NIRA

6. The Palmer Raids
   - (A) created a climate of opinion in which Senator Joe McCarthy could capture the attention of the American people
   - (B) identified over 400,000 communists who were exiled to the Soviet Union
   - (C) exposed the attorney general to such publicity that he was able to capture the Republican nomination for president in 1924
   - (D) united the country in opposing the Fascist threat of Italy and Germany in the 1930s
   - (E) reflected the anti-communist hysteria of the post-World War I period

7. Which of the following ideas was NOT incorporated in Frederick Jackson Turner's thesis on the influence of the frontier on America?
    (A) "The complex European life" had continual impact on America since the "Atlantic Coast… was the frontier of Europe."
    (B) There is a "new product that is American."
    (C) The frontier is the "outer edge… the meeting point between savagery and civilization."
    (D) A "frontier settlement" had existed until 1890.
    (E) "Democracy born of free land, strong in selfishness and individualism," has its "dangers as well as its benefits."

8. "… and he [the President] shall nominate, and by and with the advice and consent of the Senate, shall appoint… judges of the Supreme Court…"
    The passage above from the Constitution best illustrates the concept of
    (A) power of the purse
    (B) executive privilege
    (C) checks and balances
    (D) judicial review
    (E) due process

9. "I will not, I cannot, give up my belief that America must, not alone for the happiness of her own people, but for the moral guidance and greater contentment of the world, be permitted to live her own life. Next to the tie which binds a man to his God is the tie which binds a man to his country, and all schemes, all plans however ambitious and fascinating they seem in their proposal, but which would embarrass or entangle and impede or shackle her sovereign will, which would compromise her freedom of action I unhesitatingly put behind me."
    In the previous passage the writer is making a statement which could best be summarized as in favor of
    (A) isolationism and Christianity
    (B) sovereignty and socialism
    (C) freedom and nationalism
    (D) socialism and Christianity
    (E) isolationism and nationalism

(Question 10)

THE BEST THEY HAVE TO OFFER.

SOURCE: World Telegram, August 11, 1934

10. In the cartoon above the artist is
    (A) suggesting the Republican party has no effective solution to the depression
    (B) supporting the anti-communist crusade of the 1920s
    (C) advocating social Darwinism as a policy
    (D) indicating he believes in nonviolent protest
    (E) implying that the G.O.P. is being robbed by Wall St. and Rugged Individualism

(Question 11)

11. On the above map the areas colored black illustrate the
    (A) region divided into camps at the Yalta Conference
    (B) members of the Common Market
    (C) Central Powers in World War I
    (D) greatest extent of Nazi control in World War II
    (E) regions where Romance languages are spoken

12. Which of the following did NOT contribute to the reelection of Ronald
    Reagan in 1984?
    (A) Support of the pro-life movement
    (B) Congressional passage of a program based on "supply side"
         economic theory
    (C) A disarmament agreement with the Soviet Union
    (D) Support of Vice-President George Bush
    (E) Reagan's television presence

(Question 13)

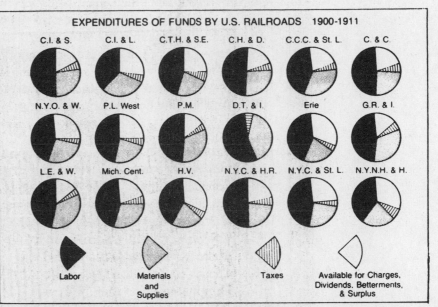

SOURCE: *Illustrated London News*, July, 1912

13. Which of the following statements is NOT correct according to information in the chart above?
    (A) In all cases the smallest percent spent by railroads was on taxes.
    (B) The largest percentage spent by each railroad was for labor (wages).
    (C) The percentage spent on materials and supplies varied, but never exceeded 50 percent.
    (D) The percentage available for dividends was never greater than the amount spent on labor.
    (E) The amount spent on taxes varied less than the amount spent on materials and supplies.

(Question 14)

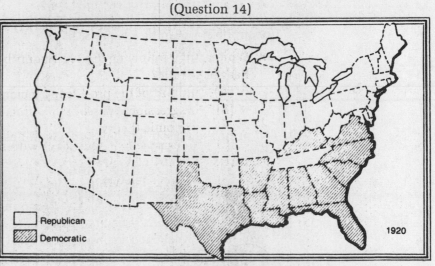

ELECTION MAP OF 1920

14. According to the map, the Democratic party in the election of 1920
   (A) nominated Woodrow Wilson for the presidency
   (B) made inroads into the Midwestern wheat belt—the traditional stronghold of the Republican party
   (C) failed to carry any states west of the Mississippi
   (D) lost every state except those that could be considered "southern"
   (E) carried New England and the South

15. Which of the following is a correct statement regarding the Vietnam War?
   (A) U.S. involvement in Vietnam began with John F. Kennedy
   (B) President Lyndon Johnson decided to withdraw from the presidential race because of his stand on Vietnam
   (C) U.S. forces never attacked across the borders of Vietnam
   (D) The Gulf of Tonkin Resolution made the Vietnam conflict legal in international law as it declared war on North Vietnam
   (E) Throughout the war the areas controlled by each side were clearly identifiable

16. An economic system in which a nation seeks to accumulate precious metals by maintaining a favorable balance of trade is most descriptive of
   (A) capitalism   (D) feudalism
   (B) socialism   (E) fascism
   (C) mercantilism

17. Under the Articles of Confederation, sovereignty was primarily in the hands of the
   (A) executive   (D) many local governments
   (B) Congress   (E) revolutionary army
   (C) states

18. A person supporting the concept of implied power in regard to the U.S. Constitution would be a believer in
   (A) limited executive power   (D) loose constructionism
   (B) strict constructionism   (E) states' rights
   (C) Jeffersonianism

19. The principal reason for the Era of Good Feeling during the presidency of James Monroe was
   (A) relative peace in the world
   (B) great economic development and general prosperity at home
   (C) a great religious revival that de-emphasized political considerations swept the United States
   (D) a very weakened opposition political party
   (E) his strong stand in favor of Latin America stated in the Monroe Doctrine

20. The main purpose of Henry Clay's American System was to
- (A) advance and implement Manifest Destiny
- (B) develop an interdependent economic system tying the East, West, and South together
- (C) curtail immigration in favor of large native population growth
- (D) integrate the native American into U.S. society
- (E) expand American investment abroad

21. Transcendentalist writers found their major source of truth and inspiration in
- (A) church dogma
- (B) the Bible
- (C) the political situation of the time
- (D) nature
- (E) history

22. The Tariff of Abominations led directly to the
- (A) specie circular
- (B) South Carolina exposition and protest
- (C) Hartford Convention
- (D) president's veto
- (E) resignation of Vice-President Calhoun

23. The major battle in the western theater during the Civil War which had the effect of splitting the Confederacy in half was
- (A) the Battle of the Wilderness
- (B) Vicksburg
- (C) Antietam
- (D) Gettysburg
- (E) Petersburg

24. The political leader most responsible for securing the passage of the Civil Rights Act of 1960 and 1964 was
- (A) John F. Kennedy
- (B) Lyndon Baines Johnson
- (C) Adam Clayton Powell
- (D) Andrew Young
- (E) George Wallace

25. Of his Fourteen Points, Wilson was most concerned with establishing
- (A) Point I: Open covenants, openly arrived at
- (B) Point II: Absolute freedom of navigation upon the seas
- (C) Point IV: Adequate guarantees given and taken that national armaments will be reduced to the lowest point consistent with domestic safety
- (D) Point V: A free, open-minded and absolutely impartial adjustment of all colonial claims
- (E) Point XIV: A general association of nations formed to provide political independence and territorial integrity of all nations

26. The Creel Committee during World War I represented the United States' first successful attempt at large-scale governmental
- (A) armament manufacture
- (B) food production
- (C) shipbuilding
- (D) propaganda
- (E) railroad management

27. Which American leader during the 20th century would most likely have made the following statement?
"We had a chance to gain the leadership of the world. We lost it, and soon we shall be witnessing the tragedy of it all."
- (A) Theodore Roosevelt
- (B) Woodrow Wilson
- (C) Franklin Roosevelt
- (D) John F. Kennedy
- (E) Lyndon B. Johnson

28. Which of the following New Deal legislation was a basic reform measure dealing with banking?
- (A) Public Works Administration
- (B) Federal Deposit Insurance Corporation
- (C) Civilian Conservation Corps
- (D) National Industrial Recovery Act
- (E) Agricultural Adjustment Administration

29. "With millions of men and women still unemployed and the whole industrialized world critically dependent upon the scope and vigor of the American economic recovery, a veto of the tax cut would be poor public policy, which political headline-hunting could not justify."
The quotation suggests all of the following EXCEPT
- (A) The United States continues to be in a depression.
- (B) A presidential veto would be harmful to the nation.
- (C) Other nations are heavily affected by the U.S. economy.
- (D) In determining policy, the president should be guided solely by the political impact of the policy.
- (E) The unemployment rate is high in the nation.

30. Which one of the following accurately describes the president's Cabinet?
- (A) It is fully described in the United States Constitution
- (B) Members are not approved by the United States Senate
- (C) Members of the Cabinet serve at the pleasure of the Chief Executive
- (D) The Cabinet must meet every Thursday
- (E) The number of Executive Departments headed by Cabinet officers can be changed by the president as he wishes

31. The political Reconstruction of the South was ended after
- (A) the impeachment of President Johnson
- (B) the Democratic presidential victory in 1884
- (C) an agreement was arranged which allowed Republican Rutherford B. Hayes to become president
- (D) the southern states indicated they welcomed military occupation
- (E) the Grandfather clause as a voting requirement was outlawed by the Supreme Court

32. "But do these people want good government? Tammany says they don't. Are the people honest? Are the people better than Tammany? Are they better than the merchant and the politician? Isn't our corrupt government, after all, representative?... Democracy with us may be impossible... but then newspaper and magazine articles, if they have proved nothing else, have demonstrated beyond doubt that we can stand the truth."

The quotation would most likely have been said by a

  (A) muckraker   (D) fundamentalist
  (B) Dixiecrat   (E) Federalist
  (C) Populist

33. When the New Deal program of Franklin D. Roosevelt was threatened by Supreme Court decisions against New Deal measures, the president responded by

  (A) giving his famous "my dog Falla" speech, which compared the Supreme Court to his dog
  (B) calling on Congress to increase the size of the Supreme Court so that he could appoint new members who approved of New Deal legislation
  (C) ordering impeachment proceedings against members of the Court
  (D) ignoring the Court decisions following the precedent set by Andrew Jackson
  (E) calling on the American people to elect only Democrats to Congress

34. Which of the following did NOT contribute to the bad relations between native Americans and the U.S. government in the forty years following the Civil War?

  (A) The slaughter of the buffalo
  (B) The corruption of many Indian Agents
  (C) The discovery and exploration of gold in the Black Hills of South Dakota
  (D) The publication of works such as Helen Hunt Jackson's *A Century of Dishonor* and *Ramona*
  (E) The disregard of treaty arrangements

35. Which of the following would NOT be considered a victory for organized labor?

  (A) Taft-Hartley Act
  (B) Wisconsin Unemployment Insurance Law
  (C) Establishment of the Committee for Industrial Organization
  (D) Wagner Act
  (E) Anthracite Coal Strike of 1902

36. All of the following major transportation developments affecting U.S. history took place in the period before the twentieth century EXCEPT

  (A) railroads   (D) airplanes
  (B) canals   (E) stagecoach
  (C) steamboats

37. Which of the following events took place first?
   (A) Calhoun's resignation as vice-president
   (B) Election of Andrew Jackson
   (C) The Peggy Eaton affair
   (D) Veto of the bill renewing the Bank of the United States
   (E) Specie circular

38. The English colony first settled by the Dutch was
   (A) New York   (D) Pennsylvania
   (B) Jamaica   (E) Delaware
   (C) Canada

39. The principal motivation for the settlement of the Plymouth Bay Colony was
   (A) economic   (D) social
   (B) political   (E) cultural
   (C) religious

40. Which of the following best explains why the earliest factories in the United States were located in New England?
   (A) its easy access to large quantities of coal
   (B) abundant water power
   (C) the availability of cheap labor
   (D) a well-developed system of canals
   (E) good harbors

41. *The Sovereignty and Goodness of God or Narrative of the Captivity and Restoration of Mrs. Mary Rowlandson* was
   (A) an account of the Salem Witch Trials
   (B) a sermon by Jonathan Edwards, which precipitated the Great Awakening
   (C) an argument used by the abolitionists in attacking slavery
   (D) the most popular story about native Americans written in the English colonies
   (E) a statement in favor of temperance

42. The era of Prohibition in the 1920s created which of the following?
   I.   A general breakdown or change in the moral attitudes of Americans
   II.   An increase in the number of gangsters and bootleggers
   III. Strong support for repeal of Prohibition throughout the South
   IV.   An awareness of the weakness of the federal government in controlling private habits of its citizens when a strong minority opposes such control
   (A) I and II only
   (B) I, II, and III only
   (C) II, III, and IV only
   (D) I, II, and IV only
   (E) I, II, III, IV

43. The fundamental thesis of Keynesian economics is that
- (A)   the government should tax highly in times of inflation and the government should spend extensively in times of deflation
- (B)   the government should keep "hands off" all economic activity
- (C)   businessmen should run the government
- (D)   the wealth of a nation is measured by the amount of gold it holds
- (E)   tax cuts stimulate and increase deflation

44. Which of the following events occurred under the government of the Articles of Confederation?
- (A)   The repeal of the Stamp Act
- (B)   Shays' Rebellion
- (C)   The suppression of the Barbary Pirates
- (D)   Daniel Boone's first trip to Kentucky
- (E)   The Boston Massacre

45. Jefferson is often accused of political inconsistency since he apparently supported states' rights in the Kentucky and Virginia resolves but acted as a supporter of federal power and loose construction of the Constitution when he
- I.   arranged the Louisiana Purchase
- II.   sent the United States Navy to attack the Barbary Pirates
- III.   ordered Lewis and Clark to explore the West
- IV.   proclaimed the Embargo in 1807
- (A)   I only
- (B)   I and III only
- (C)   I, II, and IV only
- (D)   I, III, and IV only
- (E)   I, II, III, IV

46. In the years immediately after 1825 the pattern of western settlement was greatly affected by the
- (A)   aftermath of the Battle of the Little Big Horn
- (B)   opening of the Erie Canal
- (C)   purchase of Alaska
- (D)   discovery of gold in South Dakota
- (E)   completion of the first transcontinental railroad

47. Which of the following was NOT a major event of the War of 1812?
- (A)   Battle of Fallen Timbers
- (B)   Battle of New Orleans
- (C)   Burning of Washington, D.C.
- (D)   Capt. Oliver Hazard Perry's victory on Lake Erie
- (E)   British bombardment of Fort McHenry in Baltimore

48. Which of the following authors' artistic contributions is NOT correctly summarized after his name?
- (A)   Mark Twain—great humorist who used tales of the American West and frontier to establish international reputation
- (B)   Bret Harte—writer of cynical tales of the eastern *nouveaux riches*

    (C)   Joel Chandler Harris—creator of Uncle Remus and writer of stories of the post-Civil War South

    (D)   Hamlin Garland—realistic view of prairie and agricultural life

    (E)   William Dean Howells—realistically analyzed post- Civil War economic conditions in novels

49. Which of the following is the correct chronological order for the events?

    (A)   Wilson's 14 Points; rejection of League of Nations by U.S. Senate; Washington Disarmament Conference; Dawes Plan; Kellogg-Briand Pact.

    (B)   Dawes Plan; Wilson's 14 Points; rejection of League of Nations by U.S. Senate; Washington Disarmament Conference; Kellogg-Briand Pact.

    (C)   Wilson's 14 Points; Dawes Plan; Kellogg-Briand Pact; rejection of League of Nations by U.S. Senate; Washington Disarmament Conference

    (D)   Kellogg-Briand Pact; Washington Disarmament Conference; Wilson's 14 Points; Dawes Plan; rejection of League of Nations by U.S. Senate

    (E)   Washington Disarmament Conference; Dawes Plan; rejection of League of Nations by U.S. Senate; Wilson's 14 Points; Kellogg-Briand Pact

50. The Pendleton Act was passed by Congress as a response to

    (A)   the assassination of President Garfield

    (B)   the Cross of Gold speech by William Jennings Bryan

    (C)   the declaration by the Supreme Court that the Granger Laws were unconstitutional

    (D)   the election of Theodore Roosevelt as vice-president

    (E)   the application to the United States for annexation by the provisional government of Hawaii

51. Which of the following was NOT a major issue during the presidency of Jimmy Carter?

    (A)   Iranian hostage crisis

    (B)   Inflation

    (C)   The unilateral withdrawal of U.S. troops from Europe

    (D)   SALT negotiations

    (E)   Human rights

52. All of the following were actions by the United States federal government to deal with the money supply EXCEPT

    (A)   Sherman Silver Purchase Act

    (B)   Social Security Act

    (C)   Establishment of the Commodity Dollar

    (D)   Federal Reserve Act

    (E)   Specie circular

53. In the forty years following the end of Reconstruction, fundamental changes in the American system were brought about as a result of federal legislation in all of the following EXCEPT

(A) immigration
(B) civil service
(C) civil rights
(D) interstate commerce
(E) monetary policy

54. Which of the following did NOT contribute to the decision of the United States to declare war on Spain in 1898?

(A) The sinking of the battleship *Maine*
(B) The De Lome Letter
(C) The stimulation of public opinion by the Yellow Press
(D) The acquisition of Pago Pago
(E) The need to protect American economic investments

55. The purpose of the "gag rule" adopted by the U.S. Senate was to

(A) encourage full participation in debate by all members of the Senate
(B) control unlimited filibuster
(C) limit debate on attempts to override presidential vetoes
(D) prevent debate of abolitionist proposals
(E) discourage criticism of U.S. foreign policy

56. All of the following occurred during George Washington's two terms EXCEPT

(A) election of John Adams to the presidency
(B) resignation of Thomas Jefferson as Secretary of State
(C) XYZ Affair
(D) Hamilton's and Jefferson's letters on the constitutionality of the Bank of the U.S.
(E) the negotiation of the Jay Treaty

57. Which of the following events should NOT be considered part of the expansion of the United States?

(A) Purchase of Alaska
(B) Annexation of the Midway Islands
(C) Opening of the Panama Canal
(D) Battle of Manila Bay
(E) The London Economic Conference

58. Which of the following Acts established the concept of surveying land into six-square-mile Townships and the sale of land at public auction?

(A) Homestead Act
(B) Pacific Railway Act
(C) Land Act of 1796
(D) Desert Land Act
(E) Surplus Revenue Act

59. Which of the following events occurred most recently?
  (A)   The establishment of the Congress of Industrial Organizations
  (B)   Passage by Massachusetts of the first minimum wage act for women
  (C)   Organization of the Knights of Labor
  (D)   Passage of the La Follette Seaman's Act regulating employment conditions for maritime workers
  (E)   Passage of the Adamson Act regulating railroad working conditions

60. Which of the following events finally precipitated the military activity of the Civil War?
  (A)   The establishment of the state of West Virginia
  (B)   Secession of South Carolina
  (C)   Action at Fort Sumter
  (D)   First election of Lincoln to the presidency
  (E)   The Emancipation Proclamation

(Refer to the cartoon below for question 61)

THE DEFENDER OF TRUSTS.

J. G. B. "This is only a little private matter, officer, with which you have nothing to do."

SOURCE: *Harper's Weekly,* September 1, 1888

61. All of the following ideas are presented by the cartoonist EXCEPT

- (A) Several American industries are organized as trusts.
- (B) The American market at the time the cartoon was drawn was operated under the emblem of freedom and equality.
- (C) Trusts are robbing competition in the American market.
- (D) A well-dressed gentleman does not believe the police officer should interfere with the robbery.
- (E) The law is not prepared to become involved.

62. Which of the following is NOT true regarding dollar diplomacy?

- (A) Investments were encouraged in both the Far East and in countries near the Panama Canal
- (B) It allowed Taft to spend less on the Navy
- (C) It eliminated armed intervention by United States forces in the Caribbean
- (D) Woodrow Wilson reluctantly continued the policy after his election to the presidency
- (E) United States money was used to support governments in the Caribbean and Central America rather than money from European nations

(Refer to the graph below for question 63)

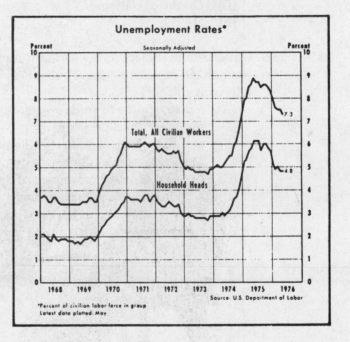

63. According to the graph on unemployment rates, all of the following statements are correct EXCEPT
    (A) During part of 1975 the percentage of unemployed household heads was as high as the percentage of the total of unemployed in 1971.
    (B) The gap between unemployed household heads and the total number of unemployed was greatest in 1969.
    (C) The gap between the total of unemployed and the unemployed household heads fluctuates but follows the same basic pattern.
    (D) Unemployment did not exceed 9 percent between 1968 and 1976.
    (E) The greatest percentage increase in unemployment took place in late 1974 and early 1975.

64. "For upwards of half a century the republics of the Western world have been working together to promote their common civilization under a system of peace. That venture, launched so hopefully fifty years ago (in 1889), has succeeded; the American family is today a great co-operative group facing a troubled world in serenity and calm... ."
    To which of the following organizations is the author referring?
    (A) Economic Development Council (EDC)
    (B) Pan-American Union
    (C) Contadora Group
    (D) League of Nations
    (E) NATO

65. United States society in the period from the end of World War II until the election of President John F. Kennedy was characterized by all of the following EXCEPT
    (A) a new attitude towards segregation in schools precipitated by Supreme Court decisions
    (B) a concern over Communist (Soviet) infiltration into the United States government bureaucracy
    (C) the start of a new movement of popular music
    (D) a voting populace that seemed uncritical and silent
    (E) a major economic recession with high unemployment for all Americans

66. "In light of facts and experience the Government of the United States is impelled to reaffirm its previous expressed opinion that imposition of restrictions upon the movements and activities of American nationals who are engaged in philanthropic, educational and commercial endeavors in China has placed and will, if continued, increasingly place Japanese interests in a preferred position and is, therefore, unquestionably discriminatory, in its effect, against legitimate American interests. Further,... the plans and practices of the Japanese authorities imply an assumption on the part of those authorities that the Japanese... regimes established and maintained in China by Japanese armed forces are entitled to act in China... to disregard and even to declare nonexistent or abrogated the established rights and interests of other countries, including the United States."

The above passage is most likely taken from the
    (A) American Declaration of War on Japan in 1941
    (B) Treaty of Portsmouth ending the Russo-Japanese War
    (C) terms of surrender signed by the Japanese at the end of World War II
    (D) "Open Door" notes of Secretary of State John Hay
    (E) United States note of protest over Japanese actions in China in the late 1930s

67. During the late 19th century and up to the outbreak of World War I the concept of spheres of influence was most often an issue in the development of United States relations with
    (A) Cuba   (D) Nicaragua
    (B) China   (E) The Philippines
    (C) Lebanon

68. "In the discussions to which this interest has given rise and in the arrangements by which they may terminate the occasion has been judged proper for asserting, as a principle in which the rights and interests of the United States are involved, that the American continents, by the free and independent condition which they have assumed and maintain, are henceforth not to be considered as subjects for future colonization by any European powers... ."

The principles articulated in the above passage are often considered the key point in the
    (A) Stimson Doctrine   (D) Monroe Doctrine
    (B) Eisenhower Doctrine   (E) Truman Doctrine
    (C) Roosevelt Corollary

SOURCE: Los Angeles County Natural History Museum Foundation, History Fund

69. The scene in the photograph above is most likely of
   (A)   Hispanic Americans in Los Angeles
   (B)   San Francisco during the Gold Rush
   (C)   the south side of Chicago during the days of black migrations to
          the cities
   (D)   Native Americans settled in Sioux City
   (E)   immigrants in New York City

70. The economic program introduced during the presidency of Ronald Reagan
and often referred to as Reaganomics included which of the following items?
   I.   Tax reduction for all payers of federal income taxes
   II.   Increased expenditures for military defense
   III.   A rapidly increasing federal deficit
   IV.   Reduction in federal expenditures for social services and aid to
          state government
   (A)   I only
   (B)   I and III only

(C) II, III, and IV only
(D) I, III, and IV only
(E) I, II, III, IV

Getting Back to a Competitive Basis

SOURCE: Saturday Evening Post, June 6, 1914

71. The political cartoonist who drew this picture was making a comment upon the

(A) popularity of organ grinders
(B) attempt to win people's support for animal rights
(C) seeking by Theodore Roosevelt and Woodrow Wilson of popular support for their political reform programs
(D) way every product in America is advertised as "new"
(E) rivalry of political candidates

(Refer to the photograph below for question 72)

SOURCE: *Harper's Weekly*, March 9, 1912

72. The tall building in the middle of the photograph shows the influence of
    (A) English Georgian architects
    (B) the Greek Revival movement
    (C) Frank Lloyd Wright
    (D) Henry Hobson Richardson
    (E) Eino Saarinen

73. All of the following occurred during the presidency of Jimmy Carter EXCEPT
    (A) the imposition by OPEC of its first oil embargo to force oil prices to rise
    (B) the seizure of Americans by Iranians and the holding of them as hostages in Teheran
    (C) the signing of the Camp David Peace Accord
    (D) the strong support for human rights and the Helsinki Accord by the president
    (E) the negotiation of new treaties with Panama which guaranteed the neutrality of the Canal

74. "If the *British* Parliament has a legal authority to issue an order that we shall furnish a single article for the troops here, and to compel obedience to *that* order, they have the same right to issue an order for us to supply those troops with arms, clothes, and every necessary; and to compel obedience to *that* order also; in short, to lay any burthens they please upon us. What is this but taxing us to a certain sum, and leaving us only the manner of raising it?" The argument presented by the author of the above statement could best be summarized as the
   (A) British Parliament has no authority to tax Americans
   (B) Stamp Act is intolerable
   (C) Americans should supply British troops with clothes, arms and all other necessities
   (D) Americans should determine the method by which they will be taxed by Parliament
   (E) Americans should pay more taxes

75. All of the following are characteristic of the African slave trade in the 18th century EXCEPT
   (A) kings of African nations along the coast sold slaves to white traders
   (B) during the "middle passage" slaves were chained and kept below deck most of the time
   (C) degradation and psychological damage occurred to all those involved, according to scholars today
   (D) the colonists relied on the English traders to supply slaves
   (E) most of the slaves sold in the Southern colonies were imported directly from Africa

76. "'The natural liberty of man is to be free from any superior power on earth, and not to be under the will or legislative authority of man, but only to have the law of nature for his rule.' This is the liberty of independent states; this is the liberty of every man out of society, and who has a mind to live so; which liberty is only abridged in certain instances, not lost to those who are born in or voluntarily enter into society; this gift of God cannot be annihilated." Which of the following documents most closely incorporates the idea expressed in the quotation?
   (A) Communist Manifesto   (D) The U.S. Constitution
   (B) Declaration of Independence (E) Northwest Ordinance
   (C) Emancipation Proclamation

77. Which of the following best characterizes the Cuban Missile Crisis during John F. Kennedy's presidency?
   (A) The presence of Soviet missiles in Cuba was discovered accidentally
   (B) The president of the United States overreacted and was restrained by his advisers from taking steps which would have meant war with the Soviets

(C) Both sides displayed a sober approach and both sides made concessions and took steps to overcome dangerous developments which could have led to World War III

(D) Nikita Khrushchev refused to accept a U.S. Naval quarantine of Cuba and forced the U.S. to board Soviet ships in order to resolve the crisis

(E) Fidel Castro was consulted by the Soviets and he followed the Soviet lead in all responses to the United States' actions during the crisis

(Refer to the chart below for question 78)

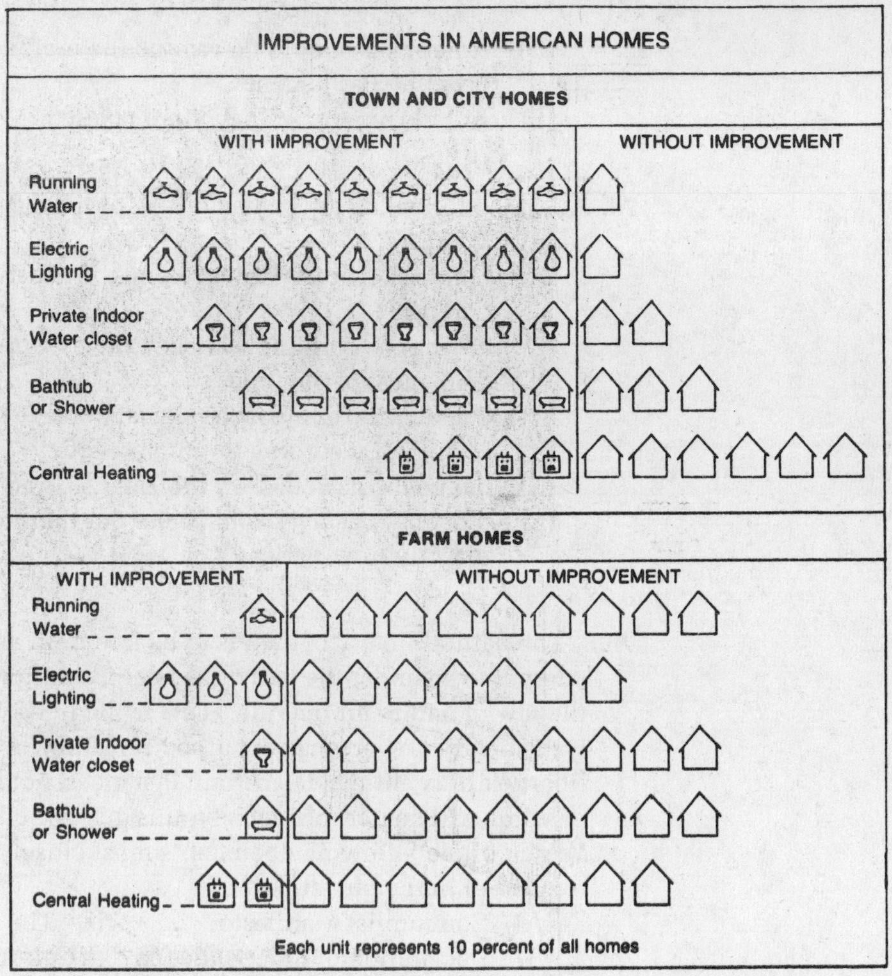

IMPROVEMENTS IN AMERICAN HOMES

Each unit represents 10 percent of all homes

SOURCE: *Building America*

78. Considering the items chosen for comparison in the above chart and the quantitative relationship between farm and city homes, one would assume the information in the chart dates from the

(A) post-World War II period

(B) Populist Era

(C) Civil War years

(D) Great Depression of the early 1930s

(E) Jacksonian period

79. All of the following occurred during the presidency of Richard Nixon EXCEPT
- (A) the fall of Saigon to the North Vietnamese
- (B) the Watergate break-in and consequent Congressional hearings
- (C) the resignation of the vice-president
- (D) diplomatic overtures to the People's Republic of China, including a presidential visit
- (E) an attempt to end the Arab-Israeli conflict in the Near East through Shuttle Diplomacy

(Refer to the cartoon below for question 80)

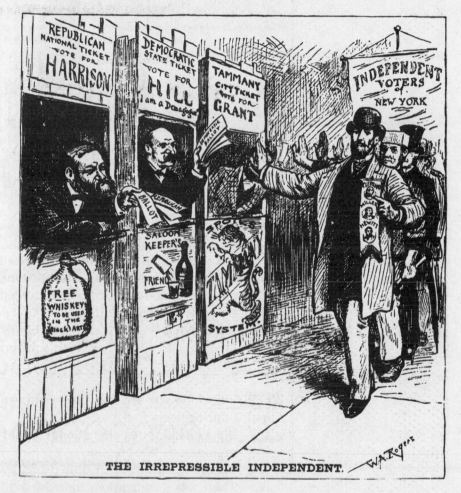

THE IRREPRESSIBLE INDEPENDENT.

SOURCE: *Harper's Weekly*, October 20, 1888

80. In the cartoon above, the spoils system referred to on the Tammany booth indicates the political system of
- (A) honoring opponents with at least one appointed office
- (B) rewarding supporters with appointed offices
- (C) declaring openly who your political supporters have been
- (D) appointing your campaign manager to the cabinet, usually as postmaster general
- (E) pointing out how your opponents spoiled your opportunity for election

(Refer to the bar chart below for question 81)

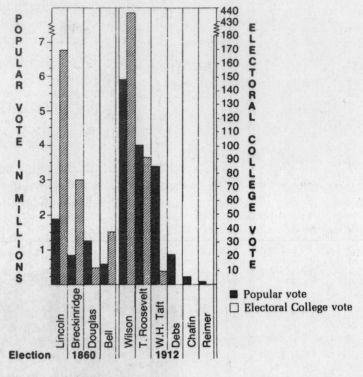

81. The bar graph above proves that
   (A)   the Electoral College is unjust
   (B)   any of the three top candidates in the 1912 election, if they had run in 1860, would have defeated Lincoln
   (C)   popular candidates cannot win in the Electoral College
   (D)   Bell was a better candidate than Douglas
   (E)   Lincoln and Wilson were both minority presidents according to the popular vote, but received a majority of votes in the Electoral College

82. Which of the following is LEAST descriptive of the educational changes in America during the period 1865-1900?
   (A)   Blacks had limited educational opportunities in spite of the work of Booker T. Washington
   (B)   The illiteracy rate for people over 10 years old steadily declined
   (C)   There was a tremendous increase in the number of colleges, including colleges for women
   (D)   Summer school courses and college extension courses were introduced to expand educational opportunities
   (E)   American research scientists and philosophers became the best and most widely known in the world, taking intellectual leadership away from Europe

83. Which statement is INCORRECTLY paired with the man who stated it?
   (A)   John C. Calhoun—"Liberty and union, now and forever, one and inseparable"

    (B)   Patrick Henry—"Give me liberty or give me death"

    (C)   Thomas Jefferson—"We hold these truths to be self-evident"

    (D)   Andrew Jackson—"Our federal union, it must be preserved"

    (E)   Franklin D. Roosevelt—"The only thing we have to fear is fear itself"

84. Which one of the following American authors was LEAST concerned with social criticism of America?

    (A)   Henry James   (D)   Upton Sinclair

    (B)   Frank Norris   (E)   Jacob Riis

    (C)   Booth Tarkington

85. Which one of the following groups is NOT made up of individuals who as contemporaries interacted to affect the direction of American history?

    (A)   Martin Luther King, Jr., Robert Kennedy, John F. Kennedy

    (B)   Theodore Roosevelt, Woodrow Wilson, Henry Cabot Lodge

    (C)   Daniel Webster, John C. Calhoun, Henry Clay

    (D)   John Marshall, Andrew Jackson, Nicholas Biddle

    (E)   Mark Hanna, William McKinley, Franklin Roosevelt

86. The term *impressment* as used by the United States in the period before the War of 1812 referred to

    (A)   the foreign policy concept of shunning alliances with other countries

    (B)   a combining together of nations in an effort to provide greater protection from attacks of the British

    (C)   the British practice of forcing American sailors into service on British warships

    (D)   an agreement temporarily uniting two or more countries

    (E)   a written plea from an individual protesting a wrong as a result of the actions of the British

87. An American political conservative in the 20th century would typically support which of the following?

    (A)   The idea that liberty is superior to equality

    (B)   Majority rule is infallible and should always prevail

    (C)   Organized religion has no place in a democratic society

    (D)   The unlimited acquisition of private property is dangerous for free government and needs to be limited

    (E)   The unity of the community is the primary goal of society

88. All of the following explorers are correctly paired with the country for which they sailed EXCEPT

    (A)   Ferdinand Magellan—Spain

    (B)   Samuel de Champlain—France

    (C)   Henry Hudson—Portugal

    (D)   John Cabot—England

    (E)   Francis Drake—England

89. "... Whereas... [the colonies] have freely declared... that a most flourishing civil state may stand and best be maintained... with a full liberty in religious concernments and that true piety rightly grounded upon gospel principles will give the best and greatest security to sovereignty and will lay in the hearts of men the strongest obligations to true loyalty:

"... we, being willing to... secure them [the people] in the free exercise and enjoyment of all their civil and religious rights... and to preserve unto them that liberty, in the true Christian faith and worship of God, which they have sought... to enjoy;... do hereby publish, grant, ordain, and declare... that no person with the said colony, at any time hereafter, shall be any wise molested, punished, disquieted, or called in question for any differences in opinion in matters of religion."

The above quotation is most likely taken from

(A) the Mayflower Compact

(B) the Rhode Island colonial charter

(C) a speech to Parliament by King James I

(D) the Albany Plan of Union

(E) the transcript of the trial of Peter Zenger

90. If an historian doing original research wished to analyze the changes made in Thomas Jefferson's original draft of the Declaration of Independence by the Committee of Five and by the members of the Continental Congress, the best way to begin would be to

(A) call the Library of Congress and ask for advice

(B) consult the final version signed by members of the Continental Congress and the letters they wrote about the Declaration.

(C) visit the National Archives to study the original draft and other early copies of the Declaration including the version signed by the members of the Congress

(D) read a book on the writing of the Declaration of Independence and analyze the author's conclusion

(E) address the National Organization of American Historians and ask the historians present at the meeting what they believe the changes were

Questions 91-92 refer to the following quotation:

"The history of mankind is a history of repeated injuries and usurpations on the part of man toward woman, having in direct object the establishment of an absolute tyranny over her. To prove this, let facts be submitted to a candid world.

Having deprived her of this first right of a citizen, the elective franchise [right to vote], thereby leaving her without representation in the halls of legislation, he has oppressed her on all sides.

He has made her, if married, in the eye of the law, civilly dead... .

Resolved, That all laws which prevent woman from occupying such a station in society as her conscience shall dictate, or which place her in a position inferior to that of man, are contrary to the great precept of nature, and, therefore, of no force or authority.

Resolved, That it is the duty of the women of this country to secure to themselves their sacred right to the elective franchise.

Resolved, That the speedy success of our cause depends upon the zealous and untiring efforts of both men and women, for the overthrow of the monopoly of the pulpit, and for the securing to women an equal participation with men in the various trades, professions, and commerce."

91. The above statement would NOT have been written after
  (A) 1898
  (B) 1919
  (C) 1865
  (D) 1848
  (E) 1800

92. The writer of the previous quotation believes all of the following EXCEPT
  (A) That men and women are equal
  (B) That women deserve the franchise
  (C) That women should be permitted to become members of the clergy and of other professions
  (D) That married women are "civilly dead"
  (E) That women alone must fight for their rights

93. A new dimension was added to the campaign for the 1988 presidential nomination when announced candidates withdrew from the campaign after
  (A) they denounced the signing of a nuclear arms reduction treaty with the Soviet Union
  (B) the Republican Administration denied them federal matching funds to pay for their campaign
  (C) the New Hampshire primary results were declared invalid
  (D) the national press revealed very personal aspects of their private lives
  (E) the Democratic Party leadership asked them to do so

94. United States policy towards Latin America under Franklin D. Roosevelt can be summarized as
  (A) the Roosevelt Corollary to the Monroe Doctrine
  (B) the Alliance for Progress
  (C) the establishment of the Pan-American Union
  (D) equal membership in the Organization of American States
  (E) the Good Neighbor Policy

95. All of the following reform movements of the pre-Civil War period are correctly paired with a leader of the movement EXCEPT
    (A) Care of the insane—Dorothea Dix
    (B) Abolition—Harriet Beecher Stowe
    (C) Women's Rights—Lucretia Mott
    (D) Education—Brigham Young
    (E) Prohibition—Neal S. Dow

96. All of the following major U.S. Supreme Court decisions are correctly paired with the decision handed down by the Supreme Court in the case named EXCEPT
    (A) *McCulloch v. Maryland*—upheld Maryland's right to tax the Bank of the United States
    (B) *Schechter v. United States*—declared the NIRA invalid, thus ending the first phase of the New Deal
    (C) *Plessy v. Ferguson*—upheld Louisiana law requiring segregated trains for blacks and whites
    (D) *Munn v. Illinois*—upheld an Illinois law fixing maximum rates for grain storage
    (E) *Mueller v. Oregon*—upheld an Oregon law limiting the maximum working hours for women

97. Which of the following events connected with the civil rights movement of the post-World War II period occurred first?
    (A) The lunch counter sit-ins
    (B) The decision in *Brown v. Board of Education*
    (C) The assassination of Martin Luther King, Jr.
    (D) Montgomery, Alabama, bus boycott
    (E) The 24th Amendment (anti-poll tax) to the Constitution

98. "United States tariffs until the 1930s established high rates of protection for industry and increased the rates of the preceding tariff."
    The quotation applies accurately to all of the following United States tariffs EXCEPT
    (A) The Tariff of Abominations
    (B) Fordney-McCumber Tariff
    (C) Underwood Tariff
    (D) Morrill Tariff
    (E) The Clay Compromise Tariff

99. "Now the trumpet summons us again—not a call to bear arms, though arms we need—not a call to battle, though embattled we are—but a call to bear the burden of a long twilight struggle, year in and year out, 'rejoicing in hope, patient in tribulation'—a struggle against the common enemies of man: tyranny, poverty, disease and war itself"

The author of the above quotation would most likely have supported all of the following EXCEPT

(A)   The War on Poverty
(B)   The Peace Corps
(C)   A flat percentage rate tax on all incomes
(D)   Medicare
(E)   The SALT disarmament agreements

100. Which of the following would NOT be considered part of the Cold War?

(A)   The U-2 incident
(B)   The Truman Doctrine
(C)   The U.N. intervention in the Congo
(D)   The attempts to impeach Earl Warren
(E)   The Bay of Pigs affair

Section II
DBQ

Part A: Document-Based Essay Question (DBQ)

Writing time—40 minutes

Directions: The following question requires you to construct a coherent essay that integrates your interpretation of documents A-H and your knowledge of the period referred to in the question. In your essay, you should strive to support your assertions both by citing key pieces of evidence from the documents and by drawing on your knowledge of the period.

1. Between 1900 and 1918 to what degree did the attitudes expressed in Supreme Court decisions concerning government regulation of business and working conditions reflect the attitudes of the political leaders of the nation? Why or why not were they in agreement?

Document A

It is settled by various decisions of this court that state constitutions and state laws may regulate life in many ways which we as legislators might think as injudicious or if you like as tyrannical.

The liberty of the citizen to do as he likes so long as he does not interfere with the liberty of others to do the same, which has been a shibboleth (accepted truth) for some well-known writers, is interfered with by school laws, by the Post Office, by every state or municipal institution which takes his money for purposes thought desirable, whether he likes it or not.

A constitution is not intended to embody a particular economic theory, whether of paternalism and the relation of the citizen to the State or of laissez-faire. It is made for people of fundamentally differing views.

> Oliver Wendell Holmes' Dissenting Opinion in *Lochner v. New York* — U.S. Supreme Court, 1905 — in which the majority of the Court declared unconstitutional a New York State law limiting the number of hours bakers could work each week.

Document B

... in the spinning and carding rooms of cotton and woolen mills, where large numbers of children are employed, clouds of lint-dust fill the lungs and menace the health. The children have a distressing cough, caused by the irritation of the throat, and many are hoarse from the same cause. In bottle factories and other branches of glass manufacture, the atmosphere is constantly charged with microscopic particles of glass.

The children who are employed in the manufacture of wall papers and poisonous paints suffer from slow poisoning. The naphtha fumes in the manufacture of rubber goods produce paralysis and premature decay.

> John Spargo, *The Cry of the Children*, 1906

Document C

... A gentleman by the name of Markham, writing a magazine article not long ago, said that he had visited the glasshouses and had seen children— boys and girls— with emaciated forms, with their eyes, as it were, protruding from their sockets, all due to overwork. He spoke of their little bodies being blistered by the hot furnaces, and a lot more of that kind of magazine stuff, for it is nothing but stuff.

I have been engaged in the manufacture of glass for thirty-five years and if Mr. Markham had come to see my factory ... (he) would not (have seen) anything like that which he described in his magazine article.

... The glasshouse boy of today becomes the glass manufacturer of tomorrow.

> United States Senator Nathan B. Scott of West Virginia, from a Speech in U.S. Congress, 1906

Document D

SOURCE: Library of Congress

Young boy working in canning factory. Early 1900s.

Document E

Constitutional questions are not settled by even a consensus of present public opinion, for it is the peculiar value of a written constitution that it places in unchanging form limitations upon legislative action, and thus gives a permanence and stability to popular government which otherwise would be lacking.

As argued in this case, the two sexes differ in structure of body, in the functions to be performed by each, in the amount of physical strength, in the capacity for long-continued labor, particularly when done standing, in the influence of vigorous health upon the future well-being of the race. This difference justifies a difference in legislation.

For these reasons the act in question is not in conflict with the federal Constitution as it respects the limitation of the hours of work done by a female in a laundry.

> *Mueller v. Oregon* 1908 Supreme Court decision in which the Court upheld an Oregon law limiting to ten a day the hours of labor for women employed in factories. Scientific, psychological, and sociological evidence was introduced by Louis B. Brandeis in winning the case.

Document F

— In this new age we find, for instance, that our laws with regard to relations of employer and employee are in many respects wholly antiquated and impossible... The modern corporation is not engaged in business as an individual. When we deal with it, we deal with an impersonal element, an immaterial piece of society...

— And do our laws take note of this curious state of things? Do they even attempt to distinguish between a man's act as a corporation director and as an individual? They do not. Our laws still deal with us on the basis of the old system.... What this country needs above everything else is a body of laws which will look after the men who are on the make rather than the men who are already made. Because the men who are already made are not going to live indefinitely, and they are not always kind enough to leave sons as able and as honest as they are...

— We used to think in the old-fashioned days when life was very simple that all the government had to do was to put on a policeman's uniform, and say, "Now don't anybody hurt anybody else." We used to say that the ideal of government was for every man to be left alone and not be interfered with, except when he interfered with somebody else. But we are coming now to realize that life is so complicated that we are not dealing with the old conditions, and that the law has to step in and create new conditions under which we may live, the conditions which will make it tolerable for us to live.

— We have been proud of our industrial achievements, but we have not hitherto stopped, thoughtfully enough to count the human cost, the cost of lives snuffed out, of energies overtaxed and broken, the fearful physical and spiritual cost to the men and women and children upon whom the dead weight and burden of it all has fallen pitilessly the years through.

> From speeches by Woodrow Wilson, 1912 and 1913

Document G

The American people are right in demanding that new nationalism, without which we cannot hope to deal with new problems. The new nationalism... is impatient of the utter confusion that results from local legislatures attempting to treat national issues as local issues... This new nationalism regards the executive power as the steward of the public welfare. It demands of the judiciary that it should be interested primarily in human welfare rather than in property, just as it demands that the representative body shall represent all of the people rather than any one class or section of people.

I believe in shaping the ends of government to protect property as well as human welfare. Normally, and in the long run, the ends are the same; but whenever the alternative must be faced, I am for men and not for property...

One of the fundamental necessities that a representative government such as ours is to make certain is that the men to whom people delegate their power shall serve the people by whom they are elected, and not the special interests... The object of government is the welfare of the people... No matter how honest and decent we are in our private lives, if we do not have the right kind of law and the right kind of administration of the law, we cannot go forward as a nation.

A National Industrial Commission would be created, which should have complete power to regulate and control all the great industrial concerns engaged in interstate business, which practically means all of them in this country. This commission should deal with all the abuses of the Trust, such supervision would put a stop to exploitation of the people by dishonest capitalists.

From speeches by Theodore Roosevelt, 1910
and 1912

Document H

Over interstate transportation, or its incidents, the regulatory power of Congress is ample, but the production of articles intended for interstate commerce is a matter of local regulations... If it were otherwise, all manufacture intended for interstate shipment would be brought under federal control to the practical exclusion of the authority of the states, a result certainly not contemplated by the framers of the Constitution when they vested in Congress the authority to regulate commerce among the states.

... In the present case. The thing attended to be accomplished by this statute is the denial of the facilities of interstate commerce to those manufacturers in the states who employ children within the prohibited ages. The Act, in effect, does not regulate transportation among the states, but aims to standardize the ages at which children may be employed in mining and manufacturing within the states. The goods shipped are in themselves, harmless...

That there should be limitations upon the right to employ children in the mines and factories in the interest of their own and the public welfare, all will admit... [However,] in our view, the necessary effect of this Act is, by means of a prohibition against a movement [of commodities] in interstate commerce..., to regulate the hours of labor of children..., [which is] a purely state authority... The Act... is repugnant to the Constitution. It not only transcends the authority delegated to Congress over commerce, but also exerts a power as to a purely local matter to which the federal authority does not extend.

> The majority opinion of the Supreme Court in Hammer v. Dagenhart in 1918 in which the Court declared unconstitutional the Keating-Owen Child Labor Act.

Section II
Free Response
Questions 2-6

Part B: Essay Question

Writing time—50 minutes

Directions: You are to answer *one* of the following five questions. Carefully choose the question that you are best prepared to answer. Cite relevant historical evidence in support of your generalizations and present your arguments clearly and logically. When you finish writing, check your work if time permits. Make certain to number your answer as the question is numbered below.

2. "Events on the frontier between 1763 and 1788 and the development of government policies in response to them were more significant for the development of the United States than the events which took place in the settled areas of the eastern seaboard between 1763 and 1788." Evaluate this statement.

3. Since the Civil War, to what extent have changes in the political control of the federal government been in response to domestic economic crises?

4. "Writers both of fiction and nonfiction often have a profound influence on the course of history." Compare the "profound influence" of one work of fiction and one work of nonfiction on the course of American history.

5. How do you account for the recurring cycles of reform movements in the United States?

6. "American history reveals that government by the majority can be divisive and that the views of the minority must be considered in executing policy." Assess the validity of this statement for the periods 1793-1812 and 1953-1974.

End of Examination

At the actual exam at this time you will be directed to circle on the back of your essay booklet in which you have written your answers the numbers of the two questions you answered.

Comments and Answers to Questions on Model Advanced Placement Examination

In this section you will find answers and answer explanations for the 100 multiple-choice questions of the model exam. The explanations of the multiple-choice questions indicate which answer is most correct and, in most cases, why the other choices should be eliminated. By reading all 100 statements, you will get a quick summary of the highlights of American history.

1.	E	2.	B	3.	B	4.	C
5.	D	6.	E	7.	A	8.	C
9.	E	10.	A	11.	D	12.	C
13.	A	14.	D	15.	B	16.	C
17.	C	18.	D	19.	D	20.	B
21.	D	22.	B	23.	B	24.	B
25.	E	26.	D	27.	B	28.	B
29.	D	30.	C	31.	C	32.	A
33.	B	34.	D	35.	A	36.	D
37.	B	38.	A	39.	C	40.	B
41.	D	42.	D	43.	A	44.	B
45.	E	46.	B	47.	A	48.	B
49.	A	50.	A	51.	C	52.	B
53.	C	54.	D	55.	D	56.	C
57.	E	58.	C	59.	A	60.	C
61.	E	62.	C	63.	B	64.	B
65.	E	66.	E	67.	B	68.	D
69.	E	70.	D	71.	C	72.	D
73.	A	74.	A	75.	D	76.	B
77.	C	78.	D	79.	A	80.	B
81.	E	82.	E	83.	A	84.	C
85.	E	86.	C	87.	A	88.	C
89.	B	90.	C	91.	B	92.	E
93.	D	94.	E	95.	D	96.	A
97.	B	98.	C	99.	C	100.	D

1. (E) The statement is typical of the Social Darwinist point of view. A Social Darwinist, Andrew Carnegie, an American businessman, and John D. Rockefeller would all have shared this viewpoint at the end of the last century. Eugene V. Debs, an American Socialist, would not have supported the view.

2. (B) For this question, you need to be able to read the chart and to understand the key. The only statement that is correct is the one about more Irish coming to America in 1850-1855 than in 1885-1890.

3. (B) This is a simple chronological question. The Connecticut Compromise was a compromise between the Virginia Plan and the New Jersey Plan at the Constitutional Convention, and it came last. The first event was the Declaration of Independence, and then the government under the Articles of Confederation was established. This government was changed by the Constitution.

4. (C) James Madison, John Jay, and Alexander Hamilton authored *The Federalist Papers* together. They all supported the Consitition. Thomas Jefferson, Patrick Henry, and Melancthon Smith all opposed the Constitution. Andrew Jackson was not involved in its ratification, and Samuel E. Morison is a 20th-century historian.

5. (D) NATO (North Atlantic Treaty Organization) was a post-World War II development. The other four choices were offered as solutions to the problems of the Great Depression. The WPA (Work Progress Administration) and the NIRA (National Industrial Recovery Act) were part of Roosevelt's solution to the problems of the Great Depression. EPIC (End Poverty in California) and the "Share the Wealth" movement were offered in opposition to Roosevelt's ideas.

6. (E) The Palmer Raids, led by the attorney general, reflected the anti-communist hysteria of the post-World War I period. The raids created a climate of opinion similar to that created by Senator Joe McCarthy in the 1950s.

7. (A) The American historian Frederick Jackson Turner, in his thesis on the influence of the frontier on America, stated all four points except the idea that "'The complex European life' had continual impact on America." In his article, Turner emphasized the uniqueness of America and the importance of the frontier in developing the American.

8. (C) Sections of the Constitution can be used to illustrate all five answers, but the quotation given is a clear example of checks and balances.

9. (E) The concepts expressed in the passage are those of isolationism and nationalism. Isolationism calls for separation of America from other nations; nationalism contains the idea that your country is the best, and its sovereign will should not be compromised in any way by following other nations. The writer is certainly in favor of freedom, but there is less emphasis on that concept than upon isolationism. Christianity, sovereignty, and socialism are irrelevant to the quotation.

10. (A) The cartoon from the World Telegram of August 1, 1934, clearly suggests that the Republican party, represented as the old man with the letters G.O.P. on his vest, has no effective solution to the Great Depression. The only ideas offered are those of a return to the programs of 1929, which were in effect under President Hoover at the time of the "great crash." It might appear that the G.O.P. is being robbed by Wall Street and Rugged Individualism, but these two figures represent the G.O.P.'s major support. They are holding on to the G.O.P. for support; they are not robbing him. To be able to interpret this cartoon, one needs an understanding of the economic situation in the United States from 1929 to 1934.

11. (D) The areas colored black on the map represent the greatest extent of Nazi control in World War II. The names of the countries on the map should help you to identify what the black represents. The name of the city of Stalingrad may be the best clue. It was at Stalingrad that the Russians finally stopped the German advance.

12. (C)   Ronald Reagan began extensive negotiations with the Soviet Union on disarmament *after* his re-election in 1984. The other four reasons are suggested for Reagan's overwhelming victory in 1984.

13. (A)   This is a very tricky question and requires a careful reading of the chart. A is incorrect because the D.T. & I. Railroad has no funds available for Charges, Dividends, Betterments, & Surplus. Therefore, the smallest amount they spent was for this and not for taxes. The other statements are clearly correct.

14. (D)   A careful reading of the map reveals that the Democratic party in the election of 1920 "lost every state except those that could be considered 'southern.'"

15. (B)   President Lyndon Johnson withdrew from the presidential race after his defeat in the New Hampshire primary in 1968. His withdrawal was attributed to the public's rejection of his policy in Vietnam. President Johnson continued to expand America's commitment to that nation. U.S. involvement began under President Eisenhower with his support of the French in that country. U.S. forces attacked both Cambodia and Laos during the Vietnam War and also bombed North Vietnam. The Gulf of Tonkin Resolution authorized retaliation by President Johnson but was not a declaration of war and did not legalize the conflict internationally. One of the identifying features of the Vietnam War was the inability to identify the enemy. There were no clear battle lines.

16. (C)   The statement is a definition of mercantilism. Check the Glossary for definitions of the other terms.

17. (C)   Under the Articles of Confederation, the states exercised sovereignty. This was the greatest weakness of the Articles of Confederation because the central government was unable to make and enforce decisions for all of the states.

18. (D)   A "loose constructionist" believes that the U.S. Constitution should not be read strictly and that when you find a power that is implied by the wording of the Constitution, that power is a legitimate power for the government to exercise. The four other choices all share the concept of "strict construction" under which the Constitution must be read literally and no extension of powers made.

19. (D)   The presidential years of James Monroe have often been referred to as the Era of Good Feeling. The Whig party, or the opposition political party, had been badly weakened by its failure to support the War of 1812. Thus, President Monroe had little resistance to his measures, something which made his presidency appear as a period of "good feeling."

20. (B)   The main purpose of Henry Clay's American System was to develop an interdependent economic system tying the East, West, and South together. He offered it after the Era of Good Feeling, at a time when sectionalism was beginning to grow. The other four choices had nothing to do with his American System.

21. (D)   The transcendentalist writers of New England, of whom Ralph Waldo Emerson is the most noteworthy, found their major source of truth and inspiration in nature. The writers—centered in Concord, Massachusetts, in the 1830s and 1840s—are considered to have begun the first native American philosophical movement, although this movement had close connections with the Romantic Movement in England.

22. (B)   The South Carolina "exposition and protest" was written but not signed by Calhoun. It supported the South Carolina legislature's resolutions declaring the Tariff of Abominations unconstitutional, unjust, and oppressive to the interest of the South. The Tariff of Abominations, passed in 1828, was a political move by Jackson's supporters to undercut President J.Q. Adams and work for the election of Jackson. The move backfired when New England voted for the tariff, which supported the protective concept. This was one step in the slow alienation of South Carolina from the Union, which culminated in secession in 1860. The other events had nothing to do with the Tariff of Abominations. Calhoun resigned as Jackson's vice-president in 1832; the Hartford Convention was called to protest the War of 1812; and the specie circular was issued by Jackson in 1836.

23. (B)   After the capture of Vicksburg in the west, the Confederacy was split in half. The other four choices are important battles of the Civil War in the east.

24. (B)   The person usually given credit for the passage of the Civil Rights Acts of 1960 and 1964 is Lyndon Baines Johnson. In 1960 he was leader of the Senate, and in 1964 he was President of the United States. John F. Kennedy was in favor of civil rights legislation, but couldn't get it through Congress. With the impact his assassination had on the country, President Johnson was able to get passed not only the Civil Rights Act of 1964 but many of the things President Kennedy believed in. Adam Clayton Powell, a black, was an important member of the House of Representatives, and Andrew Young, also a black, was U.S. Ambassador to the United Nations under President Carter, but neither was involved with the passage of the Civil Rights Acts of 1960 and 1964. George Wallace, Governor of Alabama, opposed civil rights legislation.

25. (E)   Wilson announced his Fourteen Points as a possible formula for peace at the end of World War I. He was most concerned about establishing a League of Nations, as suggested in Point XIV. The League was incorporated into the Treaty of Versailles, and the Treaty was rejected by the Senate. The other points are important ones, but Wilson was more prepared to compromise on them than on the League. He believed that if there was a League, other issues could be resolved by it before war broke out.

26. (D)   The Creel Committee organized during World War I by the U.S. government had propaganda as its purpose. During the war, the government was concerned about the four other issues, but other committees and commissions took care of those matters.

27. (B)   Woodrow Wilson would most likely have commented on the lost opportunity of the United States to take world leadership. He had hoped the

United States would take the lead in the League of Nations after World War I, and this was rejected. The idea expressed was too early for the period of Theodore Roosevelt. John F. Kennedy and Lyndon B. Johnson both rose to importance as political leaders after World War II, when America had already taken on world leadership. One might think that Franklin Roosevelt was the author, but during his administration he slowly moved the United States into a position of leadership and saw the United States through the "tragedy" of World War II.

28. (B) Although all five choices present New Deal legislation, the only one dealing with banking is the Federal Deposit Insurance Corporation.

29. (D) A careful reading of the quotation will show that the author suggests that the United States continues to be in a depression, that a veto of the tax cut would be harmful to the nation, that other nations are heavily affected by the U.S. economy, and that the unemployment rate in the country is high. The issue under discussion is a tax cut to create economic recovery at a time of high unemployment. The author does not suggest that the political impact of the policy should be the sole guide in determining policy.

30. (C) Changes in the number and function of executive departments must be approved by Congress, not the president alone, and no law states when the Cabinet must meet. The president's Cabinet is not described in the Constitution. However, the Constitution states that members of the executive branch should be appointed by the president and confirmed by the Senate. During President Andrew Johnson's administration, the Senate tried to make this constitutional provision also apply to the firing of Cabinet members. This was rejected and the idea that members of the executive branch serve at the pleasure of the chief executive, i.e., the president, was re-established and remains in force. So C is the correct answer.

31. (C) The Joint Electoral Commission Report on the disputed election of 1876 between Samuel J. Tilden and Rutherford B. Hayes was accepted in 1877, making Hayes president. As part of the report, Republicans promised to withdraw federal troops from the South and appoint at least one southerner to the Cabinet. This has traditionally been interpreted to indicate the end of the political Reconstruction of the South. The southern states never indicated that they welcomed military occupation. The other three choices all deal with post-Civil War matters but do not mark the end of Reconstruction.

32. (A) The quotation emphasizes the importance of newspapers and magazine articles for revealing truth and for supporting democracy even though "it may be impossible." This is the viewpoint of the muckrakers who in the late 19th and early 20th centuries wrote articles in magazines and newspapers pointing out the inequities and corruption in American life. Tammany was the political machine that controlled New York City at the end of the last century. Dixiecrats were supporters of Governor Thurmond in his presidential campaign of 1948 on the States' Rights ticket. A Populist was a member or supporter of the Populist Party. They wanted some political reforms but concentrated on supporting the coinage of silver and agrarian problems. A fundamentalist is a deeply religious individual who believes in a literal interpretation of the Bible.

He or she may be active politically but in general is not concerned with corruption in government. A Federalist was a member of the Federalist party and a supporter of political power in the hands of the wealthy.

33. (B) The plan which Franklin D. Roosevelt introduced to force the Supreme Court to change its decisions and begin to accept the New Deal program consisted of a proposal to the Congress that the Court be increased in size. The Constitution gives to Congress the power to set the number of judges on the Court. The plan is often referred to as the Court Packing Plan. The famous "My dog Falla" speech was a humorous speech given by Roosevelt mocking the Republicans who were attacking not only his plans and policies but his family and even his dog. This was part of the presidential campaign of 1940. The president has no power to order impeachment proceedings, the president did not ignore the Court decisions but tried to get them reversed, and he did not call on the American people to elect only Democrats to Congress as a response to the decisions by the Supreme Court.

34. (D) Helen Hunt Jackson's books *A Century of Dishonor* and *Ramona* pricked the conscience of Americans and led to a new approach to native Americans that was incorporated in the Dawes Severalty Act of 1887. The goal of the Act was to assimilate Indians into the mainstream of American life by making them citizens. The other four choices were among the causes of the intense antagonisms between the native Americans and the U.S. government which led to warfare between the two.

35. (A) The Taft-Hartley Act of 1947 banned the closed shop, permitted employers to sue unions for broken contracts, required unions to abide by a sixty-day "cooling-off period," as part of strike settlements, required unions to make public their financial statements, forced union leaders to sign a non-communist oath, and forbade unions to support political campaigns with monetary contributions. Because of these features, the Act is not considered a victory for organized labor. The other four choices are. Wisconsin passed one of the first unemployment laws in the country; the establishment of the Committee for Industrial Organization (CIO) helped industrial unionization; the Anthracite Strike of 1902 was settled by Teddy Roosevelt in favor of the workers, using the authority of the federal government to support labor; and the Wagner Act of 1935 was one of the highlights of the New Deal labor legislation. It defined unfair labor practices on the employers' part and upheld the right of employees to join unions and to bargain collectively.

36. (D) Airplanes were not developed until the 20th century. The other four choices were developed in the 19th century or earlier.

37. (B) All five choices occurred during the presidency of Andrew Jackson, and thus, his election would be the first event.

38. (A) New York was first settled by the Dutch. Delaware was first settled by Swedes, Pennsylvania by the English, Jamaica by Spaniards, and Canada by the French.

39. (C) The traditional interpretation of the founding of the Plymouth Bay Colony is that it was founded *primarily* for religious purposes. To some degree, the reasons were also political, social, cultural, and economic, but the religious were the most important ones.

40. (B) Although all the choices are important for the development of factories, it was because of abundant water power that the earliest factories in the United States were located in New England.

41. (D) *The Sovereignty and Goodness of God or Narrative of the Captivity and Restoration of Mrs. Mary Rowlandson* was the most popular story about native Americans written in the English colonies.

42. (D) The South strongly supported Prohibition and even today regions of the South have Prohibition laws. The other three choices are characteristic of the Prohibition Era of the 1920s.

43. (A) Keynes developed his economic theories in the post-World War I period, and they have had profound impact on Western society during this century. The general concept is that the government should interfere in the business cycle to counteract the highs and lows of inflation and deflation. To smooth out the extremes of the business cycle, the government should tax highly in times of inflation and should spend extensively in times of deflation. In theory, the high taxes will cut down the rate of inflation, and the government spending in times of deflation would create jobs and counterbalance the deflationary cycle. The government has found it much easier to spend extensively in deflationary times than it has to tax highly in times of inflation. Choice E presents the reverse of Keynes's view. The other three choices present other economic theory. Laissez-faire economics believes that government should keep hands off all economic activity. Social Darwinists believe business people should run the government. Under mercantilist economic theory the wealth of a nation is measured by the amount of gold it holds.

44. (B) Shays' Rebellion occurred in western Massachusetts in 1786 under the government of the Articles of Confederation. It was one of the events that led to the calling of the Constitutional Convention in 1787. The Stamp Act was repealed in 1766, Daniel Boone took his first trip to Kentucky in 1767, and the Boston Massacre occurred in 1770, all before independence was declared. President Jefferson fought and finally suppressed the Barbary Pirates during his first administration.

45. (E) Jefferson is often considered a states' rights supporter. As president, however, he often acted beyond the authority strictly given to the president in the Constitution. During his presidency, he undertook the four events mentioned, and all seemed to stretch the power of the presidency, especially the purchase of Louisiana.

46. (B) The opening of the Erie Canal in 1825 had an important effect on the settlement of the West, since it provided an easy water route west of the New England and New York areas. The canal increased the settlement in the

Northwest territories greatly. The completion of the transcontinental railroad did affect western settlement, as the other events did, but later in the century.

47.   (A)   The Battle of Fallen Timbers occurred in northwest Ohio in 1794, and helped to secure the northwest frontier from Indian attack. The other battles all occurred in the War of 1812.

48.   (B)   The five authors listed are all important 19th and early 20th century American writers. They are all linked correctly to the type of work they wrote except for Bret Harte, who was noted for his stories on the West and not for cynical tales of the eastern nouveaux riches.

49.   (A)   The following is the correct chronological order for the events: Wilson's 14 Points, which were presented in 1917; the rejection of the League of Nations by the U.S. Senate, which was done in 1919; the Washington Disarmament Conference, which first met in November of 1921; the Dawes Plan for German reparations, which was presented in April of 1924; and finally, the Kellogg-Briand Pact for the outlawing of war, which was negotiated in 1928. These are all events relating to the U.S. involvement in Europe after World War I.

50.   (A)   The Pendleton Act (Civil Service Act of 1883) was passed as a response to the assassination of President Garfield. The Act set up a three-person civil service commission with the responsibility of administering competitive examinations so that federal office holders could be appointed on a merit basis. President Garfield had been assassinated by Charles Guiteau, who was a disappointed office seeker and mentally unstable.

51.   (C)   During the presidency of Jimmy Carter there was talk of the possibility of withdrawing some U.S. troops from Europe, but U.S. troops were not withdrawn. Strategic Arms Limitation Talks (SALT) were held during his presidency, inflation was not a major problem, human rights were the guiding principle of U.S. foreign policy, and American hostages were seized after the overthrow of the Shah of Iran and the establishment of the Khomeini government. The hostages were not released until the day of the inauguration of Carter's successor, Ronald Reagan.

52.   (B)   The Social Security Act of 1935 passed as part of the New Deal provided retirement pensions and unemployment payments. While it provided an income for the old, disabled, and unemployed, its purpose was not to control the money supply. The other four choices, the Specie Circular of 1836, the Sherman Silver Purchase Act of 1890, the Federal Reserve Act of 1913, and the establishment of the Commodity Dollar in 1933, all had as their purpose the control of the money supply in some way.

53.   (C)   From the end of Reconstruction in 1877 to the outbreak of World War I in 1914, fundamental changes in the American system were brought about by federal legislation in all areas except civil rights.

54.   (D)   The acquisition of Pago Pago by treaty negotiated with the chiefs of the island of Tutuila in the Samoan Islands had nothing to do with the U.S. entry into the Spanish-American War. The other choices are often given as reasons for the U.S. entry into the Spanish-American War, the sinking of the battleship Maine being the final justification for war.

55. (D)   The "gag rule" was adopted by the U.S. Senate in 1836 to prevent debate of abolitionist proposals requesting the ending of slavery. The rule provided a complicated formula by which abolitionists could petition the Senate, but the petition would not be debated.

56. (C)   The XYZ Affair occurred during John Adams's administration. The XYZ Affair of 1797 involved a demand by French ministers for a large bribe from U.S. representatives who were in France seeking to improve relations between the two countries. The other events occurred during Washington's administration. Relations with France were strained as a result of Jay's Treaty and French interference with U.S. trade. Secretary of State John Jay negotiated the treaty with the English in 1795. John Adams was elected to succeed Washington while Washington was still president. Jefferson resigned in part because his views on the Bank of the United Sates were rejected while Hamilton's views were accepted.

57. (E)   The first four events relate to the expansion of the United States in the Pacific area. The last to take place was the opening of the Panama Canal on August 15, 1914. This gave the United States a way to move the Navy back and forth between the two oceans. Alaska was purchased and the Midway Islands annexed in 1867, giving the United States more territory. The Battle of Manila Bay took place in May of 1898 and this opened the way for taking over the Philippine Islands. The London Economic Conference of 1933 was when the United States first recognized the government of the Soviet Union but it cannot be considered part of American expansion.

58. (C)   All five choices are Acts passed by the U.S. Congress dealing with land. The Land Act of 1796 called for rectangular survey and sale of land at public auction at a minimum price of two dollars an acre. Townships were set at six square miles each, and they were subdivided into sections. The smallest section one could purchase under the Act was 640 acres.

59. (A)   These five choices all deal with labor. The most recent event is the establishment of the Congress of Industrial Organizations in 1938. The CIO grew out of the Committee for Industrial Organization established in 1935 within the American Federation of Labor (AFL).

60. (C)   These five events all relate to the Civil War. The event that occurred first is Lincoln's first election to the presidency in November of 1860. South Carolina seceded at the end of the year; Fort Sumter was fired upon in 1861, beginning the fighting of the war. The Emancipation Proclamation, which freed slaves in states still in rebellion against the United States, was a wartime measure announced in 1862 and it went into effect in 1863. West Virginia was admitted to the Union as a state on June 20, 1863. (West Virginia consisted of the fifty western counties of Virginia that had refused to acknowledge the secession of Virginia from the Union.)

61. (E)   If you carefully study the cartoon from *Harper's Weekly* of September 1, 1888, you can tell that the well-dressed gentleman was trying to prevent the law, as represented by the policeman, from interfering. The gentleman does not believe the police officer should interfere, but the cartoonist suggests he is prepared to do so by both the statement under the cartoon in which the well-dressed man wants to keep the police out and by the upraised billy club held ready for use. The individual being robbed is competition, and it is being robbed by American industries, which are organized as trusts. The American market is advertised as operating under freedom and equality.

62. (C)   In spite of Taft's replacement of Theodore Roosevelt's "Big Stick" policy with Dollar Diplomacy, the United States continued to intervene militarily in the Caribbean (Cuba and Santo Domingo) and in Latin America (Nicaragua and Honduras). The other statements are all true concerning the concept of Dollar Diplomacy. Investments were encouraged in the Far East, especially China, and in Latin America. Because the policy was to secure a peace through business investment, less money was spent on military defense. Wilson continued the policy although philosophically he opposed it. The idea of United States intervention in Latin America rather than European upheld the Monroe Doctrine.

63. (B)   This is a tricky question but by studying the graph carefully you can see that the gap between total unemployed and unemployed household heads was greater in 1971, 1972, 1973, part of 1974, 1975, and 1976 than in 1969. The other statements are true.

64. (B)   The author of the quotation is referring to the Pan-American Union, the oldest and most successful association of sovereign governments in the world, which is now known as the Organization of American States (OAS). The League of Nations was part of the Treaty of Versailles. The EDC and NATO were formed after World War II in Europe. The Contadora Group, the most recent, was formed in 1985 to bring peace to Nicaragua and end the fighting between the Contras and the Sandinista government of Nicaragua.

65. (E)   All of the items except E—a major economic recession with high unemployment for all Americans—were characteristic of the period in U.S. society between the end of World War II and the election of President John F. Kennedy. The Supreme Court knocked down segregation in the public schools in the famous *Brown v. Board of Education* decision in 1954. The McCarthy era in the late 1940s and early 1950s was another Red Scare. The start of rock 'n' roll symbolized by Elvis Presley and the introduction of other types of popular music has changed American society considerably. Finally, the voting populace in the 1950s has often been characterized by historians as uncritical and silent.

66. (E)   Although all the choices deal with relations between the United States and China and/or Japan, the quotation definitely refers to the Japanese actions in China in the late 1930s. Japan invaded Manchuria in 1931 and attacked China proper in 1937. This was in violation of many agreements, including the "Open Door" notes and the Kellogg-Briand Pact.

67.   (B)   When a nation seeks to dominate in a geographic area not part of their sovereign territory by securing preferential treatment of political, economic, and even social nature, it is considered an attempt to establish a sphere of influence in the area. The European powers attempted to establish such spheres in China after the Sino-Japanese War of 1895. U.S. foreign policy attempted to deny such spheres in China through the establishment of an Open Door Policy.

68.   (D)   The passage states the important points found in the Monroe Doctrine of 1823 that the American continents are not open for colonization and that the nations on the continents are free and independent states. Theodore Roosevelt interpreted the Monroe Doctrine to allow for the United States' intervention to maintain order in the Americas and to collect debts owed other nations. This concept of America acting either on behalf of its own nationals or the other nations of the world to collect debts and maintain order has been called the Roosevelt Corollary to the Monroe Doctrine. It is a stretching of the original Doctrine and its concept as presented in the passage. The other doctrines do not relate to the Americas so the quote would not relate to them.

69.   The photograph from the *Los Angeles County Natural History Museum Foundation* shows immigrants living in New York City. The time as revealed by the clothing is the turn of the century. Hispanic migration to Los Angeles was later than that. The population is clearly not black. The names on the buildings, the tenement-style buildings and active life on the street all point to immigrants in New York City.

70.   (D)   The economic program known as Reaganomics followed the theory of supply side economics. It called first for tax cuts, which were to stimulate the economy so no revenue would be lost to the government. Reaganomics also included increased military expenditures and reduced expenditures for social services. The program resulted in unplanned massive increases in the federal debt since the economy did not respond as anticipated and the Congress refused to cut social services as far as the president requested.

71.   (C)   In the cartoon from the *Saturday Evening Post* of June 6, 1914, the main point the cartoonist is making is that Theodore Roosevelt and Woodrow Wilson are again seeking popular support for their political reform programs. Roosevelt had run for president on the "Bull Moose" ticket in 1912, and in doing so split the Republican party, which renominated President Taft. Eugene V. Debs ran as a Socialist. With these three candidates in the field, Woodrow Wilson, the candidate of the Democratic party, was able to win. The New Nationalism was the reform program advocated by Roosevelt, and the New Freedom was the reform program advocated by Wilson in that election. Wilson won, began his reforms, and in the congressional campaign of 1914, the rivalry between the two men surfaced again. Choice E, "rivalry of political candidates," has truth in it, but C is a better answer. The other choices are irrelevant.

72.   (D)   The office building in the center of the photograph from *Harper's Weekly*, March 9, 1912, shows the influence during the last quarter of the nineteenth century of the outstanding American architect, Henry Hobson Richardson. Richardson was strongly influenced by the Romanesque architecture of southern France. He is known for his use of Romanesque elements (one being the arch) and for imaginative treatment of ornament, both of which can be seen in this photograph.

Frank Lloyd Wright's work is characterized as natural. He often blended his houses into the natural surroundings and used local materials. He was deeply concerned about the materials used and about the functional qualities of his buildings. He is considered by many to be the outstanding American architect of this century, with a strong influence on many others.

Eino Saarinen is remembered for his imaginative qualities, as seen in the residential colleges at Yale, which remind one of Italian hill towns. He, too, was concerned with structure and function. He is remembered as one of the outstanding mid-20th century American architects.

Buildings in the Greek Revival style of architecture incorporate many elements of classical Greek temples and public buildings. Columns with Doric, Corinthian, or Ionic capitals; friezes and carvings with egg and dart designs; and porticoes with columns two stories high characterize this architecture.

The Georgian style developed in England in the 18th century during the reigns of the first three Georges. In the colonies the finest public buildings (such as those at Williamsburg), the homes of wealthy colonists in Boston, Philadelphia, and Charleston, and plantation homes such as Westover in Virginia were built in the Georgian style. These constructions are all characterized by balance and symmetry and a strong emphasis on the horizontal line. In many cases, there are pediments or decorative devices above the windows, and pilasters and pediments beside and above the doors, respectively.

73. (A) The first oil embargo imposed by OPEC in order to raise oil prices occurred in 1973 during Nixon's second term. The effect of the embargo continued to be felt during the Carter and Reagan administrations. The other events all occurred during Carter's presidency and were important foreign policy issues of the period.

74. (A) In the quotation the most important argument being presented is that the British Parliament has no authority to tax Americans. The concern is that if Parliament can force the colonists to carry out this order then they can force the colonists to do everything—pay taxes, clothe and house troops—and the colonists rebelled against this concept.

75. (D) The American colonists, especially merchants from Newport and Bristol, Rhode Island, and some from Boston and Salem, Massachusetts; Providence, Rhode Island; Portsmouth, New Hampshire; and New London, Connecticut, all participated in the profitable slave trade along with many English merchants. The other statements are all true concerning the slave trade in the 18th century.

76. (B) The spirit of the philosophy expressed in the quotation is incorporated in the Declaration of Independence more than it is in the other documents.

77. (C) Both sides did make concessions during the Cuban Missile Crisis which averted a move to World War III. Both Kennedy and Khrushchev said this in reflecting upon the crisis. Recent studies show Castro did not follow every lead of the Soviets, and Khrushchev did honor the U.S. quarantine. Some believe Kennedy overreacted but that is not generally accepted and even if it were, it is not as full a description of the event as is choice C. The missiles were discovered by U.S. planes flying over Cuba. The flights were part of regular U.S. surveillance and the sighting of missiles was a surprise. Recently it has been learned that those working at the missile sites disobeyed Soviet orders to camouflage the construction sites. The discovery was a surprise but that fact is certainly not the best way to characterize the missile crisis.

78. (D) The chart from *Building America* dates from the Great Depression of the early 1930s. Electric lighting proves a particularly helpful clue for dating the chart. Electric lighting was not developed until the 1870s, with Philadelphia getting the first electric street lights in 1878. It had not spread widely by the time of the Populist Era in the 1890s. The New Deal through R.E.A. worked hard to bring electric power to rural areas, and it succeeded. Therefore, by the post-World War II period, there would be much more electric lighting in farm homes than is indicated by the chart. Of course, the Civil War years were the first half of the decade of the 1860s, and the Jacksonian period centered on the two terms of President Andrew Jackson, 1829-37.

79. (A) The Nixon administration negotiated a cease fire and a settlement to the Vietnam War. Saigon, the capital of South Vietnam, did not fall to the North Vietnamese until 1975 during the presidency of Gerald Ford. The other events took place during the Nixon years.

80. (B) In the cartoon, *The Irrepressible Independent*, by W.A. Rogers, the Spoils System referred to on the Tammany booth indicates the political system of rewarding supporters with appointed offices. Tammany was a political machine that ran New York City and was noted for its system of rewarding its workers with political jobs. The other choices do not apply. This question is simply one of knowing the definition of a political term.

81. (E) The only thing that the bar graph can prove is that Lincoln and Wilson were both minority presidents according to popular vote, but received a majority of votes in the Electoral College. The chart cannot prove that the Electoral College is unjust, although many may feel that is true. Nor can it prove that Bell was a better candidate than Douglas, or that someone running in 1912 would have done as well if he had run in 1860. Finally, the chart cannot prove that popular candidates cannot win in the Electoral College.

82. (E) While American research scientists and philosophers were beginning to be recognized as important contributors to international intellectual life, they were not the recognized leaders in the period 1865-1900. During this period, American scientists such as Thomas Edison did make great contributions in the practical application of science to daily living but were not noted as research scientists. The other statements all are indicative of the changes in the American educational climate in the post-Civil War period.

83.   (A)   The quote "Liberty and union, now and forever, one and inseparable," was said by Daniel Webster, not John C. Calhoun. Calhoun was a States' Rights advocate and would not call for union in such strong terms. His famous quotation is "The union, next to our liberty, the most dear." This is a very different idea from the Webster quote. The other quotes are correctly paired and represent the position held by the speaker. Patrick Henry, speaking about the rebellion against England, Thomas Jefferson in writing the Declaration of Independence, Andrew Jackson speaking about the Nullification Crisis, and Franklin Roosevelt speaking about the Great Depression made the statements ascribed to them in this question.

84.   (C)   This question requires you to know what these American authors wrote about. Of the five, Booth Tarkington is the one who was least concerned with social criticism of America. In fact, he is best characterized as a Victorian sentimentalist. On the other hand, Norris, Sinclair, and Riis are noted for their writings of social criticisms. Henry James's novels are of upper-class conflict, but within them, there is a strong theme of social criticism.

85.   (E)   This question requires that you know groupings of famous Americans who were contemporaries and had an impact upon each other and history. Of the five groups, the one that is not made up of individuals who were contemporaries who interacted is the one with Mark Hanna, William McKinley, and Franklin D. Roosevelt. Hanna helped make McKinley president and both were linked to Theodore Roosevelt, but Franklin D. Roosevelt was of the next generation.

86.   (C)   The term *impressment* means to take by force for public service, especially naval service. As used by the United States in the period before the War of 1812, the term referred to the British practice of forcing American sailors into service on British warships. This British practice was one of the causes of that war.

87.   (A)   A 20th-century political conservative would place the value of liberty over that of equality. Conservatives see a danger of tyranny inherent in majority rule, support organized religion as a stabilizing force, and have even gone so far as to support a constitutional amendment allowing prayers in public schools. They believe strongly in private property and the capitalist ethic and would support the rights of individuals over the rights of the community.

88.   (C)   Henry Hudson sailed for the Muscovy Company of England and for the Dutch East India Company. He did not sail for Portugal. The other men are correctly paired with the countries for which they sailed.

89.   (B)   The quotation is taken from the Rhode Island colonial charter. The founders of Rhode Island were particularly concerned about both civil and religious rights. King James I believed in the divine right of kings, which is not upheld by this quotation; the Albany Plan of Union was proposed by Benjamin Franklin as the political, not religious, framework for colonial unity at the time of the French and Indian War; the trial of Peter Zenger is famous for establishing a free press and not religious liberty; and the Mayflower Compact established a political framework of government for the Pilgrims.

90. (C) If you are doing original research, the best way to begin is to go to the original sources and find what they say. The National Archives contain the important documents of American history so that would be the best place to start. If you are an amateur, you might not know this and would need to consult a librarian or read someone else's book (a secondary source) to start. At some point, you may wish to consult the letters of the signers of the Declaration but they may not comment on any changes made. Also, it is always helpful to consult other historians about their opinions but opinions are no substitute for the information you can find in original sources.

91. (B) The statement is from the Seneca Falls Convention, which was held under the leadership of Lucretia Mott and Elizabeth Cady Stanton in 1848. If you cannot identify this statement and its date, you would know it would not have been made after 1919 because in that year the 19th Amendment to the Constitution, which provided for women's suffrage, was declared ratified. The next-to-last paragraph in the statement is calling for suffrage for women and would not have been needed after 1919.

92. (E) The writer clearly believes the first four choices and believes that women and men together must fight for women's rights.

93. (D) During the campaign for the 1988 presidential nomination the national press publicized aspects of the private lives of contenders Gary Hart and Joseph Biden which led to the withdrawal from the campaign of these two announced candidates. At the time Gary Hart was leading in the polls. This was considered a change in policy on the part of the press and it led to considerable discussion on the future of the American nomination process. Later in the campaign before the first caucuses and primary, Gary Hart reentered the race but did poorly and withdrew a second time. The other choices are invalid.

94. (E) Franklin D. Roosevelt viewed the United States as a good neighbor of the Latin American nations and implemented this concept as United States policy. The Roosevelt Corollary was Theodore Roosevelt's interpretation of the Monroe Doctrine, the Alliance for Progress was John F. Kennedy's approach to Central America, the Organization of American States was instituted after World War II replacing the Pan-American Union, whose roots date to a 1885 conference in Washington.

95. (D) All of the movements are correctly linked with their leaders except for education. Although a university is named after him, Brigham Young is noted as the leader of the Mormons, not of educational reform. Horace Mann, Henry Barnard, Elizabeth Peabody, and Mary Lyon are some noted leaders of educational reform in the pre-Civil War period.

96. (A) The last four choices correctly link the case with the decision reached. *McCulloch v. Maryland* denied the right of the state of Maryland to tax the Bank of the United States. In this famous case of 1819, Chief Justice John Marshall established the concept of loose construction of the Constitution. Although the Constitution does not give Congress the power to establish a bank, the power, according to Marshall, is implied. He went on to say that no state could tax an organ of the federal government.

97. **(B)** The decision in the *Brown v. Board of Education* case came in 1954. The other events in the civil rights movement of the post-World War II period occurred after that date.

98. **(C)** The quotation would not apply to the Underwood Tariff, which was one of the few tariffs that lowered the rates. There is a tricky aspect to this question, since there is no such tariff as the Clay Compromise Tariff. The quotation would obviously not apply to a nonexistent tariff. So, that choice would have to be eliminated as a possible answer.

99. **(C)** The quotation from John F. Kennedy's inaugural address suggests that he would have supported all four points except a flat percentage tax on all incomes. Kennedy actually reduced income taxes and would not have believed in a flat tax, which would have hit the poor more heavily than the rich.

100. **(D)** The attempt to impeach Chief Justice of the U.S. Supreme Court Earl Warren during the 1950s related to domestic issues and not to issues of foreign policy. Therefore, it would not be considered part of the Cold War. The other four events involved international conflicts between the United States and its allies and the communist nations under the leadership of the Soviet Union.

Comments on the Six Free-Response Questions

Comments follow on the six sample essay questions of Part A and B of Section II of the exam. For each essay equestion, there is a general analysis that is similar to those given for the sample essay questions in each chapter of Part III. In addition to the analyses, two sample answers— one for the DBQ (Part A) and one for the first standard essay question (Part B)— are included. In the left margin of the two sample answers there are comments on certain elements of the answers that are noteworthy.

You must be aware, as all of the analyses of essay questions have indicated, that there are many possible ways to answer each essay question— theses will differ, organizational schemes will differ, and the facts chosen to prove a point will differ. The two sample answers illustrate only one of the many possible ways to write good answers.

Analysis of the DBQ (Part A)—Question 1

The DBQ is a straightforward *To what extent . . .* type of question (see Part III, Chapter 4). In essence, you are asked to analyze how Supreme Court decisions and the views expressed by political leaders are related. The second sentence of the question adds a *Why?* (see Part III, Chapter 3) aspect to this simple *To what extent . . .* question. This should present no particular problem, since it merely requires that in your answer, after you have analyzed the relationship between the court decisions and the views of the political leaders, you explain the reasons for this relationship. You will want to keep this in mind as you analyze the question and prepare an outline of your answer.

Although the documents are chosen from 1905-18, the time period 1900-1918 is stated in the directions. Directions are extremely important, and the time periods presented must be followed. You should give some background information from the turn of the century. The vocabulary used in the question should present no difficulties.

This DBQ asks you to deal with a perennial issue of American history, that is, do or should the decisions of the Supreme Court follow or lead public opinion? As the DBQ is worded, public opinion is equated with the statements of political leaders. You may have discussed this matter at some time in your study.

As indicated in Chapter 5, the DBQ on the AP examination will relate to the "mainstream" of American history. This question certainly does that, since it asks the student to focus on one crucial aspect of that important era of reform, i.e., the Progressive Era. Several of the documents are statements from presidents who led the political reforms of the age. Nothing could be more mainstream than Theodore Roosevelt and Woodrow Wilson—two presidents who would be studied in every American history course. The other documents may be less obvious and you may not have studied these particular Supreme Court cases but enough information about the cases is included for you to understand them. You should have no difficulty relating them to the main developments from 1900 to 1918.

As you are aware, it is necessary to introduce in your answer information not found in the documents, but which is relevant to the question. In this question, knowledge from many sources might be introduced to provide a deeper understanding of the tension between the Supreme Court and the Progressive leaders. Some information you introduce might be on the Muckrakers who, at the turn of the century, pointed out unsavory working conditions and political corruption, thus paving the way for many reforms. Mention might be made of the attitude of Social Darwinists who supported laissez-faire government and opposed government regulation of business. Comments on Roosevelt and Wilson — their styles of leadership as president, their goals as developed in the New Nationalism and New Freedom Programs, legislation they supported and their views toward the individual — might be included to provide the background to the issues addresssed in the documents.

You are given 15 minutes to read the documents and organize your answer. You may use some of the time to pick the other essay question you must answer and to organize that essay, but do not rush through the organizing process for the DBQ. Organizing is a crucial step in essay writing, as has been emphasized throughout the book (see "Seven Steps in Essay Writing" in Part II, Steps 1-3). As you organize, you may wish to underline key phrases or ideas in the documents to quote or paraphrase in your answer, but be sure that you do not merely copy passages from different documents but that you use information from the documents to build support for the thesis you state in your opening paragraph. Time spent on reading the documents carefully and organizing an effective outline is time well spent and will help prepare for an effective answer.

The sample answer for this DBQ is an example that makes good use of the documents and includes sound information from American history to support the thesis presented.

Sample Answer for the DBQ

Opening sentence introduces broad topic of the question.

A continual issue in U.S. history has been how to get the Supreme Court to work together with the Executive and Legislative branches and not to block their desires. This was an important issue in the years 1900–1918, when decisions of the Supreme Court were not in agreement with the views of the best known political leaders. Two reasons can be given for this situation: first, the Court is the most important branch of government and is usually out of touch with the country; and second, the ideas of Wilson and Roosevelt were ahead of those of most political leaders.

Thesis on the To what degree . . . aspect of the question.

Two reasons that respond to the Why? part of the question follow.

Two documents are mentioned as evidence, and dates are given, setting the time period of the question.

Information from the "mainstream" of American history is introduced to support ideas in the documents.

The decisions of the Supreme Court in *Lochner v. New York* in 1905 and in *Hammer v. Dagenhart* in 1918 indicate that the Court upheld the conservative ideas of the Social Darwinists throughout the period 1900–1918. Social Darwinists applied the idea of survival of the fittest to business and wanted no government interference in the economic life of the nation. Of

Uses information in the document, but does not repeat the content of the document, thus indicating an understanding of and ability to use the information.

course, not every judge believed in Social Darwinism, as seen in Mr. Holmes's dissent in 1905 in which he is complaining about that concept. Also, a good lawyer such as Mr. Brandeis, by using special arguments, could persuade the Court to allow the regulation of the working conditions of women by a state government. But this is a major exception to the general views held by the Court.

Poor linking of paragraphs. Ideas introduced appear separated from documents, but writer ties mainstream information to documents in last sentence to support point 1 of reasons for *Why?* part of question.

Until 1913, the United States Senators were elected by state legislatures, which were often controlled by business interests. For example, the Boston and Maine Railroad controlled the New Hampshire legislature. U.S. Senators confirmed members of the Supreme Court, and the conservative views of business were thus represented both in the Senate and on the Court. This conservative view is seen in Senator Scott's statement on

Good comment on value of sources (see directions).

the working conditions he has seen—a personal view, which is not a very reliable historical source, but in this case, is illustrative of a widely held view.

Documents may be referred to by letter, but better to use author's name or some other specific identification from the document. Good use of "mainstream" history.

Repetition of "Roosevelt" helps link paragraphs.

Use of abbreviation "T.R." is not formal essay style, but permissible if time is running out.

Effective weaving together of information *in* documents, and knowledge *recalled* from study of main issues in U.S. history— supporting point 2 of reasons for *Why?* part of question.

Good use of document—brief quote with source stated is effective (also done above).

Repeats thesis.

Brings paper back to broad topic of opening sentence.

Document B presents a view of the Muckraker, a group of writers who pointed out the political corruption in the cities, the power of business monopolies (Tarbell and Standard Oil), and the horror of working conditions. These writers had an impact on certain men, such as Roosevelt, who became the leaders of the Progressive Movement, a reform movement of the first two decades of this century.

Roosevelt became president by a fluke—he was on the Republican ticket to win votes and did not represent the views of the leadership. He became president when McKinley was assassinated, and he worked for better labor conditions, as can be seen in his settlement of the coal strike. But at the same time, the Court remained conservative (see Document A). When Taft did not support Roosevelt's ideas, T.R. ran for president in 1912 on the Bull Moose ticket. He campaigned for the "welfare of the people" and for the judiciary to respond to the needs of all the people, and not just for special interests (see Document G). Roosevelt's campaign split the Republican party, allowing the Progressive Democrat, Woodrow Wilson, to win. Wilson, a minority president, was able to get some legislation passed to improve working conditions (Railroad Act), but the Supreme Court continued to lag behind the Executive and Legislative branches of government with its conservative, Social Darwinist attitude expressed in *Hammer v. Dagenhart.* This decision forbid federal regulation of child labor. The Court thus remained conservative in spite of the election of Wilson, who had expressed his desire to have the law "step in and create new conditions under which we may live" (see Document F).

The documents presented help to make it clear that the decisions of the Supreme Court were not in agreement with the expressed views of the leaders of the Executive Branch of government. The Supreme Court remained conservative while the Progressive, Woodrow Wilson, was president. The period 1900–1918 clearly illustrates the adage that the Supreme Court lags behind the Executive and Legislative branch of government in its decisions and understanding of the needs of the people.

Comment on the Sample Answer for the DBQ

The essay is a good example of what should be done with the DBQ. The writer makes use of all the documents except D. They are not discussed in order, but are used in different combinations to illustrate points. The writer uses considerable information from the period 1900-1918 to support the thesis and weaves it in well with the documents. He or she assumes the reader understands the content of the documents, so he or she does not need to summarize them or to quote extensively from them. This answer would qualify for a high score on the examination.

Comments on Question 2 of Section II

The second question is a typical *Evaluate this statement* question (see Part III, Chapter 1). The quotation presents a most unusual interpretation of the era of the American Revolution, suggesting that the events in the West (frontier) were more "significant" for the development of the United States than events on the eastern seaboard (Boston, Philadelphia, Virginia) in the years from the Peace of Paris, which ended the French and Indian War in 1763, to the establishment of the government under the Constitution in 1788. The wording of the quotation should present no problem, and most students should quickly recall many events of the era under consideration. The question lends itself to a chronological organization, discussing events on the frontier before 1776 first, and then those after 1776, with references to events on the eastern seaboard woven in. The events you pick will be ones to support your thesis.

Remember, you are free to agree or disagree with this quotation. Most students will probably disagree, citing events such as the Stamp Act Crisis; the Boston Massacre; the closing of the port of Boston; the reaction in New York to the Quartering Act; the meetings of the Continental Congresses; the writing and approval of the Declaration of Independence; the fighting at Bunker Hill, Saratoga, and Yorktown; the economic crisis under the government of the Articles of Confederation; and Shays' Rebellion, which led to the Constitutional Convention. To illustrate that there are arguments on the other side of the question, the following sample answer supports the quotation. Again, in the left-hand margin are comments pointing out good aspects of the answer. This answer presents only *one* of many possible approaches to a very interesting and provocative *Evaluate this statement* type of question.

Sample Answer for Standard Essay Question 2

Opening comment is broad—catches attention flashlight beam image of "Seven Steps in Essay Writing."

Links opening comment to thesis, and introduces the Topic of the essay.

Clearly stated thesis using quote from the question.

Admits evidence exists that might refute the stated thesis.

Main idea of paragraph

Introduces factual refutation of the evidence given at start of the paragraph—clever to admit and then to refute other view.

Points out an understanding of geography in parenthetical expression.

The role of the historian is to determine what events of the past are significant and explain to his generation why they are. For many years American historians have concentrated on the events that took place on the eastern seaboard between 1763 and 1788, suggesting that for American history they were the most significant events of those decades. These historians have often ignored the events on the western frontier in those years— events which were "more significant for the development of U.S. history" than happenings in the East.

Granted that many significant events from the Stamp Act Crisis of 1765 to Shays' Rebellion of 1786 took place in the East. Granted also that the Declaration of Independence was signed, the Continental Congresses met, and many battles of the Revolutionary War were fought in the East, but *all of these were affected by events in the West*. It must be remembered that the Peace of Paris in 1763 ended a war fought basically for possession and/or control of the Northwest Territory (Ohio, Michigan, etc.) and of the Mississippi Valley. It was in this war that George Washington gained his colonial reputation that allowed him to become the leader of the colonial army. Without his western military experience, where would the colonial armies

Paragraph is structured so major point of refutation appears at the end of paragraph. *Ties facts back to topic and thesis.*

Shifts argument to events that actually took place *in* the West.

Good linkage of paragraphs as point of argument is shifted to government.

Student's grammar is somewhat scrambled, but he makes his point, and minor grammatical errors can be expected when writing under intense pressure.

Again, ties facts to topic and thesis.

Repeated word again links paragraphs as several new arguments are added.

Cleverly presents many facts centered on the military significance of the West and its place in U.S. foreign policy.

Another good link. Saves major point to the last paragraph so that reader remembers this crucial point of the argument in favor of the thesis.

Good, brief summary of important document shows writer knows the facts, not just the name of the document.

have been? More significantly, the entire taxation issue that was argued in the East was precipitated by the need of the British to pay the expenses they incurred in the French and Indian War. Without that war, *a result of British policy on the frontier,* there would have been no need for the taxes—Stamp Act, Townshend Acts, Tea Act—which stirred up the East, and led to the cry, "No taxation without representation" and ultimately to independence.

One often-forgotten event leading to American independence is the British Proclamation Line of 1763, which closed the Northwest Territory to colonial settlement. American leaders such as Washington and Franklin had committed money to companies to organize this territory. When the British stopped this settlement, colonists had an important motive for leading an anti-British movement in the East. In 1774 the English made matters worse for colonial leaders when by the Quebec Act they established a form of government for the area and extended the boundaries of the former French province of Quebec to include the Northwest, putting it under different laws than the British colonies.

Many of these colonies, such as Virginia and Connecticut, claimed control of the Northwest. After the Declaration of Independence, as the Continental Congress struggled to govern the colonies, Maryland refused to ratify the new government arrangement—The Articles of Confederation—until all colonies gave up their claims to western lands. When Virginia finally did cede her claim in 1781, the Articles were ratified, and so, again, the West played a *significant* role in Eastern events.

Many other illustrations could be given of the *significance* of the West, such as the victories of George Rogers Clark in the Northwest, the British plan to split the West from the colonies, which was frustrated by the colonial victory at Saratoga, and victories on the frontier in Carolina, which led to Yorktown. Also, during the negotiations for peace, the future of the West was a significant issue, and the United States won control over the land from the Appalachians to the Mississippi. The British refused to evacuate forts in the Northwest, called for in the treaty, and the resulting diplomatic struggle to gain control of the frontier region was the major foreign policy issue between 1783 and 1788.

All of these illustrations of the significance of the West for U.S. history pale by comparison to the great issue that was solved by the Continential Congress, that is, *how to organize and govern the frontier region.* The plan of organization was first set forth in the Basic Land Ordinance of 1785 and developed fully in the Northwest Ordinance of 1787. This document set the pattern for the future expansion of the U.S. in creating new states coast to coast. It abolished slavery in the territory and established trial by jury and freedom of religion. Nothing could be more significant to the development of the U.S. than the establishment both of the idea that these principles would be extended to new territory, which might have been treated as colonies, and of the plan for the expansion of the U.S. coast to coast.

Again, acknowledges events in the East, but restates thesis, and adds an interpretation of history to reenforce it.

Ends by moving back to broad topic of the opening, thus framing the essay and tying it together in the construction.

Certainly, the East was important in American history from 1763 to 1788, but the events in the West were more significant. They provided the cause for so many events, and history is a cause and effect relationship. One must admit that the cause of events is more significant than the effects, and American historians should take more time to explain why from 1763 to 1788 the events of the frontier are more significant than those in the East.

Comment on the Sample Answer for Standard Essay Question 2

This was a very good answer to the question. The author introduces the topic with a broad statement and narrows it down to a clearly stated thesis in which the question is quoted. The thesis is the last sentence of the opening paragraph. As you are aware, you may argue on any side of the question, and in this case, the writer has taken the less accepted view. Since most individuals would believe that events in the East were more important and would be aware of these events, the writer refutes these in the second paragraph. This, then, paves the way for the positive data the writer will use. The most important point the writer has is kept for the last paragraph, which is a very effective technique. The organization used is basically chronological, but there is some movement back and forth in time as the main topic under discussion (war, government, land organization) is shifted. The conclusion restates the thesis and moves back to the more general topic introduced in the opening sentence of the essay. This frames the essay effectively. The "Seven Steps in Essay Writing" have been well used by this author.

Comment on Standard Essay Question 3

This is another *To what extent* . . . question (see Part III, Chapter 4). It covers a long time period. "Since the Civil War" implies that you may bring the question up to the present, but remember that the emphasis on essay questions on the AP exam is on the period before 1970. So you do not need to cover the entire 130 years. Instead, it would be wise to pick a few (two or three) changes in the political control of the federal government and discuss them in some detail, analyzing how the changes occurred as a response to domestic economic crises.

Another approach would be to consider the major economic crises since 1865 and then to decide if changes in the political control of the federal government took place as a result of them. Among the crises that might come to mind are the Panics of 1873 and 1907, the Panic of 1893 and the following Gold Crisis, the Stock Market Crash and Great Depression of 1929-33, the Recession of 1953-54, and the Inflationary Crisis of the late 1970s. A discussion of two or three of these crises in relation to political changes that did or did not follow would make a very effective answer. Whether you pick the political or economic organizational scheme may well depend on the emphasis given to these factors in your study of American history.

The question expects you to establish a relationship between two forces in history — one economic and one political. Your perception of the relationship should be stated in your thesis. While deciding on your thesis, you will have recalled many events since 1865, and you should use those events that you are most familiar with to prove your thesis.

Comment on Standard Essay Question 4

This *Compare* type of question (see Part III, Chapter 6) focuses on the literary history of the United States. As stated earlier in this book, on this examination you can expect to have questions from the social, literary, judicial, and other more specialized aspects of history. Not all of the questions will be from the traditional political, and economic aspects of history, although these will have the greater emphasis. You may not cover literature very carefully in your history course, but if you think a moment, you may be surprised at how many fiction and nonfiction works were mentioned in your study. Also, in English classes you may have studied works of literature that could be applied to this question. To answer the question, the first thing you must do is choose two works that fit the specific requirements of the question, one fiction and one nonfiction work. You must be able to explain the "profound influence" each had on the course of American history. In discussing these influences, you will need to present information from areas of history other than literary. The question, then, does provide an opportunity to discuss political or economic events and/or social or literary developments, depending on the books you pick.

Many works could be chosen to discuss. The work that may well first come to mind is Harriet Beecher Stowe's novel, *Uncle Tom's Cabin*. The importance of this 1852 novel is mentioned in every presentation of the coming of the Civil War and the Abolitionist Movement. It greatly affected public opinion and is considered a catalyst in the coming of the war and the crystallization of anti-slavery sentiment in the North. Nonfiction works you might choose range from John Dickinson's *Letters from a Farmer in Pennsylvania to the Inhabitants of the British Colonies* (1768), which had an important impact on colonial opinion before the Declaration of Independence, to Michael Harrington's *The Other Americans* (the magazine article appeared in *Commonweal 27* May 1960, and the book was published in 1962), which affected John F. Kennedy's and Lyndon Johnson's attitudes towards poverty in America.

Other examples of influential works that might be included in your answer are the following: Thomas Paine, *Common Sense* (1776); Alexander Hamilton, John Jay, James Madison, *Federalist Papers* (1788); Frederick Jackson Turner, *The Significance of the Frontier in American History* (1893); Alfred Thayer Mahan, *The Influence of Sea Power on History* (1890); Charles Austin Beard, *An Economic Interpretation of the Constitution* (1913); Walter Rauschenbusch, *Christianity and the Social Crisis* (1907). Other types of works would be Jonathan Edwards, *Sinners in the Hands of an Angry God* (1741), which is a very important sermon, or Ralph Waldo Emerson's *The American Scholar* (1837), which is an important address. Among novels that might be used are these: Upton Sinclair, *The Jungle* (1960); Frank Norris, *The Octopus* (1901); William Dean Howells' *Rise of Silas Lapham* (1885); Edward Bellamy's *Looking Backward*; and Herman Melville's *Moby Dick* (1851); or you might decide to pick as your work of fiction a work of poetry, such as Walt Whitman's, *Leaves of Grass* (1855). As you can see, the range of works from which one might choose is broad.

Once you have chosen the two books you will use, you should follow the "Seven Steps in Essay Writing." First, quickly jot what you can recall about the circumstances under which the two books were written, and then jot down the information about their influence on United States history. Using this information, you will develop your thesis. You might think that this *Compare* question does not need a thesis; that you can simply write a descriptive account of the publication of the two books and how people reacted to them. This would certainly supply a good organizational scheme, but you should develop a thesis first and write an introductory paragraph stating the topic and your thesis in it. Then you can go on to write the essay organized around the two books and come to a conclusion that agrees with your thesis. You might argue that novels rarely have profound influence immediately upon publication, but may later be regarded as of great significance, using a work such as Washington Irving's *Sketch Books* of 1820 as one example. Or you might argue the opposite, using *Uncle Tom's Cabin* or *The Jungle* as examples. There are obviously many positions to take on this question and many works from which to choose.

Comment on Standard Essay Question 5

This is a good question for which you must have a knowledge of the entire time period of American history. Within that sweep, however, the question has a clear focus on one type of event — reform. In answering this *How?* question (see Part III, Chapter 3), the first thing you must do is to determine what reform movements may have occurred in American history, and then you must decide if they occur cyclically. Finally, if you believe reform is cyclical, you must develop your arguments as to why it is. If you disagree, then you must develop an explanation as to why the assumption behind the question is incorrect.

What reform periods can you recall? The most obvious are the Jacksonian Era (1828-40), the Progressive/Populist Era (1890-1914), the New Deal (1933-40), and the Kennedy/Johnson years (1961-68). Are there factors that these periods have in common? What might lead someone to consider their occurrence as cyclical? One idea is that the concerns addressed in each period were essentially the same, so that reform keeps recurring on the same matter. Another idea is simply that there are periods in American history when reform appears to be more important than any other issue and periods when reform is of little interest. There are obviously other matters one might consider in an analysis of the question. Once you have done your own work on this, an effective thesis should follow. There are many ways to organize the answer to this question. It might be chronological, with one movement following the next, or you might trace one or two issues through several periods of reform. However you structure your answer, you must remember to address the issue of "recurring cycles" even if you decide to reject that concept and to argue that reform is not cyclical but steady or erratic.

One important point to note about this question is that it involves what is now called social history in many schools. In discussing reform movements, you may want to mention several specific reforms of a social nature: for example, the reforms in education in the 1830s and 1840s, the legislation involving food and drugs passed in the early 1900s, the laws affecting conditions of employment passed in the 1930s, the legislation concerning the improvement of the environment passed in the 1960s. These social reforms are all interwoven with economic and political history, and you should include some economic and political history in your answer even if you wish to focus on the social aspects of reform. This question illustrates, as does Question 4, how the AP exam will have questions relating to different types of history.

Comment on Standard Essay Question 6

This last question from the sample exam is an example of an *Assess the Validity* type of question (see Part III, Chapter 1), a type of question that has been very popular and widely used on recent American History AP examinations. Although you are often asked to deal with only one time period in such a question, in this case you must deal with two quite distant time periods. This illustrates the continuity one finds in history.

The first step in answering the question will be to analyze the quotation. It raises the eternal issue of democratic government — the conflict between the power of the majority and the rights of the minority. The quote states that minority rights ("views") cannot be ignored by a democratic society (the United States) when "executing policy." You must decide if the statement is true or not, but, more than that, whether it is true or not for two very specific times in American history. Therefore, once you have analyzed the quotation, you must go on to consider the two specific time periods given in the question. The first period, 1793-1812, includes such events as the XYZ Affair, the Alien and Sedition Acts, and the "Revolution of 1800." It also includes such events as the Louisiana Purchase, the Embargo of 1807 and the U.S. involvement in the War of 1812. In each of these issues there were majority and minority views. You must decide if the minority views were considered and what the results were if they were or were not. Is there a lesson to draw from how the issues were handled?

In continuing your analysis, you must ask the same question for the period 1953-74, which includes such events as the investigations of Senator Joseph McCarthy, the decision in *Brown v. Board of Education*, the civil rights movement, including the assassination of Martin Luther King, Jr., and the U.S. involvement in Vietnam. Once you decide what consideration was given to minority views on these and other issues of the time and whether there are lessons to draw from this treatment, you will have your thesis, and you will probably have an organizational scheme.

To prove your thesis, you must select several issues and not try to cover everything in the two time periods. The easiest organization of this paper would be to discuss the two periods separately and then pull the paper together with a conclusion. Of course, you might discover similarities in the two eras and organize the paper around a comparison of the issues. For example, in each period a perceived threat from a foreign power (France in the 1790s and the USSR in the 1950s) led to a curtailment of the rights of individuals. As in the case of all essay answers, there are many ways to approach the question and no one way is best. What is important is that you follow the "Seven Steps in Essay Writing" and that you use specific facts carefully selected from your study of American history to prove your thesis.

Chronological Summary of
Major Events and Developmen
in American History

**Introduction for
the Student**

This summary of major events in American History is arranged according to the time divisions of the chapters in the book.

Included in each section are the names of leaders of each era. Their importance is usually not identified. You should look up information about those you don't know. Certain events are described briefly while others are merely listed. Again you should look up those with which you are not familiar, and you can add other events that you feel are important.

This summary can serve as a quick review of American history or as an introduction to its study. It illustrates the basic factual material from the mainstream of American history one needs, but under no circumstances should it be considered a substitute for the skills developed when reading different authors with conflicting opinions of our past. You are urged to add dates, people and events to this summary as you study. The margins of this section provide space to do this.

At the end of this chronological summary is a chronological listing of events. These two chronologies provide an important introduction to your study.

**Introduction for
the Teacher**

This summary can be used effectively by the classroom teacher. Since it parallels the chapters in Part III, assignments can be given to students to look up further information on people, places, or events mentioned. Reports could be oral or written or incorporated into essays. Projects for small groups within the class can be designed around information in this section. Questions such as "What further information should be included?" or "What information could be eliminated?" would lead to an excellent review of American history and would involve the student in analyzing the significance of various events, a skill which will be tested on the examination. Students using this book outside of class could also profit from such an analysis conducted on their own.

**Chapter 1—
Colonial America
Before 1763**

REASONS FOR EXPLORATION
Search for a sea route to the Far East
Desire for glory and wealth
Quest for new lands
Adventure

FACTORS FAVORABLE TO SUCCESSFUL EXPLORATION
Invention of the astrolabe and compass
Invention of the printing press
Growth of national states in western Europe
Increase of monetary resources and the use of the joint stock company as an economic organization
The Renaissance and revival of intellectual curiosity
Invention of gunpowder

EXPLORERS AND FOUNDERS OF COLONIES

SPAIN

Columbus: First visit to America, given publicity	1492
Balboa: First Spaniard to see the Pacific Ocean from Central America	1513
Magellan: First recorded circumnavigation of the globe	1519-1522
Cortez: Conquered and claimed Mexico	1519
Pizarro: Conquered and claimed Peru	1531
De Soto: First Spaniard to explore the Mississippi River	1541

PORTUGAL

De Gama: Reached India by sailing around Africa	1498
Vespucci: Explored the coast of South America. America is named after him.	1501

FRANCE

De Champlain: Founded Quebec, the Father of New France; discovered Lakes Champlain and Huron	1608
Father Marquette and Joliet: Explored upper Mississippi River	1673
LaSalle: Explored the Mississippi River to its mouth	1682

ENGLAND

Cabot: Explored the Labrador coast	1497
Frobisher: Explored the Labrador coast	1576
Drake: First Englishman to circumnavigate the globe	1577-1580
Raleigh: Attempted to found a colony off the coast of Virginia	1584
Smith: Founder and leader of Jamestown	1607
Lord Baltimore: Founder of Maryland	1634
Penn: Founder of Pennsylvania	1681
Bradford: Leader of Plymouth Colony	1620

HOLLAND

Minuit: Founder of New Amsterdam (later New York)	1626

REASONS FOR COLONIZATION OF THE NEW WORLD

Religious freedom
Economic opportunity
Political freedom
Farming land
Social change

TERRITORY OF EUROPEAN COLONIES IN THE NEW WORLD

Spain: All of South America except Brazil, plus Central America, Mexico, Florida, California

France: All of Canada except the Hudson Bay region, plus the Great Lakes region, the Mississippi Basin, the French West Indies

Holland: The Hudson River Valley in New York

England: The eastern coast from New England to Georgia, west to the Appalachian Mountains

ENGLAND ACHIEVES DOMINATION OF NORTHERN HALF OF NORTH AMERICA

English Navy defeated the Spanish Armada, gaining control of the seas	1588
English drove the Dutch out of New York	1664

England defeated France at Quebec in the French and
Indian War, gaining control of Canada and the lands
east of the Mississippi River   1763

GEOGRAPHY AND ITS EFFECT ON SETTLEMENTS
The physical nature of the settled land usually determined the occupation and manner
of life of the period.

New England: Rocky soil and long winters prevented extensive farming; wheat, corn,
hay, and flax were the main agricultural products; colonists lumbered vast forests and
fished off the coast; because of excellent harbors and rivers they developed trade as their
chief source of income. Town provided first industrial towns small town

Middle Colonies: Level, fertile, rich land and good rainfall made for abundant farming;
wheat, oats, and barley were grown in such quantity that these states were called "bread
colonies."

Southern Colonies: Warm climate, long growing season, and fertile lands produced rich
crops of cotton, tobacco, rice, and indigo; a good river system provided easy transportation
inland; the produce was shipped to England and brought plantation owners large profits
and manufactured goods in return.

SOME CONTRIBUTIONS OF MOTHER COUNTRIES
TO NORTH AMERICA
England: Democratic forms of local government; tradition of hard-working, zealous
individuals; English language; Puritan religion.

France: Language, culture, and religion introduced to Canada and Louisiana and to many
Indians west of Appalachians.

Spain: Schools, hospitals, and printing presses established by missionaries; Spanish
language in Southwest; teaching of Christianity and handicrafts to Indians.

EVENTS THAT FOSTERED THE DEMOCRATIC IDEAL
IN THE ENGLISH COLONIES
Formation of Virginia House of Burgesses: First representative assembly
in America; the beginning of representative government in America.   1619

Signing of the Mayflower Compact: First agreement for self-government;
bound the freemen to obey "Just and equal laws."   1620

New England Town Meeting: Taught people to express themselves openly
and helped further self-government.   after 1629

Petition of Rights and Bill of Rights: Established certain rights of English
subjects vis à vis the Royal Power in England. The colonists later claimed
these rights also.   1628, 1689

Colonial Government: The governor of each colony, whether a royal or
charter colony, had to consult advisors before taking action.

Control of Purse: The settlers of most colonies voted for members of
a legislature, which in turn determined the Governor's salary. When
this control was threatened, the colonists felt threatened.

Fundamental Orders of Connecticut: Was the first written constitution
in America.   1639

Formation of New England Confederation: Connecticut, New Haven,
Plymouth, and Massachusetts formed a league of friendship for defense,
offense, and advice. This was perhaps the first step toward national
union of states.   1643

Passing of Maryland Toleration Act: Guaranteed religious freedom to
all Christians.   1649

Bacon's Rebellion: Virginia farmers revolt against corrupt and oppressive
government.   1676

Formation of New York Chapter of Liberties: This document granted freedom of religion to all Christians and gave all freeholders the right to vote.   1683

Zenger Case: Set a precedent that led to the establishment of freedom of the press.   1734

SOME IMPORTANT INDIVIDUALS OF THE PERIOD OF EXPLORATION AND COLONIZATION

Dominion of New England

Jeffrey Amherst	Thomas Fairfax	Queen Elizabeth I of England
Edmund Andros	Benjamin Franklin	Queen Isabella of Spain
Nathaniel Bacon	Anne Hutchinson	Mary White Rowlandson
Edward Braddock	Thomas Hutchinson	William Shirley
Charles II	Cotton Mather	Miles Standish
John Cotton	Montezuma	George Washington
Jonathan Edwards	King Philip	William and Mary of England
	Pocahontas	John Witherspoon

**Chapter 2—
The Era of the
American
Revolution—
1763-1789**

CAUSES OF THE AMERICAN REVOLUTION

The theory of mercantilism: Held that the colonies existed only for the profit of the mother country; caused discontent among American businessmen and traders.

Navigation Acts: Prohibited commerce with England and other countries.   1660, 1663, 1673

Concept of the Rights of English subjects: Coloniest believed their rights were being denied by Parliament.

Aftermath of the French and Indian War: British had acquired a large debt they felt the colonists should help pay; also, they acquired all of Canada, which they had to rule.   1763

The Proclamation of 1763: Tried to stop colonization of the West by closing the land between the Alleghenies and the Mississippi to protect the Indians from exploitation by the settlers until treaties could be negotiated.   1763

The Sugar Act: Taxed sugar to raise revenue, which threatened to destroy the profitable triangular trade between Britain, the colonies, and the West Indies.   1764

The Stamp Act: The colonists were forced to pay a tax on papers, pamphlets, calendars, and almanacs for the purpose of raising money to support the British army in the colonies. It was during this controversy that Patrick Henry said, ". . . Give me liberty or give me death!"   1764

The Quartering Act: Required the colonists to quarter (house) British troops while they enforced unfavorable acts.   1766

Writs of Assistance: Allowed British officials to enter any home to search for smuggled goods, which contradicted the traditional right of English subjects to protection of their homes.

The Townshend Acts: Placed a tax on imported paper, lead, glass, tea, and painter's colors in order to pay the salaries of the governors and judges in the colonies, which would eliminate colonists' control of the purse.   1767

The House of Burgesses: Dissolved by the governor of Virginia.   1769

The Boston Massacre: Some Boston townspeople were fired upon by a group of British soldiers. Several people were killed.   1770

The Boston Tea Party: Enraged by the monopoly of the tea trade held by the East India Company and by the English refusal to rescind the tax on tea, about fifty men disguised as Indians boarded the tea ships at the wharf and emptied the tea into the harbor.   1773

The Intolerable Acts: The British government, in retaliation for the Boston Tea Party, closed the port of Boston until the tea was paid for, revised the charter of Massachusetts so that the Council would be appointed by the king, and forced the colonists of Massachusetts to house British soldiers. British officers were allowed to be tried in England for crimes of violence.   1774

Summary View of the Rights of British America: Expressed views of the colonists in opposition to England and called for the ending of slavery — written by T. Jefferson.   1774

IMPORTANT EVENTS OF THE REVOLUTIONARY PERIOD

First Continental Congress: All colonies except Georgia were represented; pledged to boycott all English goods if England did not settle existing disagreements.   Sept., 1774

Battle of Concord and Lexington: Minutemen and Massachusetts militia, forewarned by Paul Revere and William Dawes, routed English in first battle of the Revolution.   April, 1775

Second Continental Congress: Met in Philadelphia, attended by all thirteen colonies; made provisions for raising a colonial army, issuing and borrowing money; appointed George Washington as commander-in-chief of army; drafted the *Articles of Confederation,* an agreement among the states outlining the operation of the united government.   1775

Declaration of Independence: Signed by John Hancock, president of the Second Continental Congress, and all the members present, stated the equality of all people, declared the right of people to rebel when denied life, liberty, and the pursuit of happiness by their governments.   July 4, 1776

Treaty of Paris: England recognized the independence of the colonies and ceded land from Canada to Florida.   1783

IMPORTANT BATTLES OF THE REVOLUTION

Battle of Trenton and Princeton: After New York was captured, Washington had fled to Pennsylvania. He recrossed the Delaware River and won these two victories, which made it clear the war would continue.   1776-1777

Battle of Saratoga: Considered the turning point of the war when Americans proved they could beat the best soldiers in the world.   1778

Battle of Yorktown: Washington cornered a British army on land, while Admiral de Grasse, a French ally, prevented British reinforcements from landing by sea. As a result, Lord Cornwallis surrendered the British Army thus bringing the war to an end.   1781

DEVELOPMENT OF THE CONSTITUTION

The Articles of Confederation: America's first Constitution had the following weaknesses:

Each state, regardless of size, had only one vote.

Congress could make laws, but there was no executive to enforce them.

Amendments could be adopted only by unanimous vote.

There was no national court to settle arguments between states.

Congress could not regulate commerce between states, collect taxes, or force states to contribute to government needs.

Congress could only ask states for troops, but could not raise an army.

Annapolis Convention: Several states met at Annapolis Maryland to consider ways of improving trade and making changes in the Articles. They issued a call for a meeting that became the Constitutional Convention.   1786

Constitutional Convention: Convened at Independence Hall, Philadelphia, to revise Articles of Confederation but decided to draw up a completely new document.

May, 1787

COMPROMISES REACHED IN FORMING THE CONSTITUTION

The Great Compromise: Resolved the conflict between large and small states by providing equal representation in the Senate and representation based on population in the House of Representatives.

Three-Fifths Compromise: Resolved the conflict between slave and free states by counting five slaves as three people in determining each states representation in the House of Representatives.

Commerce Compromise: Resolved the conflict between agricultural and manufacturing states by permitting Congress to tax goods entering but not leaving the country.

Indirect vote for president: Resolved the conflict between aristocrats and democrats by having president elected by electoral college.

THE GREAT ARCHITECTS OF THE CONSTITUTION

Known as *The Founding Fathers,* the men most responsible for its adoption were George Washington, James Madison, Alexander Hamilton, Gouvernour Morris, Robert Morris, Benjamin Franklin, and George Mason.

BRANCHES OF THE GOVERNMENT

Authority was vested in three branches that acted as a check on each other:

Legislative: The House of Representatives and the Senate make laws according to the power granted in Article I Section 8. These power include making laws concerning such items as money, commerce, courts, war, the armed forces, immigration, and taxation. The Congress may override a presidential veto of passed legislation by a two-thirds vote. The Senate confirms presidential appointments and treaties.

Executive: The president who heads the executive branch, enforces the laws, conducts foreign policy, and negotiates treaties. The president is commander-in-chief of the army and makes appointments of judges and other members of the executive branch.

Judicial: Supreme Court, and such lesser federal courts as Congress establishes, determine the constitutionality of laws and the interpretation of the Constitution. Federal judges are appointed by the President and confirmed by the Senate.

THE BILL OF RIGHTS

A written guarantee of the people's liberties, these were added to the Constitution as the first ten amendments in 1791. Several states refused to ratify the Constitution unless a Bill of Rights was added immediately. The Bill of Rights guaranteed:

Freedom of speech, press, religion.

The right of bear arms.

That people would not be forced to quarter soldiers.

Protection against illegal search.

The right to know reasons for arrest.

The right to a quick trial by a jury of peers.

The right to trial by jury in civil cases involving more than $20.

Protection against cruel and unusual punishment and excessive bail.

That no rights not listed in Constitution should be therefore denied.

That the people and states would retain powers not assigned to government.

SOME IMPORTANT INDIVIDUALS OF THE
REVOLUTIONARY PERIOD: 1763-1789

Abigail Adams	Nathan Hale	Gouvernour Morris
John Adams	Alexander Hamilton	Robert Morris
Samuel Adams	John Hancock	James Otis
Ethan Allen	Patrick Henry	Thomas Paine
Crispus Atticus	Sir William Howe	William Paterson
Daniel Boone	Thomas Hutchinson	Charles C. Pinckney
General Edward Braddock	John Jay	William Pitt
John Burgoyne	Thomas Jefferson	Edmund Randolph
George Rogers Clark	Sir William Johnson	Paul Revere
George Clinton	John Paul Jones	Daniel Shays
John Singleton Copley	Rufus King	Roger Sherman
Lord Cornwallis	John Lansing	John Trumbull
Benjamin Franklin	Ann Lee	George Washington
Joseph Galloway	Richard Henry Lee	Martha Washington
Elbridge Gerry	James Madison	Anthony Wayne
	George Mason	James Wilson

**Chapter 3—
The New
Nation—
1789-1824**

THE GROWTH OF POLITICAL PARTIES

Bank of the U.S.: Hamilton and Jefferson submitted to President Washington papers explaining their position on the bank. This involved their interpretation of the Constitution—strictly for Jefferson, loosely for Hamilton. Gradually others expressed opinions on the Constitution, and out of this discussion came the first two political parties in the nation.

The Federalists: Led by Alexander Hamilton, they became the political party representing investors, merchants, and manufacturers. It is viewed as the more conservative of the two parties. The Federalists were in power until 1800.

The Anti-Federalists, or Republicans: Led by Thomas Jefferson, the party represented the farming population, small business people, and some city workers. At the time it was the more liberal of the two parties and was dominant from 1800 to 1824. The leaders of the Republican party grew increasingly conservative and finally it was absorbed by the Whig Party.

Disappearance of Federalist Party: Passed from the political scene in 1816; the Federalists lost credibility after the Hartford Convention and they opposed the War of 1812, which lost them support outside of New England.

The Democratic Party: Emerged with the election of Andrew Jackson in 1828; it represented the western and southern farmers and workers of the East; it became the more liberal party.

The Whig Party: Formed after the Federalist and the Republican parties disappeared; Henry Clay, former Federalists, and some conservative Republicans organized the opposition to the Democratic party in the form of the newly created Whig party.

THE ESTABLISHMENT OF THE FEDERAL GOVERNMENT

President Washington developed the concept of a *cabinet* to advise him. Alexander Hamilton, Secretary of the Treasury, supported a *loose interpretation* of the Constitution to give power to the government in Washington. Thomas Jefferson, Secretary of State, supported a *strict interpretation* of the Constitution to give more power to the people and the state governments. These interpretations continue to divide people today. Congress passed laws establishing the framework of the government, including the Judiciary Act of 1789.

Whiskey Rebellion 1794: Washington used state and federal troops to crush a farmers' rebellion in Pennsylvania, giving strength to the federal government.

Washington's Farewell Address 1797: Called for no foreign alliances, two terms for the president, and no factions (parties) in political life.

Chief Justice John Marshall: Appointed to the Supreme Court, Marshall led the Court in interpreting the Constitution to give power to the federal government.

SOME IMPORTANT SUPREME COURT DECISIONS

Marbury v. Madison (1803) established that the Supreme Court had the power of judicial review.

Dartmouth College v. Woodward (1819) established the point that the charter of a private corporation is protected by the Constitution.

McCullough v. Maryland (1819) interpreted the elastic clause giving the federal government power to do those things not denied it in order to achieve legitimate goals. Also established the idea that the elastic clause applied to federal-state relations, thus extending the power of the federal government.

Gibbons v. Ogden (1824) established the concept of federal control over interstate commerce.

THE WAR OF 1812

Causes

Election to Congress of War Hawks from western states (example: Henry Clay from Kentucky) who wanted war with England to gain control of western lands and defeat Indian tribes.

British furnished native Americans with arms and encouraged them to attack settlers in the Northwest territory and on the frontier who were encroaching on tribal lands and breaking treaty agreements.

Economic warfare of the British and French symbolized in such acts as the British Orders in Council, Jefferson's Embargo of 1807, and the Non-intercourse Act of 1809.

British attacked U.S. ships and impressed American sailors into service in their crews.

British seized American ships.

British fired on frigate *Chesapeake*, killing three American Sailors.

Important Events of the War

Captain Perry's naval victory on Lake Erie, reported with the famous words, "We have met the enemy and they are ours."

Victories of the *Constitution (Old Ironsides)* at sea.
The capture of Washington, D.C., and the burning of the White House by the British.

The writing of the *Star Spangled Banner* by Francis Scott Key as the British bombarded Fort McHenry in Baltimore, Maryland.

Battle of New Orleans, won by general Andrew Jackson ("Old Hickory") after the treaty ending the war had been signed.

Results of the War of 1812

The United States Merchant Marine was almost destroyed.

Development of national pride and increase of national unity (although the *Treaty of Ghent* [1814], did not reflect a victory, it established clearly our complete independence from Britain).

Increased western migration when unemployment spread in the East as a result of the destruction of United States commerce.

Manufacturing developed in different areas of the United States since Britain's wartime embargo prevented imports.

THE MONROE DOCTRINE

Russia, Prussia, and Austria formed the Holy Alliance, after Napoleon's defeat in 1815, to crush rebellions against monarchy wherever they might arise. Spain sought their help to regain its South American possessions lost due to popular revolt by the people led by Simón Bolivar and José de San Martín.

Russia was claiming the Oregon Territory, which both the United States and Britain were also claiming.

The British, in order to protect their trade, suggested joint action with the United States against European encroachment in the Americas, but this was rejected by the United States. Instead, to prevent European expansion in America, President James Monroe, in an address to Congress in 1823, stated what became known as the Monroe Doctrine. The Doctrine, which became a cornerstone of American foreign policy, stated:

1. No part of America was open to further European colonization.
2. European attempts to interfere with any existing American (North or South) governments would be considered unfriendly acts.
3. The United States would not interfere with existing European colonies.
4. The United States would not interfere in the affairs of Europe.

THE ERA OF GOOD FEELING

The Federalists disappeared as a result of not fully supporting the War of 1812. After the war the Republicans were in control of the nation. Henry Clay from Kentucky and John C. Calhoun from South Carolina soon emerged as national leaders. Clay, the "Great Compromiser," tried to reconcile the sectional differences with his "American System"—a protective tariff to aid manufacturers and better transportation (internal improvements), paid for with money from the tariffs, to aid farmers. Presidents Monroe and J.Q. Adams vetoed all bills for such improvements. Henry Clay offered the Missouri Compromise in 1820 to admit Maine (free) and Missouri (slave) as states, thus reconciling differences between the North and the South.

SOME IMPORTANT INDIVIDUALS OF THE PERIOD 1789-1824

John Adams	Thomas Jefferson	Charles Wilson Peale
John Q. Adams	Alexander Hamilton	Charles C. Pinckney
Abigail Adams	William H. Harrison	John Randolph
Aaron Burr	Washington Irving	Susanna Rowson
John C. Calhoun	Rufus King	Sacajawea
Samuel Chase	Benjamin H. Latrobe	Haym Salomon
William Clark	Meriwether Lewis	Winfield Scott
Henry Clay	Dolly Madison	Tecumseh
George Clinton	James Madison	Mersey Warren
Albert Gallatin	John Marshall	George Washington
John Jay	James Monroe	Daniel Webster
		Eli Whitney

Chapter 4—Jackson and the West—1824-1850

THE GROWTH OF SECTIONALISM

The Industrial North: As trade and manufacturing became the most important activities of the northern section of the United States, the North developed the following political and economic needs:

A national bank that would guarantee uniform and stable currency.

The end of the sale of cheap lands in the West to workers needed for northern industry.

A high protective tariff to protect native manufactured products against foreign competition.

Internal improvements (roads and canals) to link the markets and raw materials of the West to the markets and manufacturing of the Northeast.

The prevention of the spread of slavery and the slave based economic system to new western territories where it would compete with wage labor and provide less of a market.

The Slave South: With the invention of Eli Whitney's cotton gin in 1793 unskilled slave labor became increasingly important to plantation owners whose main crop, cotton, produced almost all of southern wealth. The economic and political needs of the South were:

Cheap western lands in which more cotton could be grown.

The extension of slavery to these lands.

No internal improvements (roads and canals) because they benefited only the Northeast and West and were to be paid for by tariffs.

No high tariffs since they raised the price of manufactured goods, which the South imported from Britain, to whom cotton was sold in payment.

The Farming West: Since agriculture was the principal activity and chief source of wealth in the West, its needs were:

Access to cheap land for expansion . . .

Cheap money (much money in circulation even though, as a result, the value of that money in terms of purchasing power is lessened), which meant opposition to the national bank that was controlled by Eastern business interests . . .

Extension of voting rights to all, regardless of property holdings.

Internal improvements (roads and canals) to transport produce to the market.

SECTIONAL COMPROMISES

As each section tried to gain control of the federal government to pass bills advantageous to itself, bitterness between the sections increased and problems could be settled only by compromise. Some of the more important compromises were:

Missouri Compromise (1820): Since, if there were more free states than slave states, the North would gain political control of Congress, the South opposed the admission of free states unless they were balanced by the admission of an equal number of slave states. Likewise, the North opposed the admission of slave states. When Missouri requested admission to the Union in 1818, as a slave state, Henry Clay, (the "Great Compromiser") proposed the Missouri Compromise, which states that:

Missouri would be admitted as a slave state, Maine as a free state.

Slavery would be prohibited in the Louisiana Territory north of the 36°30′ parallel.

(Missouri was to be the one exception.)

Compromise Tariff of 1833: When the North pushed a high tariff through Congress in 1828, the South was angry. When the tariff was again raised in 1832, South Carolina, led by John Calhoun, threatened secession. After negotiating a new tariff acceptable to the South, Clay saw it pushed through Congress as well as a bill (Force Act) that would allow the president to use troops to collect the tariff. The compromise avoided civil war in 1832-1833.

Mexican War: Many Americans hoped that war with Mexico (1846) would unite the nation and prevent the sectional conflicts from breaking up the Union. Many also believed that it was our *Manifest Destiny* to expand the borders of the nation to include all of North America. They held that this expansion would bring benefits to all peoples. Unfortunately, the war added to sectional divisions as New Englanders did not support the war. The peace treaty added new territory that had to be organized as states. This created both economic tensions and problems over the spread of slavery to the new areas.

Compromise of 1850: When California asked for admission in 1850, the balance between the North and South was once again endangered. The Compromise of 1850, called the Omnibus Bill, and also written by Henry Clay, provided that:

The people of Utah and New Mexico would vote to determine whether they should be free or slave states (this idea became known as popular or "squatter" sovereignty).

California would be admitted as a free state.

The Fugitive Slave Law would be strengthened.

Slave trading would be prohibited in the District of Columbia.

IMPORTANT MILESTONES IN EXPANSION 1787-1853

Northwest Ordinance of 1787: Adopted by the government under the Articles of Confederation, it made provision for western lands conquered by George Rogers Clark in the Revolution and stated that:

No more than five and no less than three states were to be formed from the territory.

Inhabitants of a territory would be admitted as a state on equal terms when its population reached 60,000.

Slavery was prohibited in the territory.

Louisiana Purchase: Extending from the Mississippi River to the Rocky Mountains and from Canada to the Gulf of Mexico, this vast territory was purchased from Napoleon for $15 million during Jefferson's administration in 1803.

Florida Purchase: American settlers in western Florida revolted against Spain in 1810, and the land was annexed in 1812 and added to the state of Louisiana. In 1819, the United States purchased the eastern part of Florida from Spain for $5 million.

The Oregon Territory: Originally claimed by Britain, United States, Spain, and Russia; by 1818 the other two countries ceded rights to the United States and Britain, who occupied it jointly.

Marcus Whitman led American settlers into the area in 1840. A dispute developed over the territory as American settlers moved in. In 1844, the slogan "fifty-four forty or fight," which meant the United States would take over all the Oregon territory, helped elect James Polk president.

In 1846 a compromise was worked out with Britain and a treaty signed that gave the United States rights to the land south of the 49th parallel and Britain the land north from the 49th to 54th 40'.

The Mexican War: General Sam Houston defeated the Mexican leader, Santa Anna, in 1836, and Texas was granted its independence from Mexico and established as a republic. In the following nine years there were various attempts to have Texas join the union or ally with Britain. Finally, in 1845, Texas was admitted as the 28th state of the United States. In 1846, war broke out between the United States and Mexico—Mexico being angered by American annexation of Texas and claims to all land north of the Rio Grande River. United States, under the generalship of Winfield Scott and Zachary Taylor, won a series of battles in Mexico. California was captured under the combined efforts of Stephen Kearny, John Sloat, and John Fremont.

The Treaty of Guadalupe-Hidalgo: Signed in 1848, provided that the Mexican areas of New Mexico (present Utah, New Mexico, Colorado, and Arizona) and Upper California (present California) were ceded to the United States.

The Rio Grande River was fixed as the southern boundary of Texas.

The United States agreed to a payment of $15 million for the territory.

Gadsden Purchase: A small strip of land now incorporated in Arizona and New Mexico was purchased from Mexico in 1853 to provide a good southern railroad route to the West. Its purchase completed the territory of what became the 48 contiguous United States (the lower 48).

SOME IMPORTANT INDIVIDUALS OF THE PERIOD 1824-1850

John Q. Adams	Kit Carson	John C. Fremont
John Jacob Astor	Henry Clay	Margaret Fuller
John James Audubon	Samuel Colt	William Lloyd Garrison
Stephen Austin	James Fenimore Cooper	Charles Goodyear
Thomas Hart Benton	Charlotte Cushman	Angelina Grimké
James Beckwith	Dorothea Dix	Sarah Grimké
Nicholas Biddle	Frederick Douglass	William H. Harrison
James G. Birney	Peggy Eaton	Robert Y. Hayne
John C. Calhoun	Ralph Waldo Emerson	Sam Houston

Andrew Jackson	William S. Mount	Henry David Thoreau
Hannah Farsham Lee	Edgar Allan Poe	Nat Turner
Henry Wadsworth Longfellow	James K. Polk	John Tyler
Mary Lyon	Winfield Scott	Martin Van Buren
Horace Mann	John Slidell	Daniel Webster
Samuel F.B. Morse	Elizabeth Cady Stanton	Marcus Whitman
Lucretia Mott	Zachary Taylor	Brigham Young

**Chapter 5—
The Coming of the
Civil War, Civil War
and Reconstruction—
1850-1877**

EVENTS LEADING TO THE CIVIL WAR

North-South Hostility Over Regional Differences: Disagreement over tariffs and the economic systems of the two areas was a basic cause of the hostility. As new territory was added to the Union, the question of the extension of slavery became crucial to the South for both economic and political reasons.

The Abolitionists: Led by William Lloyd Garrison, publisher of *The Liberator*, the Abolitionists fought for an end to slavery.

Slave Rebellions: There were many rebellions in the South. Those led by Denmark Vesey and Nat Turner terrified slave owners and alerted northerners to the many horrors of slavery.

National Fugitive Slave Law: This law, which the South demanded, pointed out vividly to northerners some of the evils of the slave system as they saw slaves who had escaped being taken back often in chains to their owners.

Uncle Tom's Cabin: The famous novel (1852) by Harriet Beecher Stowe awakened the North to sympathy for the slaves.

The Underground Railway: Organized largely by Abolitionists, it helped slaves escape to the North. Harriet Tubman was one of the famous and effective operators of the railroad.

Kansas-Nebraska Act: In 1854, this act repealed the Missouri Compromise and stated that each new state created from the territory of the Louisiana Purchase would decide whether to be free or slave. Both Northerners and Southerners financed settlers in both the Kansas and Nebraska territories to support their positions on slavery. Small scale civil war broke out in both areas as they struggled to decide on a slave or a free status.

Dred Scott Case: In 1857, when a slave named Dred Scott demanded freedom because his master had moved from a slave state (Missouri) to a free state (Illinois), the case was taken all the way to the Supreme Court. The Court in *Dred Scott v. Sandford* decided that slaves were property that could be taken anywhere and that the Missouri Compromise was unconstitutional.

John Brown's Raid: In 1859, an abolitionist, John Brown, led a raid on an arsenal at Harper's Ferry in Virginia. He planned to seize arms, distribute them to slaves, and lead them in a revolt for freedom. He was captured, tried, and hanged.

The Election of 1860: The Democratic party split into two parts over the slavery issue. These were:

The northern wing, which ran Stephen Douglas on a platform of popular sovereignty to determine free or slave status.

The southern wing, which ran John C. Breckenridge on a policy based on the Dred Scott decision that slaves were property protected everywhere by the Constitution. The remnants of the Whig and American Parties nominated John Bell on a platform that condemned sectional parties and called for upholding the Constitution and the laws of the land.

The recently formed Republican Party nominated Abraham Lincoln on a platform that stated:

Kansas was not to be admitted as a free state.

Slavery was not to be extended to the territories.

Free farming land was to be given to those settling in the West.

A high protective tariff was to be maintained.

In the four party race no one won a majority.

Lincoln was elected by the Electoral College system, even though he received no more than 40 percent of the votes cast.

Southern Secession: With Lincoln's election, seven states (South Carolina, Texas, Louisiana, Mississippi, Alabama, Florida, and Georgia) seceded from the Union. They created The Confederate States of America with Jefferson Davis as president. Their constitution stated that:

There would be no Supreme Court.

States would have more rights than the central government.

Slavery was lawful.

Lincoln's Inaugural Address (1861): Lincoln refused to accept the dissolution of the Union, and stated that war or peace was in the hands of the South.

Fort Sumter: On April 12, 1861, Southern forces fired on Fort Sumter in the harbor of Charleston, S.C. The federal fort had been built years before to guard the harbor and was occupied by federal troops. Lincoln was determined to hold on to federal property in the seceded states and would not acknowledge the secession. Civil war therefore began. Virginia, Tennessee, Arkansas, and North Carolina seceded and joined the Confederacy.

BASIC CAUSES OF THE WAR

Economic: The northern manufacturers needed a high tariff, skilled labor, internal improvements, and a national bank. The southern planters needed low tariffs, slave labor, state banks, and opposed internal improvements.

Political: Notherners opposed extension of slavery to new states because they wanted political control of Congress, which made laws. Most Southerners favored extension of slavery because they, too, wanted to control Congress. Many Northerners believed the Constitution had created a Union—"one nation, indivisible"—that could not be dissolved. Southerners believed the states that made the Union could unmake it and secede.

Moral: Abolitionists and others felt that slavery was an evil and must be eliminated. The South defended slavery by claiming it was established by God and quoted Bible passages to prove it.

MAIN EVENTS OF THE CIVIL WAR

Blockade of the South: In order to cut the South off from supplies, the North blockaded the coast from Virginia to Texas. The blockade also succeeded in preventing the Confederacy from exporting cotton and tobacco. The iron-clad Confederate ship *Merrimac* attempted to break the blockade, but was prevented from doing so by the iron-clad Union ship, *Monitor.*

Capture of Vicksburg: Union forces captured Forts Henry (KY) and Donelson (TE) in 1862, which opened up the Mississippi River valley to invasion by the North. General Grant captured Vicksburg (MI) in 1863, cutting the West from the rest of the Confederacy since New Orleans (LA) had been captured by the Union in 1862.

Emancipation Proclamation (January 1863): Lincoln's famous proclamation freed all slaves residing in states that had rebelled against the Union. This was a military move to help win the war. Lincoln offered other plans for dealing with the problems of slavery after the war.

The Battle of Gettysburg (1863): After defeating invading northern armies, General Robert E. Lee invaded the North and was himself defeated at Gettysburg (PA) in the crucial battle of the war.

Capture of Atlanta (1864): General Sherman captured Atlanta (GA), and, in a famous march to and through Georgia, destroyed everything in his path that might help the enemy. This action, plus the capture of Vicksburg, cut the South into three sections.

Surrender at Appomattox (April 1865): Lee surrendered after steadily losing ground and after finding himself unable to lift the siege of Petersburg (VA). Petersburg fell to Grant on April 2. Lee then abandoned Richmond (VA), the Confederate capital, and fled west only to surrender a week later on April 9. This essentially ended the war, although some fighting continued until the end of May.

RESULTS OF THE CIVIL WAR

Northern business and industry: It grew and prospered during the war, and replaced southern agriculture as the principal activity of this country.

Homestead Act (1862): The act provided free land in the West for those who settled on it and developed it. The South had not supported such legislation before the war.

Pacific Railroad acts (1862 and 1864): Prior to the war southern routes for a transcontinental railroad were considered. The route approved after secession went from St. Louis to San Francisco. It would tie the industry of the East to raw materials and farm products of the West. The Acts granted rights of way and land to the builders, thus providing government subsidies for the road's construction.

Constitutional: The federal government was proven more powerful than any state government. No state could secede from the Union. Three amendments to the Constitution (numbers 13, 14, 15) ended slavery and gave equal protection of the laws and the vote to all males.

Destruction of the southern plantation economy: Based on slavery, it was destroyed forever. It was replaced by sharecropping.

Wartime rights of civilians: The Supreme Court in *ex parte Milligan* upheld the Constitutional rights of a civilian during war time. The case established civilian rule as primary over military government even in times of war.

RECONSTRUCTION

Issue I: Readmission of rebel states to the Union.

> *Solution:* Lincoln's plan was to re-admit states when 10 percent of the voters pledged loyalty to the United States and agreed to the abolition of slavery. After his assassination, northern members of Congress, called Radical Republicans, became harsher, passed the *Reconstruction Acts of 1867*, which treated the South as a conquered province. To gain admittance the seceded states had to ratify the 14th Amendment and meet other requirements. Northern troops occupied the South until the states met all conditions of re-admission. The last occupation troops were withdrawn in 1877.

Issue II: Guarantee of civil rights to Black Americans.

> *Solution:* The *Civil Rights Bill of 1866* was aimed at undoing the effects of Black codes established by southern governments. The 14th and 15th amendments were to guarantee these civil rights. None of these actions were successful in protecting civil rights and the Supreme Court limited the application of the Civil Rights Bill to national issues. Southern legislators maintained some Black Codes and found other ways, including the later Jim Crow laws, to restrict the rights of the freed slaves.

Issue III: Government of rebel states.

> *Solution:* Former slaves, but not Confederate leaders, were allowed to vote at state party conventions and in elections until states were re-admitted, after which the states again set their own rules as to who could vote. Many of the state governments passed important social legislation dealing with schooling and other issues.

RESULTS OF RECONSTRUCTION

Reconstruction problems focused on the issue of whether the southern states were ever out of the Union. The Radical Republicans held that they were, and so developed plans to re-admit the states that differed from Lincoln's plan, as he believed the states had always been part of the Union, even if in rebellion. The freed slaves were often treated as pawns in the game of power politics, especially by northerners who came south (Carpetbaggers). In many southern states ex-slaves held important political offices and helped to write new enlightened state constitutions.

Formation of the Solid South: The federal occupation troops were recalled from the South by President Hayes (1877) after he was declared the winner of the disrupted presidential election of 1876. After 1877, and the withdrawal of all federal troops from the South, for many years the southern states voted for the Democratic party on almost all occasions, as a result of the whites' dislike of Radical Republicans. This concept of the Solid South was still a consideration in elections in the post World War II period.

13th Amendment: 1865—Abolished slavery in the United States.

14th Amendment: 1868—Black Americans were made citizens of the United States. It guaranteed that no state could deny life, liberty, or property without due process of law.

15th Amendment: 1870—Stated that no state can deny the right to vote on account of race, color, or previous condition of servitude.

Ku Klux Klan: It was formed to control ex-slaves and to "keep them in their place" and not allow them to change the basic political and social structure of the South. The Klan grew, especially after 1877.

New Constitutions of southern states: They established free public schools for all children, abolished imprisonment for debt, abolished property qualifications for voting and jury duty.

Railways, highways, and national banking system strengthened the federal government.

Prevention of black voting (after 1877): To counteract influence of black voters, the South tried to deny them political rights by state measures that limited voting privileges to those:

Who could pass literacy tests

Who could pay a poll tax

Who owned property

Whose grandfather had voted

SOME IMPORTANT INDIVIDUALS OF THE PERIOD 1850-1877

Louisa May Alcott	Jay Gould	Dred Scott
Horatio Alger	Rutherford B. Hayes	Horatio Seymour
Clara Barton	Julia Ward Howe	William T. Sherman
John Brown	"Stonewall" Jackson	Thaddeus Stevens
Blanche K. Bruce	Andrew Johnson	Lucy Stone
Jay Cooke	Robert E. Lee	Harriet Beecher Stowe
Jefferson Davis	Abraham Lincoln	James E.B. Stuart
Ignatius Donnelly	George McClellan	Charles Sumner
Stephen Douglas	Herman Melville	Roger B. Taney
Mary Baker Eddy	Francis Parkman	Samuel Tilden
Millard Fillmore	Franklin Pierce	Sojourner Truth
William Lloyd Garrison	Hiram R. Revels	Hariet Tubman
Ulysses S. Grant	Carl Schurz	William "Boss" Tweed
Horace Greeley		

**Chapter 6—
Populists and
Progressives—
1877-1916**

THE INDUSTRIAL REVOLUTION

The Industrial Revolution was a change from hand manufacturing which was done in homes to machine manufacturing done in a factory. The Revolution was stimulated in the United States by:

Growing trade, especially after Revolutionary War removed British restrictions on American industry. Markets for exported goods were soon found. The United States was also free to import under our own tariff regulations.

Invention of cotton gin by Eli Whitney in 1793 provided northern textile workers with an abundance of raw material. It also established the idea of interchangeable parts in manufacturing, which standardized products.

Power from swift-running rivers and of abundant natural resources (coal, iron, and lumber) was easily available, especially in New England and along the Fall Line of the Appalachian Mountains.

Coal, iron ore, and lumber in abundance and near population centers.

Napoleonic Wars, War of 1812, and British blockade all forced American manufacture to grow, since we could not rely on imports.

Westward Expansion throughout the 19th century opened new markets and created new demands.

Labor shortage and wartime needs during the Civil War led to increased use of machinery.

Building of roads, railroads, and canals made transportation of raw materials and finished products easier and stimulated manufacturing in industrial centers.

INFLUENCE OF GEOGRAPHIC FACTORS ON INDUSTRIAL AND AGRICULTURAL DEVELOPMENT

The United States can be divided into four major geographic areas: the Atlantic coastal plain, the Appalachian highlands, the great central plain, the Cordilleran highlands.

Atlantic Coastal Plain: East of the Appalachian Mountains.
First area settled by English colonists.
Suitable for growth of manufacturing cities because of:
    Power available from rivers flowing down from Appalachian Mountains.
    Rivers also allow for some transportation inland (e.g., Hudson River).
    Excellent harbors.
Long, narrow plainland between mountains and Atlantic provides excellent areas for farming to supply food to large population centers.

Appalachian Highlands: From Adirondack Mountains through Allegheny and Cumberland plateaus to central Alabama in the South.
Mountain area, originally dense forest, provided protection for colonists during Revolutionary War.
Rich mining areas—coal and iron—in mountainous parts of Pennsylvania, West Virginia and Alabama.
Valley areas are suitable for farming.

The Great Central Plain: From the Appalachians to the Rockies, and from Canada to Mexico, this is the largest region, comprising almost half of the land in the United States.
Richest agricultural region in the world because of great fertile plains.
Lush land for stock grazing from North Dakota to Texas.
Mississippi River, great North-South waterway, drains the area and supplies excellent transportation, along with its tributaries (e.g., Ohio and Missouri Rivers).

Cordilleran Highlands: From Rocky Mountains to Pacific Ocean.
Mountainous area rich in lumber and mineral resources.
Fertile valley and lowland area near Pacific is suitable for fruit orchards and farming.

18TH-CENTURY INVENTIONS THAT SPURRED INDUSTRIAL REVOLUTION

Flying Shuttle: John Kay (English), increased speed of weaving.   1733

Spinning Jenny: James Hargreaves (English), spun several threads at one time.   1765

Water Frame: Richard Arkwright (English), machine operated by water power spun thread very fast.   1769

Steam Engine: Invented by Thomas Newcomen (English) in 1703, and improved by James Watts (English) in 1769, ushered in Age of Stream. The use of steam power transformed:

> *Transportation* because of application to water and land travel.

> *Factories,* which were no longer dependent on water power, and so could produce at much greater rates of speed and could be located in different areas nearer to raw materials and away from waterfalls.

IMPORTANT 19TH- and 20TH-CENTURY INVENTIONS

Industry: Many inventions transformed the American way of life.

Colt Revolver: Samuel Colt	1831
Electric Dynamo: Michael Faraday	1831
Rubber: Charles Goodyear	1837
Electric Light Bulb: Thomas A. Edison	1879
X-Ray: Wilhelm Roentgen	1895
Radio Vacuum Tube: Lee De Forest	1907
Bakelite (Plastic begins synthetics revolution): Lee Backeland	1909
Cellophane: Jacques Brandenberger	1912
Liquid Fuel Rocket: Robert Goddard	1926
Synthetic Superpolymer (Nylon): Wallace Carothers	1934
Mark I (computer): Howard Aiken	1937
Controlled Nuclear Fission: Enrico Fermi	1942
Power-Producing Nuclear Fission: United States Atomic Energy Commission	1951
Solar Battery: Bell Telephone and Air Research Development	1954
Demonstration of Laser Action: Theodore Maiman	1960

Agriculture: Until 1800, all farm work was done by hand with the help of draft animals and using primitive tools which had changed very little over the centuries. The following inventions revolutionized farming in the 19th century:

Cotton Gin: Eli Whitney	1793
Iron Plow: Charles Newbold	1797
Reaper: Cyrus McCormick	1834
Modern Steel Plow: James Oliver	1868

Transportation and Communication: Inventions also drastically changed the speed of travel and communication. Outstanding ones were

Steamboat: Robert Fulton	1807
Locomotive: George Stevenson	1830
Screw Propellor: John Ericsson	1831
Telegraph: Samuel Morse	1844
Sleeping Car: George Pullman	1867
Air Brake: George Westinghouse	1872
Telephone: Alexander Graham Bell	1876
Automobile: developed by Henry Ford and others	1895
Motion Pictures: C.F. Jenkins	1896
Airplane: Wright Brothers	1903

Radio: R.A Fressenden	1906
Diesel tractors and trains	1930s
Helicopter: I. Sikorsky	1939
Electric Computer: American Industry	1940s
Television: C.F. Jenkins, V. Zworykin, RCA, and CBS	1941
Jet Planes: Lockheed Company	1942
Transistor: William Shockley and Bell Telephone Team	1948
UNIVAC (Universal Automatic Computer): Eckert-Mauchly Corp.	1951
Duplicating Machine (Xerox)	1959
Manned Space Flight (NASA)	1961
Facsimile Machine	1970

Mining and Smelting: As steel became increasingly important in manufacturing, the following processes developed:

New method of making steel from iron: William Kelly	1851
Bessemer Process: Henry Bessemer, used blast of hot air to remove impurities from molten iron.	1856
Open Hearth Method used more of the iron effectively.	1868

New steel alloys with special strengths were developed to aid the growing industrial demands of car, plane, and rocket industries.

20TH CENTURY

Aluminum Industry was stimulated by World War I	1914

BASES OF U.S. INDUSTRIAL POWER

Immigration: All Americans are immigrants. Even the ancestors of the Native Americans came as immigrants from Siberia across the Bering Sea. All immigrants both as groups and as individuals have contributed to the development of the nation. The Native Americans cultivated plants, developed a special understanding of their relationship with the environment and aided the first white settlers. The first settlers on the coast carved cities and farms out of forests The slaves gave their labor to produce much wealth and capital for the later industrial development of the nation. Chinese laborers built the great railroads through the Rockies. Later immigrants from Europe supplied labor in the early factories and mines of the Northeast, working under poor conditions to build the wealth of America. After the Civil War immigration increased greatly and America was considered the Melting Pot of peoples. How closely this idea was achieved is debatable, but for generations it was the stated goal of the nation—"e pluribus unum"—from many, one. In more recent years the concept of pluralism has replaced the melting pot imagery. Pluralism suggests greater emphasis on the many, the pluribus, but pluralism still holds that the many peoples make one nation. Some individual contributions by post-Civil War immigrants to the U.S. illustrate how beneficial this immigration has been to the nation and how diversified the peoples have been.

Germany:	Carl Schurz (politics)
	Walter Damrosch (music)
	Albert Einstein (science)
	Carl Schurz (politics)
Denmark:	Jacob Riis (social reform and literature)
Scotland:	Andrew Carnegie (industry)
Canada:	James J. Hill (railroads)
England:	Alexander Graham Bell (invention)
Switzerland:	Louis Agassiz (zoology)
Yugoslavia:	Michael Papin (X-ray)
Italy:	Arturo Toscanini (music)
	Amadeo P. Giannini (banking)
Ireland:	Augustus St. Gaudens (sculpture)
Lithuania:	Sydney Hillman (labor)

Russia:	David Sarnoff (television)
Mexico:	José Limón (dance)
Japan:	Hideyo Noguchi (medicine)
	Yamasaki (architecture)

Resources: America has been blessed with rich deposits of oil, coal, iron, and other minerals needed for industry. Farmlands are rich and can produce almost every type of product needed for manufacture, except natural rubber. There have been abundant water resources and the nation is blessed with a variety of climates—none of which are truly oppressive.

Psychological Factors: Open lands, political freedom, inventiveness, individualism, and other factors created a climate of opinion that encouraged industrial growth.

RESULTS OF EARLY INDUSTRIAL REVOLUTION

Growth of great cities, as people changed their occupation from farming to manufacturing.

Rapid growth of city population, causing slums and increased crime rate.

Bad working conditions shared by many people, leading to development and growth of trade unions.

Trade unions that organized laborers to demand such items as shorter working days, safer working conditions and insurance to cover injuries.

Greater interest in social reforms and politics to provide solutions to problems.

Demand for political parties to change programs to meet new problems created by industrial change.

Increase of America's productivity and power.

Imperialism, as leaders and the people perceived a need for colonies as sources of raw materials and markets for finished products in competition with other industrializing nations.

Increased militarism, as international competition grew.

Speeding up of transportation, bringing people closer together.

Increased need for education.

More foods and materials available to a greater number of people.

New giant industries (railroad, oil, steel, etc.)

Transformation in farming techniques.

Increased standard of living of most people in industrialized societies.

Rising expectations of most people to share in the "good life" produced by material plenty.

EFFECTS OF INDUSTRIAL REVOLUTION ON AMERICAN LIFE

New Production Methods: Large-scale production in factories produced new techniques of organizing work. These were:

Division of labor: each worker performs one small task over and over again.

Assembly line: each worker adds one part to the product being made as it moves along from worker to worker.

Standardization of parts: many parts of each machine and the same part in different machines are made the same in shape and size so that, when defective or worn out, individual parts can be easily changed and replaced with new parts or parts from another similar machine. The parts are thus interchangeable.

Business Combines: Until the Civil War, most factories were small—but afterward they began growing larger and larger; railroads opened up new markets; the heavy flow of immigrants provided cheap labor, and discovery of new mineral resources increased tremendously the supply of raw materials. As a result, factories increased in size, hiring many more workers and buying more machinery. Individual capitalists were unable to finance these huge projects, and new business forms were created. They were:

The Corporation: A company sells shares of stocks; shareholders elect the management (the Board of Directors), casting one vote, usually, for each share of stock owned; the management then selects the officers of the company who run the business on a day-to-day basis but who are responsible to the Board of Directors and ultimately to the shareholders.

The Trust: As industries grew, many related corporations (such as sugar refineries) merged into one large combination, run by a Board of Trustees.
Shareholders assigned their share in the corporation to trustees who managed the new trusts as Boards of Directors did for the corportion. The trustees were often members of the Board of Directors of the corporations. Often the creating of a trust was the work of an individual such as John D. Rockefeller who created the Standard Oil Trust to control the industry.

Advantages of the Trust: Huge amounts of raw materials can be purchased more economically.
Large-scale manufacture creates more efficient production and distribution.
The industry can make gainful use of by-products.

Disadvantages of the Trust: Drives out small business and destroys competition.
Regulates prices often unfairly through price cutting wars.
Concentrates great wealth and power in the hands of a few.
May control an industry by achieving a vertical or horizontal control. A *vertical trust* or organization is one where the trust owns or controls everything—raw materials, manufacturing, distribution facilities—needed by the company. A *horizontal trust* or organization is one where the trust owns either all the raw materials or all the manufacturing or all the distribution facilities of an industry.

Other related forms of business organization were the Pools and Holding Companies. Pools were combinations of businesses that agreed to control prices; *holding companies* were arrangements in which a company controlled a portion of the stock in other corporations (e.g., U.S. Steel Corporation).

Development of Trade Unions: The early factory system was responsible for many evils such as:

Use of child labor.

Low pay and a long working day.

Unsanitary working conditions.

Forced purchase at company stores.

There were no laws to restrain abuses by employers.

Workers in America had found as early as 1793 that they could best achieve their demands and changes in working conditions by uniting. Gradually, unions grew. The most important were

Knights of Labor: Organized in Philadelphia, 1879, by garment workers, aimed at organizing all workers into one large union. Although it reached a membership of 700,000, poor leadership and internal disputes caused its gradual collapse.

American Federation of Labor (AFL): Founded in 1886, soon replaced Knights of Labor; it organized skilled workers according to their trade, or craft. Craft unions in different cities united to form national craft unions in different fields (carpenters, painters, etc.). Thus the AFL is an organization of many craft unions united under a single leadership. Noted early leaders of the AFL: Samuel Gompers, one of the founders; William Green, who succeeded on Gompers's death and remained in charge from 1924-1952; George Meany. In the early 1930s the AFL formed a Committee of Industrial Organization to consider the establishment of industry wide—rather than craft—unions. It met with limited success and there were internal disagreements. In 1936 the Committee broke away from the AFL to create a union (CIO) based on all the workers in a particular industry—for example, all workers in the steel industry became members of the Steel Workers Union. The CIO gained recognition for its new unions through a series of sit-in strikes in the late 1930s. The AFL and CIO reunited as one union in 1955.

THE POPULIST MOVEMENT

With the disputed election of 1877 settled in favor of Hayes, the Reconstruction Era ended. The nation's interests turned to issues of economics. As business grew, wealth accumulated in the hands of business people and bankers. Agricultural prices began a decline in 1884, that again intensified farm protests. Sectional antagonism intensified. A number of previous attempts to help the farmer's cause were revitalized, such as the Granger Movement, with little impact. Finally in 1892, several years of efforts to unite labor and farmers led to the formation of a third political party—the People's or Populist Party. Holding its first national convention in Omaha, the Populist Party produced a platform (Omaha Platform) that proposed significant reforms. To address the farmer's need for inflation and cheap money the Populists called for the coinage of silver at a 16 : 1 ratio with gold. The Platform also called for a graduated income tax, direct election of senators, a shorter working day and restrictions on immigration. In the presidential election James B. Weaver came in third behind Cleveland (Dem.) and Harrison (Rep.). Eventually the major features of the Omaha Platform were adopted by the federal government.

In 1896 the Populists nominated William Jennings Bryan for President. He was also the nominee of the Democrats who were won over to the 16 : 1 ratio for the coinage of silver by Bryan's stirring *Cross of Gold Speech*—one of the most famous speeches in American history. His campaign, while extensive, focused on the issue of the coinage of silver, which was considered the best way to help the farmers and workers as it would create an inflationary pattern. Bryan lost to William McKinley (Rep.) and with the return of better economic conditions and the start of the Spanish-American War the Populist Party declined and eventually died.

THE PROGRESSIVE MOVEMENT

The Progressive Movement developed at the turn of the century, largely as a response to problems created in urban areas by industrial growth. The Progressives worked within the established party framework, with the exception of Theodore Roosevelt's "Bull Moose" Party in 1912. They achieved a variety of reforms ranging from the Pure Food and Drug Laws (1906) under Theodore Roosevelt (Rep.) to the establishment of the Federal Reserve System (1913) under Woodrow Wilson (Dem.). Theodore Roosevelt and Woodrow Wilson were both leaders of the Progressive Movement as was Robert La Follette of Wisconsin. They illustrate the range of participation in the movement.

Others involved in the movement were writers and publicists such as Lincoln Steffens (*Shame of the Cities*), Ida Tarbell (*History of the Standard Oil Company*), and Upton Sinclair (*The Jungle*).

The movement died with the U.S. entry into World War I but not before it had made profound changes in America's business and political life.

LEGISLATION AND SUPREME COURT DECISIONS RELATED TO INDUSTRIAL GROWTH AND THE PROGRESSIVE MOVEMENT: 1877-1916

Munn v. Illinois: In this Supreme Court case the Court declared that the state, not the federal government, had the right to regulate business. Therefore, citizens had to resort to the polls and control of state government rather than to the federal courts for redress in cases involving control and regulation of business. The case has been grouped with several other cases as the Granger Cases; cases that worked against the interests of the people and in favor of business. These attitudes eventually led to the Populist Movement.

1877

Civil Rights Cases: In these cases the Supreme Court declared that the Fourteenth Amendment applied only to state actions involving infringement of civil rights. If one individual infringed on another's rights as guaranteed by the Fourteenth Amendment, it was an individual offense and redress had to be found in the state courts. Federal law and the Fourteenth Amendment did not apply. The reaction of Congress

to this interpretation of its limited powers was to pass no further civil
rights legislation until the 1950s.   1883

Wabash, St. Louis and Pacific Railroad Company v. Illinois: In this famous
case the Supreme Court declared that the state of Illinois could not
regulate interstate commerce. A state could only regulate intrastate
commerce. This created a great need for federal legislation, which came
in the Interstate Commerce Act.   1886

Interstate Commerce Act: Set up fair rate schedules for railway freight,
prohibiting special rates to trusts and the charging of higher rates for
short hauls than for long hauls. It also established the Interstate
Commerce Commission (ICC) to enforce the act.   1887

Sherman Anti-Trust Act: Aimed at breaking huge trusts into smaller
units, it failed because it was not enforced and because some
administrations favored big business.   1890

Plessy v. Ferguson: In this Supreme Court decison the court established
the principle of separate but equal facilities for blacks. This created a
two-tier system of rights for blacks and whites. It created a subservient
class that was forced to work on the farms of the South. As the blacks
left the South for the industrial North, they added to the unskilled labor
force in the cities. This had an impact on industrial growth and
development and established the civil rights system of America until
the 1950s.   1895

Pure Food and Drug Act: Prohibited sale of impure food and medicine;
four years later the act was amended to include the prohibition of false
advertising.   1906

Department of Labor: Was created to give labor representation in cabinet.   1913

Federal Reserve Act: Set up a system of Federal Reserve banks under
the joint control of the people, government, and the banking industry
to regulate and control credit.   1913

Clayton Anti-Trust Act: Prohibited unfair agreements that might diminish
competition; established a Federal Trade Commission (FTC) to investigate charges of unfair competition and prosecute such cases; prohibited
competing businesses from having the same men on Boards of Directors.   1914

Conservation of Resources: Greedy lumber cutting depleted woods
without replanting; unintelligent farming ruined soil, inefficient mining
methods wasted oil and gas; indiscriminate hunting and fishing
decimated wildlife. Under President Theodore Roosevelt, a conservation
program to end these abuses was begun. The following measures were
aimed at conserving our national resources:

National Forests: Under Roosevelt, millions of acres were set aside
as forests; timber cutting was regulated so that there would be a
continuous supply.

Hunting licenses: In order to regulate killing of game, laws were
passed by states requiring hunters and fishermen to purchase
licenses.

Reclamation Law of 1902 known as the Newlands Act: Irrigation
projects were made possible by the act. Projects were initiated aimed
at controlling floods (which washed away valuable topsoil and caused
much other damage), improving navigation and producing electric
power for outlying areas, and reclaiming wastelands. Most important
projects were: Boulder Dam in Arizona and Nevada, Grand Coulee
Dam and Roosevelt Dam in Washington, Shasta Dam in California,
Fort Peck Dam in Montana, Garrison Dam in North Dakota.

AMERICAN EXPANSION IN THE POST-CIVIL WAR PERIOD

In the post-Civil War period, Americans continued to move westward and settle the frontier. The railroad made settlement easier and opened new markets for eastern products and western raw materials and food. The movement led to warfare with the Native Americans and fighting on the plains continued until late in the century. The Dawes Act (1887) was an attempt to replace the tribal organization of the Indians by eventually making them citizens of the United States. In 1890 the Census Bureau reported there was no longer a definable frontier line as the country was settled coast to coast, although there were large areas with very few white settlers. The historian, Frederick Jackson Turner, developed an important thesis on what the "closing of the frontier" meant, stating that the formative years of American history were over. However, the nation continued to grow and expand. The growth of cities became the chief focus of domestic growth while expansion overseas became very important, especially after 1890.

THE GROWTH OF GREAT CITIES

Cities were founded by the earliest colonists. Transportation facilities—harbors, rivers, river fords, and later canal and railroad lines—were important in determining the location of many cities. The nearness of raw materials, the availability of a labor supply, and the convenience of cheap transportation also were important factors in city location and growth.

Some Major U.S. Cities

BOSTON
Became early shipping center because of Massachusetts Bay, proximity to mouths of Mystic and Charles Rivers

CHICAGO
Railroad center: chief market for agricultural products of central plains;
Approximate geographic center of great coal mining and steel manufacturing areas;
Harbor on Lake Michigan

DENVER
Junction of South Platte River and Cherry Creek;
Center of Rocky Mountain states; access to mineral resources and oil

DETROIT
Center of network of waterways made it terminal for shipping on Detroit River, River Rouge, St. Clair, Lake Erie, and Lake Huron;
Water power from rivers; easy access to coal and steel by river or rail transport
Birthplace of automobile industry in the late 19th century

NEW ORLEANS
Located near mouth of Mississippi River and close to Gulf of Mexico;
Proximity to external shipping (Gulf of Mexico) and internal transportation facilities (Mississippi River) made it center of cotton and later oil industries

NEW YORK
Great natural harbor;
Juncture of Hudson River with Atlantic Ocean;
Waterway to Midwest created by linking Hudson River to Great Lakes via Erie Canal

PHILADELPHIA
Junction of Schuylkill and Delaware rivers;
Proximity to coal fields;
Pennsylvania Railroad gave it a link to the West

PITTSBURGH
Junction of Ohio, Allegheny, and Monongahela rivers;
Proximity to both coal and iron ore, making it convenient for growth of smelting industry;
Oil and natural gas fields nearby

SAN FRANCISCO
Proximity to Sacramento and San Joaquin rivers;
Located on Pacific Ocean, with one of the world's finest harbors;
Near great gold fields

SEATTLE
Located on Puget Sound and Lake Washington;
Gateway to Alaskan gold fields;
Great shipping center for the Pacific;
Center for lumber and salmon fishing industries

OVERSEAS EXPANSION 1867–1917

The Alaska Purchase: Termed "Seward's Folly," Alaska was purchased from Russia upon the urging of Secretary of State Seward in 1867 for $7.2 million.

Annexation of Hawaii: Discovered by an Englishman, Captain James Cook, in 1778, Hawaii first attracted the interest of the United States in 1820 when missionaries went there

In 1884 the United States leased Pearl Harbor as a naval station.

In 1889, the native queen was overthrown by a rebellion, and the new government petitioned the United States to annex the islands.

In 1898, Congress approved annexation.

Pacific Islands: In 1867, the United States annexed uninhabited Midway Island as a coaling station.

In 1889, by negotiation with European nations the United States acquired Tutuila, Pago Pago for its valuable harbor.

Spanish-American War: In 1895 Cuban patriots revolted against harsh Spanish rule and were severely punished. Sensational American newspaper stories demanded intervention, as did American business owners who had considerble investments in Cuban sugar and tobacco.

In February 1898, the American battleship *Maine* was mysteriously blown up while in the harbor of Havana. The slogan "Remember the Maine" aroused the American public, and in April Congress declared war on Spain.

An American army was landed in Cuba and soon destroyed Spanish resistance in Santiago; meanwhile, the Spanish fleet bottled up in the harbor of Santiago, was thoroughly beaten, trying to escape. Under Secretary of the Navy Theodore Roosevelt, before leaving to lead a contingent of the Army in Cuba at the Battle of San Juan Hill, arranged for the U.S. Navy in the Pacific to be ready to attack the Philippines in case of war with Spain. When war came, the fleet attacked the Spanish Fleet in the Philippines and occupied Manila.

The Treaty of Paris, signed in December 1898, ended the war. It contained the following provisions:

Puerto Rico, Guam, and the Philippines were ceded to the United States.

Cuba was granted independence. The United States was to supervise this independence.

The United States paid $20 million to Spain for the Philippines.

The Panama Canal Zone: With possessions in the Atlantic and Pacific, the United States needed a way to get its navy from ocean to ocean without sailing around South America or Africa. A canal providing a short water passage between the two oceans was the ideal solution. Such a canal was first attempted by a French company, but it failed.

The United States under President Theodore Roosevelt in 1903 offered $10 million and a yearly rental of $250,000 to Colombia for use of land in the province of Panama where a canal could be built. The Colombian government refused the offer.

In November 1903, the Panamanian people rebelled, and with United States support, set up an independent government. 15 days later the new republic of Panama accepted the same terms offered to Colombia and gave the United States the right to build a canal and exclusive control of a Canal Zone in perpetuity. The United States paid Colombia $20 million as redress for the loss of her Province of Panama and Colombia recognized the independence of the Republic of Panama.

Virgin Islands: These islands, purchased from Denmark in 1917, provided a defense for the Panama Canal. They provided naval bases on the perimeter of the Caribbean Sea.

SOME IMPORTANT INDIVIDUALS OF THE PERIOD 1877–1916

Jane Addams	James A. Garfield	Joseph Pulitzer
John P. Altgeld	Charlotte Perkins Gilman	Thomas B. Reed
Susan B. Anthony	Samuel Gompers	Walter Reed
Chester Arthur	Mark Hanna	Jacob Riis
Ethel Barrymore	Benjamin Harrison	John D. Rockefeller
Edward Bellamy	John Hay	Theodore Roosevelt
James G. Blaine	Rutherford B. Hayes	Augustus Saint-Gaudens
William Jennings Bryan	William Randolph Hearst	Louis H. Sullivan
Andrew Carnegie	Winslow Homer	William H. Taft
George Washington Carver	William Dean Howells	Ida Tarbell
Mary Cassatt	Charles E. Hughes	Samuel Tilden
Tennessee Claflin	Sarah Orne Jewett	Mark Twain (Samuel
Grover Cleveland	Oliver Kelley	Clemens)
Roscoe Conkling	Sidney Lanier	Cornelius Vanderbilt
Eugene Debs	Mary Elizabeth Lease	Booker T. Washington
Emily Dickinson	Alfred T. Mahan	Tom Watson
Dorothea Dix	William McKinley	James B. Weaver
W.E.B. DuBois	Frank Norris	Frances Willard
Isadora Duncan	John J. Pershing	Woodrow Wilson
Jim Fisk	Gifford Pinchot	Pearl White
Henry Ford	Terrence V. Powderly	Victoria Claflin Woodhull

Chapter 7—World War I, the Inter-war Period, and World War II—1916–1945

HIGHLIGHTS OF AMERICAN FOREIGN POLICY TO WORLD WAR I

Throughout its history the United States has had contact and involvements with foreign nations. Our interest in South America stems from the founding of the nation. Interest in the Pacific was officially acknowledged as early as 1785, when still governed under the Articles of Confederation, Americans began trading with China, and, of course, the United States introduced Japan to modern times with the "opening" of Japan by Perry in 1853. There have always been foreign policy relations with Europe, but many have suggested the United States followed a policy of isolation from Europe during most of the 19th century. The War of 1812, efforts to keep England and France out of the Civil War and the Spanish-American War are three among many possible indications that United States isolation from Europe was not a fact in the 19th century but a theory.

During the first thirty-five years of the nation's history several actions were taken that provided a foundation and attitude for much of United States foreign policy.

Proclamation of Neutrality by President Washington stated that the United States would be neutral in the war between England and France. This established the precedent of United States neutrality in European affairs. 1793

Washington's *Farewell Address* urged America not to sign an alliance with any nation. 1796

Jefferson's Inaugural Address promised that the United States would seek peace, commerce, and friendship with all nations, but would enter into entangling alliances with none. This became the basis of United States foreign policy until after World War II when the NATO alliance was established. Since then, the United States has signed many treaties allying itself with foreign nations. 1801

The *Monore Doctrine* states an idea that guided U.S. policy towards the Americas. President Monroe promised that America would stay out of European affairs, and demanded that European countries stay out of the affairs of North and South America. Later presidents added their own interpretations to this basic policy as it applied to South America. 1823

Involvement in the Pacific became important for the United States after the Civil War with the rapid industrial growth that followed. Acquisition of islands as coaling stations (Samoa) and interest in new markets

(Hawaii) illustrate this early involvement. Later the proclaiming of the *Open Door Policy* in China in 1899, U.S. involvement in the *Boxer Rebellion* in China in 1900, and the fact that President T. Roosevelt arbitated the Russo-Japanese War in 1905 (for which he won the Nobel Peace Prize) showed continued concern for the U.S position in Asia and the free access to markets. The *Spanish-American War*, fought in the Caribbean (Cuba) and the Pacific (Philippines) marks the emergence of the United States as a great power on the international scene. U.S. interest in Asia was seen by the acquisition of the Philippines at the end of that war, while concern for the Caribbean was seen in the acquisition of Puerto Rico and the protectorate over Cuba.

1898

Involvement in the Americas even preceded the Monroe Doctrine. In the post-Civil War period U.S. interest in the Americas became focused on Central America and new markets. Concern over Cuba culminated in the Spanish-American War. Desire to maintain "order" and keep European powers out of the area led to the sending of U.S. Marines to several nations. A highlight of U.S involvement was the support of Panama's revolution and the building of the *Panama Canal* (completed in 1914). Involvement in the Mexican Civil War after 1911 almost led to a second war with Mexico.

WORLD WAR I

Causes: sparked by the assassination of Archduke Ferdinand of Austria-Hungary on June 28, 1914, World War I was really caused by imperialistic and economic rivalries.

Why America Joined: Although President Wilson urged a policy of neutrality, Americans sold arms to the Allies, and in 1917 abandoned its neutral position. The following events caused the United States to enter the war:

Sinking of Lusitania by German submarines aroused public opinion.

The use of unrestricted submarine warfare (sinking ships without warning) by Germany. Such warfare was stopped temporarily after U.S. protest.

Discovery of the Zimmermann Note (which demonstrated that Germany planned to urge Mexico to attack the United States).

On April 5, 1917, after Germany resumed unrestricted submarine warfare, sinking U.S. ships and those of other neutral nations despite a U.S. note of warning, Congress declared war.

The War: An army of 4 million troops was raised by a draft (Selective Service). Many volunteered. Bond drives helped to pay the huge expense of financing the war. These bonds were called Liberty Bonds.

The nation was immobilized for a total war effort including a War Industries Board and a Committee for Public Information.

American naval power broke Germany's blockade of England and helped destroy its fleet of submarines.

Two million American soldiers in Europe, added to the forces of the Allies, crushed Germany on land. The American Expeditionary Force (AEF) under General John J. Pershing participated in battles at Belleau Wood, Château-Thierry, St. Mihiel, and the Argonne Forest.

An armistice was signed on November 11, 1918.

Wilson's 14 Points: Wilson's plan for a peace treaty included 14 points that he hoped would prevent future wars. Some important points were:

Reduction of armaments.

An end to secret treaties.

Freedom of the seas.

An equitable solution to the colonial problem.

Self-determination of peoples.

Establishment of a League of Nations to arbitrate problems among nations peacefully.

Treaty of Versailles: Largely ignoring the 14 points and intending to make Germany powerless to wage war forever, the Allies formulated a treaty that was signed June 28, 1919. Some of its important provisions were:

Surrender of German Territory: Cessation of Alsace-Lorraine on the border of France and Germany to France; cessation of other territories and colonies to other European allies and Japan. The colonies were to be administered by the various victorious nations under *mandates* of the League of Nations.

Reparations: Germany was forced to compensate the Allies for war damages.

Allied Occupation: The Allies occupied the Rhineland region in Germany (between the Rhine River and the French and Belgian borders).

War Guilt: Germany was forced to admit guilt for starting the war.

A *League of Nations:* Designed to provide a forum for the nations to discuss issues of conflict and prevent war, the League failed to act effectively in disputes and proved to be ineffective in preventing the outbreak of World War II. Although the League was Wilson's idea, the U.S. Senate voted not to accept the treaty. The failure of the United States to join is considered one reason for the League's failure.

THE 1920s

The Roaring Twenties: In the immediate post-war period there were many problems of adjustment to peace. Jobs were hard to find for many returning veterans. Farm prices were depressed and remained so during the entire period until the New Deal. Industry slowly recovered, prosperity returned and there was an economic boom; but it is now clear that the prosperity was not evenly distributed. There was a great land boom in Florida in which many people lost money and heavy speculation on the stock market culminated in the crash of October 1929.

Prohibition was instituted and led to the growth of crime as criminal leaders like Al Capone organized others to supply illegal alcohol. New attitudes towards sex and morality, the growth of "speakeasies" (bars), and the development of jazz and the blues have led scholars to refer to the period as the "roaring twenties."

The Red Scare of the early 20s was directed against communism, which Americans came to fear after a communist government was established in the Soviet Union and a communist led uprising occurred in Germany. Attorney General Palmer and J. Edgar Hoover made reputations for themselves, but the actual threat to the nation was exaggerated.

Return to normalcy was the slogan of the Harding Administration elected in 1920. It supported a return to pre-war attitudes and foreign policy positions. The U.S. turned down the Treaty of Versailles with its League of Nations and returned to *isolationism*, as the policy of ignoring Europe was called. The administration ended with several scandals (Teapot Dome), and this discredited the federal government. Harding died in office. His successors, Presidents Coolidge and Hoover, basically followed the pattern of support of business and little government regulation begun by Harding. In foreign policy, although they professed a policy of isolationism, they supported negotiations over reparations from Germany and sent military forces to Central American nations on several occasions to protect the status quo and American business interests.

THE GREAT DEPRESSION AND THE NEW DEAL

Although a decade of good times and prosperity for some followed World War I, the United States was engulfed in a major depression at the end of the 1920s. Causes of the depression included:

High tariffs aimed at eliminating European competition from American markets but the reduced trade made it impossible to sell U.S. goods abroad.

Speculation in real estate and stocks caused artificial rises in prices.

Overproduction and unemployment caused in part by replacement of workers with machines.

War debts absorbed European purchasing power, lessening foreign trade.

Too much credit on easy terms caused financial collapses when borrowers were unable to pay back their loans.

The stock market crash of October 1929 is considered the starting point of the Great Depression. The federal government under President Hoover took little action to correct the economic problems believing the economy would adjust naturally without interference and that the states or local charity should help the jobless until the economy again was operating fully. It reflected the laissez-faire attitudes and Social Darwinist philosophy that had prevailed in the Republican Party in the 1920s. After two years with no economic improvement, Hoover did support some federal help (Reconstruction Finance Corporation).

In the *election of 1932* Franklin D. Roosevelt, a Democrat, defeated Herbert Hoover. As a candidate, Franklin D. Roosevelt promised action to combat the depression. The actions became incorporated in what is known as the New Deal. The various measures of the New Deal taken to combat the depression have been grouped by some historians in the general categories of: the "3 Rs"—relief, recovery, reform.

Some historians reject this classification as some acts fit in more than one category. However, the "3 Rs" provide one organizational scheme for categorizing the many New Deal measures. Examples of each type of legislation are:

1. *Relief*—direct giving of goods, clothing, shelter, and jobs to the unemployed.
   Works Progress Adminstration (WPA): The federal government gave employment to men on work projects it initiated.
2. *Recovery*—laws aimed at curing the sickness of the economy at that moment.
   Home Owners Loan Corporation (HOLC): Government made loans available to homeowners to prevent loss of their homes to mortgagees.
   Agricultural Adjustment Act (AAA): Reduced amount of crops planted to create artificial shortages and stimulate prices.
3. *Reform*—long-term changes in the economy designed to prevent future depressions.
   Tennessee Valley Authority (TVA): Comprehensive development of the production of electricity and the control of flooding in the Tennessee River valley. Opposed by many as socialism (i.e., government involvement, development, and ownership of industry), but the TVA was approved by the Supreme Court. The electricity produced proved vital to the development of the atomic bomb by the United States in World War II.
   Reciprocal Tariff Act: Removed barriers to trade by lowering tariffs through negotiation.
   National Industrial Recovery Act (NIRA): Codes of fair practices including rights of workers were drawn up by each industry involved in interstate commerce. The codes were administered by the National Recovery Administration (NRA). The Supreme Court, interpreting the Constitution very strictly, declared this and some other early New Deal legislation unconstitutional.

Supreme Court Controversy: Roosevelt attempted in 1937, after his overwhelming reelection, to change the composition of the Supreme Court. Roosevelt was upset by the failure of the Court to approve much of his legislation. Congress refused to support his "court packing" plan. With the death of several judges, Roosevelt was able to appoint new judges who supported his legislation and interpreted the Constitution more loosely.

Recession of 1937: In the first few years of the New Deal economic conditions improved in the nation. In 1937 recovery staggered and there was a little recession. With the coming of World War II the American economy improved rapidly and the Great Depression quickly receded from view.

Organized Labor: The American Federation of Labor (AFL) had organized only skilled workers. In 1935, the AFL created a Committee for Industrial Organization, headed by John L. Lewis, to organize unskilled and semi-skilled workers. The committee left the

AFL in 1936, and in 1938 formed its own labor organization, the Congress of Industrial Organization (CIO). Instead of dividing workers by craft, the CIO divided them by industry. For example, all workers in the automobile industry, whether skilled or unskilled, became members of the United Automobile Workers. The CIO made quick progress in organizing previously unaffiliated industrial workers in such fields as steel, textile, shipbuilding, and rubber. The CIO used "sit-in" strikes as a tool to gain recognition from industry.

IMPORTANT LEGISLATION AND SUPREME COURT DECISIONS
1916–1945

Adamson Act: Provided for 8-hour day for railroad workers.   1916

Norris-LaGuardia Anti-Injunction Act: Limited power of courts to issue injunctions and curtail workers' rights to strike and picket.   1932

New Deal Legislation: (See acts mentioned above) Acts were passed dealing with many issues from agricultural reform to workman's compensation; they changed the American economy. A number of the programs were reversed during President Reagan's terms in office.   1933

Federal Communications Commission (FCC): Regulates communication by telephone, telegraph, radio, and television.   1934

Securities and Exchange Commission (SEC): Protects investors by establishing fair procedures in sale of stocks; in 1935 the SEC was given power to regulate financial practices of public utilities involved in interstate commerce.   1935

Schechter Poultry Corp. v. U.S.: The Court declared the National Industrial Recovery Act unconstitutional.   1935

National Labor Relations Act (called *Wagner Act*): Safeguarded labor's rights to organize and bargain through unions.   1935

Social Security Act: Established a federal-state system of unemployment compensation and old age pension paid for by a federal tax on employee's income and employer's total payroll.   1935

U.S. v. Butler: The first Agricultural Adjustment Act was declared unconstitutional.   1936

NLRB v. Jones and Laughlin Steel Corp.: The Court, in a 5-4 decision upheld the National Labor Relations Act.   1937

Fair Labor Standards Act: Established minimum wage and work week of 40 hours with time and a half for overtime.   1938

Serviceman's Readjustment Act (GI Bill): Addressed the issue of demobilizing the 12,000,000 servicemen who had fought in World War II by providing loans to veterans for housing and education.   1944

WORLD WAR II
Background

Rise of Fascism: In 1922, Mussolini, leader of the Italian Fascists, took power. Pursuing a militaristic policy as a solution to Italy's economic problems, he attacked Ethiopia in 1935.

In 1931, Japan, led by a military dictatorship, attacked China and annexed Manchuria. In 1937 Japan invaded China.

Germany, under Hitler who took power in 1933, also embarked on a militaristic program to address economic problems. The three fascist powers—Germany, Italy and Japan—formed an alliance known as the Axis. Hitler denounced the Treaty of Versailles. He seized the industrialized Ruhr in 1936 and annexed Austria in 1938. Hitler and his Nazis Party made vicious attacks on Catholics and Jews and suppressed all who did not agree with his policies. Yet the League of Nations and the World War I allies did not join together to stop any of the aggressive moves of the Axis powers. In 1938 England and France negotiated the Munich Agreement with Hitler hoping to bring "peace in our time" by allowing Hitler to take the Sudetenland from Czechoslovakia but Hitler soon broke the agreement. Hitler invaded Poland in September 1939.

France and Britain declared war on Germany to help Poland resist the attack, but they failed. Germany speedily conquered Norway, Denmark, the Netherlands, Belgium, and then France. Great Britain and the British Commonwealth together with governments in exile from the conquered countries and the colonies of these countries continued the war. England withstood a massive air onslaught by the Germans in 1940. Finally in June, 1941, Hitler broke a treaty with the Soviet Union and attacked, bringing the Soviets into the war on the side of the Allies (i.e, those fighting against Germany and Italy and later Japan).

American Involvement in the War: Although it was on the outbreak of war in Europe in 1939, a policy of neutrality was declared by President Roosevelt. It was later repealed and replaced by the Lend-Lease Act, which gave the president power to sell or lease war equipment to any country whose defense he deemed important to the preservation of American safety. America became "the arsenal of democracy," and supplied Great Britain with arms after the Fall of France in 1940.

America Enters: Relations between the United States and Japan became very strained in the 1930s. Negotiations were undertaken in Washington to address these differences when on December 7, 1941, the Japanese air force and navy in a surprise attack on Pearl Harbor, destroyed a large part of the American fleet that was stationed there. The United States became a participant in World War II when, the next day, Congress declared war on Japan, and three days later, Germany and Italy declared war on the United States.

Wartime Government Agencies: The government quickly organized for full scale war while military forces were rapidly built up. A number of agencies were established to run the war. Among them were

> *War Production Board (WPB):* Organized industry so that war materials could be produced at the highest level of efficiency.

> *Office of Price Administration (OPA):* To prevent inflation and a black market, the OPA set prices and rationed goods such as oil and food. This assured a fair distribution of the limited consumer supplies and assured the needs of the military would be met.

> *War Labor Board (WLB):* Settled disputes between business and labor without strikes so that production would not be interrupted and morale would be high.

> *Fair Employment Practices Committee (FEPC):* Aimed at insuring morale and maximum use of the labor force by preventing employer discrimination against workers because of race or religion. The efforts of this committee laid the foundation for the civil rights movement of the 1950s.

> *Office of War Information (OWI):* Issued patriotic material and served as the propaganda branch of the government. Its goal was to maintain morale by warning people against defeatist and harmful propaganda.

Allied Wartime Cooperation: During the war the allied leaders, Churchill (England), Stalin (Soviet Union), De Gaulle (Free France) Jiang Jieshi (China), and Roosevelt (USA) held a series of conferences to plan war strategy, and at Yalta (1945) to plan for the post-war world. Different combinations of these Big Five leaders attended these meetings, which made it possible for the war effort to be unified. These wartime conferences set the precedent for post-war Summit Meetings.

The War in Asia: Japan quickly captured the Philippines, Guam, Wake, Hong Kong, and Singapore. The crippled United States fleet was unable to stop the over-running of these and other islands. By spring of 1942, the tide began to turn with aid from Australia and New Zealand.

Important naval victories in the Coral Sea and at Midway (the "turning point of the war") shattered most of the Japanese fleet. This was followed by a series of American victories in hotly fought battles on Pacific islands. Guadalcanal, the Aleutians, and Bougainville fell in 1943; the Marshalls, Saipan, the Philippines, Corregidor, and Iwo Jima in 1944 and 1945.

Meanwhile China continued to fight Japan on the mainland, and following the agreement signed at Yalta, Russia invaded Japanese-held lands in Manchuria on August 8, 1945. On August 6 and 9, 1945, atomic bombs were dropped on the Japanese cities of Hiroshima and Nagasaki. On the 14th of that month, the Japanese agreed to unconditional surrender. The official surrender document was signed on board the U.S.S. *Missouri* on September 2, 1945, ending World War II. The fighting in Europe had already ended.

The War in Europe: In November, 1942, General Eisenhower, Commander of Allied Forces, landed with Allied armies in French West Africa and captured Morocco and Algeria. In 1943 Sicily and then Italy were invaded.

The final phase of the war began on June 6, 1944 with the Allied invasion of the Normandy peninsula in France. Caught between an attack by Soviet troops on the east and Allied troops on the west, German resistance crumbled after a final attempt to stop the invasion in the Battle of the Bulge in December 1944. On May 1, it was announced that Hitler had committed suicide, and on May 7, 1945, the Germans surrendered unconditionally.

SOME IMPORTANT INDIVIDUALS OF THE PERIOD 1918–1945

Marian Anderson	Cordell Hull	Eleanor Roosevelt
Mary Bethune	Harold Ickes	Franklin Roosevelt
Willa Cather	Jiang Jieshi	George H. "Babe" Ruth
Charles Chaplin	Al Jolson	Nicola Sacco
Winston Churchill	Frank Kellogg	Carl Sandburg
Calvin Coolidge	Robert LaFollette	Alfred E. Smith
Charles DeGaulle	Fiorello LaGuardia	Josef Stalin
T.S. Eliot	John L. Lewis	Gertrude Stein
Dwight Eisenhower	Charles Lindbergh	John Steinbeck
Albert B. Fall	Henry Cabot Lodge	Norman Thomas
F. Scott Fitzgerald	Joe Louis	Jim Thorpe
Clark Gable	Douglas MacArthur	Bartolomeo Vanzetti
Greta Garbo	George Marshall	Orson Welles
Marcus Garvey	A. Mitchell Palmer	Edith Wharton
Warren Harding	George Patton	Wendell Wilkie
Ernest Hemingway	Frances Perkins	Woodrow Wilson
Adolph Hitler	John Pershing	Frank Lloyd Wright
Herbert Hoover	Mary Pickford	Richard Wright
Harry Hopkins	A. Philip Randolph	Minoru Yamasaki
Charles Evans Hughes	Paul Robeson	Mao Zedong

Chapter 8—
The Post-War Period,
The Cold War and
After—
1945–1992

THE IMMEDIATE POST-WAR PERIOD

The problem of demobilizing 12 million servicemen and returning them to civilian life was solved by the serviceman's Readjustment Act of 1944, commonly known as the G.I. Bill of Rights. Among its provisions were:

Governmental financed job training and education for discharged servicemen.

Unemployment payments for veterans.

Loans to veterans for business, farms, and home construction.

With the end of rationing and price control, prices skyrocketed. There was a period of inflation, but a post-war depression, which many people feared, was avoided. No truly satisfactory solution for the problem of inflation was found, and inflationary pressure continued to affect the nation for many years.

The United Nations

Meetings at Bretton Woods in 1943 and at Dumbarton Oaks in 1944 laid the basis for a worldwide organization dedicated to finding peaceful solutions to international problems. On April 25, 1945, delegates from 50 nations met in San Francisco to draw up the charter for a new organization, the United Nations, to replace the League of Nations. The main provisions of the charter were:

Member nations would not help an aggressor nation.

Member nations would settle disputes peacefully.

Member nations would use neither force nor the threat of force to settle disputes.

Member nations would use the armed might of an international police force to fight against aggressors.

The Charter of the United Nations: created the following governing bodies:

General Assembly: Composed of delegates from each member nation, it discusses and recommends solutions to international problems, but must refer all solutions regarding the use of force to the Security Council. Each nation has one vote.

Security Council: Consists of 15 members, five permanent members—the Big Five: (the victors in World War II over Germany and Japan) the United States, Great Britain, France, China (the government of Jiang Jieshi on Taiwan held the seat until 1972 when the People's Republic was given the seat), Soviet Union (replaced by Russia in 1991)—and ten non-permanent members elected for a two-year term by the General Assembly. Decisions may be passed by the vote of nine members, but must include all of the Big Five. That gives any one of the great powers veto power over the Council's decisions.

The Council bears primary responsibility under the U.N. Charter for the maintenance of international peace and security. Situations may be brought to its attention by any nation and the Council can investigate it or initiate action. Peace keeping missions are voted on by the Security Council.

The Economic and Social Council: Studies and makes suggestions for economic and social betterment of countries.

The Secretariat: The U.N.'s administrative arm, headed by the Secretary General, who is elected by the General Assembly. Its task is to carry out those policies adopted by the Assembly and Council. It oversees peace keeping forces. The headquarters is in New York City. Other offices are in Geneva, Switzerland, former headquarters of the League of Nations, the Hague, the Netherlands, seat of the International Court of Justice, and other cities.

There are many other important organizations and committees connected with the United Nations. Among the more important are:

Trusteeship Council, International Court of Justice, International Labor Organization, and World Health Organization.

THE COLD WAR

At the end of World War II, previously amicable relations between the United States and the Soviet Union deteriorated. President Truman, who had become president after the death of Roosevelt in April 1945, reacted quickly, and the basis of the U.S. post-World War II foreign policy was set by the end of 1947. The focus was a struggle with the Soviet Union blocking their expansion while protecting the interests of the United States and its allies. Nuclear weapons held by both sides after 1948 deterred a "hot war" between the superpowers. The antagonisms remained between the two superpowers until the mid-1980s although there were times of improved relations such as the period of *Détente* under President Nixon. With the introduction of the policy of *Glasnost* by President Gorbachev in 1985, relations between the two powers changed rapidly. Presidents Reagan and Gorbachev held several Summit Meetings and negotiated arms reductions. With the fall of the Berlin Wall in 1989 and the subsequent break-up in 1991 of the Soviet Union into the *Union of Independent States*, the Cold War was declared ended.

MAJOR COLD WAR EVENTS

Truman Doctrine: Truman announced a pledge of aid to the governments of Greece and Turkey, which Truman believed were being threatened by Soviet-led communist interests. The doctrine was later interpreted to mean the United States would oppose the overthrow of any democratic government. 1947

"X" Article: George Kennan of the State Department published an article in the magazine *Foreign Affairs* that outlined as the goal of U.S. policy the containment of the Soviet Union to prevent its expansion and spreading doctrines of communism. Known as the *Containment Policy*, it was adopted as the basis of U.S. Cold War policy and underlay many of the events of the Cold War. 1947

National Security Act: This Act established the National Security Council as an advisory body to the president and the CIA as an information gathering/spying organization. 1947

Marshall Plan: At a speech at Harvard University, Secretary of State Marshall introduced his European Recovery Program, known as the Marshall Plan, which made provision for United States' financial assistance to European countries whose failing economies made them targets for communism. 1947

Berlin Blockade: The Soviet Union blocked land access to Berlin and the U.S. responded with an airlift of supplies. 1948

North Atlantic Treaty Alliance (NATO): The approval of the first U.S. peacetime military alliance rejected George Washington's advice of 1797 to avoid permanent alliances. NATO was designed to block or contain communist, especially Soviet, expansion. It brought the nations of the North Atlantic and northern Mediterranean together for mutual defense. 1949

Communist Victory in China: After a struggle dating back to the 1920s, the Chinese communists under Mao Zedong defeated the Nationalist forces of Jiang Jieshi. The Nationalists fled to Taiwan, establishing a government there that was recognized as the Chinese government by the United States and the U.N. until the Nixon administration reversed the policy and officially recognized the mainland government of Mao Zedong as the government of China. In the early 1950s this "loss of China" was a divisive issue in U.S. domestic politics. 1949

Korean War: Communist North Korea attacked South Korea; the United States and other nations under the United Nations flag fought for three years to block aggression. The armistice terms essentially restored the status quo. 1950-53

Southeast Asia Treaty Organization (SEATO): Designed to contain communist, especially Chinese, expansion in Asia. 1954

Fall of Dien Bien Phu and *Geneva Conference on Vietnam:* After the French lost their important base at Dien Bien Phu to the Vietnamese communists, the United States considered military intervention. Instead, at Geneva, a peace plan was developed for the region. It was later rejected by Ngo Dinh Diem, premier of South Vietnam.

1954

Involvement in Vietnam: The United States became more and more involved in Vietnam as U.S. foreign policy focused on the containment of communism in Southeast Asia. (See Vietnam War below.)

1955

Hungarian Revolt: Hungary's attempt to throw off Soviet domination was crushed by Soviet military intervention.

1956

Aswan Dam: Foreign aid became a tool of the Cold War. The United States and Great Britain offered to help Egypt build a high dam at Aswan to aid economic development of the nation. They later withdrew the offer and Egypt received funding from the Soviet Union.

1956

Suez Canal Seized: Responding to Egypt's seizure of the Canal in an attempt to raise money for development, France, England, and Israel invaded Egypt and were stopped by the United States and the U.S.S.R. This provided a rare example of superpower Cold War cooperation.

1956

Eisenhower Doctrine: Approved by Congress, this permitted the United States to extend economic and military aid to Near Eastern countries who wanted it because they believed they were threatened by communists.

1957

Lebanon: United States sent troops to keep communists from seizing power.

1958

U-2 Spy Plane: The Soviets shot down a U.S. spy plane over Soviet territory, which ended a move towards rapprochement at the end of Eisenhower's presidency.

1960

Independence of African Nations: The United Nations admitted 13 new African nations to membership. Civil War broke out in the Republic of the Congo and the United Nations intervened. Many of the nations were caught in the Cold War seeking financial and military aid from both sides.

1960

Cuban Revolution: Castro's guerrilla troops finally seized control of Cuba. Relations with the United States rapidly deteriorated. Many Cubans fled to the United States and finally the United States broke diplomatic relations with Cuba.

1961

Bay of Pigs: Unsuccessful attempt by Cuban refugees backed by United States to invade and overthrow Castro's communist regime in Cuba.

1961

Berlin Wall: East Germans sealed off their part of Berlin from the West. The wall became the symbol of the Cold War.

1961

Cuban Missile Crisis: Soviet attempt to set up intermediate range missiles in Cuba was blocked by a U.S. blockade and political maneuvering. Nuclear war was narrowly avoided.

1962

Hot Line Agreement: Established direct rapid communication between Moscow and Washington, suggesting cooperation was possible between the superpowers. First used during the Six-Day War of 1967 between Israel and its Arab neighbors.

1963

Li   Nuclear Test Ban Treaty: After many years of bomb testing and u   l stopping of tests, a treaty was signed banning the testing of nuclear weapons in the atmosphere, in outer space, or under water. Underground tests were permitted.

1963

Dominican Republic Intervention: President Johnson sent U.S. troops into the Dominican Republic to crush a "band of communist conspirators" who the President claimed had gained control of a revolution against an authoritarian president.

1965

Outer Space Treaty: Banned military bases, weapons, and weapons tests in space and established principles for peaceful development of space.

1967

Pueblo Seized: A U.S. intelligence gathering ship was seized off Korea. After a U.S. officer signed a statement accepting guilt for spying, the ship was released by the North Korean government.

1968

Nuclear Nonproliferation Treaty: The Treaty banned the spread of nuclear weapons among signatory nations. It approved of access to nuclear energy for peaceful uses.

1969

Nixon's Visit to China: A new era in relations between the U.S. and China was confirmed with President Nixon's visit to the People's Republic of China. Changes had been underway for several years including the U.S. acceptance in the U.N. of the People's Republic, not Taiwan, as the holder of the Security Council seat.

1972

Moscow Summit: President Nixon visited Moscow and signed several agreements including the ABM (Anti-Ballistic Missile) Treaty. An easing of Cold War tensions was obvious and was given the name *Détente* by the press.

1972

Yom Kippur War and Shuttle Diplomacy: After the overwhelming Israeli victory in the Six-Day War of 1967 an uneasy truce settled in the Near East. War erupted again in October 1973, which resulted in a costly Israeli victory. Secretary of State Kissinger undertook a series of visits to the Near East ("Shuttle Diplomacy"), which resulted in cease-fire agreements between Israel and Syria. The Soviet Union sought influence in the Near East to balance that of the U.S. and Israel. Arms were sold to both Arab nations and Israel by the U.S. and to the Arab nations by the Soviet Union, which led to further Cold War tensions.

1974

SALT II Agreement: The agreement limited the number of missiles and long-range bombers held by the U.S. and Soviet Union. It was signed at a summit meeting in Geneva but President Carter asked the Senate to delay ratification after the Soviet Union invaded Afghanistan.

1979

Afghanistan Invasion: The Soviet Union sent troops into Afghanistan to maintain Soviet influence over the government. President Carter responded with a grain embargo, cutting off Soviet food supplies from the U.S. With the advent of Glasnost, an agreement involving the Soviet Union, the U.S., and various Afghan factions was negotiated and Soviet troops were withdrawn. The invasion has been referred to as the Soviet Union's Vietnam and it had major ramifications on its society.

1979

Iran-Iraq (Gulf) War: War broke out between these two oil-producing Muslim nations on the Persian Gulf. Both the U.S. and the Soviet Union have important interest in the region and the conflict added tensions to relations between the superpowers. The war became a stalemate with neither side able to win. With the change in U.S.-Soviet relations after 1985, a ceasefire was finally negotiated in 1988.

1980

The "Evil Empire": In a speech President Reagan declared his view of the Soviet Union as the "evil empire" responsible for the evils of the world. The policy dominated his administration's foreign policy in the first five years and led to such policies as the Anti-Soviet Trade boycott that followed Reagan's declaration that the Soviet Union was responsible for repression in Poland.

1981

El Salvador/Nicaragua: Early in the Reagan years concern was shown for guerrilla movements in El Salvador and their relationship to the Sandinista-controlled government of Nicaragua, which the U.S. viewed as controlled by Soviet and Cuban communists. How to deal with the issues became a major foreign policy concern of the Reagan administration with many Cold War ramifications. The administration established a guerrilla organization, the Contras in Nicaragua to oppose the Sandinista government and asked Congress for funding, which was alternately given and denied.

1981

Iran Contra Affair: When denied funding for the Contras and frustrated by the continued holding of hostages in Lebanon by groups friendly to Iran, the Reagan Administration developed a complex plan to free the American hostages held in Lebanon by selling arms to Iran thus getting Iran's support and then using the monetary profits to fund the Contras fighting against the Sandinista government of Nicaragua. The plan was developed secretly and lacked Congressional approval. When the plan was exposed, Congress established a Special Prosecutor to investigate the situation, which was grounded in the fear of the spread of communism in Central America. Several individuals involved in the plan, including President Reagan's National Security Advisor, Admiral Poindexter, and White House Aid Marine Lt. Col. Oliver North, were indicted on several counts of lawbreaking. Found guilty, the judge dismissed charges because testimony freely given before Congress by North and Poindexter was used•to convict them thus encroaching on their Constitutional rights. The special prosecutor was still investigating the situation in 1992 trying to determine who knew what about the sales, what Constitutional rights were broken, and what abuse of power took place, if any.

1987

END OF THE COLD WAR

Glasnost and Peristroika: Mikhail Gorbachev emerged as the leader of the Soviet Union after several older communist leaders died having served brief terms as head of the Soviet government. As a member of the younger generation, Gorbachev addressed domestic reform (peristroika) and changes in foreign policy (glasnost). His goal was to create limited reforms while maintaining communism, but changes came rapidly in foreign affairs yet too slowly for many within the Union. The reform movements led to the collapse of the Soviet Union and the fall of communism in Eastern Europe.

1985

Fall of the Berlin Wall: President Gorbachev refused to suppress reforms and changes in Eastern European nations militarily as had been done during the Cold War. Changes in Poland led by *Solidarity,* a nationalist, anti-communist Labor Union, and the *"Velvet Revolution"* in Czechoslovakia are examples of the changes. East Germans began fleeing to the West through neighboring countries that had opened their borders with the West. Finally the East German government announced in November that the Berlin Wall, symbol of the Cold War, would be torn down and Germans could travel freely between East and West. Within a year the two Germanies voted for reunification, thus ending the division created by the "Iron Curtain" after World War II.

1989

Persian Gulf War: Iraq invaded Kuwait and the U.S. led a united effort through the U.N. to reverse the aggression. While not supplying troops, the communist states, the Soviet Union and China, supported the move in the Security Council. After considerable debate in the country, on January 12 the Senate narrowly passed (52-47) the *Resolution on Use of Force Against Iraq,* which authorized the use of U.S. military force. Operation Desert Shield, designed immediately after Iraq's attack to protect the Gulf States, became Operation Desert Storm. On January

15, 1991, President Bush ordered air attacks on Iraq. A ground attack followed February 22, which ended with a cease-fire on February 27. The U.N. continues to oversee the cease-fire, and the Big Five Security Council members continue their support for its strict enforcement and the control of Iraq's nuclear and biological warfare capacities.   1990

United Nations Negotiated End to Military Conflicts: With the Cold War ending, an end to several international conflicts with roots in the Cold War were negotiated including an end to the War in Afghanistan and an agreement ending the conflicts in Cambodia and El Salvador.   1990

Coup against Gorbachev: Upset by the Gorbachev reforms, communist conservatives led a coup against Gorbachev in August. It failed and led to the emergence of Boris Yeltsin, popularly elected President of Russia, as leader. He was invited to the White House. Gorbachev resigned by the end of the year.   1991

Commonwealth of Independent States: The Soviet Union broke up into its separate states. Russia under Yeltsin appeared the strongest. Age old tensions between the states led to military clashes in several, removing the focus from the Cold War confrontation between the U.S. and the Soviet Union. The Communist Party was declared unconstitutional in Russia and other states, thus ending the 74 years of communist rule.   1991

Nuclear Arms Negotiations: With the breakup of the Soviet Union, four successor states held nuclear weapons. President Bush invited the leaders of the four newly independent nations to Washington to negotiate arms reductions and controls. Tentative agreements were reached that would reduce arms by half. Russia was identified as the sole successor nuclear power, but the three other nations seemed unwilling to accept this position. The future of Soviet nuclear weapons remained unclear. Russia was allotted the Soviet Union's seat in the Security Council.   1991

Yeltsin Visit to Washington: Yeltsin visited Washington, spoke before Congress, asked for U.S. economic aid and announced the end of the Cold War. The former Soviet states requested admission into the International Monetary Fund (IMF) and promised to continue economic reforms headed in the direction of capitalism.   1992

VIETNAM WAR

Starting in 1945, the U.S. showed an interest in a non-communist Vietnam. The area soon became a battle ground in the U.S. effort to contain communism. The United States encouraged and gave limited support to the French in their fight against the communist Viet Minh. When the French were defeated at Dien Bien Phu in 1954, their withdrawal was negotiated in the Geneva Accords and the nation was split into North and South. The U.S. secretly aided South Vietnam in a small way under Eisenhower. As war between the communist North Vietnamese and their Viet Cong allies and the South Vietnamese intensified, the U.S. continued to expand its involvement to block communism's spread. The *"domino theory"*—if one nation in Southeast Asia goes communist, the others will also—was followed in establishing U.S. policy.

Although President Kennedy insisted it was the Vietnamese's war to "win or lose," he increased U.S. aid and sent in more troops. President Johnson continued the policy and after a confusing incident in the Gulf of Tonkin involving U.S. naval vessels, he obtained support from Congress for the *Gulf of Tonkin Resolution,* which gave the President full power to protect South Vietnam from further aggression and to protect U.S. forces. Johnson used the Resolution as a declaration of war.

Lyndon Johnson's support for the war put strain on his Great Society program. Protest against U.S. involvement grew steadily and led to Johnson's defeat in the New Hampshire primary in 1968. He then withdrew from the presidential race. Hubert Humphrey, Johnson's Vice-President, was unable to extricate himself from the taint of war support.

Nixon won the election and sought ways to end U.S. involvement in the Vietnam War. The massacre of civilians by U.S. troops at My Lai in 1969 and the shooting of student demonstrators by the National Guard at Kent State intensified U.S. protests against the war. Nixon desired to end the war but "with honor." Negotiations were begun. He authorized the invasion of Cambodia in 1970, and in 1972 he ordered the bombing of North Vietnam to put pressure on North Vietnam to negotiate. A reduction of U.S. forces was begun with the South Vietnamese gradually taking over responsibility for defending their nation. After lengthy negotiations that began in 1969 a settlement was reached in 1973, and U.S. forces were completely withdrawn.

In 1975 the governments of South Vietnam, Cambodia, and Laos all fell to the communists. In 1974 President Ford offered clemency to Vietnam War Draft Dodgers and in 1977 President Carter granted a full pardon to Americans who fled to Canada rather than be drafted to fight.

This war, which some Americans see as the first war the U.S. "lost," continues to have a profound effect on the nation. Many refugees, including the so-called "boat-people," fled Vietnam and some have found asylum in the U.S. Many veterans felt the lack of support from the nation and felt alienated. During the Reagan and Bush administrations contacts with the communist government of Vietnam gradually increased but relations remained strained over the issue of missing American soldiers. The "lessons of Vietnam" were referred to in debates over policy for Central America in the 1980s, but there was often disagreement as to what these lessons were—to interfere or not to interfere in foreign civil wars, to fight against native communist movements or not, to subsidize guerrilla warfare in other nations or not, the validity of the "domino theory." President Bush seized the victory in the Persian Gulf War as a way of "putting Vietnam behind us." He claimed the successful U.S. intervention in the Middle East to stop aggression proved that the U.S. could pull together as a nation in support of the "right" and be successful in a war. Immediately after the Persian Gulf War the President received the strong support of the American people and he announced the tragedy of Vietnam had been replaced by a new sense of American spirit and nationalism. However, in the 1992 presidential election campaign, service in Vietnam was made a major issue by the Republican Party.

MAJOR LEGISLATION AND SUPREME COURT DECISIONS—1945–1992

Taft-Hartley Law: Aimed at making unions more responsible in relations with management, it prohibited unfair labor practices.   1947

Presidential Succession Act: Revised the 1886 law making the Speaker of the House and then the President pro tempore of the Senate successors after the Vice-President.   1947

National Security Act: Reorganized the army, navy and air force and established the cabinet level Department of Defense.   1947

Internal Security Act (McCarran Act): Required registration of communists and all communist front organizations.   1950

Department of Health, Education and Welfare: Created new cabinet level department to handle these areas of social concern.   1953

Atomic Energy Act: Permitted private power companies to own reactors for the production of electric power.   1954

Brown v. Board of Education: Supreme Court decision reversed the concept of separate but equal in race relations and ordered the integration of schools to provide equal educational opportunities for blacks and whites.   1954

Highway Act: Established the federal interstate highway system.   1956

Civil Rights Act: First act dealing with civil rights and their guarantee passed by Congress since Reconstruction. Established a six-person Commission on Civil Rights to investigate civil rights violations.   1957

Landrum-Griffin Act: Included provisions to curb labor racketeers.   1959

Peace Corps: Program to aid economically undeveloped countries by sending volunteers to help in the development of their economy by doing many things from teaching farming techniques to building schools.

1961

Gideon v. Wainwright: The Supreme Court determined that a lawyer must be provided by the state for all those charged with committing a felony.

1963

Escobedo v. Illinois: The Supreme Court ruled that if requested, a lawyer had to be present during police interrogration before an indictment is made.

1964

Voting Rights Act: Act guaranteeing to all the right to vote in federal elections—directed towards southern blacks who flocked to register supported by federal marshals.

1965

Medicare Act: Provides medical service to those over 65 under the administration of the Social Security System.

1965

Office of Economic Opportunity (OEO): Catchall office set up to operate Job Corps, Operation Head Start, and other parts of Johnson's Great Society program to benefit depressed areas and underprivileged persons.

1965

Elementary and Secondary Education Act: Provided federal money for certain programs in public and parochial schools to improve the quality of education in the U.S.

1965

Water Quality Act: Allows federal government to set water purity standards for states to force industry to clean up the lakes and rivers of the nation.

1965

National Traffic and Motor Vehicle Safety Act: Sets some federal safety standards for the auto industry.

1966

Freedom of Information Act: Made certain documents and records available to citizens who asked to see them, including some secret documents.

1966

National Committee on Product Safety: Commission to study potentially hazardous products and evaluate laws to protect consumers.

1967

Civil Rights Act: Directed towards toppling racial barriers in most of the nation's housing.

1968

Consumer Credit Protection Act (Truth in Lending): Requires lenders and retailers selling merchandise for credit to make full disclosures of the total cost of such credit to the consumer.

1968

Washington Omnibus Anti-Crime Law (No-Knock Law): Designed to give more authority to police enforcement officials in the District of Columbia and to serve as a model of tough reform police laws for the nation.

1970

Environmental Policy Act: Established a commission in the White House to report on environmental quality and to oversee the enforcement of environmental legislation.

1970

Furman v. Georgia: The death penalty was held unconstitutional. Later decisions modified this opinion to make it permissible in some circumstances if applied fairly.

1973

Roe v. Wade: Declared state laws denying abortion during the first trimester of pregnancy unconstitutional, a violation of a woman's privacy to determine to end a pregnancy.

1973

Energy Policy and Conservation Act: Set control limits on car exhaust and gave President more control over energy policy.

1973

Department of Energy: In response to the OPEC energy crisis of the 1970s, the Department of Energy was created, taxes on oil increased, and conservation measures were instituted.

1977

Civil Service Reform Act: These measures were part of President Carter's attempts to streamline and increase the efficiency of the government's bureaucracy. The Act reduced the Civil Service.
                                                                    1978

Air Transport Deregulation Act: Airline fares and routes were no longer to be controlled by government regulation.
                                                                    1978

Bakke v. Board of Regents: The Supreme Court held that Bakke, a white who had been denied admission to medical school in California, had been discriminated against since his scores were higher than those of persons admitted to positions at the school reserved to minorities. The Court also upheld the University of California's use of race as a criterion for admission to achieve a mixed student body.
                                                                    1978

Department of Education: As part of the streamlining efforts of President Carter, the various government offices dealing with education were consolidated in one department.
                                                                    1979

Peacetime Draft Registration: Draft registration was required of 18-year-olds to have the country prepared for any international emergency. No one, however, was actually drafted into the armed services.
                                                                    1980

Toxic Waste Superfund: Established to treat quickly dangerous spills of toxic wastes and to clean up toxic waste dumps.
                                                                    1981

Economic Recovery Tax Act (ERTA): A supply-side tax program that reduced taxes and cut the budget, changing the long-standing taxing policies of the government.
                                                                    1981

Anti-Drug Legislation: Each session of Congress from 1982-1989 passed drug legislation reflecting the continuing concern with drug use and traffic. The 1989 law established a cabinet level position of *Director of National Drug Policy* (Anti-Drug "Tsar") to coordinate President Bush's war on drugs. The 1989 legislation included the death penalty for major drug trafficking and the 1988 law required schools to implement programs aimed at preventing illegal substance use and provided assistance to Colombia, Peru, and Bolivia to fight drug traffickers.
                                                                    1982

Clean Water Act: Authorized a 10-year extension of the federal program for subsidizing building of sewer plants. It was passed over President Reagan's veto.
                                                                    1987

Savings and Loans (S & L's) Bailout Legislation: Congress provided funds and approved a program to buy or shore up financially failing S & L's.
                                                                    1987

Repeal of the Catastrophic Health Care Act of 1988: In a major change of policy and under heavy pressure from AARP (American Association of Retired Pesons) Congress repealed the expansion of the Medicare program which it had passed the previous year. This was the first time Congress had repealed a major social benefit it had enacted. The act had extended Medicare to cases of extended hospital care and catastrophic illness to be paid for by a sur tax on Medicare enrollees. Their objection to this tax led to the repeal of the law. Health care costs continued to be a major political issue for Congress and the nation at the start of the 1990s.
                                                                    1989

Crime Control Bill: In this compromise bill Congress continued to reject tight gun control provisions. The law increased support of police training.
                                                                    1990

Board of Education of Oklahoma City v. Dowell: Supreme Court held that a school district could end busing to achieve integration if it had done "everything practical" and the schools were single race because of local housing patterns. The case illustrated the continuing importance of the courts in the struggle for civil rights.
                                                                    1990

Americans With Disabilities Act: The act prohibits discrimination against disabled persons in employment, public services, and accommodations, and requires that telecommunication be made accessible to those with speech and hearing impairments. Employers are required to make reasonable accommodations for disabled workers.

1990

Immigration Bill: The first major revision of immigration policy in 25 years changed visa requirements, allowed for more immigrants, especially those with education and skills needed in the U.S., and made it harder to exclude foreigners because of their sexual persuasion.

1990

Clean Air Act: After 10 years of inaction the 1977 Clean Air Act was revised and updated with support from President Bush. Deadlines for control of harmful emissions by cities and motor vehicles were revised. Provisions to control acid rain and chlorofluorocarbons, which harm the earth's ozone layer, were also made.

1990

Rust v. Sullivan: The Supreme Court by a 5-4 vote upheld regulations issued in 1988 by the Department of Health and Human Services that barred federally funded health and family planning clinics from providing information on abortion. It was one more case in the ongoing struggle over abortion rights fought out in the courts.

1991

Civil Rights Act (Job Bias Bill): After several years of debate and struggle between Congress and President Bush, the President signed a bill that reversed several recent Supreme Court decisions that had made it more difficult to achieve redress in cases of job discrimination in employment—issues of so-called "quotas."

1991

Planned Parenthood v. Casey: The Supreme Court by a 5-4 vote upheld several Pennsylvania laws restricting a woman's access to abortion, but the Court affirmed the basic right to abortion established in *Roe v. Wade.*

1992

PRESIDENTIAL ADMINISTRATIONS 1945–1992

Harry Truman: Truman became President upon the death of Franklin Roosevelt in April 1945. Not well informed on issues by Roosevelt, he quickly took control supporting the establishment of the United Nations at the San Francisco Conference, making the decision to drop atomic bombs on Japan, and presiding over the end of World War II. His foreign policy focused on containing the perceived communist threat, which became the key element of the Cold War. He announced the Truman Doctrine of containment, supported Foreign Aid (the Point Four Plan) and the Marshall Plan, and responded to communist North Korea's invasion of South Korea by sending troooops and appealing to the U.N. In a very close election, he won a second term defeating Governor Thomas Dewey of New York. His stance on the communist threat and his support of labor in vetoing the Taft Hartley law (passed over his veto) gained him support.

Dwight D. Eisenhower: Eisenhower defeated Adlai Stevenson in the 1952 election. The Koran War was a major issue in the campaign. Eisenhower's foreign policy was one of Cold War confrontation and Brinkmanship. John Foster Dulles served as a forceful Secretary of State. Domestically, after Joseph McCarthy's "witch hunts" against the domestic threat of communism ended and he was censured by the Senate, the Eisenhower years were quite peaceful. The civil rights movement was stimulated by the *Brown v. Board of Education* Supreme Court decision on school integration. Eisenhower gave only moderate support to the movement but did finally send federal troops to support the integration of the high school in Little Rock, Arkansas. His administration held to a high standard of honesty in government. Sherman Adams, his White House Chief of Staff, was asked to resign after it was revealed he had accepted a vicuna coat as a gift. The most far-reaching domestic legislation of his presidency was the National Highway Act, which set up the interstate highway network.

John F. Kennedy: Elected president in 1960 by a narrow margin over Richard M. Nixon. He was the first Catholic to win the office and the youngest ruler of a major world power. His administration supplied much polish and glitter, but little substantial domestic legislation. Kennedy's administration is most noted for foreign policy developments, among them the Alliance for Progress, the Peace Corps, the Bay of Pigs, the Cuban Missile Crisis, the start of the Space Race, and the extension of the U.S. commitment to Vietnam. Kennedy was assassinated on November 22, 1963 in Dallas, Texas.

Lyndon Johnson: In the aftermath of Kennedy's tragic death, Johnson initiated a number of domestic reforms including a Civil Rights bill.

The extension of civil rights was an important aspect of the Kennedy/Johnson years. Supreme Court decisions, congressional legislation, and the efforts of many workers and leaders led to a great breakthrough in the extension of rights to blacks. However, the assassination in 1968 of Martin Luther King, Jr., a believer in nonviolent protest, was followed by outbreaks of violence, and the movement lost momentum. More militant leaders called for Black Power. The eventual success of the movement inspired many other minority groups to seek power, with the result that Mexican-Americans (Chicanos), Native Americans, homosexuals (Gay Power), and women organized to have an impact on political affairs.

Johnson initiated a War on Poverty in an attempt to eradicate poverty in America and create a Great Society. In many ways it was an updating and extension of Franklin Roosevelt's New Deal. It began well and included such diverse programs as Head Start and Medicare. His concept of the Great Society was hampered by increased involvement in the war in Vietnam and the need for military expenditures there.

Student unrest in the mid-60s reflected a change in attitude among some young people and culminated in anti-war protests that forced President Johnson to announce he would not run for a second term. The unrest took many forms, including the "Hippie" movement, greater use of illegal drugs, establishment of communes, anti-war demonstrations in Washington and elsewhere, and violence at the Democratic Convention in Chicago in 1968. One hero of the movement, Robert Kennedy, was assassinated in Los Angeles in 1968 while campaigning for the Democatic presidential nomination, removing an important political leader of the protest.

Richard M. Nixon: Elected president in 1968, Nixon promised to "bring the nation together" and end the Vietnam War. Anti-war protests increased and there were periodic outbursts of anti-war violence (e.g. Kent State, 1970) during his presidency that led his administration to seek ways to prevent it. He gradually withdrew troops from Vietnam while expanding the war into Cambodia. With his Secretary of State, Henry Kissinger, he negotiated an end to the war in Vietnam.

As the Vietnam War was winding down, the Nixon administration made moves to end the Cold War and to reverse the policies of the previous 25 years. His actions collectively have been referred to as *Détente*. Nixon met with Brezhnev, the premier of the Soviet Union, both in Moscow and Washington. He also made a trip to Communist China, opening diplomatic relations with that nation for the first time since the communists seized control of mainland China in 1949. Nixon's successor, Gerald Ford, continued the policy of détente and some observers saw this as the beginning of the end to the Cold War. Nixon's negotiations with the Soviet Union and recognition of the People's Republic of China were the most important developments in foreign policy during his administration.

Domestically Nixon pursued a conservative political agenda trying to cut federal programs under a program of New Federalism. The Watergate was the most memorable event of his presidency domestically. Nixon was concerned by the anti-war protests and the possibility of a Democratic victory in 1972. He approved of "dirty tricks" including a break in at the Democratic Headquarters in the Watergate apartment complex in Washington. A cover up unraveled through newspaper exposés, the appointment of a Special Prosecutor, and Grand Jury inquiries. Vice-President Spiro Agnew was forced to resign as a result of illegal acts on his part. Finally, tape recordings of White House meetings revealed that Nixon was aware of the breakin and coverups of illegal acts. Congress began impeachment proceedings and President Nixon resigned in August 1974. He was the first president to be forced from office. He was succeeded by Gerald Ford, who had been chosen to succeed Agnew as vice-president, following the procedure set forth in the 25th Amendment, which was ratified in 1967. Nelson Rockefeller, four-term governor of New York, was chosen as vice-president following the same procedure.

Gerald R. Ford: President Ford, the first man to come to the presidency by appointment rather than election served the remaining years of Nixon's term. Nelson Rockefeller, four-term governor of New York, was chosen as vice-president following the procedure established in the 25th Amendment. Ford continued the policy of détente, holding a summit conference in Vladivostok in 1974 and visiting China in 1975. The aftermath of Watergate, including Ford's pardon of Nixon, colored his administration. There was high inflation and Ford introduced his WIN (Whip Inflation Now) policy to combat it with limited success. OPEC (Organization of Petroleum Exporting Countries) and its oil pricing policies affected domestic affairs and led to large increases in oil costs. Ford was defeated in his re-election campaign by Governor Jimmy Carter of Georgia.

James E. Carter: Jimmy Carter considered himself a "born again" Christian. Elected in 1976 as an "outsider," President Carter found it difficult to be effective in dealing with the established bureaucracy of Congress and government. He desired to streamline the government and make it more efficient. He began the deregulation of business (Air Transport Deregulation Act), which intensified under Reagan. Domestic issues of inflation and energy crises together with the international crisis of the Iranian Revolution and the seizure of American hostages clouded his administration. His foreign policy focused on the issue of human rights. The highlight of the administration of Jimmy Carter was the establishment of the Camp David Peace Accord, which finally brought peace in the Near East between Israel and Egypt, although it did not solve all of the outstanding issues in the area. He also negotiated a new treaty with Panama, which will eventually give that nation control over the Panama Canal.

Ronald Reagan: Viewed by many as an extreme conservative Republican, Ronald Reagan overwhelmed Jimmy Carter in the election of 1980. The Republicans gained control of the Senate; Reagan's goals were to reduce inflation, reform the tax structure, reduce taxes, deregulate business and industry, cut social welfare programs, and build up the military. A major debate developed about the need for a balanced budget and military versus social welfare expenditures. Supply side economics, the philosophical position behind the Reagan reforms, did not operate as expected and a huge government budget deficit and a large trade deficit developed, although the inflation rate slowed dramatically. Reagan appointed conservatives to the Supreme Court and the court's views on privacy, especially the right to abortion, began to shift.

Reagan's foreign policy centered on the concept of the Soviet Union as an "evil empire" and their responsibility for the Cold War and world unrest. This view lay behind the 1983 invasion of Grenada, where the Cubans and Soviets appeared to be building a major airstrip. It was also seen in the support given to the Contras against the Sandinista government of Nicaragua. Democrats in Congress did not agree with the Reagan view and Congressional support for the Contras was erratic, leading the White House to resort to extra-legal methods of funding them. These illegal attempts were exposed and dubbed the Iran-Contra Affair. A special prosecutor was appointed and charges were brought against several of the President's advisers. The investigation was still continuing in 1992 and became an issue in the election with questions raised as to how much then Vice-President Bush knew about the illegal acts.

Reagan followed a policy of peace through strength: He introduced SDI—Strategic Defense Initiative, commonly known as Star Wars—which antagonized the Soviets but led to negotiation with them for a disarmament agreement. When Mikhail Gorbachev came to power, his policies of glasnost improved relations. Negotiations led to Summit Meetings at Geneva, Reykjavik (Iceland), and Washington—where in 1987 an Intermediate Range Missile Treaty (INF) was signed marking the beginning of a new phase of the Cold War.

Other highlights of the Reagan years were the release of the American hostages by Iran on his inauguration day, the Israeli invasion of Lebanon, which left that country divided and led Reagan to send in Marines, who were later withdrawn after 237 were killed in a terrorist bombing of their barracks, and the Iran-Iraq War, which led to unrest in the Persian Gulf and caused the U.S. to put the American flag on Kuwaiti oil tankers and escort them through the Gulf with U.S. Navy ships, in order to assure the flow of oil to Europe and Japan.

George Bush: In 1988 Reagan's Vice-President, George Bush, overwhelmingly defeated Democrat Michael Dukakis, Governor of Massachusetts, in a negative campaign that addressed such issues as the environment, crime, patriotism, and family values. The public's alienation from politics grew during the first term reinforced by the deadlock between the Democratic Congress and the Republican president, the battle over conservative Supreme Court appointments, the S & L bailout, continued investigations of the Iran-Contra Affair, and several scandals involving Congress (Keating Five, House of Representatives Post Office and Bank Scandals).

Announcing he would be both the education and environment President, Bush supported a Clean Air Act but allowed his administration to loosen environmental regulations and gave limited support to the work of the U.N. Conference on the Environment and Development (Rio Conference). His education plans called for local effort, not federal government involvement. The appointment of Judge Clarence Thomas to the Supreme Court seemed to assure a conservative majority on the Court for the future. The administration, led by Vice-President Quayle supported the conservative agenda of pushing family values and overturning *Roe v. Wade*. What began as a mild recession continued to worsen and was seen as a depression by 1992. Differences between Congress and the President led to near deadlock in response to the economy, and the trade and budget deficits continued to grow. Bush was unable to present a balanced budget to the Congress.

President Bush had extensive foreign policy experience and used it to deal directly with world leaders. The great success of the first term was the organization of a U.N. led coalition against Iraq after its president, Saddam Hussein, had seized the country of Kuwait. Operation Desert Shield and then Desert Storm forced Iraq's withdrawal, but Hussein, still leading Iraq, continually tested the U.N.'s enforcement of the cease-fire, dimming the early success of the Persian Gulf War. In 1992, questions were raised whether the Bush administration had supported Hussein and led him to believe he could seize Kuwaiti oil fields. A formal investigation of Iraqgate was called for by Congress.

Bush developed a close relationship with Gorbachev and his successors after the Soviet Union collapsed in 1991. Improving U.S.-Soviet relations and then the end of the Cold War allowed the U.N. to settle a number of international conflicts with strong support from the Bush administration. The end of the Cold War heightened the domestic argument over military defense vs. social welfare spending. Outbreaks of fighting in former states of the Soviet Union and in Yugoslavia based on nationalistic interests indicated the "New World Order" proclaimed by President Bush after the success in the Persian Gulf War would not be peaceful. Other foreign policy events included: the invasion of Panama to seize accused drug dealer General Manuel Noriega; the freeing of all hostages held in Lebanon; and the opening of Arab-Israeli peace talks. In 1992 the Democratic Party nominated two southern, middle-of-the-road white men, Bill Clinton, Governor of Arkansas, and Al Gore, Senator from Tennessee, as their presidential candidates. The Republicans renominated Bush and Quayle.

In 1992 a politically unknown businessman, H. Ross Perot, announced he would run for the Presidency and his supporters got his name on the ballot in all 50 states. He suddenly withdrew from the race in July when he was leading in some polls. Perot reentered the race on October 1 but seemed to have little effect on the lead in the polls developed by Clinton. On November 4 Clinton was elected with 43 percent of the popular vote but with a large majority of electoral votes. Perot surprised many pollsters getting well over 20 percent of the vote in many states.

SOME IMPORTANT INDIVIDUALS OF THE PERIOD 1945–1992

Edward Albee	Warren Burger	Geraldine Ferraro
Muhammad Ali	George Bush	Diane Fienstein
Woody Allen	Jimmy Carter	Betty Friedan
Jerry Apodaca	Rosalind Carter	William Fulbright
Neil Armstrong	Eldridge Cleaver	Barry Goldwater
Pearl Bailey	Bill Clinton	Albert Gore
Leonard Bernstein	John Connally	Mikhail Gorbachev
Humphrey Bogart	Archibald Cox	Martha Graham
Edward Brooke	Bing Crosby	H.R. (Bob) Haldeman
H. Rap Brown	Thomas Dewey	Joseph Heller
Jerry Brown	John Foster Dulles	Anita Hill
Anita Bryant	Dwight Eisenhower	Oveta Culp Hobby
Pat Buchanan	William Faulkner	Hubert Humphrey

Saddam Hussein	Walter Mondale	Frank Sinatra
Daniel Ken Inouye	Marilyn Monroe	Joseph Stalin
Jesse Jackson	Toni Morrison	George Steinbrenner
Lyndon B. Johnson	Philip Murray	Gloria Steinem
Vernon Jordan	Ralph Nader	Charles Stengel
Louis I. Kahn	Richard M. Nixon	Edward Stettinius
Helen Keller	Manuel Noriega	Adlai Stevenson
Jack Kemp	Sandra Day O'Connor	David Stockman
John F. Kennedy	Rosa Parks	Robert Taft
Robert Kennedy	I. N. Pei	Margaret Thatcher
Billy Jean King	H. Ross Perot	Clarence Thomas
Martin Luther King, Jr.	Jackson Pollack	Harry Truman
Henry Kissinger	Elvis Presley	Paul Tsongas
John Lennon	Daniel Quayle	Ted Turner
Douglas MacArthur	Ronald Reagan	Arthur Vandenberg
Malcolm X	Walter Reuther	Kurt Vonnegut
Louis Muñoz Marin	Ann Richards	George Wallace
George Marshall	Eliot Richardson	Andy Warhol
Willie Mays	Nelson Rockefeller	Tennessee Williams
Eugene McCarthy	Eleanor Roosevelt	Wendell Wilkie
George Meany	Dean Rusk	Boris Yeltsin
Arthur Miller	Alan B. Shepard	Andrew Young
Patsy Takemoto Mink		

Chronology of Important Dates

The following Time-Line of United States History provides an overview that should prove useful in a quick review. You may wish to add your own dates to this Time-Line as you study.

Time-Line

about 50,000 years ago—First Native Americans cross land bridge from Siberia

about 500 A.D. Pueblo culture develops in Southwestern United States

1492 — Columbus's first voyage to America

1497–98 — Voyage of John Cabot

1519–21 — Magellan circumnavigates the globe

1565 — St. Augustine founded by Spanish

1580s — Colony at Roanoke by Sir Walter Raleigh

1607 — Colony at Jamestown by English

1608 — Santa Fe founded by Spanish

1609 — Quebec founded by French

1619 — House of Burgesses

1619 — First slaves brought to Virginia

1620 — Mayflower Compact — colony at Plymouth

1630 — Boston founded

1634 — Maryland founded

1638 — New Sweden founded by Swedes

1639 — Fundamental Orders of Connecticut

1664 — Dutch driven from New York

1675 — King Philip's war

1682 — Pennsylvania founded

1689–97 — King William's war

1692 — Salem witch trials

1696 — Navigation Acts restated

1702 — Cotton Mather publishes *The Ecclesiastical History of New England*

1702–13 — Queen Anne's War

1718 — San Antonio founded

1733 — Molasses Act

    — Georgia, last of original 13 colonies, founded

1739–42 — War of Jenkin's Ear

1740–48 — King George's War

1754 — Albany Plan of Union proposed

    — Fort Necessity (Pitt) built

    — Jonathan Edwards, noted preacher and writer, dies

1754–63 — French and Indian War

1759 — Fort Ticonderoga captured

    — Quebec captured

1763 — Treaty of Paris — France loses Canada and Northwest Territory

    — Pontiac's Rebellion

1764 — Sugar Act

1765 — Quartering Act

    — Stamp Act/Stamp Act Congress

1766 — Stamp Act repealed

    — Declaratory Act passed

1767 — Townshend Acts passed

    — New York Assembly suspended

    — Nonimportation of British goods

1768 — Massachusestts Assembly dissolved

    — Troops stationed in Boston

1769 — San Diego founded by Spaniards
     — First California mission
1770 — Townshend Acts repealed
     — Tea Tax maintained
     — Boston Massacre
1772 — Massachusetts Committee of Correspondence
     — Gaspée burned
1773 — Boston Tea Party
1774 — First Continental Congress
     — Intolerable Acts
     — Quebec Act
     — Galloway's Plan of Union
1775 — Battles of Lexington and Concord
     — Lord North's Conciliation Plan
1776 — Second Continental Congress
     — Declaration of Independence
1778 — Battle of Saratoga
     — France becomes U.S. ally
1781 — Battle of Yorktown
     — Articles of Confederation ratified
1783 — Treaty of Paris
1785 — Basic Land Ordinance
1786 — Annapolis Convention
1786–87 — Shays' Rebellion
1787 — Constitutional Convention
     — Northwest Ordinance
1788 — Nine states ratify Constitution
1789 — George Washington elected first president
     — 13 states join federal union
1790 — Alexander Hamilton's financial program
1791 — Bill of Rights adopted
     — Bank of the United States chartered
     — Benjamin Franklin's *Autobiography* first published
1792 — Gilbert Stuart portrait *George Washington*
1793 — Proclamation of Neutrality
     — Citizen Genêt affair
1794 — Whiskey Rebellion
1795 — Jay's Treaty
     — Pinckney's Treaty
1796 — John Adams elected second president
1797 — XYZ Affair
1798 — Alien and Sedition Acts
     — Kentucky and Virginia Resolutions
1800 — Thomas Jefferson elected third president
1801 — John Marshall Chief Justice
1803 — Louisiana Purchase
     — *Marbury v. Madison*
1804–07 — Lewis and Clark Expedition
1807 — Embargo
     — Fulton invents the steamboat
     — Aaron Burr conspiracy trial
1808 — James Madison elected fourth president
     — Slave trade stopped by Congressional law
1810 — Annexation of West Florida
1812–15 — War of 1812
1815 — Battle of New Orleans
     — Hartford Convention
     — Treaty of Ghent
1816 — James Monroe elected fifth president
     — Second Bank of the United States chartered

1817 — Rush-Bagot agreement
1818 — Convention of 1818
1819 — Washington Irving's *Sketch Book* published
    — Knickerbocker School of New York writers
1820 — Missouri Compromise
    — Greek Revival architecture dominates
1823 — Monroe Doctrine
1824 — John Quincy Adams elected sixth president
1825 — Erie Canal opened
    — *Self Portrait in His Museum* painted by Charles Willson Peale
1828 — Tariff Act
    — Andrew Jackson elected seventh president
1830 — Webster-Hayne debate
1831 — Alexis de Tocqueville visits U.S.
    — Eaton Affair
    — Nat Turner slave rebellion
    — Maysville Road bill vetoed
1832 — Tariff Act
    — Nullification controversy
    — Jackson vetoes bill to recharter Second Bank of the United States
    — Telegraph invented
    — Reaper invented
1834 — Whig party formed
1836 — Texas Revolution
    — Martin Van Buren elected eighth president
    — Ralph Waldo Emerson's *Nature* published
    — Transcendentalism
1837 — Panic of 1837
    — Gag Rule in Congress
    — Specie Circular
1840 — William Henry Harrison elected ninth president
    — Independent Treasury Act
1841 — Harrison dies; John Tyler becomes tenth president
1842 — Webster-Ashburton Treaty
1844 — James K. Polk elected eleventh president
    — Oregon Dispute
1845 — Texas annexed
1846 — Oregon settlement
1846–48 — Mexican War
1848 — Treaty of Guadalupe Hidalgo
    — Gold discovered in California
    — Zachary Taylor elected twelfth president
1849 — California gold rush
1850 — Taylor dies; Millard Fillmore becomes thirteenth president
    — Compromise of 1850
1851 — Melville's *Moby Dick* published
1852 — Harriet Beecher Stowe's *Uncle Tom's Cabin* published
    — Franklin Pierce elected fourteenth president
1854 — Republican party formed
    — Kansas-Nebraska Act
    — Japan reopened by Admiral Perry
1856 — Violence in Kansas
    — James Buchanan elected fifteenth president
1857 — Dred Scott decision
1858 — First transatlantic cable
    — Lincoln-Douglas debates
1859 — John Brown's raid on Harper's Ferry
    — First oil well drilled
1860 — Abraham Lincoln elected sixteenth president
    — South Carolina secedes

1861 — Confederacy formed
— Fort Sumter attacked
— Morrill Tariff
1862 — Morrill Act
— Pacific Railways Act
1863 — Emancipation Proclamation
— Battle of Gettysburg
1864 — Homestead Act
— Sherman's march through Georgia
1865 — Wade Davis Bill
— Lee surrenders
— Lincoln assassinated; Andrew Johnson becomes seventeenth president
— 13th Amendment passed (abolished slavery)
1866 — Civil Rights Act
1867 — First Reconstruction Act
1868 — President Johnson impeached
— 14th Amendment passed (equal protection of the laws)
— Ulysses S. Grant elected eighteenth president
1870 — Ku Klux Klan formed
1871 — Tweed Ring in New York
1873 — The "Crime of '73"
1875 — Rutherford B. Hayes elected nineteenth president
1877 — Last federal troops removed from South
— *Trinity Church* Boston by Henry Hobson Richardson
1878 — Bland-Allison Act
1880 — James A. Garfield, elected twentieth president
1881 — James A. Garfield assassinated; Chester A. Arthur becomes twenty-first president
1883 — Pendleton Civil Service Act
1884 — Grover Cleveland elected twenty-second president
1885 — Mark Twain's *Huckleberry Finn* published
1886 — American Federation of Labor formed
1887 — Interstate Commerce Act passed
— Dawes Act
1888 — Benjamin Harrison elected twenty-third president
1889 — Oklahoma opened for settlement
1890 — Frontier "closes" according to Census Bureau
— Sherman Anti-Trust Act
— Sherman Silver Purchase Act
1892 — Bering Sea Dispute
— Homestead Steel strike
— Populist party nominates James B. Weaver for presidency
— Grover Cleveland elected twenty-fourth president
1893 — Panic of 1893
1894 — Eugene V. Debs leads Pullman strike
— Carey Act Passed (Reclamation)
— *Chicago Stock Exchange* building by Louis Sullivan
1895 — Venezuela Boundary dispute
1896 — William McKinley elected twenty-fifth president
1897 — Diesel Engine
1898 — Battleship *Maine* sunk
— Spanish-American War
— Edward Bellamy's *Looking Backward* published
1899 — Open Door Policy announced
1901 — President McKinley assassinated; Theodore Roosevelt becomes twenty-sixth president
1902 — Newland Act passes (conservation movement)
— Owen Wister's *The Virginian* published
1903 — Panama Revolt
1904 — Roosevelt Corollary to Monroe Doctrine
1905 — Russo-Japanese War ended by Treaty of Portsmouth
1906 — Pure Food and Drug Law passed
— Hepburn Act

1907 — Gentlemen's Agreement with Japan
1908 — William Howard Taft elected twenty-seventh president
      — White House Conservation Conference
1911 — U.S. Intervention in Nicaragua
1912 — Woodrow Wilson elected twenty-eighth president
1913 — Underwood Tariff passed, reducing tariff rates
      — Federal Reserve Banking Act passed
      — 16th Amendment Passed (Income Tax)
      — 17th Amendment passed (direct election of senators)
      — *Cliff Dwellers* by George Bellows painted
1914 — Federal Trade Commission established
      — Clayton Anti-trust Act passed
      — World War I begins in Europe
      — Panama Canal opened
1915 — Sinking of the Lusitania
      — Re-election of Woodrow Wilson in "He kept us out of war" campaign
1916 — Mexican border campaign by U.S. Army
      — Keating-Owen Child Labor Act passed
      — National Defense Act
1917 — U.S. enters World War I
      — Virgin Islands purchased
      — Law limiting European immigration passed
1918 — Wilson announces 14 Points
      — World War I ends
1919 — U.S. Senate rejects treaty of Versailles
      — 18th Amendment passed (Prohibition)
      — Palmer raids
1920 — Warren G. Harding elected twenty-ninth president
1920 — 19th Amendment passed (women can vote)
      — Prohibition begins
      — *Main Street* by Sinclair Lewis published
1921 — Quota System for immigration introduced
      — Washington Disarmament Congress
1923 — President Harding dies; Calvin Coolidge becomes thirtieth president
      — Ku Klux Klan exposés
1924 — National Origins Act passed
      — Dawes plan on German reparations
      — Harding administration scandals revealed
1925 — Scopes "Monkey" trial
      — *The Great Gatsby* by F. Scott Fitzgerald published
1926 — *Eleven A.M.* by Edward Hopper painted
1927 — Geneva Disarmament Congress
      — Sacco-Vanzetti case
      — *The Jazz Singer* — first talking motion picture
1928 — Herbert Hoover elected thirty-first president
      — *Strange Interlude* by Eugene O'Neill published
1929 — Stock market crash, start of the Great Depression
      — *A Farewell to Arms* by Ernest Hemingway published
1931 — Hoover debt moratorium
1932 — Franklin D. Roosevelt elected thirty-second president
      — Reconstruction Finance Corporation established
      — Glass-Steagall Act
1933 — New Deal Begins: 1st AAA, NIRA, TVA, FERA, HOLC, RDIC, CCC, SEC, FHA
      — 18th Amendment (Prohibition ends)
      — Good Neighbor Policy announced
1934 — Philippine Independence Act passed
      — Nye Committee munitions investigations
1935 — "2nd New Deal"
      — Social Security Act
1937 — Supreme Court "packing" plan
      — *Falling Water* house by Frank Lloyd Wright

1938 — 2nd Agricultural Adjustment Act
1939 — Limited national emergency declared as World War II begins in Europe
  — Neutrality Act
  — New York World's Fair
1941 — Four Freedoms speech
  — Lend Lease Act passed
  — Japanese attack Pearl Harbor
  — U.S. enters World War II
  — *Citizen Kane* produced (Orson Welles)
1942 — Bataan and Corregidor captured by Japanese
  — Battle of Midway
  — U.S. forces invade North Africa
  — Price control and rationing
1943 — Invasion of Philippines
  — Invasion of Sicily
1944 — D-Day invasion of France
  — Battle of the Bulge
  — G.I. Bill
1945 — End of World War II
  — President Franklin D. Roosevelt dies; Harry Truman becomes thirty-third president
  — Atomic bombs dropped on Hiroshima and Nagasaki
  — Yalta conference
1946 — First meeting of General Assembly of United Nations
  — Cold war begins
  — Philippine independence
1947 — Truman Doctrine
  — Marshall Plan
  — Taft-Hartley Act passes
  — *Cathedral* by Jackson Pollock painted
  — Jackie Robinson becomes first black player on major league baseball team
1948 — Berlin Blockade and airlift
  — Organization of American States formed
  — Hiss case
  — *Sexual Behavior of the Human Male* by Kinsey published
1949 — NATO formed
  — Fall of mainland China to Chinese communists
1950 — McCarran Internal Security Act
1950–53 — Korean War
1951 — Japanese Peace treaty
  — West German Peace contract
  — Internal Security Act (McCarren Act)
  — 22nd Amendment (two terms for president) ratified
  — J.D. Salinger's *Catcher in the Rye* published
1952 — U.S. explodes first H-Bomb
  — Dwight D. Eisenhower elected thirty-fourth president
  — Ralph Ellison's *Invisible Man* published
1953 — Execution of Julius and Ethel Rosenberg
  — Department of Health, Education, and Welfare created
1954 — *Brown v. Board of Education* decision by Supreme Court
  — Senator Joseph McCarthy censored by Senate
  — SEATO formed
  — Dien Bien Phu captured by Vietminh
  — Atomic Energy Act
  — Elvis Presley introduces his style of rock 'n roll
1955 — General Summit conference
  — Austrian Peace Treaty
  — AFL and CIO merge to form AFL-CIO
  — Montgomery, Alabama, bus boycott
  — *Target with Plaster Casts* by Jasper Johns and *Bed* by Robert Rauschenberg painted

1956 — Suez crisis
— Hungarian revolt
— Federal Aid Highway Act
— Allen Ginsberg's poem *Howl* introduces the "Beat Generation"
1957 — Eisenhower Doctrine
— First Sputnik launched by Soviet Union
— Civil Rights Act
— Little Rock, Arkansas, school integration riots
— Defense Reorganization Act
— Jack Kerouac's *On the Road* published
— Post-war Baby Boom peaks
1959 — St. Lawrence seaway opened
— *Black on Maroon* by Mark Rothko painted
— Xerox machine available
1960 — John F. Kennedy elected thirty-fifth president
— U-2 incident
— The Beatles tour the U.S.
— John Updike's *Rabbit Run* published
1961 — Berlin Crisis
— Bay of Pigs
— First man in space
— Advisory group sent to South Vietnam
— Peace Corps formed
— 23rd Amendment (District of Columbia voting rights)
1962 — Cuban Missile Crisis
— Trade Expansion Act
1963 — President Kennedy assassinated; Lyndon Johnson becomes thirty-sixth president
— Supreme Court (Warren Court) declares prayer in public schools unconstitutional and supports rights of criminal suspects
— Civil Rights March on Washington
— *The Feminine Mystique* by Betty Friedan published
1964 — Civil Rights Act passed
— War on Poverty begins — Economic Opportunity Act
— Warren Commission report on Kennedy assassination
— 24th Amendment (No Poll Tax)
1965 — U.S. Troops engage in combat in South Vietnam
— Voting Rights Act passed
— Great Society programs: Elementary and Secondary School Act; Medicare; Water Quality Act: Omnibus Housing Act; Higher Education Act
— Assassination of Malcolm X
— Selma to Montgomery, Alabama, civil rights march
— *Sixteen Jackies* by Andy Warhol painted
1966 — Department of Transportation
— NOW (National Organization for Women) founded
1967 — Urban Riots (Detroit, Newark, Rochester, Milwaukee, Washington)
— 25th Amendment (Presidential Succession Amendment) ratified
1968 — Dr. Martin Luther King, Jr., assassinated
— Robert Kennedy assassinated
— Riots at Democratic Convention in Chicago
— Richard M. Nixon elected thirty-seventh president
— Columbia University students seize the campus (SDS)
— Non-Proliferation Nuclear Treaty Passed by U.N.
— Anti-Vietnam War protests
— *U.S.S. Pueblo* seized by North Korea
1969 — Men land on the Moon
— My Lai massacre revealed
— Nixon Silent Majority speech
— Woodstock rock concert
— *La Grande Vitesse* sculpture by Alexander Calder

1970 — U.S. troops invade Cambodia on orders of President Nixon
— Independent U.S. Postal Service established
1971 — 26th Amendment (Voting Age) ratified
— Amtrak (train) service initiated
— Pentagon Papers published
— New Economic program — price control
— Devaluation of U.S. dollar
1972 — Watergate break-in by agents of the Republican White House; "cover-up" begins
— President Nixon visits Communist China
— Senate passes Equal Rights Amendment (ERA) but it is not ratified by states
— SALT disarmament treaty signed
1973 — Vice-President Agnew forced to resign; Gerald Ford chosen as vice-president by Nixon with Congressional approval
— Roe v. Wade (abortion decision of the Supreme Court)
— Wounded Knee incident
— Existence of White House tapes revealed as part of Watergate Investigation
— "Saturday Night Massacre" — Resignation of Attorney General Eliot Richardson and Special Prosecutor Archibald Cox over Watergate
— U.S. negotiates withdrawal from Vietnam
1974 — Presidential impeachment hearings
— President Nixon resigns presidency; Gerald Ford becomes thirty-eighth president
— Nelson Rockefeller confirmed as vice-president
— Ford pardons Nixon
— Ford Vietnam War Amnesty program
— Oil shortages due to embargo and OPEC
1975 — Oil price controls ended
— President Ford visits mainland China
— Government of South Vietnam surrenders to the North Vietnamese Communists
— Former Attorney General Mitchell and Nixon presidential aides Haldeman and Ehrlichman sentenced to prison for roles in Watergate scandals
1976 — Bicentennial Year
— 200-mile fishing limit proclaimed by United States
— Supreme Court upholds busing in Boston to achieve integration
— Copyright Revision Bill is passed
— Jimmy Carter elected thirty-ninth president of the United States
1977 — Carter opens presidency by granting a pardon to draft evaders and proposing a large government spending program to reduce unemployment
— Trans-Alaska Pipeline opens
— Clean Air Bill passed
— President Sadat of Egypt visits Israel
— Government Reorganization Bill
1978 — California tax cut (Proposition 13) approved by voters
— Air Transport Deregulation Act
— Civil Service Reform Act
— Bakke v. University of California (affirmative action) decision by Supreme Court
— Humphrey-Hawkins Employment Bill
— Camp David meetings (Israel-Egypt peace talks) and accord
1979 — U.S.-China diplomatic recognition finalized
— Egypt-Israel Peace Treaty
— Space vehicle Voyager II photographs Jupiter
— Three Mile Island nuclear plant accident
— Pope John Paul II visits United States
— Iranian students seize U.S. embassy in Teheran and make employees hostages
— Boat people leave Vietnam
1980 — Inflation continues as consumer prices rise 13.3%
— Attempt to rescue Iranian hostages fails
— John Anderson announces independent race for the presidency
— Polish workers strike under leadership of solidarity labor union
— Peacetime draft registration is begun
— Ronald Reagan is elected fortieth president

1981 — Inflation continues as consumer prices rise 12.4%
  — Reagan economic plan reduces taxes, cuts welfare benefits, and increases spending for defense
  — Soviet grain-embargo lifted by President Reagan
  — AIDS identified
  — U.S. increases aid to El Salvador
1982 — President Reagan proposes "New Federalism," transferring major welfare programs to states
  — Inflation rate slows as unemployment reaches post-World War II record
  — Equal Rights Amendment to Constitution (ERA) defeated
  — U.S. troops ordered to Lebanon due to civil war and fight between Israel and P.L.O.
  — Congress passes budget with a projected deficit of $100 billion
  — START talks open
  — Reagan introduces Strategic Defense Initiative (SDI or "Star Wars")
1983 — U.S. troops invade Grenada
  — Terrorists bomb U.S. Marine barracks in Beirut, Lebanon, killing 237
  — Congress passes bill to reform Social Security System
  — Unemployment rate goes over 10%
1984 — Representative Geraldine Ferraro (Democrat, N.Y.) becomes first woman vice-presidential candidate for a major party
  — Ronald Reagan overwhelmingly reelected, defeating Walter Mondale
  — Record defict in balance of trade payments
1985 — Shiite Moslems hijack plane and hold Americans hostage
  — President Reagan signs Gramm/Rudman Act (Balanced Budget)
  — Mikhail Gorbachev becomes leader of Soviet Union and introduces reforms (Glasnost and Peristroika)
  — First Summit Meeting in Geneva between Mikhail Gorbachev and Ronald Reagan
  — Supreme Court bars "moment of silence" in schools
  — S & L (savings and loan) failures upset economy
1986 — Challenger space shuttle explodes
  — Chernobyl nuclear power plant accident in Soviet Union
  — Helsinki Summit Meeting between Mikhail Gorbachev and Ronald Reagan
  — 100th Anniversary of the Statue of Liberty
  — Iran-Contra affair revealed
1987 — Iran-Contra Congressional Hearings
  — Stock Market collapses in over 500-point loss on the Dow Jones in one day
  — Washington Summit Meeting of Mikhail Gorbachev and Ronald Reagan
  — INF Treaty signed
  — Congress approves S & L bailouts program
  — Clean Water Act passed over Reagan's veto
  — Toni Morison's *Beloved* published
1988 — Governor Michael Dukakis of Massachusetts (Democrat) and Vice-President George Bush (Republican) win party presidential nominations
  — George Bush elected forty-first president
  — Anti-Drug Act passed (fourth act in six years)
  — First Drug Tsar, William Bennett, resigns
  — Peace accord signed in Nicaragua and Sandinistas are voted out of office
  — Medicare Catastrophic Health Care Bill - repealed in 1989
1989 — Fall of Berlin Wall
  — U.S. invades Panama to seize accused drug dealer General Noriega
1990 — Second Earth Day celebration heightens environmental concerns
  — Iraq invades Kuwait—Bush organizes anti-Iraq coalition in U.N. (Operation Desert Shield)
  — Non-communist governments established in all of eastern Europe
  — Cold War ends
  — Keating Five Investigation begins
  — Americans With Disabilities Act
1991 — Iraq invaded and defeated by U.N. coalition led by U.S. (Operation Desert Storm)
  — Bush's popularity in polls reaches highest level ever for a president
  — Economic downturn continues and slips into a major recession

1991 — Coup against Gorbachev fails
   — Soviet Union breaks up—replaced by Commonwealth of Independent States
   — Yugoslavia breaks up as Slovenia and Croatia declare independence—warfare breaks out
   — Guilty charges against Lt. Col. Oliver North in Iran-Contra case dropped by Judge Gesell
   — Judge Clarence Thomas nominated and approved for Supreme Court
   — Cambodian Peace Accords; El Salvador Peace Pact; Afghanistan Peace Agreement; Namibia Accord—all arranged through U.N.
   — Last U.S. hostages freed in Lebanon
   — Arab-Israeli Peace conference meets in Madrid
   — *Rust v. Sullivan* Supreme Court decision
   — BCCI Scandal revealed—charges brought by Justice Department
1992 — U.N. Conference on Environment and Development (Rio Conference)—U.S. refuses to sign Bio-Diversity Treaty
   — Budget deficit continues to grow as recession worsens—bankruptcies increase
   — Legislative stalemate between Democratic controlled Congress and Republican president continues as Bush continues to veto legislation
   — House of Representatives Bank check scandal
   — Rodney King Case followed by riots in Los Angeles
   — *Planned Parenthood v. Casey* (abortion) decision by Supreme Court
   — Governor Bill Clinton of Arkansas and Senator Albert Gore of Tennessee nominated by Democratic Party
   — President Bush and Vice-President Dan Quayle renominated by Republican Party
   — H. Ross Perot enters race as independent presidential candidate and names General James Stockdale as his vice-president
   — Bill Clinton elected forty-second president of the United States.

Appendix

The words listed in this glossary are ones you should have encountered during your study of American history. Read the list and see how many are familiar. It is important to know the vocabulary of history, so be certain you understand those words that are new to you.

Glossary

Abolitionist — before the American Civil War, one who believed in the abolition of slavery

Abrogation — the terminating or voiding of a treaty or agreement

Absolutism — control of a people or nation with no checks on the authority of the ruler

Admiralty Court — a court that has jurisdiction over maritime cases

Aggression — attack on or invasion of territory of another country

AIDS — Acquired Immune Deficiency Syndrome — A fatal disease that has become a worldwide epidemic and for which a cure is being sought. It is thought that the cost of treating AIDS patients and of research to find a cure will have a major impact on national budgets in the 1990s

Alien — someone not a citizen of the country

Alliance — a formal temporary union of two or more countries

Amendment — a change or proposed change in a bill or in the Constitution

Amnesty — a forgiveness en masse

Anarchy — a government without law or order, or in which no central authority is obeyed; or a state of society in which law and order are absent

Appeasement — the act of giving in to a potential enemy in hope that his appetite for further plunder or aggression will be filled

Appropriation — setting aside funds for a particular use, especially as applied to government expenditures

Arbitration — settlement of a dispute by a hearing before one or more persons chosen by the conflicting parties

Aristocracy — the theory of practice of government rule by an elite considered the best. In common historical usage it implies an inherited nobility

Armistice — a cease-fire in anticipation of negotiations for a more durable peace

Assassination — the killing of a politically important individual by surprise attack

Autocracy — government by one person who exercises supreme authority

Automation — use of machines to take the place of labor

Autonomy — the right of self-government within a framework of a larger political unit

Axis — the alliance of Germany, Italy, and Japan in World War II

Balance of Payments — specie, credit, or exchange of goods needed by one nation to clear its accounts with another nation over a set trading period

Balance of Power — policy that attempts to balance a nation's power either by alliances or by national action against a combination of nations that might threaten the nation's national interests

Belligerent — a country that is at war or is openly supporting another country at war

Bicameral — a legislature that has two chambers or houses; e.g., the American Congress is bicameral, having a House of Representatives and a Senate. Nebraska's legislature is unicameral, having but one legislative chamber

Bilateral — two-sided, as opposed to unilateral, one-sided, or as compared to multilateral, many-sided action or treaty

Bi-Metallism — backing a nation's currency with both gold and silver

Black Code — a series of laws relating to the control and dehumanization of black Americans during the Reconstruction period and after, largely in southern states

Black Power — a political and social concept that blacks should exercise control over their destiny without pressure from members of the majority; assumes the group needs political and economic independence to achieve this goal. The concept can be applied to other groups, such as Chicano Power

Bloc — a group of political parties temporarily joined to work for the same goal

Blockade — use of ships or troops to prevent entrance to or exit from a country

Bloody Shirt — used as a symbol of the rebellion of the Confederate states by the Republican party to discredit the South in the years after 1865

Blue Laws — laws written to enforce moral behavior

Boondoggling — word invented during the New Deal period and used primarily by conservative forces to describe what they termed wasteful expenditure of public money

Bourbon — very conservative southern Democrat

Bourgeoisie — the middle class — particularly merchants and industrialists in that period when nobility was the upper class. Used by Marx in his analysis of the class struggle

Boycott — to refuse to have business dealings with a firm or person

Brinkmanship — a term coined in respect to the foreign policy approach of Secretary of State John Foster Dulles, and used since to describe a gambler's attitude in the management of foreign relations. Dulles said that one must be prepared to go to the "brink," presumably atomic war, if a nation were to be taken seriously in international affairs

Budget — a financial statement that estimates and limits future expenses

Cabinet — advisory council of a president or other ruler — usually appointed

Capital — money that can be used for building factories, railroads, etc.

Capitalism — the economic system in which means of production and distribution are privately owned under competitive conditions

Carpetbagger — a northerner who traveled to the former Confederacy during the Reconstruction period to participate in the political reorganization of the South, often to profit therefrom

Cartel — a business monopoly that extends beyond national boundary lines

Caucus — a private meeting of leaders of a political party to determine policy

Cavalier — a supporter of Charles I of England, particularly a soldier defending his reign; now someone of aristocratic leaning

Charisma — magnetic personality, charm, leadership, attractiveness; used in reference to political candidates

Charter — a document issued by a government or ruler granting rights and privileges to an individual or group

Charter Colony — a corporate colony operating under a charter obtained from the king by a company's stockholders

Chauvinism — extreme or exaggerated patriotism or commitment to a position; it comes from Nicolas Chauvin, who supported Napoleon in the extreme

Chicano — Individuals of Mexican ancestry; Mexican Americans

Civil Rights — the liberties and privileges of citizens — especially those granted in the Bill of Rights

Closed Shop — a factory or place of business at which only union members may be employed

Coalition — a temporary union of individuals or political parties to attain some common aim

Cold War — a state of hostility between nations not involving physical contact. Applied specifically to U.S.-U.S.S.R. relations between 1946 and 1990

Collective Bargaining — settlement of labor management disputes by discussion between representatives of the workers and the employer

Colony — an inhabited region politically dependent on and dominated by a more powerful nation

Collective Security — combining nations in an effort to provide greater protection from aggression

Communism — an economic system in which all means of production and distribution are owned and controlled by the government

Compact — an agreement, a contract

Computer — a machine that can solve problems very quickly because of its ability to do calculations as fed into it by operators

Conscription — compulsory enrollment for military service; draft

Conservation — official care and protection of natural resources

Conservative — in politics, one who wishes to keep conditions basically as they are with little or no change

Continental — a soldier in the Revolutionary army; paper money issued by the Continental Congress, which continually depreciated in value

Contras — those forces opposing the Sandinista government of Nicaragua and funded and supported by the Reagan administration

Convention — a body of delegates meeting for some reason

Copperhead — a northerner in sympathy with the South and active in its cause or one in favor of a negotiated peace with the South

Corporation — a firm (usually in business) operating under a government charter that legally authorizes it to act as a single person with all the rights of a person under the law, but actually composed of two or more people who share ownership

Coup d'Etat — a sudden, forceful overthrow of government at the top

Culture — the way of living and ideas a people share

Delegate — a representative of a group to a meeting or convention

Democracy — government by the people, by majority vote

Depression — time of unemployment and financial collapse. The depression that began in 1929 was so long and hard that it is known as the Great Depression

Desegregation — ending of segregation, usually by integration

Despot — a ruler with absolute power — usually a tyrant

Dictator — a ruler who has supreme and absolute power — one who has usurped that power by force or legal trickery

Diplomacy — the conduct of negotiations to achieve agreements between countries; international contacts

Discrimination — a majority's denial of advantages to certain minority groups

Displaced Person — one who is uprooted from his or her native land by war and forced to move elsewhere

Divine Right — the belief — especially prevalent in the 16th and 17th centuries in Europe — that kings ruled and held power because of God's will

Dollar Diplomacy — a type of economic imperialism whereby the United States sought to insure its investment abroad, particularly in Latin America, by using military power or threat of military power

Due Process — traceable in English and American legal tradition to Magna Carta, due process has come to mean the procedure guaranteed to all citizens, that affords them their "day in court"

Duty — a tax, usually on imports

Ecology — the study of the relationship between individual organisms and their environment

Edict — an order issued by a governmental authority that has the same effect as a law

Electoral College — the procedure by which the president and vice-president of the United States are elected. Every state has as many votes in the Electoral College as it has senators and representatives combined, and the electors are voted for at the November presidential election every four years. The electors collectively (the college) then vote for president and vice-president

Embargo — a government order preventing the movement of merchant ships and/or the prohibition of trade

Emigrant — someone who leaves his or her country to settle in another

Empire — many lands under the control of one ruler or nation

Entente — an agreement temporarily uniting two or more countries, usually informal and unsigned

Environment — surroundings; all the conditions around us for living

Equality — everything being equal or everyone having the same rights

Excise Tax — an internal tax on the manufacture, sale, or consumption of goods, e.g., tobacco, alcohol, etc.

Executive Agreement — an agreement between the president and the head of a foreign country

Expansion — as applied to countries, the acquisition of additional territory

Exports — goods sent out of the country for sale in another country

Extraterritoriality—the state or privilege of exemption from the laws of local courts, particularly in the case of diplomatic representatives to a foreign country

Fair Deal — the slogan used to describe the domestic program of President Truman

Fascism — originally Mussolini's philosophy of dictatorship and conquest, now any system modeled on that of Mussolini

Featherbedding — retaining workers on unnecessary jobs, or paying workers more than necessary to do a job, or hiring more workers than necessary to do a job

Federal—the central government or authority as contrasted with state or local government

Federalism — a system of government in which a central authority divides or shares power with its regional parts

Feudalism — the social structure of the Middle Ages, based on the relation of a lord to his vassals, who held land (called fiefs) granted by the lord in return for obedience and loyalty

Fifth Columnist — a traitor who aids the enemy

Filibuster — private imperialistic adventure by unauthorized individuals out for their own profit and in some cases their own sovereignty; extended debate in the U.S. Senate designed to prevent a vote on a bill of which the filibusterer (speaker) disapproves but the majority of Senate members approves

Fourteen Points — Wilson's statement of war aims, delivered to Congress during the course of World War I. Among the points were freedom of the seas, self-determination of subject peoples, reduction of armaments once the war was successfully ended, and, most important, a League of Nations to keep the peace in the post-war world

Frontier — that boundary or border of a country that faces either another country or unsettled land

Gay Rights — a movement demanding civil rights for homosexuals

Genocide — the deliberate murder, or attempted murder, of a whole people. May be based on racial, ethnic, religious, cultural, or political concepts

Ghetto — place where people of one minority group live together

Good Neighbor Policy — part of the New Deal's foreign policy, which aimed at strengthening United States ties with Latin America

Guerrilla — one who carries on or assists in an irregular war

Guild—an association of persons in the same trade or craft, formed for mutual aid and protection

Hegemony—leadership, paramount influence, or military-economic overlordship of one nation over another, or over other nations or regions

Holding Company — a company that usually does not produce anything or perform any service except to control other companies through the ownership of controlling shares of stock

Hostage — a civilian seized by a group or individual and held captive to force an enemy to negotiate and make changes in policy; a form of blackmail

Immigrant — someone who comes to make his or her home in a new country

Impeach — to indict a public official for misbehavior. The case is then tried before a jury assigned to the case

Imperialism—a government policy of annexing territory by force or political pressure, or gaining political control over weaker lands

Implied Powers — powers suggested but not specifically listed in the Constitution and exercised by the national government and its three branches

Imports — goods brought into one country from another

Impressment—the practice of the British of forcing American sailors into service on British warships under the assumption that they were escaped British seamen

Inalienable — nontransferable, irrevocable. As associated with rights it means that there are certain rights that humans cannot cancel; they are God-given, or derived from nature

Industrial Revolution — that phase of economic development characterized by a change from home to factory production

Inflation—a large rise in prices due to increase in the money supply and/or expansion of credit

Injunction — a court order preventing a person or group of people from carrying on some activity — usually applied to an order preventing a union from picketing

Insurgent — a rebel

Integration — bringing together or making as one, unification; applied especially to blacks and whites in a number of social areas

Internationalism — an ideology that emphasizes the unity of the world's peoples, and that deplores restrictive national boundaries and competing national sovereignties

Irangate — name given to the policy followed secretly by the Reagan Administration to sell arms to Iran to help free hostages in Lebanon while using the profits from the arms sales to support the Contras in Central America

Isolationism — a foreign policy that shuns alliances and compacts with other countries

Jim Crow Law — a law enforcing segregation, or control of blacks in such a manner as to make them unequal

Jingoism — super-militaristic patriotism

Journeyman — worker who is learning a craft under a master; such individuals work for a daily wage

Judicial — that branch of government related to the courts and their decisions concerning the legality of laws and acts

Judicial Review — the power of a court to accept appeals of legislative and executive action and decisions of lower courts with the possibility of modifying or nullifying such action as being "unconstitutional"

Jury — a group of people in a court who hear and decide a case

Keynesian Economics — ideas of John Maynard Keynes, British economist. Essentially Keynes believed in government spending during depression periods and retrenching with economy budgets and high taxation during periods of boom

Labor Theory of Value — a central part of Karl Marx's scientific socialism. Marx contended that economic value is derived from labor acting on materials of production. The concept was also expressed by John Locke

Labor Union — organization of workers to improve their wages and working conditions

Laissez-faire — noninterference by government in private enterprises

Lame Duck — an official (congressperson, etc.) defeated in an election but continuing to serve because his or her successor is not scheduled to take office until a later date.

Law and Order — a vaguely defined political concept held by those who oppose violence and anarchy; an important campaign issue in many elections

Legal Tender — any kind of money that is declared official by act of government

Legislative — branch of government concerned with making laws

Liberal — in politics, an individual who is not tied to tradition or party lines and welcomes experimentation with new ideas

Logrolling — mutual assistance in the passage of legislation so that one member of Congress votes for a colleague's bills in return for similar assistance in his or her desired legislation

Lynching — execution or killing by a mob, with no proper trial

Majority — more than half of the votes, or the larger part of the population

Mandate — a vote of confidence from the people. A mandate also refers to a colony held in trust by a major power under the League of Nations

Manifest Destiny — the belief that it was the destiny of the United States to expand to the natural boundary of the Pacific

Marxism — the economic and political theories of Karl Marx as interpreted by Lenin, Stalin, Mao Tse-tung, and many others. The main features of Marxism are world revolution, removal of the exploiting class, a dictatorship of the proletariat during the transition period of the "withering away" of the state, and a goal of the classless communist society where everyone shall contribute according to his abilities and take according to his needs

Master Craftsman — a worker who has learned a trade and produced a masterpiece to become a member of a guild

Masterpiece — an object produced by a journeyman. If approved of by the guild, the journeyman would be admitted into the guild as a master

Megalopolis — a very large urban region

Mercantilism — the practice of achieving a favorable balance of trade (exports exceed imports) through government acts to benefit the commercial interests of the country (example: English Navigation Acts of the 1680s)

Metropolitan Centers — big cities with smaller cities around them

Middle Class — that part of society between the fairly affluent upper class and the poor lower class

Migrant — person moving from one place to another

Militarism — the overvaluing of the military establishment, its leaders, their aims and ideals. Also, the substitution of military for civilian control of the state

Militarist — one who believes in an aggressive foreign policy backed up with well-prepared armed forces

Military Industrial Complex — a phrase used by President Eisenhower to refer to the relationship between the military and business in the United States; he warned against their power in his farewell address to the nation

Monarchy — system of government with king as ruler

Monopoly — control of the entire supply of some product, giving the power to set prices and/or limit production

Moratorium — a period of suspended activity

Most-Favored-Nation Clause — a common treaty provision that grants to the recipient all privileges granted to any other nation by the granting nation. It often applies to trading agreements

Muckraker — one who exposes, usually in writing, misdeeds of business or politics, hoping to bring reform

National (or Public) Debt — the sum total of all financial obligations that result from borrowing by a nation-state

Nationalism — ardent and sometimes excessive devotion to national interests and prestige

Natural Law — rules that appear to be true and are argued as true because they are either rational or because they are ordained by God

Natural Right — a right assumed to be protected by natural law

Nazism — Fascist philosophy of Hitler's Germany

Negotiation — in international affairs, the practice of settling disputes by means other than the resort to armed force, or by judicial or arbitrational or diplomatic mechanisms; in domestic affairs, the settling of disputes by discussion and compromise

Neutral — a country that neither assists nor allies itself with another country at war

Neutralism — a nonpartisan or nonattached view of policy in regard to competing systems or states

Neutrality — a policy of a nation that seeks to maintain impartiality between two opposing states or groups of states, but at the same time to fully protect its own international rights

New Deal — the domestic reform program of President Franklin Roosevelt

New Federalism — President Nixon's domestic program, which centered on returning some power to the states at the expense of the national government under the assumption that the federal bureaucracy had grown too large and unresponsive to local needs. Also endorsed by President Reagan

New Freedom — the domestic and foreign policy programs of Woodrow Wilson

New Frontier — the domestic and foreign policy programs of President John F. Kennedy

New Nationalism — slogan for the reform program of Theodore Roosevelt and the Bull Moose Party

Nonviolence — a peaceful kind of protest connected with Gandhi and Martin Luther King, Jr.

Nullify — to cancel or destroy the legal effectiveness of a law, tradition, or agreement

Oligarchy — government by a few

Open Door — American foreign policy in regard to Asia that was initiated by Secretary of State John Hay on September 6, 1899. The policy was to persuade nations having interests in Asia, and particularly having business in China, to deal with China as an equal. The policy sought equal commercial opportunity for all nations and the abolition of restrictive spheres of influence as well as other supranational privileges such as extraterritoriality

Open Shop — factory in which employment is not dependent upon being a member of a union

Ordinance — a rule or regulation issued by a nonsovereign body (usually a city, country, or township)

Panic — financial crisis followed by unemployment and hard times, but not as severe as a depression

Patronage — appointing people to government positions as a reward for political services while disregarding merits such persons might have for the jobs assigned

Petition — a written plea from an individual or organized group protesting some wrong, personal or societal, in hopes of gaining a redress

Plebiscite — a vote by the people of the country on some measure submitted to them for acceptance or rejection. It was originally considered an extension of the democratic principle, but has recently been used by dictators to gain support for their autocratic decisions

Plutocracy — government by the wealthy

Police Power — the broad power of government to regulate and restrain individuals and groups in the use of their life, liberty, and property in order to protect and promote peace, order, health, safety, good morals, and general welfare

Policy — the course followed by a government or one of its representatives

Pollution — the dirtying of the environment; something unclean or poisonous

Pork Barrel — the money and public works Congress distributes and the spending of public money through logrolling techniques to benefit particular localities and enhance the election possibilities of representatives at the expense of the general public good

Poverty — lack of money or goods; condition of being poor

Precedent — in American and British law, it is a previous ruling in law that is so important it requires subsequent cases to take it into account and usually abide by the earlier decision

Prejudice — dislike for a person or group without good reason

Proclamation — a public announcement of official policy

Propaganda — ideas, beliefs, and information either untrue or exaggerated spread by an organized group or government

Proportional Representation — a system of electing legislators that results in representation approximately proportionate to the strength of each political party as determined in a vote

Proprietary Colony — a colony run and controlled by an individual or group of individuals as their private estate, e.g., William Penn's Pennsylvania

Protective Tariff — a tax on imported goods designed to increase their price to the level of similar home-produced goods

Protectorate — a country protected by a more powerful state that shares in its government

Protestant Ethic — the extolling of work and the abhorrence of waste by Calvinists and their descendants. Connected in the United States with the Puritans

Purge — to free a state or party of disloyal elements

Quorum — the minimum number of members who must be present in order for business to be transacted by a group, usually of elected representatives

Racism — the doctrine that some races are inherently superior to others because of supposed cultural and intellectual inheritance

Radical — one who favors basic changes in the structure of society

Ratify — to approve a bill or law

Reactionary — one who favors a return to an older, more conservative way of life

Reaganomics — President Reagan's plan of reduced taxes to stimulate economic activity and cut inflation

Rebate — a percentage of the cost returned ostensibly for services performed or commodities sold

Recall — a petition signed by a large percentage (usually 25 percent) of the voters that recalls an elected representative from his or her position and thus leaves vacant the office held; the official so removed may run again

Recession — panic or slight depression

Referendum — a petition signed by a small percentage (usually 10 percent) that permits the public to vote on a law the legislature has passed

Renaissance — a rebirth of interest in culture, especially as applied to art and literature in the 14th to 16th centuries in western Europe. The term has been used for other periods of rebirth such as the 12th century Renaissance in France or the Harlem Renaissance of the 1920s in New York City

Reparations — payment in compensation for damages, caused usually as a result of war or war-connected activity

Representative — a person elected to represent others; a member of the U.S. House of Representatives or some other legislative body

Republic — a nation in which the people elect representatives to govern; from the Latin "res publica," or public thing

Resources (natural) — the natural wealth of a country — minerals, farmlands, forests, etc.

Revenue — money a government collects by taxes and duties

Revolution — a sudden end of one government and the start of a new one; any dramatic and somewhat sudden change

Royal Colony — a colony directly controlled by a king and governed by the king's appointed representative

Rule of Law — a fundamental principle of American and British legal systems and constitutional government. It involves three points: (1) the absolute supremacy of law over arbitrary power — no person above the law, not even the chief executive; (2) equality before the law; (3) the Constitution is the supreme law of the land and the protective force of inherent or natural rights

Satellite — an object orbiting another and commonly used to describe objects sent into space from earth. The term has also been used to refer to nations that are dependent on another country for defense or political direction

Scalawag — contemptuous name for a southern white who cooperated with northerners or blacks during Reconstruction

SDS (Students for a Democratic Society) — a youth group formed in the 1960s to force changes upon American society by political and/or violent means

Secession — withdrawal of a constituent member from a political group

Sectionalism — devotion to the interests of a state or some particular section of it over and above the interests of the country itself

Sedition — actions that encourage disrespect for law and government that fall short of treason but go beyond normal legal and political opposition

Segregation — as applied to blacks and whites — isolating one group from the other in various social activities

Serf — in feudal society, a peasant permanently attached to land owned by a lord

Settler — one who makes his or her home in a new, usually sparsely settled area

Sharecropping — a type of farm tenancy in which the tenant agrees to share part of the crop in lieu of rent, seed, and other necessary capital

Social Contract — a theory that primitive societies were first brought into being by a voluntary agreement between the ruled and the elected ruler in order to provide for mutual protection and welfare

Socialism — belief in a society based on government ownership and control of means of production and distribution

Sovereignty — supreme power. In the United States ultimate sovereignty is invested in the people and exercised by the federal government, which they control. Under the Articles of Confederation it was in the hands of several states, and prior to the American Revolution, in the British Crown. In the U.S., each level of government exercises degrees of sovereignty, but since the Civil War ultimate sovereignty has rested in the federal government

Soviet — Russian word for "council"

Specie — money in the form of coins — usually gold or silver

Speculation — legal gambling on stocks, real estate, farm commodities, etc.

Sphere of Influence — a geographic area in which a nation seeks to dominate to the point of securing preferential treatment of a political, economic, and even social nature

Spoils — in politics, the influence and jobs the winning party distributes to its workers

Spoils System — the awarding of government jobs or the granting of favors or advantages by government officials to political partisans and workers

Square Deal — the slogan used to describe the domestic program of President Theodore Roosevelt

Squatter Sovereignty — (similar to popular sovereignty) the professed right of settlers in an area to determine for themselves solutions to key problems affecting them

Status Quo Ante Bellum — the situation as it existed before a war, especially used to refer to the period before the U.S. Civil War

State's Rights — a belief that the federal government should be limited so that the individual states may exercise more power; it supports the concept of state as opposed to federal sovereignty

Statute — laws: one may distinguish four important types of legal restraint that are embodied in American and British legal systems: *Statutory law* is law established by a legislative body with the approval of the executive (or passed over his veto). *Common law* is the so-called unwritten law that has been established by custom, tradition, or precedent. *Constitutional law* is the overriding legal principles embodied in the basic governing document (e.g., the U.S. Constitution); *ordinances* are rules or regulations established by bodies — cities, counties, townships — not having full sovereignty, but existing as subdivisions of a sovereign body

Strict Construction — philosophy that holds that the Constitution should be narrowly or literally interpreted, which leads to the concept that government should be limited

Strike — walk-out by workers, or general refusal to work, in hope of forcing an employer or government body to offer better contract terms or change policies

Suburb — residential neighborhood at the edge of a city

Suffrage — the right to vote

Surtax — an additional tax; a graduated income tax added to the normal tax depending on a person's wealth

Tariff — taxes, usually referred to as duties, imposed by governments on imports and exports

Tenement — unsafe, unsanitary, and crowded apartment building

Theocracy — a church-ruled government, local, regional, or national

Totalitarianism — a government whose leadership excludes all opposition and opposing political parties and exercises complete control over all phases of national life

Treaty — a formal agreement between two or more countries

Trust — an organization composed of different companies united under one board of trustees, whose purpose is to eliminate competition and thereby control an industry by creating a monopoly

Unification — as applied to nations, the process of joining different self-governing states into one central government

Union Shop — a limited closed shop

Unwritten Constitution — customs, traditions, and practices in government that have become the way of life of a society

Urban — having to do with a city

Vassal — in feudalism, one who swears loyalty to a higher lord in return for protection and privileges

Veteran — one who has served in the military forces of the United States

Violence — attacks that harm or damage a person or thing. Politically it is usually associated with anarchy and revolution and often is a result of poverty or extreme, either conservative or radical, ideology

Veto — to refuse approval (usually of a bill, law, or motion) or forbid

Watergate — a term used to refer to the scandals of the Nixon Administration that led to his resignation as President. The scandal began with a break-in at the Democratic Party Headquarters in the Watergate Building — a condominium complex—in Washington, D.C.

Writ — a formal written document; an order or mandatory process in writing issued under seal in the name of the sovereign or of a court or judicial officer commanding the person to whom it is directed to perform or refrain from performing an act specified therein

Xenophobia — a fear or hatred of foreigners

Youth Groups — organizations of young people, often for political action